The Italian Labor Movement

DANIEL L. HOROWITZ

Harvard University Press

CAMBRIDGE · MASSACHUSETTS

1 9 6 3

To Loucele, Sanda and Paul

Foreword

There are growing signs of fundamental changes in Italy. The "opening to the Left" has become a reality with the Nenni Socialists supporting the government; the conflict between the Socialists and their allied trade unions over joining a moderate government had been a divisive issue within the Italian Left at least since the turn of the century. Collective bargaining has become more active at the plant level or in narrow groupings of firms, tending to diminish the role of the traditional broad industry and the significance of minimum wages and conditions bargained at confederation levels of labor and management. The level of unemployed for Italy as a whole, on comparable definitions, has fallen below that in the United States. Thus, long-established features of the Italian industrial relations system appear to be in transition. Moreover, the new conditions themselves are likely to accelerate and extend the break from the past.

This volume contributes both to an understanding of the Italian labor movement of the past, which has so often appeared as an enigma to students of comparative industrial relations, and provides insights into the changes only now emerging. Mr. Horowitz portrays the history of the Italian labor movement against the background of social, political and economic developments in Italian society. "The pattern of Italian trade unionism has sharply demonstrated a fundamental instability in broad institutional relationships throughout the history of modern Italy . . . The changes which have occurred in the economic and social structure, in the character of the political forces, and in the trade union movement itself, were, in their nature and degree, not sufficient to bring the three into enough congruence to achieve stability in Italian society. It is this lack of congruence which appears to be the outstanding characteristic of Italian trade unionism and of Italian society." While a high degree of congruence or consensus is yet to be achieved in Italian society, Mr. Horowitz concludes with the view that "slow as the process may be economic progress in Italy may gradually have its impact upon the social structure of the country." It may well be that this generation will see the fruition of the historic mission of the Italian working class to transform Italian society, brought about by economic progress and related pluralistic center political forces rather than by revolution.

This study is particularly noteworthy because of its illumination of the interrelations between trade unions and political parties. The delayed Italian economic development was directed by an elite characterized as dynastic rather than as middle class. The protest of the emerging industrial working class took both trade union and political forms. The interactions among these forms of labor organizations is one of the major themes of the volume. Mr. Horowitz concludes that "there existed a basic generic control by the political party which had nothing to do with controlling the trade union machinery or dominating its leadership. It was actually not a control, but a moral leadership and supremacy of the party in the allegiances of the members of the trade union movement, and to a certain lesser degree of the trade union leadership itself."

The Italian subject and the author are happily well matched. Mr. Horowitz brings to this study a career concentrated upon the interrelations among labor movements and political parties and economic developments in many countries. He was the first Labor Attaché appointed by our government; his first assignment was to Chile. Aside from periods devoted to this study in Italy, he has served in our Embassies in Paris and New Delhi. This breadth of experience and familiarity with other labor movements has enriched the present history and analysis of the Italian labor movement.

The present volume is the twelfth in the Wertheim series dealing with industrial relations systems outside the United States. These volumes taken as a group provide rich material from which to study industrial relations systems comparatively and particularly to analyze the way in which industrial relations systems evolve in the course of economic development.

This volume was begun as a companion study to Professor Val R. Lorwin's *The French Labor Movement* (1954) under the Harvard University project of foreign trade union studies and was completed under the Inter-University Study of Labor Problems in Economic Development.

December 1962   John T. Dunlop

Contents

Author's Preface

I.	The Climate of Italian Trade Unionism	1
II.	The Political Atmosphere of Trade Unionism	10
III.	Socialism and Trade Unions Till 1914	48
IV.	Catholic Trade Unions Before Fascism	95
V.	The Rise of Fascism	127
VI.	The Trade Union Movement After Fascism	181
VII.	The Communists and the Trade Unions	244
VIII.	Trade Unionism in the Fifties	274
IX.	The Pattern of Italian Trade Unionism	324
	Bibliography	343
	Index	349

Contents

Author's Preface

The present study is an analysis of the evolution of the Italian trade union movement in its relation to Italy's social, political and economic institutions. When I started my research I had intended to focus on the specific problem of Communist domination of the Italian trade union movement in the postwar period. As I proceeded, however, I became convinced that the "how" and "why" of Communist domination could fully be understood only by a broader analysis of political relationships in the labor arena and by a wider analysis of the historical background and evolution of labor organization in Italy. In recasting and broadening the scope of the study, analyzing the Communist trade union domination in the postwar period became one part of the problem of seeking to understand the nature of the Italian trade union movement and the elements which conditioned it throughout its history.

A basic characteristic of the history of modern Italy — perhaps the most basic characteristic — has been concern with the problem of national stability in seeking a congruence among its principal institutions. Such a congruence of political, economic, social and trade union forces has been tragically lacking during almost the entire period since the unification of modern Italy a century ago. I found that in attempting historically to analyze and understand the nature of the trade union movement, other related principal forces had to be given prominent attention, and their interrelationships weighed. This was particularly the case with Left political movements and with the Catholic social movement. It is hoped that this study has succeeded in furnishing some understanding of the broad historical problems of instability in Italian society resulting from this lack of congruence.

The reader will recognize that I have not surveyed systematically the full range of labor and industrial relations categories which have become traditional in American studies of trade union movements. In my opinion rigid adherence to the traditional survey approach would have obscured an understanding of the nature of the Italian trade union movement. The attempt was rather to study the trade union movement in its own terms and within the particular framework of the specific elements conditioning it in Italian society.

I have not covered the period of fascism in the same systematic fashion as other periods in modern Italian history. Unlike other periods, a large body of literature is readily available in English dealing with the social, political and economic aspects of Fascist rule. For this reason, I have assumed familiarity with the period on the part of the reader and have limited the discussion to the rise of fascism and to its aftermath and its repercussions upon the postwar period.

I began this study more than twelve years ago. The long period between inception and completion was largely due to pressure of other professional commitments. On the whole, the long period of "gestation" has been an asset, as I have had the benefit of considerably broadened experience in the intervening years. I hope the additional experience is reflected to advantage in the study itself.

I gratefully acknowledge the financial assistance granted to me by the Harvard University project of foreign trade union studies which made possible a leave of absence from the Department of State of approximately twenty months in 1950 and 1951. I am also appreciative of the financial assistance from the Inter-University Study of Labor Problems in Economic Development, which made possible a second leave of absence of approximately ten months from the Department of State during 1954 and 1955. I am also grateful to the Department of State for these extended leaves of absence. The Wertheim Committee of Harvard University has arranged for the publication of this volume.

Much of my historical and field research was conducted during these two periods. I have returned to Italy several times for short periods in more recent years and, in addition, have benefited greatly from conversations with leading participants in Italian labor affairs during their visits to Washington, Paris, Geneva and Brussels where our paths have crossed over the years.

During my first extended stay in Italy I spent a large part of my time travelling widely and concentrating on long and frequent trips to the industrial areas and the north-central agricultural regions. For most of this time I made Milan my headquarters. It was my purpose to absorb the atmosphere within which the competitive trade union and Left political forces vied for support and to learn at first hand how the trade union and political organizations functioned. I am deeply indebted to scores of local and provincial trade union officials who in this period and during visits in later years made a generous contribution toward my understanding of the Italian labor scene.

I was fortunate during this period in becoming closely acquainted with most of the national trade union leaders and many political leaders and observers, all of whom gave generously of their time and experience during those years and on the many occasions when I have met them since, in Italy and elsewhere. I have over the years cherished the many warm friendships which developed out of these relationships. In Italian fashion, they will no doubt find it easier to forgive any opinions with which they disagree or inaccuracies they may find than to forgive any lack of analytical sophistication they may discover in these pages. I hope they will find little to forgive in this regard although many may find opinions with which they disagree. The opinions are naturally my responsibility, but I want to thank the many Italians, too numerous to mention, whose help has been invaluable to me.

I want particularly to express my gratitude to Professor John T. Dunlop for his sound advice and his cheerful patience during the years when it appeared problematical whether the book would be finished. I want also to thank Professor Val R. Lorwin for his helpful comments on an early draft of sections of the manuscript. In addition, for the many helpful discussions during various phases of the study I wish to thank Professors Walter Galenson, Clark Kerr, Charles A. Myers, and Frederick H. Harbison.

I offer my gratitude and apologies to my wife, Loucele, and my children, Paul and Sanda, who have for a number of years been subjected to the consequences of my having added the writing of this book to an already full professional schedule.

Needless to say, the responsibility for the entire manuscript is solely mine, including the many translations I have made from Italian sources which are used in the text. I have written this book in my personal capacity and the Department of State bears no responsibility for any of the opinions and judgments expressed.

Daniel L. Horowitz

CHAPTER I

The Climate of Italian Trade Unionism

It has often been said that Italy is a good country for revolutionaries but a poor one for revolutions. The history of the Italian labor movement, both in its trade union and political aspects, supports the assertion.

It is a history of tumultuous battles against "the enemy" — sometimes the foundations of society itself — and of unrelenting warfare within its own ranks; of impressive achievements, but also of dramatic failures. Whether it be the "cyclone" labor unionism of the Revolutionary Syndicalists or the "transmission belt" unionism of the Communists, whether it be the "Reformist unionism" of Rigola or Viglianesi or the "modern unionism" of Pastore or Storti, the support each development has received among workers in industry and agriculture reflects in some measure the ancient unresolved power conflicts in a society tormented by incompatible traditions, and, until recent years, rigid in its structure. The history of the Italian labor movement is the subhistory of modern Italy, demonstrating the fundamental lack of consensus in the evolution of the nation's political, social, and economic institutions and in the distribution of power within these institutions.

The Italian trade union movement during much of its history has not been able to focus upon those problems — the market place problems — which have been the overwhelming concern of the trade union movements of countries like the United States, Great Britain, or the Scandinavian countries. Conflict over the foundation and structure of society has remained too strong an element in the dynamics of the movement in Italy to permit such a primary focus. While some other western countries were led by a middle-class elite in their modern industrialization process, there has been too much of the dynastic elite involved in Italy to make the response of labor completely analogous to that of these other countries.[1] The deeply felt sense of age-old injustices, the tenacious desire to preserve privilege and authority, the reluctance to adjust or compromise on issues too often raised to sacrosanct levels of principle and ideology, have set the stage upon which the drama of Italian social movements has been enacted.

Italy is a relatively poor country. This has been rightly underscored many times. But it is not this fact alone, by far, which provided the scaffolding upon which the labor movement was built or the basic traditions the work-

1. For development of the industrialization elite concepts *see* Clark Kerr, et al, *Industrialism and Industrial Man* (Cambridge, Mass., 1960), particularly pp. 47–76.

ers developed. Italy has a glorious ancient past. It has a proud heritage of artistic and cultural leadership in the world. Its people's exuberant zest for living is one of their most striking characteristics to a foreigner. But modern Italy has not had a gradual development of pluralistic power relations and evolution of democratic institutional continuity, as had Great Britain. It has not had a revolution, as had France, to give it a heritage of fundamental conceptions of individual freedom in its society or a revolutionary redistribution of land, upon which to build a diffusion of social privilege.

In recent years, as the Fascist experience has faded into the past, as the Communist internal threat has become less imminent, and as the economy has rapidly surged forward, an evolution toward the gradual resolution of historic conflicts and of healthy shifts in social balance has become possible. But the inherited basic conflicts, unfulfilled popular aspirations, and traditional social rigidities have left a heavy imprint upon the unfolding of the contemporary scene.

National unity in modern Italy is barely a century old. Political unification did not represent the fulfillment of the political and social aspirations of a people as much as the national centralization through the extension of the kingdom of Piedmont and the rule of the House of Savoy over all Italy. The national heroes of the epoch, Mazzini and Garibaldi, important a role as they played in arousing national sentiment for a unified Italy, resoundingly denounced as betrayal the actual unification, its methods and its announced principles. But the political and social principles, urged by them for transforming Italy in the process of unifying it, left their mark. It was a mark left not on a transformed Italy, but within dissenting groups, speaking in the name of the mass of disillusioned and discontented, which sought by diverse means to wield influence over events during the following generations.

The cleavages within Italian society included violent antagonisms between church and state, the inevitable concomitant of the victory of arms of the House of Savoy in eliminating the sovereignty and temporal power of the Catholic church over large parts of central Italy. To the church the kingdom of Italy was a sacrilegious usurper. In a land where the presence of the church had been felt for many centuries in multifarious forms and contexts, the conflicts and traditional divergences in attitudes already deeply rooted were given a new dimension. Even as the temporal power question receded into the realm of history, the older conflicts over the role of the church and its official and unofficial spokesmen in the questions of political, economic, social, and civic life remained.

On the political scene, while the forms of democratic parliamentary government existed, its substance did not evolve sufficiently in the decades after unification to insure continuity through consensus. Even as suffrage was widened in stages from its original base — one half million voters in a population of 27,500,000 — the parliamentary dictatorship of Depretis with its skilled *trasformismo* shortly after unification to the unparalleled masterful manipulations of Giolitti left frustrated the burgeoning pressures for diffusion of power in society. The Giolitti period of the first decade of the twentieth century, nonetheless, had gradually opened the gates to permit the start of an evolution toward a wider consensus in the community. The tide of events beginning with the Libyan imperial adventure and then the First World War proved too powerful, however, and the country succumbed to Fascist rule for a generation. The full-scale parliamentary democracy since the last war has functioned, too, under severe handicaps for achievement of reform through consensus. It has been strained by differences of doctrine and policy among the democratic parties, despite the achievements of the powerful Christian Democratic Party. More fundamentally, it has had to contend with the powerful Communist movement whose goals and methods permitted no alternative to the immediate danger the Communists represented to the democratic regime itself other than diversion of focus away from other objectives. Even more complicating was the impact of the Nenni Socialist Party position, which firmly embraced the cause of Communist alliance for most of the period. While loosening its embrace in recent years, the party engendered too little confidence that it genuinely sought effective return to democratic goals to be accepted as a legitimate participant in the game of parliamentary cooperation. It was only in 1962 that an experiment in such cooperation got under way.

Division has not only been a characteristic of society; it has also been a product of geography. Each of the regions of Italy has its own heritage, of which it has rightly been proud. The centralized regimes after national unification, by ignoring or even stifling the differences, created attitudes toward the national government which have left a heritage of psychological separatism. Above all, the division between north and south is striking. Northern Italy has been within the mainstream of western European evolution, while the south has remained a backward area with centuries of misrule, neglect, and misery carved deeply into its consciousness. Unification of Italy only brought additional burdens to the south, in the form of additional taxes and tax collectors, but offered no prospect for economic development or hope for social transformation. Only in recent years have systematic programs begun to obtain a more equitable land distribution, to reclaim and transform rural regions and develop the prerequisites for industrial development.

Meanwhile, however, even as significant progress is made, the striking difference between north and south continues. Not only are the people of northern Italy frequently ethnically closer to their neighbors to the north than to their fellow Italians in the south and in Sicily, but their way of life and their economy remain fundamentally different. The overwhelming proportion of industry is concentrated in the north, mostly in Lombardy, Piedmont, and Liguria. The large Po valley agricultural regions are relatively modern and prosperous. By contrast, the south and the islands remain for the most part more akin to North Africa as barren, agricultural regions in a pre-industrial atmosphere.

Italy as a whole has not been richly endowed by nature, if one uses the criteria relevant to economic well-being in an industrial society. Its natural attractions are world-renowned, but basic raw materials and mineral resources are few, and, until the discovery in recent years of natural gas and to a lesser extent petroleum, its power resources were limited. With a total land area little more than half that of France, its population of approximately fifty million exceeds that of its neighbor by about 10 percent. In addition, with approximately one third of Italy mountainous and another third hilly, its agricultural area is only about one quarter that of France.

The fundamental pressing fact of existence for an overwhelming number of Italians in the modern Italy of the last century has been grinding poverty. In terms of per capita calory availability, Italy is only slightly better off than Portugal and slightly less well off than Greece and Turkey. Per capita national income has shown a steady rise in recent years, but it is still about half that of France.[2]

The inability of the Italian economy to absorb its increasing population over the years during the last century is sharply pointed up in its labor force statistics. From 1881 to 1936, the population ten years of age and over increased by 11.2 million, while the employed labor force increased only by 3.2 million, equivalent to 28 percent of the total potential increase. This contrasts with a 75 percent absorption rate in Germany (1882 to 1925), a 54 percent rate in Great Britain (1881 to 1931), and 50 percent in the United States (1900 to 1940). In Italy, the inactive population of working age from 1881 to 1936, despite the economic development which took place during that period, more than doubled, going from 7.6 million (26.2 percent of total population) to 15.4 million (35.8 percent of total population).[3] The trend is underscored even more heavily if one uses the 1861 statistics as a starting point, since in that year the figure was 6.3 million or 24.1 percent of the total population. While the population as a whole increased by 62 percent between 1861 and 1936, the labor force increased by only 26 percent. Interesting to note is the fact that the employed labor force during this period increased by 40 percent in north and central Italy (where population had increased by 66 percent) and only by 4 percent in the south where population had increased 57 percent.[4]

2. Istituto Centrale di Statistica, *Annuario statistico italiano, 1961* (Rome, 1962), Table 454B, p. 438.
3. A. Jacobini, *L'Industria meccanica italiana* (Rome, 1949), pp. 4–5.
4. P. Saraceno, *Elementi per un piano economico 1949–1952* (Rome, 1948), p. 242.

The population of Italy has almost doubled since its first census after unification in 1871, increasing from 27.5 million to approximately 50 million. The increase would have been sharply greater had there not been a steady series of waves of emigration out of Italy through the years, prompted by the lack of economic opportunity at home. The greatest wave, during the years of this century before the First World War, witnessed the overseas emigration of over 5 million Italians and an additional 3.5 million who emigrated to other European countries. While approximately 2.4 million returned to Italy during this period, it left a net total emigration of approximately 6.3 million during a time when the total population of the country amounted to about 35 million.[5]

While Italy has generally been regarded as a country with a high birthrate by European standards, this reputation is contradicted by reality during the postwar period. As a matter of fact, the birthrate has been falling steadily over the last seventy-five years. While it had averaged 38.0 per thousand per year in the period 1881 to 1885, it fell to an average annual rate of 32.7 per thousand during the first decade of this century, and to 23.8 per thousand in the early thirties. During the 1950's it ranged between 17 and 18 per thousand, lower than France (18 to 19 per thousand) and very significantly lower than the United States (24 to 25 per thousand).

But the relatively low average birth rate for the country as a whole obscures the difference in rate between the north and the south. During 1960, for example, in the north, Piedmont had a birthrate of 12.3 per thousand, Lombardy 15.6, and Liguria 11.8; in the south, Calabria had a rate of 23.6 per thousand, Puglia 23.5, and Campania 24.9.[6]

The industrialization which began in the nineteenth century and set the stage for the emergence of a labor movement was concentrated almost entirely in the north. By comparison with other western European countries, industrialization began late in Italy and moved forward slowly. Until political unification of the country was achieved in the 1860's, the numerous subdivisions into which the territory was divided represented a limiting factor upon the development of industrial enterprise. The brief interlude of the Napoleonic era had not promoted enterprise in Italy, since in Napoleon's plans Italy was regarded simply as a source of primary products, principally foodstuffs, for France.[7]

While the situation changed slowly, during most of the following decades leading to unification, little spirit of enterprise manifested itself in Italy.

5. Confederazione Generale dell' Industria Italiana, *Annuario di statistiche del lavoro, 1949* (Rome, n.d.), Tables 317, 318, pp. 404–405.

6. Istituto Centrale di Statistica, *Annuario, . . . 1961,* Table 24, pp. 27–29; Table 417, p. 403.

7. Corrado Barbagallo, *Le origini della grande industria contemporanea (1750–1850)* (Perugia-Venice, 1930), vol. II, p. 17.

Roberto Tremelloni, commenting on the middle years of the century, says that little had changed from fifty years before when "the few dedicated to industries limit their initiatives to requests for subsidies and for tariff protection: all are accustomed to wait on the Prince . . . They thus develop and frequently abandon productive enterprises supported by privileges or guaranteed with legal monopolies and for which the paternal eye of the *Royal Signore* assists in cutting through complications . . . All this . . . certainly does not encourage individual initiative." [8]

As the century progressed, however, Lombardy under Austrian suzerainty and Piedmont under the reign of the House of Savoy[9] became the scene of ferment of liberal economic ideas, and progress was made toward the transformation and development of industry. In fact, as unification of Italy progressed, critics complained that "national independence is not a cry of revolution, but a principle of political economy." On the other hand, by contrast with what happened in England, it was writers on political and economic affairs who led the movement toward economic liberalism while the most directly interested, the entrepreneurs, appeared "more dragged than leading in this process." [10]

When the unification had been completed, the forward movement in Italy did not match comparable periods in the economies of other European countries. Railroad construction, largely with foreign capital, went forward as it did in other countries. However, in the years following 1861, rail traffic fell in Italy, by sharp contrast with what was happening in England. During the period 1861 to 1868, rail traffic per kilometer increased by more than 70 percent in England, while it fell by almost 20 percent on the northern line and by more than 50 percent on the southern line in Italy during the same period.[11]

While economic progress and industrial advance took place in the following decades of the nineteenth century, it was a very uneven process, characterized by sharp reversals as well as slow gains. Professor Gerschenkron, in an analysis of industrial growth in Italy,[12] points out that Italy had its period of "great push forward" during the years 1896 to 1908.[13] The annual

8. Roberto Tremelloni, *Storia dell'industria italiana contemporanea* (Turin, 1947), vol. I, pp. 23–24.

9. For the development in Lombardy, *see* Kent Roberts Greenfield, *Economics and Liberalism in the Risorgimento* (Baltimore, 1934). *See also* Epicarmo Corbino, *Annuali dell'economia italiana (1891–1900)* (Città di Castello, 1934), vol. IV, for later developments in regions of north Italy.

10. Quoted in Tremelloni, *Storia dell'industria italiana,* vol. I, pp. 158, 159.

11. Gino Luzzatto, *Storia economica dell'età moderna e contemporanea* (Padua, 1948), vol. II, pp. 366–367.

12. Alexander Gerschenkron, "Notes on the Role of Industrial Growth in Italy, 1881–1913," *Journal of Economic History* (December 1955), pp. 360–375.

13. There is general agreement among those who have constructed indices of industrial production for Italy upon the period of Italy's "great push forward," although

rate of growth during this period was lower than that which characterized other countries at an equivalent stage of development. Italy's rate was only half that of Sweden during its "push forward" in 1888 to 1896 and was only about three quarters that of Japan between 1907 and 1913 or Russia during the nineties. Furthermore, during the period 1896 to 1908 in Italy, progress was not steady, but proceeded in more jerky fashion than was true in other countries, reflecting "perhaps a more delicate state of public confidence and greater entrepreneurial uncertainties and hesitations."

Aside from its lack of natural resources, there were other retarding elements which contributed to the slowness of Italy's progress. According to Gerschenkron, in cases of very considerable backwardness, the policies of the state tended to play a very important positive role during the years of the big "upsurge" of industrial development in European countries. Nothing like this happened in Italy. There was state intervention in various forms but "what strikes the observer of these policies is not only their desultory character, not only the fact that they were rather less than more in appearance during the period of the great push of 1896–1908, but primarily the one-sided nature of the government's interest in industrial development, that is to say, its concentration on the least deserving branches of industrial activity." [14] The principal example is the tariff policy of the government, which became one of the obstacles to industrialization rather than an aid. Industrial growth was subjected to a protectionist climate in agriculture. On the industrial side, cotton textiles, an old industry which had already introduced technological advances and had limited possibilities of expansion, was protected. So, too, was ferrous metal-making, a heavy coal-consuming industry, while the machinery industry was only in part compensated for the duties accorded to iron and steel. Gerschenkron comments that only in the case of the engineering industry — which had the greatest potential for development — did government spokesmen find it advisable to pay their respects to the liberal tradition inherited from Cavour during the parliamentary debates on the tariff of 1887. The chemical industry was entirely ignored in the tariff arrangements, and machinery subsequently became the principal area of tariff concessions, leaving the industry entirely to its own devices, while iron, steel, and textiles remained heavily protected.

Cavour's liberal doctrines were a thing of the past by the 1880's. Protectionism served mainly as an instrument of vested interest in the absence of

---

considerable variation exists in the different findings on rate of growth. While Gerschenkron found a compound annual rate of 6.7 percent for the period, an official government study concluded that the rate was 9.8 percent (Ministero per la Costituente, *Rapporto della Commissione Economica, II Industria, I Relazione* (Rome, 1947), vol. II, p. 52. A lower rate was found, on the other hand, by G. DeMaria (*Giornale degli Economisti,* September–October 1941).

14. Gerschenkron, "Notes on the Role of Industrial Growth," p. 367.

a specific industrialization ideology. Nor was available capital drawn into industry very readily. The "veneration of 4 percent" which Professor Luigi Einaudi deplored at the turn of the century was far more prevalent than a venturesome spirit of enterprise. Finally, the last years of the nineteenth century were hardly conducive to confident growth, with their political disorders and repressions, nor was the industrial strife of the early years of this century reassuring to the less than bold spirits who sought guaranteed gain.

It is principally during the last decade that the Italian economy has expanded at a consistently rapid rate. The period of fascism between the two great wars succeeded in building up heavy industry to meet its imperial designs during the late thirties, but accomplished little toward a balanced economic development. The immediate years after the last war were concentrated in rebuilding the war-devastated economy. Since then Italy has forged ahead at rates which compare favorably with those of its own past and those of other European countries.

In the eight years between 1953 and 1961 industrial production almost doubled (197 percent).[15] The industrial expansion was accompanied by rapid strides in increased productivity and relatively less increase in use of manpower. The total employed labor force increased by 15 percent between 1954 and 1960, with the employed labor force in industry increasing by 34 percent during these years.[16] Real wages increased appreciably during the postwar period, but labor share of net industrial product decreased from 60 percent in 1948 to 53 percent in 1955.[17]

After the disastrous inflation during and after the last war which had carried prices to fifty times their prewar level, it is understandable that monetary stability should have been made a fundamental objective of government economic policy in the late forties. Economic orthodoxy was, however, carried to an extreme which earned the criticism of the United States European Recovery Program Administration,[18] and later the United Nations Economic Commission for Europe. The latter commented in 1953:

> Since 1947, the overriding aim of the economic policy of the Italian government has been to prevent a relapse into inflation and to make possible the abolition of controls, rationing, subsidies, and an economic functioning with a minimum of government interference. The main regulator of economic life has been a restrictive credit policy enforced by severe reserve requirements on commercial banks . . . The existence of a large State-controlled industry . . . gives

15. New York *Times,* International Edition, January 15, 1962, p. 16.
16. Cesare Vannutelli, *Labour in Italy in the "Sixties,"* p. 10, reprinted from Banco di Roma, *Review of the Economic Conditions in Italy* (Rome), XV, 1, January 1961.
17. United Nations Economic Commission for Europe, *Economic Survey of Europe in 1956* (Geneva, 1957), chapter VII, p. 21, footnote 30.
18. U.S. Economic Cooperation Administration, *European Recovery Program, Italy, Country Study* (Washington, 1949).

the Italian government considerable potential influence over industrial development . . . The government has been reluctant to interfere and make use of its
controlling share of ownership in business enterprise. Even State enterprises are
run as if they were separate private enterprises. In order to cover costs, they set
prices at a level too high to permit an expansion of production, although, given
the large unemployment, the social cost of an expansion would be small.[19]

Since 1953 the Italian government has hewn less closely to traditional
economic liberalism and has particularly emphasized its Vanoni plan for
general economic expansion and its plan for the economic development of
the south. The efforts have borne fruit in more rapid economic expansion.
In the south, progress with land redistribution, land reclamation, and efforts
at creating the prerequisites of industrialization has been made in recent
years. Nevertheless, as pointed out by the United Nations Economic Commission for Europe, the growth of national product "is increasingly dominated by the industrial situation in the North and less by the course of
agriculture . . . A fundamental purpose of the Vanoni plan — *viz* the
gradual elimination of the gap between the North and South — is not being
fulfilled." [20]

The rapid relative growth of industry in recent years is pointed up by the
shift in relative distribution of the labor force. For the first time, employment in industry moved ahead of that of agriculture in 1957. While 39.5
percent of the labor force had been devoted to agriculture and 32.5 percent
to industry in 1954, by 1958 the distribution was 32.3 percent in agriculture
and 36.2 percent in industry.[21] The trend continued in the next years, and,
in 1960, 31.2 percent of the labor force was devoted to agriculture, while 37.8
percent was devoted to industry.[22]

The development of the Italian labor movement, its characteristics, its
aspirations, and its frustrations, has been heavily conditioned by the political,
economic, and social characteristics of the country itself. The following
chapters trace the development of the movement in the context of the forces
which conditioned its nature.

19. United Nations Economic Commission for Europe, *Economic Survey of Europe
since the War* (Geneva, 1953), p. 76.
20. United Nations Economic Commission for Europe, *Economic Survey of Europe
in 1957* (Geneva, 1958), chapter 11, p. 38.
21. Computed from Istituto Centrale di Statistica, *Annuario. . . . 1958,* tables 335
and 336, pp. 306–307.
22. Vannutelli, *Labour in Italy, p.* 10.

CHAPTER II

The Political Atmosphere of Trade Unionism

The evolution of trade unionism in Italy is inextricably bound up with the ideologies current both before and after fascism which were vying for working-class support.

The psychology of scarcity, of lack of opportunity, of a hostile environment is rooted deeply in the consciousness of the people, reflected in their attitudes not only toward their economic environment, but toward their total environment, social, economic, political, cultural and even ecclesiastical. This has sometimes led to cynicism, a paralysis of will, or abject submissiveness. But mostly it has resulted in sporadic revulsion and rebellion, an overwhelming solidarity of class, a Herculean effort to make one's own individual way, a nihilism and an idealism, bursts of group enthusiasm, and then again, utter disinterest. These inconsistent reactions spring basically from the same background and are only different phases of the effort to obtain a somewhat more tolerable existence, to obtain recognition as individuals and as a group, to conquer the right to belong.

Through the period of the *Risorgimento* the ferment of liberal ideas and of economic change, so ably described for the Lombardy region by Kent Roberts Greenfield in his *Economics and Liberalism in the Risorgimento,*[1] was a phenomenon concentrated in the north. The unification of Italy, however, was achieved with a minimum of the social upheavals which so frequently characterized such processes in other countries. Agrarian reforms, social reorganization, a new society were far from the programs of those in control of the national unification process. As the Prussian state became the German state, so in Italy the Piedmont monarchy expanded to all of Italy. In the name of a united Italy, the Piedmont government wrested the land from its foreign and church rulers.

On the other hand, the unification process inevitably led to an awakening of the agrarian and city proletariat. Of the three national heroes of the unification of modern Italy there were two who refused to make peace with the result obtained, Giuseppe Garibaldi and Giuseppe Mazzini. The third, Count Camillo Benso di Cavour, who was Prime Minister during most of the unification period, represented the Monarchist liberal views which prevailed.

1. Baltimore, 1934.

Both Garibaldi and Mazzini were involved, separately, in the process of widening the new national community beyond the stratum of the governing group and the emerging industrial class. For Garibaldi this was an instinctive reaction of the knight errant in support of the little fellow. Having lent his sword to liberation movements half-way round the world, from Montevideo to Rome, this incarnation of the chivalry of past ages, the leader of the Expedition of the Thousand which brought southern Italy into the monarchy, lent his prestige and name indiscriminately to any movement which operated in the name of the underprivileged. His much quoted remark that "Socialism is the sun of the future" was typical of his support of movements which he never coldly analyzed but which appealed to him as symbols of revolt against oppression. Contributing mightily to the military phases of the unification, he drew his volunteers from among young intellectuals, as well as from the lower middle class and artisan groups. He never had the confidence or support of the ruling groups, but he did earn the adoration of the more idealistic young patriots and the neglected multitude.

Mazzini, on the other hand, not only developed a general philosophy of man's relation to society, but was in the forefront of the principal international political currents of the nineteenth century. An ardent patriot whose writings and activity forced him to spend most of his mature years in exile, his participation in public affairs in Italy, starting from membership in the early secret patriotic societies, the *Carbonari,* continued for more than forty years. His Young Italy movement, organized in 1831, spearheaded the patriotic movement for many years under the slogan of "unity, republic, democracy." With profound religious convictions, he was a leader in the fight against the temporal power of the church and for a short time, under the protection of the sword of Garibaldi, was head of the Republic of Rome during the tumultuous days of early 1849. The social content of his philosophy and his activity among wage-earner organizations will be briefly discussed in the next section. His basic effort, throughout his active political life, however, was devoted to obtaining the inclusion of all groups, including the underprivileged, in the patriotic movement and in a movement for the establishment of wide democratic reforms.

Despite the role of Garibaldi and Mazzini in the Italian unification process, however, the mass of people in the country did not feel involved in the events as they unfolded toward unification; in the agricultural areas, that is, in most of the country, they were even hostile to it. Rosselli, for example, in discussing this point says:

The Italian rural multitude, debased by misery and by degrading ignorance, did not participate in the efforts toward national unification, or if they manifested in some case their sentiments, they were almost everywhere and almost always hostile to the "innovation" desired by the *"signori,"* requested by the city and imposed on the countryside.

And later:

Let us abandon once for all the idea that in the toil for national unity and independence, the *people* or even an important fraction of the working classes had participated actively. The truth is that on the grey foundation of ignorance, of indifference and in many cases of the downright hostility of the masses, a tiny minority, belonging to the middle and upper classes, more or less conscious of their goal, sometimes in disagreement over the means to employ and the immediate objectives to be achieved, in part obeying an idealistic impulse, in part impelled by more modest concrete interests, hurt by the political fragmentation of Italy, carried the national problem to a solution.[2]

Mazzini and the Friendly Societies

The trade union and labor movement in Italy is not a linear descendant of the guilds. More similar to the British than to the Scandinavian experience in this regard, the gap in time between the effective functioning of the guilds and the emergence of the economic prerequisites for a trade union movement was too great in Italy to make possible a direct transition. The guilds were abolished over a fifty-year period, first in Tuscany in 1770 and last in the Bourbon Neapolitan kingdom in 1821. As in other countries, there was little left of strength and vigor in the guilds by the time they were abolished. The first trade unions in a modern sense did not develop until many years after the guilds had ceased to exist.

The linear predecessors of the trade unions in Italy were the friendly societies or mutual aid organizations (*Società di mutuo soccorso*), although, here too, only in some cases were the friendly societies transformed into trade unions. The friendly societies began developing through the early part of the nineteenth century and particularly in the forties and fifties. They generally had religious overtones, a patron saint, and financial support was common from among the wealthy and nobility. The benefits were commonly for illness, old age, funeral expenses, and sometimes covered accident and widow and orphan assistance. The societies were, during the early period, more frequently organized according to area than occupational groups, although as time went on the latter type began to predominate.

Perhaps more important than the transformation of some friendly societies into trade unions was the function which the friendly societies gradually assumed as meeting places for the discussion of the new ideas which began creating ferment among wage-earner groups in the wake of the revolutions of 1848.

2. Nello Rosselli, *Mazzini e Bakounine, 12 anni di movimento operaio in Italia, 1860–1872* (Turin, 1927), pp. 16 and 38.

The first promulgator of ideas which set the stage for the character of the trade union movement as it developed later was the Mazzini Young Italy movement. As a patriotic movement it was strongly Republican and anti-clerical (but not anti-religious). The monarchy issue alone was great enough to prevent Mazzini from making peace with the institutions which emerged out of the Italian unification process. Mazzini's differences, however, with the dominant groups in the new Italian government were much deeper, including political issues like his support of universal suffrage, economic issues like his rejection of liberalism, and social issues such as his insistence upon protective social legislation and education. Mazzini's social doctrine differed sharply from that of all the Socialists who competed in the First International. Mazzini rejected class conflict and collectivism. His basic social orientation, within the framework of a "free church in a free state" with the widest political liberty and freedom, was the participation of workers in ownership and the fruits of property rights in industry. Workers' cooperatives was the answer but not the entire answer offered by Mazzini. Private ownership was not to be entirely eliminated. Rather the two would compete, and as a result of such competition, and above all as a result of education, the private enterprise would accept such modifications in its habits as to make it conform to the standards of justice of the new society. Profits would be shared with workers; ownership, too, would be similarly shared, and exploitation would thus be eliminated. The key to Mazzini's approach was the opposite of that of Marx. Not class struggle, but class collaboration, not destruction of the *bourgeoisie*, but education. His emphasis was on responsibilities as much as on rights. Significantly, his principal work was entitled *Of the Duties of Man*. It is doubtful that the following which he acquired among wage earners in Italy understood much of what he taught, but he inspired confidence and a warm sympathetic admiration.

The friendly societies became the organizational instrument through which Mazzini tried to spread his political and social doctrine and to organize support for his position on the basic questions arising out of Italian unification. The early societies, mainly concentrated during the late forties and the fifties in Piedmont under the pre-unity liberal reign of the monarchy, but also in Lombardy and Tuscany, were for the most part in the hands of those who shared the dominant liberal thinking of the *Risorgimento* and repudiated efforts to draw the societies into the general political arena.

The societies during the early period were heavily under the influence of their honorary membership, drawn from groups and individuals who either contributed financially to the organizations, or who were favored politically by the membership.[3] During this period, honorary members frequently amounted to as much as 20 percent of the total membership. The officials of the organizations were frequently drawn from the middle and upper

3. *Ibid.*, p. 102.

classes. For example, even at Milan where worker participation was relatively high, in 1864 the president was a count, the secretary was a professor and one of the two vice presidents was a lawyer. The second vice president was a bookbinder. On the other hand, in this case the other minor officials were largely drawn from among the actual membership.[4] The membership largely comprised artisan journeymen. Only in the large cities were laborers beginning to participate in the organizations. The public authorities looked with favor upon the development of these self-help organizations, although they lent little direct assistance to them.

The beginning of a coordinated movement among friendly societies dates from 1853, when for the first time thirty societies from the Piedmont area met at Asti and established machinery to discuss common problems.[5] Thereafter a Congress of Worker Societies was held each year for a period of nine years, and at less frequent intervals in succeeding years. During the period of 1853 to 1859 the moderate liberal views prevailed. The congresses formed little continuing machinery: merely a commission to make arrangements and prepare an agenda for the following congress. Complete independence and autonomy was left to the individual organizations. The regulation of the congresses approved at the Third Congress held at Genoa in 1855 set out the purpose of the organization as follows: "The principal scope of the congress is to promote the moral and material welfare of the working class through education and mutual aid; to spread useful knowledge of social and private economy relative to the conditions of the industrial and working classes; to compare the practical experiences of the various societies in order to utilize them for the general interest." [6] In addition to the problems concerning assistance and reciprocal aid to traveling members, the most frequently discussed subject was that of education, both general and technical.

4. *Il Giornale degli Operai* (Genoa), II, 11, p. 85, March 12, 1864.

5. For text of official summary of the proceedings of the congress *see, Sunti degli atti del congresso generale delle Società degli Operai dello Stato tenutosi il 17, 18, 19 Ottobre 1853, in Asti,* originally published at Asti by Tipografia dei Fratelli Paglieri, 1853, and reprinted in *Movimento Operaio,* II, 11–12, pp. 314–324 (Milan, August–September 1950). Earlier, in 1850, representatives of several societies (from Pinerolo, Casale and Alessandria) met at Turin and agreed in "provisional articles of temporary association" to furnish assistance reciprocally to workers who emigrated from one city to another. During the following year at the inauguration of the Society of Turin, thirty-three societies adopted a revision of the earlier pact and decided upon the establishment of a continuing organization. While a second meeting was held at Turin in 1852, it was the Asti Congress which officially began the continuing existence of the organization. Gastone Manacorda, *Il movimento operaio italiano attraverso i suoi congressi (1853–1892)* (Rome, 1953), pp. 27–30.

6. Article 7. Text given in *Sunti degli atti del Terzo Congresso Generale dell Associazioni Operaie dello Stato tenutosi il 23, 24, 25 Novembre, 1855 in Genova,* originally published at Genoa by Tipografia di Andrea Moretti and reprinted in *Movimento Operaio,* III, 14 (Milan, December 1950 and January–February 1951), pp. 450–472 at p. 460, *see also* pp. 316–321.

At the First Congress, it was recommended that societies should set up classes on evenings and Sundays and require all members to attend. It was also agreed to petition Parliament and the municipalities for the expansion of elementary technical education to children. At the Fourth Congress at Vigevano in 1856, it was agreed to ask the Parliament to make elementary education compulsory.[7]

The tone and general social view taken at these early congresses is illustrated by the 1857 Congress' approved text of a petition to Parliament for compulsory education:

Yes, oh *signori,* compel the worker to educate himself and instruct himself and he will become independent: becoming independent he will be able to provide for himself honestly, and will regard — of this we are certain — impassively and no longer with envy, the wealth of the rich. Compel the worker to educate himself, to instruct himself and you will have, in a word, dissipated all the phantoms of the Socialist school.

The congresses reflected the views prevalent among the societies on the subject of agitations and strikes. For example, the First Congress adopted a resolution condemning the demonstrations taking place at the time against the high cost of living; two years later the Genoa Congress turned down an appeal for support from the longshoremen of the city who were agitating for a wage increase.

At the Milan Congress held in 1860 (after the unification of all Italy except Rome and Venice) there were 64 societies represented from all parts of Piedmont and Lombardy and from Emilia and Tuscany.[8] At this congress there was substantial representation of the Mazzini viewpoint, largely by societies participating for the first time. In the context of the Congress of Worker Societies the clash of views between the *Mazziniani* (Republicans) and the Moderates was on the basic issue of whether the societies and the congress should enter politics. In addition, the Mazzini view was that societies should be organized along craft or industry lines and not on a general geographical basis, that the societies and the congress should concern themselves with and work toward establishment of universal suffrage, immediate completion of Italian unification, establishment of a republic, and that the congress should set up a stronger, more centralized organization.[9]

At the Milan Congress the Moderates were able to keep a nominal control and obtain a majority view that geographical organization of worker

7. Manacorda, *Il movimento operaio italiano,* p. 38.
8. Rosselli, *Mazzini e Bakounine,* pp. 60–65. The Milan Congress was the first to call itself "Italian" rather than Piedmont. As pointed out by Rosselli, the view that the societies should be concerned with politics was supported at the congress by many who were not under Mazzini's influence.
9. *Ibid.,* pp. 58–84.

societies was preferable to craft or industry form of organization. On the other hand, they were forced to compromise by expressing a concern with the suffrage problem, in a resolution asking that the electoral law be modified so that "the working class have its just part in the naming of deputies." [10] The atmosphere was still one of moderate liberal thinking on economic questions characterized by the slogan which decked the platform in the hall of congress: "To you, who with heart and brain provide work by encouraging industry, the worker is assiduously grateful." [11]

The *Mazziniani* continued to gain support and at the Ninth Congress of Florence in 1861 they were able to win control of the organization. Their victory was at the cost of a split which, while healed for a time, became final at the next congress in 1863.[12] The Mazzini victory was a costly one for the organization. Less than half the number of societies represented at Milan were left after the 1863 Parma Congress.[13] On the other hand, in the succeeding years the number of societies attending congresses increased until, in 1871, 153 organizations were represented at the congress held in Rome. During the 1860's there was a three-fold increase in the friendly societies throughout the country. The 153 societies attending the Rome Congress represented only approximately 10 percent of the societies in existence at that time.[14]

The Florence Congress split had been precipitated by a vote on the motion that political questions were of interest to the organizations. The congress then proceeded to set up a committee to study the best means of extending organization among the workers into societies, obtaining universal suffrage and "compulsory secularized education." [15] The congress expressed concern with the problem of low wages but, reflecting the views shared by both the Mazzini followers and the Moderates, condemned strikes as disastrous

10. Manacorda, *Il movimento operaio italiano,* pp. 43–47; Rosselli, *Mazzini e Bakounine,* p. 64, characterizes the congress as a Mazzini victory.

11. Reported in *L'Unità Italiana,* October 29, 1860, and referred to in Manacorda, *Il movimento operaio italiano,* p. 42.

12. *Ibid.,* pp. 48–62. After the Florence split, a reunification process began to succeed since the political forces within the new government of the time were supporting the "Rome and Venice" unification campaign of Mazzini. However, within a few months a government reaction set in against the Mazzini movement which even resulted in the shutting down of some friendly societies. The result was that the anti-Mazzini societies definitely broke away from the Congress organization.

13. The delegates from the Milan Society reported to their organization after the Parma Congress "It is painful to say so, but the Tenth Congress of Parma was not dissimilar from the preceding ones and the conclusions were as empty as were the discussions." *Il Giornale degli Operai* (Genoa), I, 5, pp. 35–37, December 12, 1863.

14. Rosselli, *Mazzini e Bakounine,* pp. 126 and 373. At the Naples Congress of 1864 the proportion represented was also about 10 per cent. *Il Giornale degli Operai* (Genoa), II, 45, p. 353, December 5, 1864.

15. Rosselli, *Mazzini e Bakounine,* pp. 81, 83.

to the workers' interests. Greater coordination among societies, urged by the Mazzini groups, was voted at the 1863 Congress and confirmed at the Naples Congress of 1864, where an elaborate constitution was adopted, the *"Atto di fratellanza delle società operaie italiane."* As a matter of fact, despite the lengthy discussions on the document which had extended over a two-year period, its single important achievement was to provide for greater centralization in the organization.

The Mazzini forces had taken control of the congress. Not only did they weaken the organization in the process, but they did little with the organization once they gained control. There were no congresses for seven years after 1864. The organization was in fact dormant, with the energies of Mazzini and his close followers concentrated almost exclusively in the national political field. The development of individual friendly societies, however, continued at a rapid rate. By 1871 there were more than 1500 such societies throughout the country. Their mutual-assistance benefit plans, their educational programs, and the opportunities they presented for political and economic discussions flourished without specific central leadership.[16] While the 1871 Rome Congress of the societies was a Mazzini-staged performance,[17] and the Moderates staged a similar competing congress during the following year,[18] the underlying political and economic situation was already beginning to shift the stage from the friendly societies to political and, later, trade union organization. The central federation forged by the Mazzini forces first at Naples and confirmed at Rome, however, continued for a number of years, with as many as three hundred societies affiliated in 1874.

Bakunin and the International

During the sixties and early seventies the expectations which had been built up around the economic fruits of Italian unification suffered a rude disappointment, particularly in the seven years following the unification of all Italy save Rome and Venice. It was during these years that those who had opposed unification popularized the slogan, "It was better when it was worse." Prices kept rising, taxes were increasing, wages remained low. Discontent was widespread among wage earners, farmers, and artisans. The church and its clerical supporters, particularly in the areas over which the church had formerly exercised temporal power, carried on a widespread and energetic campaign of undermining the government, creating discontent and provoking anti-government activity. The myth of the "Revolution betrayed" was created. Among the wealthy, temporal power of the church

16. For discussion of the functioning of the individual societies, *see* Egisto Romani, *L'organizzazione del ceto operaio nelle società di mutuo soccorso* (S. Benedetto, 1895), esp. pp. 61–65.

17. Rosselli, *Mazzini e Bakounine*, pp. 357–385.

18. Manacorda, *Il movimento operaio italiano*, pp. 71–75.

— which they confused with religion — was described as the only force which could keep the poor on the proper road, while the Italian government — "the negation of God" — was bringing social chaos and revolution.[19] To the lower classes in the cities and particularly in the countryside a stream of anti-patriotic propaganda flowed from pulpits, in popular newspapers, in pamphlets, in meetings, and in proclamations. The propaganda took the form of depicting a betrayal by the government, a worsening of conditions under an uninterested government, a cynical use of the poor for the ends of the governing groups. The clerical propaganda contributed significantly, particularly in central Italy, to preparing the ground, already made fertile by the basic economic situation, for the success of the Socialists in later decades. Its purpose was that of strengthening its own forces to regain temporal power. Its only concrete result, according to Rosselli, "was to provoke in the poor classes the natural rancor against the moneyed class, pressing the workers toward the idea and the practice of the class struggle and of accentuating their indifference toward the political events of the country and instinctive diffidence toward the powers of the State, held to be expression of interests antithetical to theirs by the privileged classes." [20]

During this period the democratic Mazzini movement, as we mentioned in the preceding section, had succeeded in taking control of the Worker Society Congresses and of a large proportion of the individual societies. On the other hand, its preoccupation with pressing for the completion of the unity of Italy lessened its interest in immediate programs in the social field. Despite its success in capturing control of the Worker Society Congresses, its principal political support came from the patriotic youth, from intellectuals, from the middle classes. The impression, a lasting one, which it made upon workers was its promotion of cooperation, education, and organization.

Into the turbulent scene of the sixties came the figure of Michael Bakunin.

19. *See, for example,* various quotations from contemporary sources in Elio Conti, *Le origini del socialismo a Firenze (1860–1880)* (Rome, 1950), pp. 24–31.

20. *See* Rosselli, *Mazzini e Bakounine,* pp. 47–51. Typical of the tone used is the following quotation from *La Vespa* of Florence during 1864:

"The wolves in sheep's clothing preach liberty, equality, respect for law and at the same time close every avenue for honesty and skill in order to assure a sumptuous income to the hangmen and their helpers, who precisely in the name of this liberty, of this equality, plunder us, bleed us, exploit us . . . while thousands of workers are . . . oppressed by misery and cannot find work . . . the high functionaries relax in the comforts of a blissful life and the parasites, under the pretext of supporting the masses, fatten themselves at the trough of the State . . . If the people, who are the greatest of all powers, learn sometime to use their authority . . . they will not so often be trampled on, laughed at and cheated."

Rosselli, among others, has pointed to the fact that in many of the strikes in southern Italy during the years following Italian unification there is strong evidence to support the thesis that they were instigated by "clerical-reactionary" elements.

Arriving in Italy in 1864, he lived intermittently there for ten years.[21] The revolutionary socialism or anarchism of Bakunin was based upon ethical assumptions. Every organized power, by whomever represented, eliminated the liberty of the people. Capitalism was the principal evil. In this he was in agreement with Marx. But for Bakunin, unlike Marx, the state as such was incompatible with socialism since the very existence of the state must mean domination of one class by another. A loose system of free cooperative societies would be the method of organizing society in freedom and equality after a revolution had destroyed property and the state.

Bakunin, during much of the period of his activity in Italy, was engaged in a bitter struggle with Marx over control of the International Association of Workmen (the First International) organized at London in 1864. To Bakunin, Marx was an authoritarian, and his methods and ideas were the contradiction of the libertarian and federalist ideas of Bakunin's anarchism. In his conflict with Marx, Italy became one of the principal sources of his support. The first widespread efforts at the diffusion of Socialist ideas in Italy was thus not Marxist, but Bakunin's version of revolutionary socialism. On the other hand, during the ten-year period following Bakunin's arrival in Italy, these Socialist ideas were not placed primarily in an anti-Marx context. The ground was prepared for the spread of Marxism later in the century through the generic and vague Socialist ideas as spread by Bakunin and his followers, based upon concepts such as historical materialism, which were common to both Bakunin and Marx.[22]

In Italy Bakunin had to contend with the Mazzini influence. Despite the basic clash on the level of ideas and on the practical level of organization, Bakunin and Mazzini, in the early years of Bakunin's efforts, maintained a relatively good relationship. Mazzini himself had a representative at the first meeting of the International Working Men's Association at London, who proposed the Brotherhood Pact adopted at the Workers' Society Congress at Naples earlier that year as a model for the new organization. But Mazzini's bid for influence in the International failed from the start through the successful maneuvering by Marx. Mazzini, critical as he was of the Marx influence in the International, nevertheless did not fight it during its early years.[23]

21. See Max Nettlau, *Bakounine e l'Internazionale in Italia dal 1864 al 1872* (Geneva, 1928).

22. Roberto Michels, *Storia critica del movimento socialista italiano dagli inizi fino al 1911* (Florence, 1926), pp. 46–53.

23. For example, Mazzini in 1865 answered an inquiry concerning his attitude toward joining the International: "Join the International Association. The English elements are excellent; the others not so good. But you should guard against the influence of those who seek to increase the open antagonism between the working classses and the middle classes, which would be harmful without helping to gain our objective." Quoted in Rosselli, *Mazzini e Bakounine*, p. 149 from Aurelio Satti, *Cenni biografici e*

Bakunin, in agreement with Marx, in 1864 viewed as his principal task the winning away of popular support from the Mazzini movement.[24] His method, however, was not to direct his attack openly upon Mazzini himself. During his first years in Italy, with headquarters first at Florence and then at Naples and Sorrento, Bakunin concentrated upon intellectuals, middle-class students, professional groups, adventurous souls, to obtain a leadership group for his movement.[25] In this task he was singularly successful, although much less so in the early years at Florence than in the south.[26] He gradually, particularly in the Naples area, succeeded in drawing into his movement a considerable number of middle-class intellectuals, especially from among the student groups who became dedicated apostles of Anarchist insurrection.[27] Among the most important converts of this early period was Carlo Cafiero, a Neapolitan nobleman who turned over his entire wealth to the movement and became one of its most courageous and prominent leaders.

It was not until 1869 that the movement actually took root in Italy. The agitations of the intellectual youth attracted to it were combined with the economic conditions which were dramatized in 1869 in the revolts, demonstrations, and general unrest growing out of the protest against the new tax on flour milling. These activities among both the rural and city population were frequently without leadership, certainly uncoordinated, but spread widely in the country. The Anarchists had no role in the leadership or in the instigation of these agitations. In some areas the clergy encouraged the discontent. For the most part, however, the demonstrations were spontaneous.[28]

The 1869 disturbances resulted in considerable violence and suppression by the government. The Anarchists took advantage of the situation as best they could in organizing into sections of the International those drawn to their movement by the events of the year. Naples remained the principal center of the movement, with considerable activity in Sicily and the Puglie area in the south. Gradually drawn into the movement, however, were

---

storici a proemio del testo di Giuseppe Mazzini, scritti editi ed inediti (Milan–Rome, 1861–1891), vol. XVII, p. XII.

24. Rosselli, *Mazzini e Bakounine*, p. 173.

25. Michels explains the Bakunin approach as growing out of his attitude that "the proletariat, both urban and rural, is everything: force, life, intelligence, humanity and future; one thing alone they still lacked, thought," and this would be furnished by the student disciples of Bakunin. Michels, *Storia critica*, p. 14; *see also* Roberto Michels, *Il proletariato e la borghesia nel movimento socialista italiano* (Turin, 1908), p. 22.

26. Conti, *Le origini del socialismo*, pp. 76 and 81.

27. Bakunin in a letter to Francesco Mora wrote that he found in Italy "all those elements which elsewhere are missing; a youth energetic and easy to enthusiasm, without security of existence or career who, while coming from the *bourgeoisie*, has not yet reached the moral and intellectual exhaustion as it has in other countries." Quoted in Michels, *Il proletariato e la borghesia*, p. 28.

28. *See* Rosselli, *Mazzini e Bakounine*, pp. 230–247.

groups in Florence, Bologna, and the Romagna area. The event which added considerably to the attraction toward the movement was the Paris Commune in 1871. Garibaldi, with his immense popular following, threw himself on the side of the Commune. While Garibaldi's commitment to socialism was a generic one rather than a commitment to Bakunin, the Anarchist movement profited from his position. In addition, Mazzini's attack upon the Commune and his repudiation of its leadership and its conception indirectly helped the Anarchists. The Commune had so popular an appeal in Italy that Mazzini's position among the working population suffered drastically.

In 1871 the Internationalists claimed 10,000 members.[29] By 1874 they claimed 26,704 members in 129 branches.[30] By 1870 there were thirty newspapers and periodicals being published in support of the Italian International movement.[31] In 1872 the First Congress of the Italian Federation of the International Working Men's Association was held at Rimini. Twenty-one sections were represented. Of these only one — from Naples — was affiliated with the London International. The others were either branches formed directly by Bakunin followers or worker societies which had passed from Republican to Anarchist influence. Condemning Marx's ideas as "German authoritarian Communism," the congress voted to break all relations with the London General Council and not to send representatives to the next congress of the International.[32]

By this time the Anarchist movement was a strange combination of open workmen's organizations — sometimes purely political, sometimes primarily mutual-aid organizations and sometimes a combination which included some trade union functions — and small conspiratorial groups which were secretly organized for insurrectional purposes. The former, except for the tone of their pronouncements, were in fact moderate in their activity and their interests. For example, Michels points out that "nothing would be more mistaken than to think that the Revolutionary Socialists of southern Italy in the first years of the International were wild rebels . . . Frequently they used the most conciliatory methods toward employers. Rather the Revolutionary Socialists appeared sometimes to permit themselves to be attracted to very reformist ideas" such as arbitration and limits on strikes.[33] On the

29. Michels, *Storia critica*, p. 27.

30. Conti, *Le origini del socialismo*, p. 146, cites the statistics given by the Commission of Correspondence of the Italian Federation of the International to the Central Commission at Brussels. Michels, *Storia critica*, p. 42, claims that there were more than 300 branches in 1872 and that only two (Lodi and Aguila) sided with Marx against Bakunin.

31. Michels, *Storia critica*, p. 29.

32. Manacorda, *Il movimento operaio italiano*, pp. 82–86.

33. Michels, *Il proletariato e la borghesia*, pp. 30–31. Michels points out, for example, that when the anarchists tried to set up a worker organization in Naples in

other hand, the secret conspiratorial groups were the ones relied upon for the planning of insurrections.

As the movement grew in the atmosphere of fear following the Paris Commune, intermittent and widespread efforts at suppression of the Anarchist movement were made by government authorities. It is of interest to note how much attention was paid to the Anarchist movement by the police in Italy. The heavily documented study of the origins of socialism in Florence by Conti, cited previously, draws predominantly upon police reports of the period. The police and their agents had systematically infiltrated the movement; their information was detailed and, it would appear, was reported to headquarters in objective and accurate fashion.

The movement continued to grow. The agitations and demonstrations in 1873 which resulted from the economic crisis of that year were ascribed at the time to the Anarchists, with only small justification.[34] The economic crisis and the growth of the movement caused the Anarchists to feel that they could stage a successful insurrection. In 1874 they planned to begin one in Bologna. The insurrection proved a complete fiasco since the plans were obviously known in advance by the police. Sections of the International were closed down by the government, arrests were widespread, and the leaders of the movement tried in a much publicized trial two years later. Meanwhile, other attempts at insurrection, such as the famous Benevento episode of 1877, took on the aspects of comic opera performances rather than serious social movements. The trials of 1876 and the revolts of 1877 represented the last large splash of the Anarchists in Italy. During the following years the movement declined. Many of its most prominent leaders and most of its followers ended up in the Socialist movement as it evolved in the next decade.

The fact that the Anarchist movement had drawn into its circle many middle-class intellectuals had caused Marx during his conflict with Bakunin cynically to describe the Italian Internationalist movement as follows: "The 'Alliance' in Italy is not a worker organization but a troop of dispossessed,

---

1869 it made plans to build up strike funds and provided that strikes could be called only under the following conditions:

"Only a general and regular assembly of all the members of the Strike Fund have a right to declare and sanction the strike" and could only do so, "1. If the Fund is in a condition to distribute to each member and for at least three months a daily subsidy of two lire; 2. If the General Council at London is informed of the question and has given its consent; 3. If notification of the strike has been given in all places from where workers could be drawn to make the strike useless; 4. If there has been correspondence with all the principal centers of the industry; 5. If the vigilance service of the strike, the 'Surveillance of the Workers,' has been well organized." (p. 30, note 6)

34. The second Congress of the Italian Federation of the International Working Men's Association held in Bologna in 1873 was forced to meet secretly after the police broke up the open sessions and arrested the leaders. Manacorda, *Il movimento operaio italiano*, pp. 89–93.

the refuse of the *bourgeoisie*. All the so-called sections of the International in Italy are led by lawyers without clients, physicians without patients and without qualifications, students devoted to billiards, peddlers and shopkeepers and especially journalists of the small press, of more or less dubious fame." [35]

It is true that the Anarchists had practically no following in the cities of the north, where the new industries were developing a discipline and an evolution in thinking that rejected "revoltism," and in the decades that followed gave strength to the Socialist movement. For similar reasons, it had no appeal in the few large factories which existed at the time in the Florence area. It did have considerable appeal, however, in the rural and urban areas in the south and in north central Italy which were economically backward, or were in a state of transition between an artisan society and an industrialization which was only falteringly moving forward. Anarchism, for those who suffered in this process, was an expression of protest in the generic revolt traditions of the people.

The Workers' Party

The economic conditions of the late seventies favored the development of a more moderate Socialist movement in northern Italy. By 1878 the economic crisis which had begun in 1873 had been overcome. Monetary stabilization had been achieved in 1877, and in the following years there was considerable expansion of investment in industry and in construction. The modern factory system was taking hold in the large centers of the north. Private domestic investment and foreign capital combined in the late seventies and early eighties to create a boom atmosphere in the industrial part of the economy. In addition, the declining prices of agricultural products throughout Europe during this period were reflected in Italy in the declining cost of living for industrial workers.[36] It is during this period that the real beginnings of trade union and worker political activities became established in the north.

The Anarchist movement began to decline and was replaced on the political side with divergent movements, socialism on the one side and "worker exclusivism" on the other. Many of the Anarchist leaders turned to socialism in these years. Andrea Costa, the most important and popular of the Anarchist leaders in north central Italy was converted to socialism in 1879, convinced by the failure of the revolts of the previous years that it was neces-

35. Quoted in Michels, *Il proletariato e la borghesia*, p. 63, from Karl Marx, *L'alliance de la democratie socialiste et l'Association internationale des travailleurs, Rapports et documents* (London–Hambourg, 1873), p. 48. This quotation long was the standard reference for a characterization of the Italian Internationalist movement led by Bakunin.

36. *See, for example,* Gino Luzzatto, *Storia economica dell' età moderna e contemporanea*, vol. II, pp. 377–398.

sary to move more slowly and be concerned more directly with problems of immediate interest to the people.[37] The defecting Anarchist leaders brought new strength to the emerging Socialist forces which had been promoted in north central and northern Italy during the late 1870's by Benoît Malon, a veteran leader of the Paris Commune who came to Italy after the fall of the Commune, and Erico Bignami whose newspaper *La Plebe* became an important rally point for socialism, and Osvaldo Gnocchi-Viani.

In the Lombardy region, while the socialism of Enrico Bignami and Osvaldo Gnocchi-Viani made little headway among the industrial workers, significant organizational developments of a different form were taking place. The friendly societies had continued to grow, many were being converted into "leagues of resistance" or labor unions. With increased interest in political affairs, a "worker exclusivism" began to develop as a form of increased repudiation of "Moderate" parties on the one hand and distrust of intellectuals who spread the Socialist doctrines on the other. The General Association of Workers' Mutual Aid of Milan, which had existed since 1860, continued as an association of friendly societies with no industrial or craft differentiation and was controlled by conservative elements. On the other hand during the 1870's, a *Consolato Operaio* had developed in each of various areas of the Lombardy region, made up of societies organized on the basis of arts or crafts. The societies were mostly friendly societies, but included also many which were performing some trade union functions, others which were organized as labor unions, and some which were organized for educational and recreational purposes. In 1881, the Radical Party supporters who predominated in the societies of the *Consolati* organized a constituent convention for the formation of a *Confederazione Operaia Lombarda* (Confederation of Lombardy Workers). The convention reflected the democratic Radical orientation of the majority in its support of friendly societies: popular credit banks, consumer and producer cooperatives, the need for spreading popular lay education and support for universal suffrage. In addition, while suggesting that labor disputes be submitted to private arbitration, it committed its support for labor pressure on management for improvement of conditions. Considerable sentiment for rejecting nonworker leadership was expressed by many participants, although no strong issue was raised on this subject.

The *Consolato* of Milan had set up a recreation and study group, a *Circolo Operaio,* which became the center of worker exclusivism. The widening of political suffrage for the elections of 1882 for the first time gave large sectors of workers in industrial areas of the north an opportunity to participate in a national election. Led by a glove maker, Giuseppe Croce, the Milan *Cirolo Operaio* in May 1882 issued a manifesto calling for the

37. For text of Costa's letter explaining his repudiation of anarchism *see* Michels, *Storia critica,* p. 75.

formation of a workers' party made up exclusively of workers and concerning itself solely with problems of direct interest to workers. The manifesto was signed by a provisional committee made up, besides Croce, of a cabinetmaker, a typographer, a barber, and a goldsmith. It said, in part:

Workers! Our interests are in fact different from those of all the other classes, therefore, it is natural that the section and the party can be organized only by the individuals directly interested, that is, by workers. The workers, let us keep well in mind, O comrades, will never be respected, as they deserve, until they make known to the world that they want and are able to study and treat with all questions which directly affect them by themselves . . . We conclude: our scope is the material and moral improvement of the working multitudes to be obtained through their own efforts, organized into a workers' party, independent of all other parties.[38]

Within two months a "Milan section of the Workers' Party" had been set up and issued its program. The program took the position that on matters in which the state was urged to take action, cooperation with other political parties was possible since the proposed reforms had a universal and humanitarian importance not exclusively of interest to workers. In the case of action toward capital it was held that the opposition of interests made interference or "begging for support" from other parties undesirable. On the subject of state action its program included: the right and freedom to strike, universal suffrage, absolute freedom of the press, right of association, right of assembly, freedom of education, abolition of a permanent army, complete communal autonomy, institution of a single progressive tax based upon capital and income excluding basic necessities, abolition of religious subsidies.

The Workers' Party program in its section dealing with problems of capital said, in part:

The Workers' Party, indignant and concerned by the universal predominance that capital exercises over labor, supports the workers who individually or collectively, because of the length of working hours beyond just limits or because of reduction of wages beyond the limits of necessity, abandon the fields, the workshops, the factories, the mines, the quarries, feeling solidarity with them and helping them with the moral and material means at its disposal, and proposes:
To establish local leagues of resistance, federated among themselves by a pact of solidarity and independence for the purpose of forming a single worker organization, the prime objective of their party.
To obtain the participation in profits derived from labor.

38. Text of manifesto and program in A. Angiolini, *Cinquant' anni di socialismo in Italia* (Florence, 1903), pp. 157–159.

To organize worker societies, credit, production and consumer cooperatives.
To found at party headquarters an employment placement section for un-
employed workers.
To have the communes construct worker housing.
To secure that all public works be performed by workers' associations.

In the elections of 1882 the Workers' Party received but modest support.
It is of interest to note that Socialists of all hues participated in the elections
and did not make common cause with the Workers' Party. Andrea Costa
was the only Socialist elected to Parliament. While the Lombardy Socialists
were not hostile to the Workers' Party, the program of the party, concerned
as it was with a combination of labor and specific political reforms with
little Socialist ideological content, was regarded as too far removed from
Socialist doctrine to be viewed favorably.

Actually the party and its related League of the Sons of Labor in Milan
were hybrid affairs, concerned in fact much more with promoting the development of labor unions and the industrial interests of workers than
general political objectives. While the Workers' Party and its branches
maintained their worker exclusivism, their activity in both the industrial
and political field brought them increasingly close to the Socialists in specific
orientation.[39] A representative of the Workers' Party was sent to observe the
1886 Congress of the Lombardy Socialists and the Congress adopted a resolution expressing sympathy and a willingness to cooperate with the Workers'
Party's efforts.[40] The Socialists in the Milan area agreed to support the candidate for Parliament named by the Workers' Party in the 1886 elections. The
Workers' Party did not reciprocate by supporting a second candidate named
by the Socialists themselves.[41] Neither the Workers' Party nor the Socialist
Party showed great strength, although the former gained considerably over
its showing in 1882. The Radical Party candidates were strongly supported
by the *Consolato* in Milan, and most were elected.

Shortly after the elections, the government "for reasons of public order"
closed down the headquarters of the Workers' Party and arrested a number
of its leaders. While some historians have claimed that the government was
prompted to take action because of the growing strength of the movement
and the increasing indications that the Workers' Party and the Socialists
were moving closer together,[42] it appears more likely that the very weakness
of the movement rather than its strength precipitated the action: the govern-

39. Michels, *Storia critica*, pp. 92–93.
40. Angiolini, *Cinquant' anni*, p. 171.
41. There is some controversy on this point. Angiolini, *Cinquant' anni*, p. 173,
says the Socialist candidate, Gnocchi-Viani, was not supported by the Workers' Party
and appears to be correct. On the other hand, Michels in his *Storia Critica*, p. 95, gives
the impression that the party supported the candidacy of Gnocchi-Viani.
42. Angiolini, *Cinquant' anni*, pp. 173, 174.

ment had looked with favor on the movement as a means of weakening the Radical Party in the Lombardy area, but the 1886 elections showed that the Workers' Party had not sufficient appeal to neutralize worker support for the Radicals. Its repeated demonstrations of independence from government influence were probably an additional factor[43] as well as the beginnings of a tendency for the Socialists and the Workers' Party to move closer together.

The crackdown on the Workers' Party was of short duration, but the conventions of the party in 1887, 1888, and 1890 witnessed the gradual break-up of the party as more and more of its leadership and followers began to favor cooperation with the Socialists.[44] "The Workers' Party did not die either a violent or a natural death. With a slow organic process, protracted for an entire decade, it passed almost inadvertently into the Socialist Party." [45]

To understand the decline of the Workers' Party it is necessary to take into account the Socialist activities of the late eighties. A national Socialist Party had not yet been organized. On the other hand, the Socialist ideas, the formation of local and regional Socialist groups, the increasing tempo of propaganda and activities in the enormously expanding leadership circle already gave it the importance of a national movement. The anarchism of Bakunin had given way to a socialism which, while frequently generic and humanitarian, as with Bignami and Malon, became more and more Marxist in its ideology. The spread of Marxist ideas during this period and during the next decade among the intellectuals of Italy was a phenomenon of gigantic proportions. The background of an economy which seemed to lack the spark of individual initiative to break clean with its feudal past and create a dynamic forward motion; a political atmosphere of personalized rule in government through "deals" which well earned the name of *"trasformismo"*;[46] the disastrous government adventure into colonialism (the defeat of the Italian forces in Ethiopia); all these combined into an atmosphere ripe for new social ideas. Some of the best-known writers, scientists, artists, and professors became converted to socialism.[47]

43. Michels, *Storia critica*, p. 95.

44. Angiolini, *Cinquant' anni*, pp. 185–186, 188–197.

45. Michels, *Storia critica*, pp. 95–96.

46. Depretis as Prime Minister, beginning in 1887, was responsible for the development of the system, used also by his successors until the First World War, of governing through combinations based on exchange of favors with parliamentary representatives. The combination pork barrel and log-rolling resulted in support for government in power with little regard for principles or parties upon which parliamentary candidates had been elected. This rule by transformation became known as *"trasformismo."*

47. A poll was conducted in 1895 by Gustavo Macchi, a newspaperman, among a group of prominent writers, scientists and artists. The results of the poll showed 75 percent of the writers, 78 percent of the scientists, and 90 percent of the artists as favorable to socialism. Reported in Michels, *Storia critica*, p. 191.

Benedetto Croce in his history of Italy comments on the phenomenon of that period:

If one passes in review the intellectual world of those days, one is forced to conclude, not indeed that all those who embraced socialism were chosen spirits, for the movement, like all movements, attracted all kinds of people; but that socialism won over all, or almost all, the flower of the younger generation; and that to remain uninfluenced by and indifferent to it, or to assume, as some did, an attitude of increasing hostility toward it, was a sure sign of inferiority.[48]

The emerging leadership of the Socialist movement was a dedicated group with an evangelical spirit sparing little in its devotion and energy in propagandizing its ideas. While it had at first viewed with considerable suspicion the development of the Workers' Party, it soon realized that it had a great deal to gain in wooing the group. Its own following among workers was as yet relatively modest.

The Workers' Party had crystallized for many of the workers in the north the idea of resistance to employers, and of repudiation of existing political parties as of no service to workers. If the group were eventually won to socialism, as seemed probable, then the Socialists had much to gain by encouraging the Workers' Party. This they did, while they increasingly tried to demonstrate — and eventually succeeded — that they supported all the causes of direct interest to labor, whether this involved a labor dispute with an employer or a demonstration against a government action hostile to labor.

The followers — and most of the leaders — of the Workers' Party gradually came around to the support of socialism and a willingness to drop their worker exclusivism. The exclusivism had been a transitional stage in the development of the institutions for their own protection; it had represented a growing self-confidence which repudiated both the interest of the traditional political parties to act in their behalf or the need for dependence on these parties; it had represented a repudiation of the psychology of humble dependence upon *noblesse oblige* of employers and had been prompted by a self-confident attitude toward their own ability to form and lead trade union organization. It must be remembered that the organizers and supporters of the party were from among the most educated, skilled wage earners in the part of Italy which was in the forefront of industrial development. The exclusivism which repudiated assistance or participation by non-wage earners was a repudiation of the semifeudal attitudes which still prevailed in the economic and political spheres in the country. As in other countries, worker exclusivism was a normal stage in the early evolution of the labor movement.

48. Benedetto Croce, *A History of Italy 1871–1915* (Oxford, 1929), p. 148.

As time went on, however, exclusivism was dissipated between the dynamism of the Socialist ideas and the practical assistance which the "intellectuals" of the Socialist movement rendered to the wage earners in their agitations for better conditions. The wider horizons offered by the Socialist ideas and Socialist movement made exclusivism seem illusory and unnecessarily limiting.

By the time the Seventh Worker Congress was held at Milan in 1891, the Workers' Party was for all practical purposes dead. Its former adherents, together with the Socialists, were able to command a majority in contrast to previous congresses where Radicals and moderate democratic groups had predominated.[49] This Worker Congress was a continuation of those begun as the congresses of the Lombardy Worker Confederation. They were assemblies of various types of organizations, predominantly friendly societies, but also cooperatives, worker education and study circles and political groups, and, increasingly, trade unions. Many of the societies combined several of these functions. There was practically no continuing machinery between congresses. While the congresses were not representative of a continuous movement, they did represent at the time the principal gathering of worker organizations in northern Italy. The 1891 Congress, with Socialist ideas prevailing, helped crystallize the determination to form a Socialist Party on a national scale.[50] Among the more significant resolutions were ones which strongly supported the right of association into trade unions and criticized the Italian legislation on the subject of strikes; a resolution which favored the promotion of protective labor legislation; an attack on militarism and the military; and, most important, a resolution with obvious Socialist orientation supporting the creation of a national political party.[51] On the latter subject, it is interesting to note that while some of the language of the resolution still contained some vague exclusivist phraseology, it represented, particularly if taken in combination with the other resolutions adopted at the congress, an endorsement of the program which had been elaborated and launched with much publicity earlier in the year by the Socialist League of Milan.[52]

49. Angiolini points out, *Cinquant' anni,* p. 198, that non-worker Socialists attended and played an important role — as representatives of various organizations. *See also* Rinaldo Rigola, *Storia del movimento operaio italiano* (Milan, 1947), pp. 114–115.

50. For the official summary of the congress proceedings and text of resolutions, see, *Congresso operaio italiano tenutosi in Milano nei giorni 2–3, Agosto 1891–Riassunto delle discussioni e deliberazioni* (Milan, n.d.); pages 18 and 19 list the organizations represented at the congress.

51. Texts given in *ibid.,* pp. 8–10 and 15.

52. This program became the model for the program of the Socialist Party when it was later organized. The full text is given in the April 30, 1891 issue of *Critica Sociale* (Milan). Parts are quoted by Angiolini, *Cinquant' anni,* pp. 203–205 and by Rigola, *Storia,* pp. 107–114.

The 1891 Worker Congress was a significant milestone. The differentiation between the economic organizations and the political organizations concerned with workers' interests had reached a stage in which within one year a national Socialist political movement was launched, and within two years the first national organization of trade unions was established. With the 1891 Congress, the history of the pre-labor movement was closed. One could from 1892–93 onward speak of a national Italian labor movement, both political and trade union.

The Socialist Party and Government Suppression

The national political movement was launched at a congress in Genoa in August 1892.[53] The approximately 400 delegates, mostly from north and north central Italy, represented all shades of Socialist opinion. The Anarchists also attended, but walked out of the session over the basic issue of whether the new party would participate in parliamentary elections. The Milan Socialists led by Filippo Turati, together with the Workers' Party group led by Giuseppe Croce, were the dominant elements at the congress and were relatively cohesive, with a Reformist Socialist orientation. The other delegates were a heterogeneous lot, representing a wide spectrum of Revolutionary and Reformist Socialist convictions. All agreed upon the establishment of a national party. Agreement upon a program, however, was more difficult. As a result, the program adopted was general in language and vague on objectives and means. It nevertheless remained the official program until 1919.

The launching of the new party[54] gave new impetus to the extension and growth of the Socialist movement. Within one year the party claimed 107-830 members, based upon the 299 organizations — most of which were trade unions, cooperatives and friendly societies — which had affiliated.[55] The congress held at Reggio Emilia in 1893 set the pattern of the party's relationship to other parties and defined the limits of autonomy of its parliamentary representatives.[56] Socialist candidates would run for public office independently, and no electoral "deals" would be made with any other parties. Socialist deputies in Parliament were prohibited from ever supporting a vote of confidence to a government. The deputies were to be required to form a disciplined group, support only those measures approved by the party, always obtain the views of the party on all issues, always in debate

53. For a detailed account of the congress *see* Angiolini, *Cinquant' anni*, pp. 205–217.

54. The name adopted at Genoa was *Partito dei Lavoratori Italiani* and did not become the *Partito Socialista Italiano* until 1895, with the transitional name *Partito Socialista dei Lavoratori Italiani* used in 1893–1894.

55. Angiolini, *Cinquant' anni*, p. 217.

56. For a complete account of the congress and text of the resolutions, *see ibid.*, pp. 219–230.

emphasize that they "have no faith in adulterated reforms which the *bourgeoisie* may concede in the interest of its own preservation" and always take inspiration from the party program which "is in fact and in essence revolutionary."

In the general parliamentary elections of 1892 several Socialist deputies had been elected, and, while the number was not significant, it underlined the growing importance of socialism on the national scene.[57] In the local elections of 1892 and 1893 the Socialists received wide support in Turin, Milan, Bergamo, Cremona, Pavia, and in many communes in Emilia and Tuscany.[58]

During the preceding several years, the government had from time to time obstructed the activities of the Socialists in some localities but had not attempted any general suppression of the movement. Developments in Sicily during the early 1890's, however, became the occasion for several years of general repression on a national scale which had a profound effect upon the Socialist movement in the following years.

In 1891 a movement had begun in Sicily among the farm population and among wage earners in the large cities calling itself *Fasci dei Lavoratori*. The organizations had a heterogeneous character. In some urban areas they were centers to which existing mutual aid, trade union, cooperative and other worker organizations were affiliated. In other areas they were directly organized as political organizations. They had no well-defined character, and, while many of the leaders were Socialist, the movement was by no means entirely a Socialist-oriented one. In its rapid spread throughout the island it was a manifestation of the traditional incendiary relations between the poor peasants and the large landholders, combined with immediate economic grievances. Sicily was one of the most backward areas in Italy.[59] The living standards, even by comparison with the rest of Italy, were appallingly low. A landless peasantry was constantly confronted with extreme contrasts in wealth, but in the immobile social structure had no hope of obtaining land or improving its lot. More than 70 percent of the population was illiterate. Consumer taxes levied by the local authorities were several times as high as those in the north of Italy with its sharply higher income

57. The exact number of Socialist deputies becomes a matter of definition. Michels, for example, in *Proletariato e borghesia*, pp. 90–92, lists twelve as having Socialist ideas (listed originally by the Socialist newspaper of Reggio Emilia, *La Giustizia,* and quoted in Angiolini, *Cinquant' anni,* p. 230). On the other hand, only six became part of the Socialist parliamentary group established as a result of the Reggio Emilia Congress decision, and of these six only four had been elected as Socialists — the other two joined the Socialists after election to Parliament.

58. Angiolini, *Cinquant' anni,* p. 218.

59. For a discussion of the economic conditions in Sicily at the time, *see, for example,* Salvatore Carbone, *Le origini del socialismo in Sicilia* (Rome, 1947), pp. 3–33. For other bibliographical references, *see ibid.,* pp. IV–IX.

levels. Added to these basic underlying elements was the specific worsening of economic conditions at the time resulting from the world-wide fall in agricultural prices, combined with the disastrous tariff war between Italy and France which had closed the French markets to such products as wine, upon which the Sicilian economy depended.

During the two years following 1891, the *Fasci* movement spread throughout the island with remarkable rapidity. At the height of the movement there were about 200 *Fasci* with about 200,000 members.[60] For the most part the movement during this period had a strong economic-protest character.[61] In many cases specific demands for economic improvement led to disputes, strikes, and sometimes concessions from landholders, and, in the cities, from industry management. An attempt was made by some of the leaders who were Socialists to give the movement a Socialist character. Basically, however, even though some of the *Fasci* became affiliated with the Socialist Party, it remained a more generic social-economic protest movement to which the superstitious, illiterate, dissatisfied peasantry responded with emotional fervor, making it an outlet for their religious ardor and the pent-up hatred of their squalid lives. An observer visiting the island in 1893 wrote the following concerning the heterogeneous nature of the movement:

In some regions it had spread like a kind of contagion; the populace was obsessed with the belief that a new reign of justice was imminent, it met in the rustic meeting halls of the *Fasci* with a fervor with which the followers of Spartacus must have met in the great forests or the early Christians in the catacombs.

Not everywhere did the *Fasci* have a modern Socialist character. In some places they were nothing else than a collection of poor ignorant people organized by some ambitious person against the dominant party in the municipality. In other villages the *Fasci* were organized by instinct of imitation; in still others instead of Socialist ideas one found a kind of religious mania — at Lazzaretti this is so much the case that in the offices of some *Fasci* I saw the crucifix hanging with lights over it; in others, finally, the *Fasci* was nothing else than a gathering of scoundrels, who christened with the new name of *Fascio* the same associations of delinquents which once had called themselves *mafia* or *camorra*.[62]

60. Michels, *Storia critica,* p. 160. Estimates vary considerably, ranging generally between 200,000 to 300,000.

61. For detailed account of the *Fasci* movement, *see* Napoleone Colajanni, *Gli avvenimenti in Sicilia* (Palermo, 1895); N. Colajanni, "I Fasci di Sicilia," *Riforma Sociale,* I, 1–2, March 10–25, 1894, and reprinted in Salvatore Francesco Romano, *Storia della questione meridionale* (Palermo, 1945), pp. 145–169; Francisco De Luca, "I Fasci e la questione Siciliana," in *Critica Sociale,* IV, 11 and 12 (1894), reprinted as pamphlet with same title by *Critica Sociale* (Milan, 1894); Carbone, *Le origini del socialismo;* Angiolini, *Cinquant' anni,* pp. 264–281.

62. Quoted in Angiolini, *Cinquant' anni,* p. 251.

It was not infrequent that *Fasci* demonstrations displayed with unsophisticated impartiality pictures of the Virgin Mary, Karl Marx, and King Humberto I. Their slogans of protest were frequently interspersed with cries of "Long live the King."

The mixed economic-social nature of the movement resulted in decisions by the *Fasci* to participate in the local Sicilian elections of 1893. The growing economic pressures of the *Fasci* had already frightened the dominant social groups. The numerous successes of the *Fasci* in the municipal elections of 1893 were an even more frightening development for the dominant political cliques. Above all, fear was generated by the fervid spirit with which the lower classes were responding to the movement. The increasing demonstrations of strength created pressures upon the national government to do something to counter the *Fasci*. While there had been local repression and interference in the activities of the organizations on various occasions during this period, the national government did not regard the problem of the *Fasci* as a threat, and in 1893 Giolitti, who was at the time the interim Prime Minister, had dispatched his Director General of Public Safety to study the *Fasci* and their threat to public order. Giolitti, who was to dominate the political scene during the first years of the twentieth century until the First World War, described his own evaluation of the movement in his memoirs years later:[63]

I perceived at once that the movement was an economic one, fully justified by the disastrous conditions in which the peasants and miners found themselves, as was then fully demonstrated by inquiries conducted by important papers like the *Tribuna* and the *Corriere della Sera*. The revelations as to the miserable conditions of the Sicilian workers and the atrocious abuses made of child labor in the mines produced a lively impression on public opinion.

Without allowing myself to be too much alarmed, I had given the prefects instructions corresponding to the reality of the situation. I ordered them to maintain public order and prevent in any way the use of violence, but they were to allow the peasants and miners to obtain better conditions and were even to try and persuade the proprietors to come to a peaceful settlement.

But in my opinion, and according to the reports I received from the authorities, all the rumors that were going around of revolutionary danger and threats to the national unity were without foundation. The movement in conclusion was much less grave than others which followed it, but it was the first, and the wealthy classes, not yet accustomed to this kind of struggle, mistook economic agitation for social revolution.

I remember also that after the dissolution, a congress of large owners at Caltagirone, which congress had the courage to propose, by way of reform, the abolition of elementary instruction, so that the peasants and miners, not being able to read, would not be able to absorb new ideas.

63. Giolitti, *Memoirs of My Life,* translated by Edward Storer (London and Sydney, 1923), pp. 88–89.

The point of view and the conduct of the government changed later, when, for other reasons, I resigned.

When Crispi returned to power late in 1893, however, he took a much more serious view of the situation. The continued worsening of the Sicilian economic situation and the growing strength of the *Fasci* meanwhile had increased the number of violent incidents. Crispi, who was obsessed with fears of foreign intrigue against Italy, claimed that the *Fasci* were a movement in league with France and Russia to separate Sicily from Italy and that revolt was imminent. He embarked on a systematic campaign of suppression in December 1893. Innumerable instances of violence occurred, headquarters and newspapers were closed down, hundreds were deported from Sicily, scores of leaders of the movement were jailed.

There is little doubt that some of the demonstrations of the *Fasci* had degenerated into occasional violence. The extent of reaction, particularly after Sicily was placed under martial law early in 1894, was out of all proportion to the provocation. That the situation was serious and could get out of hand unless improvements were made for the peasants was recognized even by those who participated in the leadership of the movement. For example, Napoleone Colajanni as early as 1892 had said in Parliament, "I do not know if Sicily could be the scene of a civil war, but I know that the hatred of the peasants against the so-called gentlemen is most sharp. Wherever the *latifondo* exists this hatred is generated. In Sicily the danger of agrarian rebellion is permanent and if we do not do something about it, we may witness a really painful awakening." [64]

Crispi did not stop at suppression in Sicily. He used the situation as an excuse to strike out at the Socialists throughout Italy during 1894 and 1895, closing headquarters and newspapers, placing Socialist leaders under house arrest, and creating a general state of repression. All organizations having the most tenuous relation to the Socialists or to what was officially regarded as extremists suffered the same fate. Trade unions and other worker organizations were indiscriminately shut down and prevented from functioning. While Crispi fell from power in 1896 as a result of the disastrous defeat of the Italian forces at Adua in Italy's imperialist adventure in Ethiopia, and was replaced by Antonio di Rudinì, his violent suppression policy created the atmosphere for a public reaction of widespread sympathy for the Socialists which had an important effect in winning adherents and support for the Socialist movement.

Important, in addition, was the support and cooperation offered in Parliament and in public by other parties of the so-called extreme Left: the Republicans and the Radicals. Even the Liberals came to the defense of

64. Quoted in Panfilo Gentile, *Cinquant' anni di socialismo in Italia* (Milan, 1948), p. 62.

the Socialists. The Socialists continued to reject cooperation with the Republicans and Radicals as a matter of principle. The wave of sympathy for the party, however, resulted in the election of twelve Socialist deputies in the general elections of 1895, with an increase to fifteen in the elections of 1897.[65]

Even more impressive was the increase in the number of votes for Socialist candidates, considering the still restricted suffage with about one million votes cast. From an estimated 26,000 votes in 1892, the number increased to approximately 76,000 in 1895, and to approximately 135,000 in 1897.[66]

The repression of 1894–95 was followed within a few years by a still greater wave of violent repression. The early nineties have been referred to as the Black Years in Italy because of the serious repercussions of the economic warfare with France.[67] Both industry and agriculture were put in difficult straits. In the late nineties economic conditions gradually began to improve. Grain shortages and increased bread prices which resulted from the Spanish-American war, however, became the focal point of discontent. During 1898 there were demonstrations in most of the large cities, particularly in the north, as part of a campaign to eliminate the tax on flour milling. As the demonstrations spread, the government began using violence to suppress them. The most dramatic clash took place during May 1898 in Milan when over a four-day period the military carried out a campaign to clean out the demonstrators. The official figures claimed that two policemen and eighty demonstrators were killed with 450 demonstrators wounded during what became known as the "Four Days of Milan." [68] Others have claimed that up to 400 demonstrators were killed.[69]

Milan had only been the dramatic culmination of demonstrations and violent countermeasures in other areas, particularly in the north.[70] The government pursued its repression policy with the shutting down of the headquarters of any group even remotely suspected of having any responsibility for the demonstrations; trade unions, Socialist, Radical and even Catholic organizations. Thousands were arrested and more than six hundred were given prison terms by special military tribunals. A censorship was established for all newspapers and publications. The official violence and repression exceeded by far the measures taken less than four years before. With great reluctance, the Socialists as a matter of self-preservation were

65. Michels, Il proletariato e la borghesia, pp. 90–94.

66. Spartaco Cannarsa, Il socialismo e i XXVIII congressi nazionali del Partito Socialista Italiano (Florence, 1950), p. 93; Rigola, Storia, p. 172.

67. See, for example, Gino Luzzatto, Storia economica, vol. II, pp. 396–411.

68. Rigola, Storia, pp. 183–184.

69. Ibid.; also, Angiolini, Cinquant' anni, p. 352.

70. For detailed discussion of this period see ibid., pp. 328–396; Michels, Storia critica, pp. 199–206.

pushed by events into cooperation with the Radicals and Republicans. The general revulsion against the government rapidly spread much wider than among the three Left parties and forced the resignation of Rudinì.[71]

The government of Luigi Pelloux which followed lasted only one year. As a liberal general with a reputation for moderation, he had been expected to reverse the policies pursued by Rudinì. Instead, he issued only a limited amnesty and pressed for legislation to limit public meetings, authorize suppression of organizations under specified conditions and regulate the press. Under the circumstances the Socialists in Parliament began working closely with the Radical and Republican parliamentary groups. Since their combined strength, even with scattered support from other parties, was insufficient to prevent passage of Pelloux's program, they embarked on an extended filibuster. The tactic of obstruction succeeded in dramatizing the issues to a point that Pelloux felt compelled to dissolve Parliament and call for general elections during June 1900.

The election resulted in a repudiation of Pelloux and his supporters. The Socialists more than doubled their parliamentary strength by electing 33 deputies and receiving 13 percent of the popular vote.[72] The Radicals and Republicans with whom the Socialists, despite their doctrinal hesitations, jointly fought the electoral campaign, made significant advances. Other moderate opposition parties also gained strength. The interim ministry of Saracco lasted about six months in 1900 during which time the last attempt at suppression was tried in the Genoa area, this time exclusively against the trade unions.[73] But suppression as a means of fighting the rising tide of labor organization and the increasing strength of the Socialists had been tried too often during the preceding years and had failed. The temper of the times called for a different approach and the naming of Giuseppe Anardelli as Prime Minister in 1901 with Giolitti as his Minister of Interior heralded

71. Giolitti commented upon the events in his *Memoirs* as follows (Giolitti, *Memoirs,* p. 125):

"The disturbances of 1898 were originally occasioned by the misery which harassed the country, after a long and critical period which had affected the economic system of the whole world, followed by the unforeseen heavy increase in the price of bread, due to a bad harvest. Moreover, the government had not even taken the precaution of temporarily removing the *octroi* tax on corn. In my opinion, it was an error to suppose that we were in the midst of a great subversive political movement; it was rather an expression of discontent. But there still existed among the governing classes a state of mind that denoted a great fear of any popular agitation and its consequences, and the government, reflecting this feeling allowed itself to order measures of repression that were excessive."

72. Istituto Centrale di Statistica e Ministero per la Costituente, *Compendio delle statistiche elettorali italiane dal 1848 al 1934* (Rome 1947), vol. II, pp. 116–117 and 128–129, tables 44 and 47.

73. For details, *see* Rigola, *Storia,* pp. 193–199.

the basic change to an acceptance of labor organization and Socialist activity as a legitimate part of the political and economic scene in Italy.

The Formation of Trade Unions

The gradual transformation of many mutual-aid organizations into trade unions during the eighties has already been mentioned. Strikes for economic improvements and even trade union activities — generally as a by-product of mutual-aid organizations — however, had not been infrequent during the preceding twenty or more years, even before the unification of Italy.

As early as 1848 the printers of Turin had organized and obtained agreement from the printing shops of the city to a "price list." [74] The Society of Compositors of Turin, as the organization called itself, had a continuous existence from that time on. It had many features common to mutual-aid organizations of the time. Its concern with wages and working conditions gradually overshadowed its mutual-aid activities. The agreement of 1851 with the Turinese printing establishments contained detailed wage provisions and provided for time and one-half for overtime.[75] The printers of other cities gradually imitated their Turin colleagues. By 1870, eight other societies had already been founded,[76] and were dividing their energies between trade union and mutual-aid problems.

In some areas, the printers had greater difficulty than in Turin in establishing recognition of their "price lists" and agreements. For example, in Milan when the Society of Typographical Artists was organized, an agreement was reached in 1860 only after a strike, and the organization went out of existence for five years in 1867 as a result of employer opposition to a continuation of the agreement which led to an unsuccessful strike and gradual disintegration of the organization.[77]

After several false starts in 1868 and 1869, a national federation of typographical workers was formed in 1872 with which printers' organizations from thirteen cities were affiliated. The organization defined its purpose to include (1) observation of price lists of labor; (2) subsidies to unemployed members; (3) subsidies to traveling members; (4) establishment of stand-

---

74. See the interesting history of the National Printers' Federation: Tomaso Bruno, *La Federazione del Libro nei suoi primi cinquant' anni di vita* (Bologna, 1925).

75. A photostatic copy of the agreement is in *ibid.*, opposite page 24.

76. In Genoa (1852), Milan (1860), Florence (1864), Bologna (1865), Brescia (1868), Venice (1866), Treviso (1867), and Rome (1870). *Ibid.*, p. 20.

77. Ufficio del Lavoro della Società Umanitaria, Publication No. 18, *Origini, vicende e conquiste delle organizzazioni operaie aderenti alla Camera del Lavoro di Milano* (Milan, 1909), pp. 29–30. For an early history of printers' organization in Milan, *see ibid.*, pp. 129–224. The Umanitaria publication referred to here is a valuable compendium of information on the origins and early activity of more than two hundred local labor organizations in the Milan area.

ards for working conditions and admission of apprentices, and (5) maintaining contact among the affiliated organizations.[78] The national federation gradually became more centralized and was one of the most important trade union federations throughout the pre-Fascist period.

Another organization which reached back into the early history of Italian trade unionism was the hatters. Here the long history of mutual aid in a strongly organized association gradually turned to concern also with trade union problems. Some of the features of *compagnonnage* were preserved from an earlier day. An identification card system was used among the membership, which included exchange of cards and subsidies for traveling members. "Price lists" were decided locally and enforced through strikes if necessary. As early as the eighties the local organizations were enforcing union shop conditions by refusing to permit members to work alongside nonmembers. The hatters, through this period, remained a much more decentralized organization than did the printers' federation. While the local organizations came together for national congresses regularly and established requirements for admission of new locals, they set up no continuing national machinery. By 1885 the hatters' congresses assembled 85 local organizations with a total membership of 5000.[79]

Although there are strikes recorded during the sixties and seventies, most of these were not accompanied or followed by trade union organization. More frequently an organization sprang up spontaneously during a strike and gradually disappeared afterwards, or a mutual-aid organization lent itself to further the spontaneous demands of workers and then returned to its mutual-aid functions. Bakers were among the groups frequently involved in disputes in those years.[80] Construction craft workers, particularly bricklayers, were another group among whom strikes were not uncommon in the sixties.[81] One of the most important strike movements of this period occurred among the woolen textile workers of the Strona valley in the Biella area in 1863–64 in protest against what were considered intolerable factory regulations. The strikes, which involved about 3000 workers, were successful in obtaining new regulations in the plants of the area. These regulations remained in effect for thirteen years. When the employers' association tried to institute new regulations in 1877 without consulting the workers, a three-and-one-half-months' strike, closing down twenty-four establishments,

78. Bruno, *La Federazione del Libro,* pp. 17–20.

79. Direzione Generale di Statistica, *Statistiche degli scioperi avvenuti nell' industria e nell' agricoltura* (Rome, 1892), pp. 14–16.

80. *See for example,* report of the bakers' strike at Leghorn in 1864, *Il Giornale degli Operai* (Genoa), II, 38, p. 304, September 18, 1864.

81. For example, the successful strike, accompanied by considerable violence in Milan in 1860 (*Origini, vicende e conquiste,* p. 79) in which bricklayers obtained a 20 percent wage increase, and the strike of bricklayers in Brescia which also won a wage increase in 1864 (*Giornale degli Operai,* II, 33, August 14, 1864, p. 263).

successfully prevented management from doing so. These strikes in the Biella region were led by mutual-aid organizations which normally had little active concern with working conditions but which found themselves thrust into leadership as the only existing organizations of workers.[82]

The 1877 strike in Biella, with its violence and dramatic resistance against strikebreakers and management, helped focus government attention on the problem of strikes and the fact that repression alone was no solution. The government appointed a public commission to investigate the causes of strikes and to recommend means of avoiding or settling them.[83] The commission made a thorough inquiry into the question and concluded that freedom of organization should be guaranteed by law to permit collective bargaining under the new economic conditions prevailing in Italy. The commission, in its conclusions, stated:

Being aware that no special provisions can be proposed which would hasten the restoration of the ancient harmony between capital and labor, the commission has, in its proposals, placed at the top of its list, a law which recognizes, without restrictions of any kind, the right of workers and industrialists to organize themselves for the protection of their respective interests and which protects this right from violence and fraud which tend to take away from the organizations their character of a free will agreement and transform them into means of compulsion for the profit of the greedy or into instruments of disorder at the service of those who are disturbers and ambitious.[84]

While attempts were made to enact legislation along the lines of the commission's report, Parliament voted against it, and the questionable legality of trade union organization and strikes continued.

During the period of 1860 to 1878, according to the commission's study, there were 634 strikes. The majority of these took place in the north, principally the Lombardy and Piedmont regions, and were for the most part related to wage questions. The greatest number of strikes took place in the textile and dyeing industry; rural public works and railroad construction workers, construction workers, printers and bakers were also prominently represented.[85]

According to the investigation commission, Socialist and Anarchist agitation played no role in the vast majority of these strike situations. They were concentrated in those industries, principally textiles, which were in the

82. Rigola, *Storia*, pp. 147–149; Rigola, *Rinaldo Rigola e il movimento operaio nel Biellese,* autobiography (Bari, 1930), pp. 6–50; *Il Giornale degli Operai,* II, 36, September 4, 1864, p. 287; *Ibid.,* II, 48, November 27, 1864, p. 383; *Ibid.,* II, 51, December 18, 1864, p. 408.

83. *Statistiche degli scioperi,* p. 3.

84. Quoted in Rigola, *Storia,* p. 151.

85. For details *see Statistiche deli scioperi,* pp. 4–5.

forefront of industrial transformation and in the crafts which have traditionally been among the first to organize and attempt to improve their
conditions. The textile industry is particularly worth mentioning. Despite
the seeming victories of the strikes of 1864 and 1877 in the Biella area, the
workers in the industry were increasingly at the mercy of the employers as a
result of the rapid basic transformation of the industry and the government's
willingness to use force against the workers. In the seventies, according to
Rinaldo Rigola who lived in the area and later led the national trade union
movement, to identify oneself as a weaver was to be marked as an agitator,
so widespread was the agitation against the transformation of the industry.[86]
But the introduction of machinery, the home work system, and increased
use of female and child labor were decisive. For the Biella area, one of the
largest textile areas, in the late seventies "the final balance sheet of those
great manifestations," wrote Rigola, "closed with an enormous deficit for
the working class: the invincible Textile Mutual shut down, the heads of the
movement fugitives or in prison, the laid-off workers forced to change
occupation or to emigrate to America, and a general misery. For ten years,
that is, until the work had been adapted to the new industrial system, there
were to be no more strikes of any importance in the woolen textile industry."

During the eighties the process of transformation of mutual-aid organizations into trade unions[87] and the establishment of new trade unions were
accelerated, particularly in the Lombardy and Piedmont regions. Rapid industrial expansion and a construction boom characterized the period until
1887, followed by the Black Years of 1888 to 1894.[88] In the industrial areas
and large cities of the region it was the Workers' Party more than any
other group which promoted organization of workers along trade union
lines.

In the agricultural areas, it was the Socialists who had the greatest influence in this regard. In the Po Valley an enormous economic and social
transformation took place in agriculture during the 1870's and 1880's. Increased taxes and falling agricultural prices created impossible financial
burdens for small landholders who lost their land by the tens of thousands
during this period. In Mantova alone there were 4700 court ordered expro-
priations in the five-year period from 1874 to 1879. The result was gradual
consolidation of land into large estates which began using modern large-
scale farming methods. In turn this resulted in an enormous increase in day

---

86. Rigola, *Rinaldo Rigola*, p. 15.

87. The mutual-aid organizations, however, continued to increase rapidly during
this period. In 1885 there were 5000 in the country as a whole. In 1894 there were 6722.
From that year on the number began to decline. *Rigola, Storia*, p. 49.

88. Epicarmo Corbino, *Annuali dell' economia italiana* (1881–1890), (Città di
Castello, 1934), vol. III.

laborers under conditions which made them responsive to Socialist ideas and organization.[89] They were also increasingly drawn into the trade unions sponsored by the Socialist leaders active among them.

During the decade of the 1880's the number of strikes increased steadily from a low of 27 in 1880 to 139 in 1890, exclusive of agricultural strikes.[90] Most strikes were concentrated in the north, with the textile industry and construction among the most frequently affected.[91] While 16 percent of the strikes were fully successful, 43 percent ended in compromise with some concessions to the workers. Organization was spreading, and as the Workers' Party gradually disintegrated and was absorbed into the new Socialist Party, the leadership for the slowly emerging trade unions increasingly came from individuals of worker origin with Socialist orientation.[92]

The spread of local trade unions during the 1880's reached sufficient magnitude to make trade union coordination inevitable. In some few industries this was already taking place. The typographical workers, the leather workers, bakers, railroad engineers and firemen were already establishing national federations.[93] The majority of unions, however, were organized only locally and in the larger cities, as in Milan, were joined together into generic undifferentiated central worker organizations as the *Fascio dei Lavoratori* or the *Consolato Operaio* which included cooperatives and trade unions, but were made up primarily of mutual-aid organizations.

A spur to coordination was the example of the *Bourse du Travail* formed by French workers in each of a number of the principal French cities. The first of these had been established in Paris in 1886. That same year several

89. See, for example, Biagio Riguzzi, *Sindacalismo e riformismo nel parmese; L. Musini — A. Berenini* (Bari, 1931), pp. 20–66; Giovanni Zibordi, *Saggio sulla storia del movimento operaio in Italia: Camillo Prampolini e i lavoratori reggiani*, 2nd edition (Bari, 1930), pp. 58–68; Emilio Zanella, *Dalla "barbarie" alla civiltà nel polesine: L'opera di Nicolò Badaloni* (Milan, 1931), pp. 13–19.

90. Statistics cited for this period are from *Statistiche degli scioperi*, pp. 21–30.

91. A breakdown by somewhat non-homogeneous categories has been made in the official statistics for the total number of strikes from the second half of 1878 through 1891 (*ibid.*, p. 27):

Textile	240
Mining, metallurgical, and mechanical industries	144
Day laborers, bricklayers, and allied industries	260
Printers and lithographers	27
Hatters, tanners, and clothing industry	85
Bakers and other food industries	77
Carpenters, glass makers, cabmen, truckers	117
Miscellaneous industries	125
Total	1075

92. Osvaldo Gnocchi-Viani, *Dieci anni di camere del lavoro* (Bologna, 1899), p. 10.

93. Rigola, *Storia*, p. 157.

other *Bourses* were formed (at Nîmes and Nantes) and one was formed at Marseilles in 1888.[94] It was the Marseille *Bourse* which came to the attention of trade unions in Milan and developed interest in similar organization in Italy. The moderate Socialist Osvaldo Gnocchi-Viani became the most active propagandist in favor of the establishment of such coordinating bodies in Italy. A meeting was organized among the Milan trade unions in November 1888 which discussed the Marseille *Bourse* and urged its imitation in Italy;[95] the typographical national union printed a long article on the subject in its official organ;[96] Gnocchi-Viani wrote a pamphlet on the *Bourses* which was printed by the Workers' Party and received wide circulation.[97] Gnocchi-Viani also led a worker delegation to the 1889 World Exhibition at Paris as a result of which firsthand information was carried back to Milan on details of the Paris *Bourse*.[98] The principal initiative was left to the typographical union and to Gnocchi-Viani to move the project forward in Milan. After a successful appeal to the municipality of Milan for an annual subsidy and free quarters, the Chamber of Labor (*Camera del Lavoro*) of Milan began functioning in 1891.[99] In that same year, following a parallel development, Chambers of Labor were set up in Piacenza and Turin. Two years later when the first Congress of Chambers of Labor was held, there were twelve already established, and, one year later, in 1894, there were sixteen in existence.[100]

As we have seen above, the state of organization among local trade unions had reached a point in the north where coordination was inevitable. While in a few trades and industries national organizations had been formed, the local geographic coordination of the unions into Chambers of Labor fit more closely the state of organization at the time and explains the rapid spread

94. For history of *bourses de travail* in France, *see* Fernand Pelloutier, *Histoire des bourses du travail* (Paris, 1901) (reprinted 1946, Costes, Paris); Louis L. Lorwin, *Syndicalism in France,* 2nd ed. (New York, 1914); Val R. Lorwin, *French Labor Movement* (Cambridge, Mass., 1954), pp. 21–23.

95. Gnocchi-Viani, *Dieci anni,* pp. 11–12. A meeting of twenty-four worker associations was held on November 18, 1888.

96. The article appeared in *Il Tipografo* on April 1, 1889. Reprinted in *ibid.,* pp. 12–14.

97. Osvaldo Gnocchi-Viani, *Le borse del lavoro* (Allessandria, 1889), printed under auspices of the Central Committee of the Workers' Party.

98. Gnocchi-Viani, *Dieci anni,* p. 14.

99. *Ibid.,* pp. 21–22. For history of early years of the Milan Chamber, see *Origini, vicende e conquiste,* pp. XLVII-LII.

100. Gnocchi-Viani, *Dieci anni,* p. 22, says there were 16 already formed. Angiolini, in *Cinquant' anni,* p. 219, says there were 14, while Rigola, *Storia,* p. 158, says there were 14 already formed or in process of formation in July 1893 when the congress was held. The 16 listed in Gnocchi-Viani, p. 22, were at Milan, Turin, Piacenza, Venice, Brescia, Rome, Bologna, Parma, Padua, Pavia, Cremona, Florence, Verona, Monza, Bergamo, and Naples.

and important role of the Chambers of Labor from the very beginning of their existence. This is similar to developments in trade union movements of other countries at a parallel stage. For a series of diverse reasons which will be discussed later, the Chamber of Labor continued throughout the history of the Italian labor movement to play a far more important role than similar local coordinating bodies in the trade union movements of other European countries or the United States. They have been described by Rigola as "The most dynamic and fighting element of Italian trade unionism." [101]

The Chambers of Labor as adapted from the French *Bourses* described themselves as parallel organizations to the Chambers of Commerce which had long been in existence throughout Italy. Beside performing coordination functions among the local organizations, they operated as an employment service and also promoted organization, education, and successful settlement of labor disputes. On the basis of their claims to performing a public service, particularly with respect to employment placement, the Chambers of Labor, as did the French *Bourses,* appealed for subsidies from the municipal authorities and were in the early years generally successful. In fact no municipality refused financial support to chambers organized during 1891 to 1893.[102]

The statutes of the Milan Chamber of Labor, which served as a model for the other chambers, provided that "There can absolutely not be any meeting within the Chamber of Labor having a political or religious character, since the Chamber of Labor is completely extraneous to such questions and must remain so." [103] The fact is, however, that an increasingly large proportion of the leadership of the local unions and the Chambers of Labor were Socialists and inevitably gave a Socialist orientation to their activity. In addition, the Socialist Party until 1895 was organized on the basis of affiliation of organizations, and local trade union organizations frequently were directly affiliated to the party. Finally, the Socialists were urged by their party to promote union organization, support workers in labor disputes and in general to participate in the economic protective activity of labor.[104] So far as the Chambers of Labor were concerned during this period, while they concentrated on the tasks which they had announced in their statutes, they were widely identified as part of the general rising tide of strength of the combined Socialist and labor movement. The political

101. Rigola, *Storia,* p. 159.
102. Gnocchi-Viani, *Dieci anni,* pp. 23, 25. The municipal Council of Bergamo, however, refused a subsidy in 1894 because the Catholics, who opposed the Chambers of Labor, were in the majority in the Council.
103. Article 3 of Statute. *Ibid.,* p. 18.
104. Angiolini, *Cinquant' anni,* p. 224.

identification of the Chambers of Labor was, in fact, so strong that some trade unions — even beyond the Catholic-controlled organizations which will be discussed later — refused to join them.[105]

As described in the previous section, the government's repressive action against the *Fasci* in Sicily in 1894 was only the first phase of its repression in that and the following year. Throughout the country Socialist organizations and trade unions were closed down. The Chambers of Labor suffered the same fate. The suppression of the chambers followed a series of limitations set by the government including the ruling that the municipalities exceeded their powers in granting subsidies to the chambers.[106]

One of the by-products of the suppressions of 1894-95 was a reorganization of the basic structure of the Socialist Party. It was felt that individual personal affiliation to sections of the party itself instead of affiliation of organizations might offer some protection to the trade unions and other organizations against suffering the same fate as the party in the event of a recurrence of government suppression. The 1895 Socialist Party Congress therefore decided upon such a reorganization.[107]

During 1896 and 1897 the Chambers of Labor, as the trade unions affiliated to them, began rebuilding their organizations. These were years of recovery from the "Black Years" of the tariff war with France and the collapse of the building boom. Industrialization proceeded at an increased tempo.[108] The strike level which had fluctuated between 109 to 139 in the years 1889 to 1895, rose to 210 in 1896 and 217 in 1897.[109] The years 1897 and early 1898 were made more turbulent by the shortages in bread and flour and their sharply rising prices. The violence and repression which took place in the country in 1898 have already been described. The suppressions of 1894-95 had had no lasting effect upon the trade unions; they continued

105. For example, in 1892, the League for Improvement among Metal Turners refused to join the Milan Chamber "because, according to the leaders, they did not regard it as desirable, at least at the moment, to give the League that almost political character which the Chamber of Labor would like to give it." *Origine, vicende e conquiste*, p. 4.

106. Gnocchi-Viani, *Dieci anni*, pp. 32–33. Angiolini, *Cinquant' anni*, p. 219, gives the strength of some of the Chambers of Labor at the time of the First Congress of Chambers of Labor in July 1893. The Milan Chamber had 40 sections with 10,000 members; the Bologna Chamber had 60 sections with 16,000 members (20 of the sections were farm labor cooperatives); Rome had 29 sections with 8000 members; Turin had 12 sections with 3900 members; Parma, 60 sections with 1200 members; Pavia, 19 sections with 600 members; Brescia had 14 sections with 1200 members.

107. For text of resolution, *see ibid.*, p. 286. Another reason for the change was that affiliation through organizations frequently meant only that the leadership of these organizations were sympathetic to the party and did not result in a disciplined or active political movement. Rigola, *Storia*, pp. 143–144.

108. Corbino, *Annuali dell' economia italiana* (1891–1900), vol. IV, pp. 107–110.

109. Confindustria, *Annuario di statistiche del lavoro 1949* (Rome, n.d.), pp. 378–379.

to grow after a short period of reorganizing their forces. The suppressions of 1898–99 were much the same. Trade unions and Chambers of Labor were shut down together with political party organizations. They were not permitted to function.[110] But as we shall see, the tremendous upheaval and growth of the first years of the twentieth century made the suppressions only a parenthesis in the expansion of the trade union movement. Even during the years of suppression the number of strikes continued to increase: in 1898 they rose to 256 and in 1899 to 259.[111]

The Chambers of Labor had early established a federation to coordinate their activities. Their very development had been a process of spreading a common form of organization rapidly among the more developed centers of the country. In 1893, within two years after the first chambers had been set up, a congress of twelve chambers was held at Parma at which there was established *La Federazione Italiana delle Camere del Lavoro* (Italian Federation of the Chambers of Labor). The congress adopted a program for the new organization, identical with that of the Milan Chamber, but gave the organization no specific powers of its own and little financing. The federation in fact developed little activity before it was drowned out in the repressions of 1894–95. A second congress of Chambers of Labor was held in August 1897 after the revival of that year. It was a repetition of the earlier congress with little of note accomplished.[112] Again, this time within less than a year, the general government repression also closed down the federation, seized its records and arrested its leaders. It was only with the reorganizations of the Chambers of Labor and the trade unions at the turn of the century that the need for genuine coordination and national trade union activity was generally enough felt to give real life to a national organization.

The one last effort — before fascism — to use wide repressive measures against the trade union movement occurred in 1900 when the Chamber of Labor of Genoa was ordered closed on the claim that the government orders of previous repressive actions were still in effect. The immediate reaction, first of the port workers, and then of others throughout the city, was a strike which closed down activity throughout the port and the city. Negotiations then started which resulted in a complete vindication of the workers and the Chamber of Labor.[113] It also resulted in the fall of the Saracco government and the opening of an era of trade union freedom.

One of the basic results of the repressions of the nineties among the workers of the north was to bind them more closely to the Socialists. Until

110. For a description of the suppression of Chambers of Labor and their efforts to get permission to reorganize, *see* Gnocchi-Viani, *Dieci anni*, pp. 38–68.
111. Confindustria, *Annuario di statistiche . . . 1949*, p. 379.
112. Rigola, *Storia*, pp. 234–236.
113. *Ibid.*, pp. 192–199; Angiolini, *Cinquant' anni*, pp. 413–421.

that period, the Socialists had had relatively large success in rural areas of north and north central Italy. They had had only modest influence among the mass of workers in urban areas, though their influence among the worker leadership had been considerable. The fact that the workers' labor organizations suffered the same fate as the Socialists at the hands of the government dramatized the sense of identification and the personal appeal of Socialist doctrine. Socialism, even more than trade unionism, became the point of identification for most workers. It is particularly the repercussions of this period that gave substance to the complaint heard so frequently at trade union conventions in the early part of the twentieth century, that the workers had little trade union consciousness compared with their sense of political identification.

Luigi Einaudi, the famous Liberal economist who was President of Italy for a time after fascism, described the situation as he saw it during a visit to the Biella area in 1897. The situation he described had become typical in many areas of the north by the end of the last century:[114]

The conversion to socialism was effected by the workers on a mass basis. "All among us are Socialists," a worker told me, "after Crispi and after the battle of Adua. The only newspapers which we read are those of the party . . ." Among the workers there remain outside of socialism only the old men, immune to new ideas, afraid to compromise themselves, and those workers who have come from the lower Vercelli, to whom, accustomed as they are to fifteen cents per day, to touch two lires appears a holiday. The women are the most fervent. When the deputy arrives in the area, or a Socialist orator arrives in a village, there is delirium among the female part of the population; they push themselves to him to touch him and sometimes to kiss his hand. The men do not go to church any longer; the women continue to attend on Sunday; but during Mass they read *Avanti!* [the Socialist newspaper] The fifteen-year-old children are already Socialist.

Like all propaganda which appeals to the heart and to the intelligence socialism has assumed in the Biella Valley the form of a new religion. It serves the function for the worker population of school and church. It is a school because the leaders of the party are interested in enrolling the greatest number of voters and to get the workers enrolled in the electoral lists it is necessary to give them that elementary instruction which will permit them to pass the examinations before the magistrate. Then, in order that they may better absorb the principles of socialism, it is necessary that the workers know how to read and acquire the habit of reading. The transformation which has been achieved in the intellectual culture of the workers is truly very great. Formerly, to read the newspapers was considered a task of pure luxury, now it is very widespread; and along with the newspapers come the leaflets, the pamphlets and the books. Already from among the working class itself new personalities are arising, not belonging to the

114. The articles appeared in *Gazzetta Piemontese* of Turin and are quoted at length in Rigola, *Rinaldo Rigola*, pp. 155–158.

bourgeoisie, who live the same life as the workers and because of their greater intellectual level become the pioneers of the working class.

Socialism is substituted for the church with respect to the moral side of their lives.

The maximum program leaves the workers indifferent up to a certain point; what touches and moves them is the minimum political and economic program. They have started winning in their district, sending their representative to Parliament; and now they are working for the conquest of the municipal offices.

"We are too cautious, however, to take it over immediately as we could," one of them told me: "we must first study to familiarize ourselves well with all the communal administrative law; when this self-instruction is finished, all the communes will fall into our hands."

Above all, however, the workers want to seize the economic part of the minimum program: the organization of leagues of resistance for reduction of the work day, increase in wages, modification of the internal regulations in the factories.

CHAPTER III

Socialism and Trade Unions Till 1914

The period of 1901 to 1914 is usually referred to as the Giolitti period in Italian history. First as Minister of Interior until 1903 and then almost continuously as Prime Minister until 1914, Giovanni Giolitti ran the government on the basis of his own particular brand of liberalism which set the tone for economic and social advances.

This was the period when the rate of economic development in the country proceeded rapidly, real incomes increased, the economy expanded at a pace which had not been achieved before. This was the period when most of Italy's protective and social labor legislation was enacted; it was the period when for the first time the labor movement could carry on its activity in an atmosphere of freedom without fear of government suppression.

In his famous speech in Parliament on June 21, 1901, as Minister of Interior, Giolitti became the champion of liberty, in contrast to the reaction of the preceding years. "It is my profound conviction," he said, "that socialism can be fought only on the field of freedom; the other road has been tried and you have seen the results!" [1] In his autobiography, Giolitti, writing many years later about the attitudes toward labor organization at the beginning of the century and his own evaluation of the problem and the role of government, said:[2]

The principal reason for the opposition to the Chambers of Labor was just this: that their activities tended to increase wages. But even though keeping down wages may have been to the advantage of the employers, the State could have no interest in it. We may say this without considering the fact that it is an error and prejudice to believe that low wages help the progress of industry . . . in my opinion, when the government intervened to keep down wages, as it used to do, then, it committed an injustice as well as an economic and political error; an injustice because it was failing in its duty of absolute impartiality between citizens . . . an economic error because it upset the working of the law of supply and demand which is the sole legitimate regulator of the measure of wages . . . Finally, it was a political error because it made those classes which constitute the great majority of the country enemies of the State. The only equitable and useful role of the State in these struggles between capitalism and labor is to exercise a pacifying and even sometimes a conciliatory action. In case

1. L. Salvatorelli, ed., *Giolitti* (Milan, 1920), p. 41.
2. Giolitti, *Memoirs,* pp. 143–146.

of strike, its duty is to intervene only in one case: that is, to safeguard the right to work, a right not less sacred than that of a strike.

I believed, in fact, that after the failure of reaction we were at the commencement of a new historical period, which anyone who was not blind would perceive. New popular currents were entering into our political life, new problems were facing us every day, new forces were arising which the government had to take into account. The uprising of the working classes continued to gather speed, and it was an unconquerable movement both because it was common to all civilized countries and because it was based on the principle of equality between men. No one could any longer delude himself with the idea that it was possible to prevent the working classes from attaining their share of influence, both economic and political. It was the duty of the friends of the country's institutions to persuade those classes, and persuade them not with words but with facts, that they had much more to hope from the existing regime than from dreams of the future . . . It was only by means of such an attitude and such conduct on the part of the constitutional parties towards the working classes that it was possible to bring it about that the advent of these classes, instead of being a disturbing factor, should have the effect of introducing a fresh conservative force into existing institutions and of increasing the prosperity of the nation.

Giolitti is a most controversial figure in modern Italian history.[3] For some, the predominant aspect of his regime was that he extended and refined the *trasformismo* of the preceding years to such a point that democratic institutions, still at an early stage of development, were so corrupted that the post-World War I period of disturbances and the final victory of fascism were made much easier by the regime which had preceded it. For others the Giolitti era, with all its sordid political side, made an outstanding contribution to the strengthening of democratic institutions. There is little doubt that, while Giolitti was personally honest, he remained in power for as long as he did through control of constituencies in the south where the most corrupt election practices were used and through the most flagrant use of political favors and personal deals. As against this, however, political freedom, legal processes, equality of the individual before the law were established and practiced. It is true that there were still deaths which resulted from violence in labor disputes and demonstrations, but these were exceptions; labor organizations were in fact permitted freedom to organize, bargain, and strike.

So far as the trade union movement, the Socialist Party, and the labor movement in general were concerned, Giolitti, having decided that these were movements which were an inherent part of the contemporary social

3. For an excellent discussion of the various evaluations of the period and a thorough analysis of the period itself, *see* A. William Salomone, *Italian Democracy in the Making* (Philadelphia, 1945).

and political scene, explicitly set for himself the task of "domesticating" them, making them feel that there was enough of a stake in existing institutions and enough promise of improvement so that they would become committed to constitutional government.

In a narrow sense, and for the period of his regime, he succeeded in large measure in his basic objective. The trade unions, as they grew and began consolidating their strength prior to the First World War, were predominantly and increasingly Reformist in outlook and in action, always, however, in a context of competition with a vociferous and active minority of Revolutionary Syndicalists on their left. The consumer and producer cooperatives, which grew particularly strong and important during this period, represented a conservative force in the labor movement. By his legislation, which made special concessions to cooperatives, and particularly by the system he developed of granting the major part of public works projects in many areas, especially in the Emilia-Romagna area, to producer cooperatives, Giolitti helped this process immeasurably.

The tendency toward greater conservatism among the different parts of the labor movement during this period was, of course, a complex process with the atmosphere and actions of government a part of the combination of circumstances which included rapid economic advance. This was the only period prior to the Second World War during which the economy expanded at a greater rate than that of other European countries. Industry was flourishing, prices were relatively stable, wages were increasing. Even the depression of 1906–1907, which strongly affected the economies of other countries, was relatively unimportant in Italy where the internal expansion of economic forces was great enough to minimize the domestic effects of the world trend of the time.

On the other hand, the period was relatively short, too short to stamp the labor movement completely with its effects. It had been preceded by a period of complicated and painful social and economic adjustments caused by the emergence of industrial production methods; a period which was also characterized by repression and apparent cynicism toward the aspirations of the emerging wage-earner class. It was followed by the castastrophic period of maladjustment flowing from the First World War and its immediate aftermath.

It should also be pointed out that although the labor movement became institutionalized into constitutional form during the Giolitti era, it did not become so completely. To a minor extent this may have been a fault of leadership. To much greater extent, however, the fault rested with the inheritance of the preceding decades and the attitudes of workers and leadership toward the changes of the early twentieth century. To this should be added the basic effects of the differences of expanding Italian economic institutions from those of other countries as well as the atmosphere of *combinazioni* and of fraud which so frequently characterized the functioning of the government. The Italian Socialists, even during this period, and even Reformist leaders like Turati or Treves, to keep their following, were unable to take positions as consistently moderate as they would have liked. In fact, the Reformist rule of the Socialist Party was ended even before the First World War, as we shall see, in part as a reaction against what was regarded as excessively moderate policies.

Socialist Developments under Giolitti

The Socialist Party Congress of 1900 was the first held after the suppressions of the previous years. The party had only recently rebuilt its machinery. There was as yet no certain conviction that the new government would respect political and civil liberties and not return to the policies of the previous decade. On the other hand, the Socialists earlier in the year had more than doubled their parliamentary representation, winning 33 seats as a result of a popular vote of 165,000 out of the 1,270,000 votes cast. The Socialists were divided in their basic thinking between Revolutionaries and Reformists, but even within these groups themselves there was as yet no clear-cut position or ideological common basis for action. The congress, in an effort to keep unity and to satisfy the pressures from the various Socialist groups, adopted two programs, a maximum program and a minimum program. The maximum program, a reiteration of the 1892 Socialist program, spoke of conquest of power, expropriation and socialization of the means of production. The minimum program spoke of immediate reforms in the political field, of universal suffrage, remuneration for deputies, civil liberties, and impartiality of the government in labor disputes; in the economic and social field it spoke of protective labor legislation, rights of cooperatives to bid on public works, nationalization of transportation and mining, and expropriation of uncultivated land; in other fields it spoke of compulsory free lay education, development of public health services and abolition of indirect taxes with substitution of progressive income and inheritance taxes.[4]

The official committee report to the congress defined the minimum program as the means to ends defined in the maximum program and tried to distinguish both from so-called *bourgeois* reform programs.[5] The fact is these were not two complementary programs, but inconsistent separate programs each of which represented objectives of different groups which had as yet not completely solidified.

The few years which followed the adoption of the maximum and minimum programs witnessed the establishment of a government which had

4. For text, *see* Michels, *Storia critica,* pp. 212–213 and 217–222; or Angiolini, *Cinquant' anni,* pp. 407–409.

5. The report was prepared by Turati, Treves and Carlo Gambucco. Michels, *Storia critica,* p. 217.

turned its back on the reaction of the nineties. So eager were the Socialists to insure the continuation of the new liberal atmosphere that on two occasions, first in June 1901 and again in March 1902, the Socialist deputies joined in the vote of confidence given to the government, when it appeared that their abstention or opposition would swing the balance in overthrowing the government.[6] The Socialist and trade union propaganda of this period spread throughout industry and agriculture.

The social scene was characterized by tremendous strike waves in agriculture as well as in industry, which will be discussed in the next section. The sensation of social revolution felt so strongly by the conservative forces, employers in industry, and particularly employers in agriculture, caused an uproar in Parliament out of which Giolitti emerged as the defender of freedom of association and of strike activity. He was sufficiently certain of the economic nature of the strikes to be confident that they were no threat to the government. He was also convinced that the strikes were justified.[7]

By the time the Socialists held their congress in September 1902, they could look with satisfaction upon the very significant growth of their movement and of the trade unions in an atmosphere of government tolerance. At the congress it became apparent that there had been further crystallization of the two wings of the party, the "transigents" and the "intransigents," as they were called at the time. But neither had yet reached a clear-cut position, though the language used against each other had become increasingly violent. Roberto Michels, who studied this period closely at first hand, has said of the first years of the century that:

much of the intemperance of language and of action, committed by the two factions, can be pardoned for a very plausible reason. In fact the change of tactics toward them on the part of the dominant political class was for the Italian Socialists, habituated to all kinds of storms but unaccustomed to enduring the bright rays of the sun, an enormous surprise which found them completely unprepared, morally and intellectually. This fact, without precedent in the history of their movement, thus had an intoxicating effect upon some and was rejected by others, depending upon their temperaments. The Socialist Party knew well how to comport itself against the old oppressive policy, having learned from bitter and incessant experience; in the face of the new conciliatory policy, however, the party was left stupefied.[8]

The intransigents were not a homogeneous group. There were those who had no faith in a program of reform and wanted to orient the party toward a straightforward revolutionary program. Also emerging and taking form beginning about 1904 was a revolutionary syndicalism based upon the writ-

6. Angiolini, *Cinquant' anni*, pp. 427 and 430. See Rigola, *Storia*, p. 257, for discussion of balance of considerations which went into 1902 vote of confidence decision.

7. For Giolitti's views *see* Giolitti, *Memoirs*, pp. 153–154.

8. Michels, *Storia critica*, p. 247.

ings of Georges Sorel and adapted to the Italian experience. In this view reform was a snare which made only more difficult the task of ultimate revolution. The labor unions, not political parties, were to be the vehicle of revolution. Direct action through trade unions, strikes on every occasion, were to educate the masses ultimately to the revolutionary general strike which would bring on the era of socialism.

The French Syndicalists were completely opposed to political parties, including the Socialist Party, and were opposed to participation in political elections. The Italian Syndicalists, on the other hand, remained in the Socialist Party until they were faced with expulsion, and their representatives, including Arturo Labriola, ran for Parliament in the 1904 elections.[9]

There were strong reasons for the Italian Syndicalists' political action in contradicting their doctrines. It was clear from 1905 onward that the Syndicalists had lost out in their bid for control of the trade union movement. In addition, the Socialist Party had a strong hold on a large part of the wage earners, had considerable parliamentary representation and a strong tradition of unity and Socialist cooperation which antedated the formation of the national party itself. What is more, most of the Syndicalist leaders had themselves been inside the Socialist Party for many years. Under these circumstances to have followed the French lead would have been political suicide as well as psychologically difficult. They could not afford an approach as pure as the French in rejecting political party action and depending solely on revolutionary trade unions.

To agree to participation in political parties, however, was not necessarily to agree to tolerance of differences in approach to socialism. By 1904 the struggle between the Reformists and the Revolutionaries within the party — as well as in the trade unions — had reached a point when it was expected that the party would split at the congress held that year.[10] Early in the year the Revolutionaries had gained control of the regional party apparatus in Lombardy at a congress held at Brescia. With the national party apparatus in Reformist hands and located at Milan, the polemics and the struggle for party control took on intensified form.

The split, however, was postponed for almost four years through intervention at the 1904 Socialist Congress by a new bloc, calling itself Integralist, and led by Enrico Ferri.[11] The Integralists tried to represent themselves as

9. For discussion of Italian syndicalism and comparison with French, *see ibid.*, pp. 312–314.

10. For history of this period *see* Angiolini, *Cinquant' anni*, pp. 912–947; Michels, *Storia critica*, pp. 256–272, 339, 344.

11. The Integralists, in fact, developed no new approach to a program. They simply combined the two extreme programs into one. Salomone wrote, *Italian Democracy*, p. 67, of the program of 1906, "It was in fact a restatement of issues, not their solution, and as such its only positive result was to furnish all factions with material for arguments for the next two years."

a compromise group half-way between the two extremes in a combination program. They held control of the party for the next four years with an uneasy compromise, during which time the Reformists, who controlled most of the Socialist parliamentary seats, were able to have their own way for the most part, with, however, more revolutionary verbiage than they themselves would have chosen.

By 1908, the Reformists were able themselves to take over control of the party. The Revolutionary Syndicalists had by then clearly lost their battle with the Reformists. The 1908 Congress explicitly declared syndicalism incompatible with the principles and methods of the Socialist Party.

The strong feelings and bitter battles between the Reformists and Syndicalists during this period had frequently given the appearance that the Socialists were more concerned with fighting each other than fighting in common against other political groups. This was in fact frequently the case. It was more than ideological differences and competition for leadership. For the Reformists it also involved suffering the consequences of Syndicalist actions. For the Syndicalists it meant that in their specially chosen ground, the trade unions, they had come out very much second best to the Reformists. In 1904 the revolutionary faction, which at the time included primarily the Syndicalists, had been responsible for precipitating a general strike in the entire country in protest against several deaths resulting from violence used against demonstrators in the south.[12] It was a success — the first successful general strike in history, some have claimed. It had no purpose, however, other than as a demonstration. After several days the workers drifted back to work and the principal immediate result in the country was increased antagonism against the Socialists.

The government had carefully refrained from violence or a show of force. After the end of the strike, however, Giolitti dissolved Parliament and called national elections. The Socialists lost several seats while the Giolitti forces gained sufficiently to make them independent of the need for Socialist support in Parliament. Turati, who had been offered a cabinet post the previous year and had turned it down[13] — on the grounds that it was premature and would be misunderstood and condemned by the masses — and the other Reformist Socialists in Parliament thus found their importance sharply reduced as a result of actions of the Revolutionaries. Another major instance occurred in the summer of 1908 when the Parma Chamber of Labor, which was a stronghold of the Syndicalists, called a general agricultural strike in the area. The strike lasted more than two months and was lost to the accompaniment of violence. Both the Socialist Party and the General Confederation of Labor had reluctantly supported

12. See Rigola, Storia, pp. 269–270; Salomone, Italian Democracy, pp. 50–51; Angiolini, Cinquant' anni, pp. 916–917.
13. Salomone, Italian Democracy, p. 49.

the strike. In the aftermath of defeat, the Syndicalists and Reformists bitterly attacked each other in recriminatory accusations of responsibility for the result.[14]

The Reformists controlled the Socialist Party until 1912. In the 1909 national elections the party had received about 20 percent of the votes cast and had increased its parliamentary representation to 41, compared with the twenty-nine deputies it had had during the previous five years. During these years the Socialist influence in municipalities primarily in the north and north central part of the country increased enormously. Their success in local elections was even greater than in the national elections. The success of the party was accompanied by the development of vested interests in existing institutions and the consequent weakening of the militancy of the party leadership. This in turn gradually strengthened the hand of those within the party who, while not going as far as the Revolutionary Syndicalists, claimed to be the true bearers of the intransigent revolutionary tradition of socialism.

At the 1910 Socialist Party Congress, the dominant Reformist group obtained majority support for its view that immediate reforms were of principal concern, and listed four of its immediate objectives: (1) universal suffrage, with proportional representation and salaries for deputies; (2) decrease in military expenditures; (3) extensive development of lay schools; (4) social insurance, beginning with old age and invalidity insurance for all workers.[15] It was evident at the congress that the old Integralist bloc was disintegrating, while the revolutionary Intransigents were being rebuilt under the leadership of the old Workers' Party leader Costantino Lazzari. The Reformists, however, dominated the congress and showed little inclination toward making concessions to the Left.

During the following two years, the situation changed dramatically. Responding to mounting pressures, Giolitti in 1911 announced his support for a program of universal manhood suffrage. Under the program as recommended to Parliament, the electorate would be expanded from approximately three million to a total of eight million voters. The program later approved by Parliament extended suffrage to include illiterate males who had performed military service or had reached the age of thirty. In his characteristic manner, Giolitti felt confident that the enlarged suffrage would represent no threat to the stability of his government. His corrupt election methods assured him of minimum support from the south. His deals and concessions assured conservative support. He was confident that he could — and did, in 1913 — obtain further active election support against the Left

14. *See, for example,* Angiolini, *Cinquant' anni,* pp. 941–943. A later section discusses the strike further.

15. For text *see* Filippo Meda, *Il socialismo politico in Italia* (Milan, 1924), pp. 47–48.

from the Catholics, as he had in 1904. So far as the Socialists were concerned, he felt that they had been sufficiently "domesticated" during the previous decade so that they would not represent a serious threat to established government. On the other hand, his success in drawing Catholic support would help to neutralize the Socialists. As part of the general program, Giolitti had hoped to draw the Socialists into participation in his government, and in forming his new government in 1911 he had unsuccessfully offered a cabinet post to Leonida Bissolati, one of the Socialist leaders of the extreme Right who enthusiastically favored collaboration with Giolitti.

All this, it turned out later in the year, had been preparation for a step which had serious repercussions upon the Socialists and their attitude toward the government. On September 29, 1911, Italy declared war on Turkey to obtain Tripoli. Four days before the declaration of war, when the enterprise was already known, the Socialist parliamentary group met with the leadership of the party and of the trade unions and decided upon a national twenty-four-hour general protest strike. Not only was it too late, the strike itself was far from complete. The Tripoli adventure, however, gave the Revolutionaries within the Socialist Party — and the Syndicalists outside the party — their opportunity to take the initiative on the Left away from the Reformists. Here was the culmination of the effects of collaboration, "ministerialism," reformism. What purpose was served by moderate programs and the growth of Socialist Party influence under such programs if they still led to imperialist wars? For many among the Reformists, too, the Libyan War was a rude awakening. The complacent sense of gradual progress and achievement which had developed during the previous decade was torn away to expose a government embarked upon an acknowledged imperialist venture.

All the frustrations and recriminations felt by the Socialists of various hues were aired at a Socialist Congress held two weeks after the beginning of the Libyan War. The congress delegates were split into five different positions, and only the extreme political dexterity of the predominant leadership kept the party machinery from falling to the Revolutionaries.[16]

The fireworks at the 1911 Socialist Congress were but a prelude to the activity of the following year. The Revolutionary Socialists, with Benito Mussolini emerging as one of the most fiery and uninhibited, carried on a violent campaign both against the Reformist Socialists and against the government. Many, including Mussolini, in the Emilia-Romagna area, traditionally the area of violence and immoderation, were imprisoned for their incitement and participation in sabotage efforts against the military. The impact of the Libyan War, and the Revolutionary Socialist condemnation of the Reformist program in the context of the war, rapidly lost support for the Reformists among the ranks of the Socialist Party members.

16. Angiolini, *Cinquant' anni*, pp. 1031–1033; Michels, *Storia critica*, p. 404.

When the Socialist Congress met in 1912, the Revolutionary Socialists were able to gain control of the party.

The principal action taken by the new majority at the congress was to expel Bissolati, Ivanoe Bonomi, and Angiolo Cabrini, three so-called Extreme Right Reformist Socialist deputies for having joined with other deputies in paying a visit to the King to congratulate him on his escape from a recent attempted assassination. Even the so-called Left Reformists, headed by Turati and Giuseppe Modigliani supported expulsion.[17] The chief spokesman for the Revolutionaries was Mussolini, whose violent attacks upon compromises with *bourgeois* society and militarism won him an important place in the new Socialist Party hierarchy. He was made editor of *Avanti,* the official Socialist daily newspaper, a few months after the congress. The party, as a result of its congress decisions, was committed to a policy of intransigent opposition to the government.

The control of the Socialist Party by the Revolutionaries created serious problems of relationship with the trade union movement which remained in Reformist hands and which resisted attempts of the Revolutionaries, frequently in cooperation with the Syndicalists, to wrest control from the dominant group or to dictate local trade union policy, particularly by promoting general strikes. The problem of these relationships and struggles for control will be developed in a later section.

The use of the strike weapon for political pressure and demonstration purposes now had support not only from the Syndicalists but also in large measure from the intransigent Revolutionary leadership which controlled the Socialist Party. The innumerable local general demonstration strikes during the period between 1912 and 1914 had their culmination in a national general strike during June 1914 which later became known as "Red Week." This will be discussed in a later section.

The 1914 Socialist Party Congress, held at Ancona two months before the beginning of "Red Week," consolidated the predominance of the Revolutionaries in the party. As a prelude to "Red Week" and in recognition of the gathering war clouds in Europe, a strong resolution was adopted attacking militarism and urging anti-militarist activity and propaganda both on a national and international level.[18] It was on two other issues that the complete control by the Revolutionaries was manifest. The more publicized and dramatic subject was the decision that freemasonry and socialism were in basic conflict and that freemasonry membership was incompatible with membership in the Socialist Party. This issue was forced to a decision despite the considerable number of important respected Socialists who were

17. A fourth Deputy, Podrecca, was also expelled because of his "nationalist and war-mongering positions." For summary of the congress *see* Cannarsa, *Il socialismo,* pp. 183–190; Angiolini, *Cinquant' anni,* pp. 1055–1056.

18. For text, *see* Angiolini, *Cinquant' anni,* p. 1129.

known to be Masons and had been drawn into freemasonry because of its libertarian and democratic position in Italy. The second important decision made by the Revolutionaries was that in the municipal elections to be held that year the Socialists would not enter into any electoral combinations.[19]

The shift in leadership of the Socialist Party in 1912 had marked the end of the era of "domestication." The Reformists never again had an opportunity to rebuild their strength in the pre-Fascist period. Those expelled from the party in 1912 formed a party of their own, but it remained a small group with little following or importance even though Bissolati later became a cabinet minister. The war and its aftermath with its repercussions upon ideologies, its economic disruption and political upheavals, was not propitious for the return of moderate leadership. It would be a mistake, however, to underestimate the residue effect of the preceding decade even upon many among the Revolutionary Socialists. For many, even with sincere conviction in the revolutionary slogans which were currently popular, there was a basic reluctance to commit themselves and their party too far or to cut themselves off too completely from the immediate benefits and advantages which accrued from cooperation within the existing society.

Trade Union Developments under Giolitti

The early years of the twentieth century witnessed the emergence of a trade union movement in modern form. As the country moved into the Giolitti era, the economic transformations of the previous years had their full impact upon wage earner reactions to these changes. In industry, the forward movement of economic expansion was particularly strong. In agriculture, primarily in north and north central Italy, profound changes had already been taking place in the preceding years which had greatly modified pre-existing social relations and had steadily increased the proportion of day laborers, the *braccianti,* working in agriculture. In addition, the propaganda of the Socialists, as we have seen, had spread a message of worker organization and Socialist orientation which sank deep roots among the rural population.

In the opening years of the century, the expansion of labor activity was a phenomenon of gigantic proportions. In industry strikes had gradually increased from 109 in 1894 to 259 in 1899 and 383 in 1900.[20] In 1901, the number jumped to 1042 involving 196,540 workers and although the number of strikes fell to 810 in the following year, 197,514 workers were involved. The expanded number of labor disputes was even greater in agriculture. While the 62 strikes in 1885 had been the greatest number reached in any

19. For summary of the congress' discussion of the issue and the role of Freemasonary in Italy, *see* Salomone, *Italian Democracy,* pp. 81–84.

20. Strike statistics from Confindustria, *Annuario di statistiche . . . 1949,* pp. 379 and 387.

year in the previous century and had averaged 15 per year in the last decade of the century, there were 27 in 1900 and 629 in 1901, involving 222,985 workers in the latter year. As in industry, the number of strikes fell in the following year in agriculture, totaling 221, with 146,592 workers involved.

The fever of organization spread rapidly into areas and among workers who had never before participated in trade unions. While organization had become increasingly common in the preceding two decades among workers in the large cities — mostly among craft workers, during the opening years of the century organization spread rapidly among workers in industry generally and even more spectacularly among agricultural workers. There are no statistics on national trade union membership during the last decades of the nineteenth century. It is doubtful, however, whether at any time during that period membership in organizations devoted primarily to trade union objectives was as high as 150,000. By 1901, membership was well over 200,000.[21] By the following year the figure had risen to more than 500,000.[22] Characteristically, during these years, however, the new organizations had little staying power and the mortality rate among the organizations in the years immediately following was very high. This was particularly true in agriculture, where within a two-year period trade union membership spread to about 250,000 workers, primarily in the Po Valley area, but fell again in the following years. Nonetheless, while membership turnover was relatively high in the early years of the century, the over-all level of membership throughout the country during those years receded little from the high level mark of the 1902 period and increased somewhat in the middle years of the decade.

It was natural that during the early years of the century the organizational ferment should give rise to many strikes. The official statistics list demand for wage increase as the principal issue in most strikes during the period.[23] Trade union recognition by employers was not listed separately

21. The data reported to the Fourth Congress of the Chambers of Labor (October 19–20, 1901) by the Federal Committee of the *Federazione Italiana delle Camere del Lavoro* on 48 out of 55 chambers, gave a membership total of 210,450, for example, for these chambers alone. *Federazione Italiana delle Camere del Lavoro, IV Congresso delle Camere del Lavoro, Reggio Emilia, 19–20 Ottobre 1901, Resoconto delle discussioni e testo dei deliberati, con aggiunta la relazione della discussione e del voto sul tema "Ufficio del Lavoro" nella seduta dei tre Congressi riuniti (Camere del Lavoro, Cooperative e Mutue)il 21 Ottobre, 1901* (Milan, 1902), pp. 36–37.

22. Angiolo Cabrini, secretary of the *Federazione Italiana delle Camere del Lavoro,* for example, estimated trade union membership, on the basis of a detailed breakdown, to be more than 675,000, in a report to the Central Committee of the organization in September 1902. *See* statistical table in "Una Proposta" dated September 20, 1902, reproduced on pp. 109–120 in Angiolo Cabrini, *La resistenza nell' Europa giovane (Viaggi e Congressi)* (Imola, 1905), p. 115.

23. For example, in 181 strikes out of 383 in 1900, 657 out of 1042 in 1901, 469

in the official statistics, but there is evidence that this was an important issue in many strikes.[24] On the other hand, in 1901, when strikes expanded to large proportions, a combination of circumstances made possible the success of a high percentage of the strikes. In that year 71 percent of the strikes in industry, accounting for 76 percent of workers involved in strikes, were either fully successful or obtained substantial concessions. The freedom to organize and assurance of lack of intervention by the government represented an altogether new situation both for workers and employers. The workers responded with an organizational and strike spree. The employers, unaccustomed to depending upon their own resources, pleaded vainly for government assistance and only slowly in the following years developed their own defenses. Most important of all, however, was the fact that the economy was expanding rapidly and unprecedented prosperity made wage demands seem natural to the workers and relatively easy to concede for the employers.

Furthermore, communication among workers in various industries and areas had developed sufficiently that even without coordination and central leadership, strikes with basically similar objectives spread through the country. Giolitti, commenting upon this period, wrote:

> Since, both in the industrial and agricultural world, there was a great difference in the rates of pay between one industry and another, there resulted a kind of rotation strike. The workers struck from province to province, from commune to commune, from trade to trade and finally from firm to firm in order to obtain the concessions already won by their companions in other businesses, trades and provinces. I remember a time when there were more than eight hundred strikes going on at once.[25]

The enthusiasm and immediate success of the trade unions during 1901 created an atmosphere which did more to turn the trade unions toward moderate objectives than all the preaching of the Reformists. What was happening within the Socialist Party as a result of the new liberal atmosphere at the opening of the Giolitti era, was even more strongly felt in the trade unions.

The year 1901 was, however, but a beginning of the period of mass organization. The successes of that year set in their own reaction. Beginning during the following year employers were better prepared to resist the trade unions. Employer associations for the first time began to take on importance and were organized to deal with the problem of trade unions. Before the First World War, however, with the continued rapid rate of expansion in

out of 810 in 1902, and 264 out of 549 in 1903. *See* Confindustria, *Annuario de statistiche . . . 1949*, p. 379.

24. *See, for example*, Rigola, *Storia*, p. 222.

25. Giolitti, *Memoirs*, p. 172.

the economy, employers did not make an all-out drive to destroy the unions. While blacklisting was not unknown, and strikes to obtain union recognition not infrequent, collective bargaining did gradually become an established pattern in many industries. On the other hand, after 1901 the opposition of employers who were learning that they had to depend upon their own devices to resist specific union demands was more effective. Even here, however, the economic prosperity of the time made moderation easier for many employers to accept.

During 1902 and 1903 strikes met with considerably more employer resistance than during the previous year. The proportion of strikes settled completely in the workers' favor fell significantly, and those in which employers made no concessions rose.

As demonstrated in detail by a careful study made of the affiliates of the Milan Chamber of Labor for the period from its inception through 1905,[26] the rate of formation and dissolution of local unions during the early years of the century was extremely high. Frequently the union survived only one labor dispute, whether the dispute was successfully settled or not. The unions which survived from the period ending in 1890, according to the Milan study, were almost all organizations derived from the mutual-aid organizations, all had mutual-aid plans and benefits, and were predominately craft organizations. Starting with the period from 1891 and particularly after the turn of the century, the major portion of the new organizations did not have mutual-aid characteristics. In addition, after 1900, the tendency was away from craft organization toward industrial organization.

On the national level, rapid strides were made in the first years of the century in the formation of National Unions. The very impetus to organization and its rapid spread to substantial numbers of workers in industry after industry gave rise to the recognition that horizontal geographic organization was not enough to protect adequately the new mushrooming local organizations. The Chambers of Labor generally still remained the principal focal point and authority for local unions, but the need for direct relationships among organizations in the same industry or trade had become sufficiently recognized that National Federations, as they were and are still called in Italy, rapidly grew in the early years of the century. With the exception of the printers, only a few of the attempts during the latter part of the nineteenth century to form National Federations had succeeded in the establishment of strong continuing national organizations. National organization among railroad engineers and firemen in 1890 had succeeded regional organization of the previous decade and had subsequently given rise to a general Railroad Workers' National Federation. The metallurgical workers had on a modest scale begun experimenting with national organiza-

26. The Società Umanitaria study, *Origini, vicende e conquiste.*

tion from 1891 onward. The hatters had had national meetings of local hatters' organizations during the eighties and nineties, but without continuing national machinery until 1901.[27]

The spread of the National Unions occurred principally during 1901 and 1902. Their growth was extraordinary. By August 1902 there were 27 National Union Federations with a total membership of approximately 480,000.[28] Recognition of the importance of National Federations was particularly true of the emerging leadership of the trade union movement which pressed for the formation of National Federations and urged the reluctant Chambers of Labor to encourage their affiliates to join existing federations or help form new ones. In fact, at the 1901 Congress of the Italian Federation of Chambers of Labor, one of the purposes of the organization was defined to be "to assist in the formation of National Federations, taking an interest in inducing the Chambers to get their own sections to affiliate with the appropriate trade Federation." [29] While many of the Chambers of Labor were not enthusiastic about the prospect of organizations which might threaten their own authority, Angiolo Cabrini, who was named secretary of the Federation of Chambers of Labor in 1901, worked with other trade union leaders, including particularly Dario Tomasini, Felice Quaglino, Ettore Reina, Rinaldo Rigola and Pietro Chiesa in furthering the goal of the formation of National Federations.

The National Federations, springing up in great numbers in 1901 and 1902, faced many of the same organization problems as those discussed earlier for the local unions during those years. There was some turnover, some additional federations formed during the following years, and others disappeared. The extension and growth of the National Federations inevitably made them competitors for authority with the Chambers of Labor. As will be discussed in the next section, the struggle over relative authority, however, was in some ways sharpened and in others weakened, but certainly

27. *Statistica degli scioperi . . . dal 1884 al 1891*, pp. 14–16; Ministero dell' Agricoltura, Industria e Commercio, Ufficio del Lavoro, *Le organizzazioni di lavoratori in Italia, Federazioni di Mestiere. 1. La Federazione dei Cappellai, Pubblicazioni dell' Ufficio del Lavoro*, series B, no. 10 (Rome, 1906), pp. 5–6.

28. Agricultural workers accounted for 240,000 of the total. The other federations were chemical workers (6000 members), textile workers (18,000), leather workers (3,964), construction workers (29,000), metallurgical workers (50,000), seamen (12,-000), railroad workers (41,00), secondary railroad lines and street railway (6,400), shoemakes (3,461), typographical workers (9,600), lithographers (1,000), zincographers (155), glass workers (2,880), bakers (3,000), woodworkers (6,000), hatters (5,220), barbers (2,000) clerks and white-collar workers (4,500), gold workers (659), gas workers (3,500), state monopoly workers (10,000), postal telegraph workers (4,700), telegraph messengers (1,000), port workers (7,000), cooks and waiters (8,000), and nurses (no data). Cabrini, *La resistenza*, p. 115.

29. *IV Congresso delle Camere del Lavoro*, pp. 16, 18, 30, and 124.

distorted, as a result of the developing ideological struggle within the trade union movement.

The Federation of Chambers of Labor

The Italian Federation of Chambers of Labor which had been formed at the 1893 Congress played a minor role in the trade union picture until 1900. It had no authority, took little initiative, had practically no funds, and despite pious congress resolutions had been unable even to finance a publication of its own. Each Chamber of Labor retained its individual authority.

The first few years after the turn of the century, however, witnessed the concentrated development not only of significant organization on the local level, the development of National Unions, and rapid spread of additional Chambers of Labor to most of the country, but also the development of a national central organization with considerable influence and able to exercise considerable leadership over its constituent parts. The central organization, as it emerged by 1906, however, was the product of a struggle which had gone on for several years.

The Third Congress of the Italian Federation of Chambers of Labor held in July 1900 at Milan took place in an atmosphere of reconstruction and hope.[30] Trade unions and Chambers of Labor were in the process of reconstitution after the repressions of 1898–1899. Furthermore, it was becoming evident that the unions were on the threshold of a new era of trade union liberty. At the time of the congress, nineteen Chambers of Labor had been reorganized or were in the process of reorganization. Little was accomplished at the congress on the question of the Federation's authority or financing. But the congress acted as the spur to organization encouraged by the enthusiasm of its participants. There was discussion of the extension of organization in agriculture. In addition, after considering the question of seeking legislation granting legal recognition to trade unions, the decision was taken to oppose such a step.

By the time the next congress was held in October 1901 there were 55 Chambers of Labor in Italy, of which 39 sent delegates to the congress and another eight notified the federation of their adhesion to the organization. In the first flush of its own accomplishments and the immediate gains the trade unions were making throughout industry and agriculture, the congress rejected any statement in its constitution that it was dedicated to the class struggle, on the grounds that it would be "absurd to apply a declaration of principle to a modest regulatory stipulation."[31] No ideological declaration

30. Rigola, *Storia*, pp. 236–238.

31. *IV Congresso delle Camere del Lavoro*, p. 21. For text of constitution, see *ibid.*, pp. 123–126, or *Statuto della Federazione Italiana delle Camere del Lavoro* (Milan, 1902). Article 1 provided that the organization shall have an essentially economic character.

was adopted. The principal note on which socialism or Socialists were discussed was a critical one. There were numerous complaints made that many of the agricultural unions had not joined the appropriate Chambers of Labor and were kept out primarily because they were also serving as Socialist political centers with the Socialist leaders anxious to retain their leadership rather than lose it to the Chambers of Labor.[32] The congress discussions and reports made many references, however, to Socialist support for various types of labor legislation desired by the trade unions. When resolutions were adopted calling for presentation of specific bills in Parliament, the deputies who were members of Chambers of Labor were the ones who were asked to take the initiative and not the Socialists as such. Several of the trade union leaders were Socialist deputies at the time, including Cabrini, Chiesa, and Rigola.

All this understates, of course, the relationship between the trade union movement and the Socialist Party. It does, however, indicate that the problem of relationship was becoming a far more complex matter than any simple dependence of trade unions upon political party leadership for support and guidance.

The 1901 Congress faced the problem of giving the Federation sufficient financing to permit a full-time official and a publication of its own. The movement had become sufficiently large to require a degree of central leadership and authority. While the financing was on a very modest scale, it did allow a greater measure of initiative and independence than was possible when the organization had been largely dependent upon voluntary contributions, mainly from the Milan Chamber of Labor.

As discussed in the preceding section, the rapid development of National Unions during 1901 and 1902 created a new problem of coordination and of operation for the trade union movement. The National Unions had no official representation within the central trade union body, nor was there any mechanism for coordinating their activities with the Chambers of Labor to which their members were almost universally affiliated. Cabrini made a detailed report on the problem to the Federal Committee of the Italian Federation of Chambers of Labor in September 1902 recommending that a special conference be called to establish machinery for coordinating the various National Unions among themselves as well as with the Federation of Chambers of Labor.[33]

The conference, held in Milan in November 1902, was attended by representatives of twenty-five National Unions, in addition to the Chambers of Labor affiliated with the federation. By avoiding any attempt to define the relative authority of the National Unions and the Chambers of Labor, and concentrating instead upon the establishment of new central coordinating

32. *IV Congresso delle Camere del Lavoro*, pp. 110–117.
33. *See* Cabrini, *La resistenza*, pp. 109–127.

machinery, agreement was obtained without difficulty.[34] A National Council of Resistance was set up to represent the National Unions on the basis of one member for each affiliated National Union. In turn a Central Secretariat of Chambers of Labor and Federations of Resistance was established to co-ordinate the activities of the Federation of Chambers of Labor and Council of Resistance. The Secretariat was made up of eight members, four each from the two bodies, and was to have a full-time official paid by the Federation of Chambers of Labor. The National Unions were to negotiate with the Federation on contributions they were to make. As a practical matter, Cabrini became secretary both of the Secretariat and the Federation and his efforts were directed in general to strengthening the National Unions. On the other hand, it is clear from the regulation adopted and from the controls kept by the Federation that the Chambers of Labor felt that they were protecting their interests adequately.

The problem of getting the Chambers and the National Unions to insist that their sections join both appropriate bodies continued to be a problem of some importance for a number of years. In 1903 a referendum among the Chambers of Labor obtained majority approval for a change in the constitution of the Federation of Chambers of Labor requiring that Chambers make it obligatory that their affiliated sections join the appropriate National Union where such existed, provided that the National Union belonged to the Secretariat of Resistance and its constitution required its own sections to join the appropriate Chamber of Labor.[35]

The second conference of National Unions and Chambers of Labor, held in November 1903, avoided most controversial problems.[36] The problem of relative emphasis in trade union structure was beginning to be submerged in the troublesome issue of basic orientation which was coming to the fore within the Socialist Party. The issue of Reformist socialism versus Revolutionary socialism, as we have seen in a previous section, was at the time becoming serious within the party. The same struggle was taking place within the trade unions. Here the issue was the use of the trade unions for political purposes, the tactics and policies to be used in labor disputes and in strikes. The Revolutionary Syndicalist doctrine, as applied in Italy, was only slowly clarified in the years 1903 to 1906. During the early part of this period little differentiation was made between Revolutionary socialism and Revolutionary syndicalism, with those on the Left in the political and trade union fields still sorting out and developing their doctrines. So far

34. See Rigola, *Storia*, pp. 245–248. For complete summary of actions taken at the conference, *see* Angiolini, *Cinquant' anni*, pp. 714–716.

35. *Cronaca del Lavoro* (official organ of Italian Federation of Chambers of Labor) II, 20, August 1903, pp. 131–132. The vote was 43 Chambers in favor, 2 against with 25 refraining from answering.

36. For reports to the conference and resolutions adopted, *see Cronaca del Lavoro*, II, 23, November 1903 and III, 25, January 1904.

as the trade unions were concerned, the upsurge of revolutionary influence was made easier by the setbacks in labor disputes from 1902 onward.[37]

To the Revolutionaries in the trade union movement, strikes as such had intrinsic value. The achievement of the ultimate general strike for the transformation of society and the need to "energize" the workers through practice were only part of the story. It was partly an approach to industrial relations, which assumed the inevitability and, therefore, necessity of violent clashes and class struggle against the ruling class as represented by individual employers and the government. These general strikes were necessarily more political in their impact than economic.

The Revolutionary approach within the trade unions did not seem a strange doctrine to the workers. The repeated appeals to sympathetic strike action seemed a natural one at the time. The militancy and willingness to strike was a symptom both of the heightened expectations of workers and of their frustrations at their modest advances.

The general report of Cabrini and Premoli to the 1905 Congress of the Chambers of Labor and National Unions commented on this problem as follows:[38]

Taking over the government of the Federation of Chambers at the end of 1901, we found the worker and peasant movement in that state of feverish exaltation which supported in many the illusion of an approaching social transformation through the action of the Leagues themselves. On the other hand, it did not succeed in hiding from the eyes of more experienced organizers how much there was of hysteria and infantile impulsiveness in a great part of that improvised resistance, against which there was being formed capitalistic coalitions, who were experienced, strong in institutions already rooted in custom, and forced by a new political situation to make use of their own *direct action.*

Therefore our double preaching in that flood of strikes and in that flowering of Leagues — : Advice to the organizers against the abuse of the strike, making them conscious and mindful of the relationships which exist between the development of industrial society and the possibility for the wage earners of winning better conditions of sale for the labor force; to persuade them, in addition, of the insufficiency of the instruments of struggle improvised during the struggle itself.

And when in some cities the blunder was made of committing the strength of the entire organized proletariat against the resistance of a single employer or

37. For experience of the Milan Chamber of Labor in this regard and the 1904–06 control of the Chamber by Revolutionary leadership, *see Origini, vicende e conquiste,* pp. LI to LIV. For membership statistics of Milan Chamber see *idem* and Ministero dell' Agricoltura, Industria e Commercio. *Supplemento al Bollettino dell' Ufficio del Lavoro, No. 15, Statistica delle organizzazioni di lavoratori al 1 Gennaio 1912* (Rome, 1913), p. 65.

38. *V Congresso delle Camere del Lavoro—III Convegno della Resistenza* (*Genova 6-7-8-9 Gennaio 1905*) *Azione Triennale* (*Novembre 1901-Dicembre 1904*) *del Comitato Federale e Segretariato della Resistenza* (*A. Cabrini e P. Premoli, relatori*), (Milan, 1904), p. 11.

a group of employers of a given industry — and the appeal was launched for a general strike extended to the entire nation for a strictly economic conflict — we did not refrain from condemning such movements, lacking in common sense and destined to generalize the local disasters.

During the years 1903 to 1906 the Revolutionary doctrines and tactics spread more successfully in the Chambers of Labor than in the National Unions. Even the Milan Chamber fell to the Revolutionaries in 1904 and remained in their control for two years. While increasing numbers of Chambers of Labor were taken over by Revolutionary leadership, the National Unions remained in Reformist hands with the principal exception of the National Union of Railroad Workers. In general, the very nature of the Chambers of Labor, dealing with problems of all workers in a locality, more closely allied to political currents and influences, less impelled to concentrate on problems of workers in particular industries, made them easier targets than the National Unions with their continuing responsibility for and concentration on the problems in a specific industry and the pressures for immediate gains.

The problem of the relations and relative authority of the Chambers of Labor and the National Unions was thus colored in great part by the ideological and tactical struggle which happened to coincide with the structural units in the labor movement. It became, for example, not simply a question of who would offer leadership and advice to local unions, but also what kind of leadership and advice would be offered. In this type of struggle, with but few exceptions (such as the printers, or the hatters, or to some extent the construction workers), the Chambers of Labor had the great advantage over the National Unions. The Chambers were the traditional home of labor. The National Unions were new, weak, inexperienced and not anything like the identification symbol to workers that the Chambers were.[39]

Those Chambers of Labor which had fallen into Revolutionary hands became the implacable enemies of the National Unions and were able in most cases to obtain support for their tactics among the local unions even beyond their direct strength in the local organizations. The tactic of general sympathetic strikes was used with abandon. It is true that provocation for labor protest sometimes was great in the face of government violence against strikers and demonstrators, primarily in the south. Rigola had estimated that in the years 1901 to 1904 there were 40 workers killed and 202 wounded. These were not, however, the result of a policy of repression, but rather the result of excess of zeal on both sides. Even Rigola admitted that the fault was not all on one side.[40]

39. See Rinaldo Rigola, Manualetto di tecnica sindacale (Florence, 1947), p. 26.
40. Rigola, Storia, p. 267.

As a dramatic protest against the growing number of victims of police violence, the Revolutionary elements in Milan took the lead in calling a general strike on a national scale in September 1904. The strike was successful in shutting down the economy for four days. Even the Secretariat of Resistance and the Federal Committee of the Federation of Chambers of Labor were forced to go along with the general strike, although their limit of three days led to acrimonious recriminations from the Revolutionary elements.[41] The restraint exercised by the government during the general strike and the reverses of the Socialists in the national elections called shortly after the strike have already been discussed. The strike led to a strengthening of employer opposition to unions and at the same time to the sharpening of the factional fight within the trade union movement itself.

When the Congress of Trade Unions was held early in January 1905, the Reformist and Revolutionary forces among the delegates were about equally represented.[42] Representation was on a dual basis, through Chambers of Labor and through National Unions.[43] The debate was long and turbulent on a resolution proposed by the Milan Chamber of Labor, which would have insisted upon obstruction tactics in Parliament by the Socialist, Radical and Republican deputies until the government would resign and a law be passed prohibiting the intervention of the armed forces in labor disputes. While the resolution did not carry, the atmosphere of the congress was such as to indicate that a splitting of the organization was a genuine possibility. No attempt was made to review the structure of the Central Secretariat and its two wings, the National Council of Resistance and the Italian Federation of Chambers of Labor. The time was obviously inappropriate to tinker with the machinery, unsatisfactory as it was.

The dispute of the railroad workers which developed shortly after the congress helped precipitate the dissolution of the existing central trade union coordinating machinery. In 1902 there had also been a railroad dispute which had threatened a shutdown of the lines. At that time the grievances were sufficiently serious and had been sufficiently publicized by the trade unions, the Socialist Party and its parliamentary deputies that public sympathy had largely been won by the workers. The government was generally sympathetic to the demands as well, and the unions had obtained a reasonable compromise settlement.[44]

41. For a discussion of the strike from the point of view of the Secretariat and Federal Council see *V Congresso delle Camere*, pp. 18–20.

42. For a discussion of the congress see Rigola, *Storia*, pp. 287–291. For official general report to the congress made by the Secretaries Cabrini and Premoli, see *V Congresso delle Camere*.

43. There were 53 Chambers of Labor represented at the congress and 17 National Unions. Rigola, *Storia*, pp. 287, 290.

44. For the government's handling of the situation see Giolitti, *Memoirs*, pp. 168–169.

On the other hand, by the time the 1905 dispute developed, the Reformist policies of the railroad unions had been replaced by a Revolutionary Syndicalist orientation. The unions lost public support, already dubious as a result of the 1904 general strike, as a result of flaming Revolutionary statements and particularly the application of a technique of "noncollaboration" or obstruction on the job. The technique consisted simply in doing nothing more than was literally required by the terms of one's job description. Disruption of railroad schedules and of smooth operation was the logical result. Furthermore, the Revolutionary Syndicalist contempt for the parliamentary process and particularly for the Reformist Socialist deputies caused them to turn their backs upon the conciliatory methods used in 1902 to obtain a settlement, and made a strike inevitable. When the strike came in April 1905, less than half the organized railroad workers responded to the strike call and the strike collapsed completely within four days.[45]

At the beginning of the strike, when the railroad union officials realized their difficulties, they appealed to the Central Secretariat of Resistance for a general sympathetic strike to be called in all other industries. It was the refusal to call such a general strike which finally destroyed the Secretariat. The Revolutionary members of the Secretariat resigned. New elections through a referendum were then called, but there was very little participation in them. The newly elected members, with a Revolutionary majority, bickered for some time about the calling of a new congress to attempt to resolve the issues, but found it impossible to obtain sufficient support to proceed. Several members of the Secretariat resigned. By this time, for all practical purposes, the Secretariat was dead.[46]

Commenting upon this period Brocchi has written:[47]

The evangelical enthusiasm which had aroused so much energy is exhausted in almost all the organizations and lack of confidence and fatigue paralyze the best forces of the Italian proletariat. The Revolutionaries attribute the decomposition of the leagues to the submissive attitude of the Reformists toward the state; the Reformists, on the other hand, accuse the Revolutionaries of having managed the ruin of the unions with frantic incitement to strikes and with the systematic disparagement of every action of slow, positive, gradual conquest. But it is certain that the continuous crises of the Secretariat of Resistance, the conflict of jurisdiction between Chambers of Labor and National Unions are the principal causes of the phenomenon.

45. Rigola, *Storia*, pp. 292–294.

46. *Ibid.*, pp. 292–295, 307; *see* also Serafino Cerutti, "Dal Congresso della Resistenza Operaia," *Edilizia*, reprinted in *Vita Operaia* (independent labor periodical edited by Rinaldo Rigola) I, 6 (Biella), September 15, 1906, pp. 41–43; *Origini, Vicende e Conquiste*, p. LXVIII.

47. Quoted from R. Brocchi, *L'organizzazione di resistenza in Italia* (Macerata 1907), in Rigola, *Storia*, p. 295. For another view *see* editorial entitled "Confederazione del Lavoro e Partito Socialista" in *Vita Operaia*, I, 2, July 15, 1906 (Biella), pp. 9–10.

The Formation of the CGL

The breakdown of the Central Secretariat machinery represented a basic turning point in the history of the Italian trade union movement. The initiative now fell to the Reformist trade unionists who grasped the leadership of the movement and, until the free unions fell under the onslaught of fascism, remained in majority control. Under their leadership a trade union movement began to take shape which in its conception, structure and functioning moved in much the same direction as the trade union movements of northern Europe. The basic problems of Italian society, the competing political currents stirred up in part by these problems, and its relatively short span of years prevented the evolution of the trade union movement from running such a course. It did, however, succeed in sinking its roots sufficiently deeply in the traditions of the Italian workers to leave a strong heritage manifest in the trade unions of post-Fascist Italy, despite the intervening twenty years of trade union restrictions.

The National Metallurgical Union called a conference of National Union representatives in March 1906 where it was agreed that a congress should be held later that year for the purpose of establishing a confederation of labor. The conference claimed that it did not plan to replace the Secretariat of Resistance, but to work with it in arranging for the congress. But efforts to obtain cooperation from the Secretariat failed because of the basically different objectives of the National Union group representatives, who were Reformists, and the Secretariat, which at this time was controlled by the Revolutionaries. The Secretariat, however, gradually realizing that it could no longer function, eventually reluctantly agreed to permit the initiative to fall to the committee already established for the calling of the congress.[48]

That the problem at this stage was no longer primarily one of Chambers of Labor versus National Unions, but rather reformism versus Revolutionary syndicalism, is indicated by the fact that of the seven members of the organizing committee, four were officials from Chambers of Labor and only three from National Unions. All seven, however, were Reformists.[49] Representation at the congress was not based on the Chambers of Labor and the National Unions as such, and instead was based upon individual local unions. Each local was permitted to send delegates varying in number on the basis of membership in its organization. When the congress met on September 29

48. For text of convocation order issued by the organizing committee of the congress *see* inside back cover of *Vita Operaia*, I, 5, September 1, 1906. For earlier circular of Secretariat of Resistance, *see* inside back cover, *Ibid.*, I, 3, August 1, 1906.

49. The members were E. Verzi (Metallurgical Union), F. Quaglino (Construction Workers Union), E. Gondolo (Typographical Union) and A. Vergnanini, L. Calda, C. Della Valle and P. Bellotti (of the Chambers of Labor of Reggio Emilia, Genoa and Milan), *Ibid.*, I, 5, September 1, 1906, inside back cover.

to October 1 there were delegates from approximately 700 local unions representing about 250,000 members.[50]

The Revolutionary Syndicalists were divided on the issue of attending the congress, and while some of the organizations controlled by them refrained from attending, others sent representatives. At the congress the Revolutionary Syndicalists joined forces with the Republicans and the Anarchists, who also opposed the Reformist Socialists. Together, however, the opposition at the congress could muster no more than about one-third of the votes, and when the majority approved a resolution establishing the *Confederazione Generale del Lavoro* (General Confederation of Labor) along Reformist lines, the opposition walked out of the congress. Shortly afterward the unions controlled by the Republicans, who had considerable strength in the Romagna area but relatively little national strength, decided to join the Confederation of Labor rather than continue to make common cause with the Revolutionary Syndicalists.[51] The Revolutionary Syndicalists, as we shall see below, found it difficult to make up their minds whether to oppose the CGL from outside the organization or from within it.

The 1906 Congress, after the walk-out of the opposition groups, adopted a constitution for the new organization[52] and elected a Directive Council and a Committee of Vigilance. The former body was authorized to name an executive committee from among its members and together were given the responsibility of seeing that the constitution was observed, carrying out the decisions of congresses and seeing that affiliated organizations did likewise, keeping workers informed of developments through an official publication, cooperating and assisting Chambers of Labor and national trade unions in propaganda and organization and taking an interest, when it seemed appropriate, in the resolution of labor disputes, administering the funds of the organization, and carrying out the program of the organization as spelled out in the constitution. Affiliation to the organization was to be through local unions, provided the local unions were themselves affiliated with the appropriate Chamber of Labor and National Union where they existed.

On the important question of relations with political parties, the organization declared that the confederation would have "the absolute general leadership of the industrial and peasant proletarian movement above all political distinctions." It did provide that the organization should make "the necessary and appropriate agreements with the parties which defend, in the political field, the interests of the workers, so that every partial dispute be-

---

50. Rigola, *Storia*, p. 307.

51. *Ibid.*, pp. 308–309. See also R. Rigola, *Ventun mesi di vita della Confederazione del Lavoro, Rapporto al VII Congresso Nazionale delle Società di Resistenza* (Turin, 1908), pp. 43–44.

52. For text of constitution, *see* Rigola, *Storia*, pp. 309–313.

tween capital and labor be defined justly and every general campaign, determined by the sharpness of the class struggle, be oriented toward practical ends."

The congress made no attempt to spell out the relative responsibilities of the Chambers of Labor and the National Unions. The 1905 Congress of the Central Secretariat of Resistance had recognized the equal legitimacy of both forms of organizations and had declared that the National Unions had responsibility for leading labor disputes while Chambers of Labor had such responsibilities only where the local unions involved were in fields where no National Union existed.[53] The 1906 Congress apparently did not regard it as an issue which would be further clarified by any additional resolutions at the time. In fact, even the constitution proposed by the opponents of the Reformists accepted the general import of the 1905 resolution. None of this meant, of course, that there had been a satisfactory division of responsibility acceptable to all. There was still to continue throughout the pre-Fascist period a struggle between the two types of organizations in many areas. But the legitimacy of the National Unions had gradually and in many instances, grudgingly, been accepted. This was more true, as one would expect, among the Reformists than among the Revolutionary Socialists. It also applied more uniformly to the stronger National Unions like the printers, hatters, and railroad unions. In fact, the CGL did find it advisable at its 1908 Congress to amend its constitution to provide that "the functions of the two organizations are understood to be limited, for the Federations [National Unions] to the orientation and leadership of resistance activities of the category of its own affiliates — having heard the opinion of the Chambers of Labor and possibly in agreement with them — and, for the Chambers to the protection and coordination of the local interests of the working classes."[54]

The leadership of the new organization, solidly Reformist — or Federalist, as it was called in a trade union context — chose Rinaldo Rigola as secretary and head of the organization in 1907. Rigola left the indelible stamp of his personality upon the CGL during the entire period of its existence until it was destroyed by fascism, although Rigola himself resigned from leadership in the organization in 1918.

Rigola brought to his task a keen sense of the independent role of trade unionism, a basically moderate approach which was in the mainstream of

53. *Ibid.*, p. 314; *also* Rigola, *Manualetto*, p. 27, footnote 1, has text of resolution on responsibilities of Chambers of Labor and National Unions to have their sections join the appropriate Chamber or National union, as the case might be. For text of the principal points in the resolution sponsored at the 1905 Congress by the Typographical Workers' Union *see* Bruno, *La Federazione del Libro*, p. 113.

54. Rigola, *Storia*, p. 368. For discussion of the amendment, *see* Confederazione Generale del Lavoro, *Resoconto stenografico del VII Congresso della Resistenza (II della Confederazione Generale del Lavoro)*, Modena, 6, 7, 8, e 9 Settembre 1908 (Turin, 1910), pp. 100, 127–132.

the slowly evolving unionism of countries further to the north, and a strength of personality and conviction. The position he attained and held for many years was all the more remarkable since he had become totally blind before his selection as head of the CGL.[55] He had been born on February 2, 1868 of a working-class family in Biella, the principal textile center in Piedmont. More fortunate than most, he had succeeded in completing the five-year elementary school course and had learned the trade of cabinetmaker. In accordance with the custom of the time, he had traveled and worked in other parts of Italy, in France, and in Switzerland. At Biella, where he returned frequently and finally settled down, he worked as an independent artisan; in his travels he had usually worked in factories.

He had acquired through his own experience and through self-education an extensive knowledge of social movements and trade unionism, and after a period of Republican sympathy had early become a Socialist. His work at Biella permitted him more freedom than factory work would have, and in 1895, using his cabinetmaker's shop in his home as an office, he began editing a Socialist paper, *Il Corriere Biellese*. In 1897, while still under the legally eligible age of thirty he ran unsuccessfully for Parliament. In the repressions of the following year he had been forced to flee from Italy, and after a short stay in Switzerland, settled in Lyon where he continued to work at his trade and to mingle with other Italian Socialist exiles in the city.

In the Italian parliamentary election of 1900, while still in exile, he was elected deputy from the Biella district and returned to Italy. In that same year the Socialist Congress decided to set up a special section in its secretariat to be concerned with trade union labor matters, and Rigola was named secretary in charge (Andrea Costa was secretary in charge of political affairs). Late that year, however, Rigola, who had in his youth suffered from lesions in the eyes, found the condition of his eyes rapidly deteriorating as part of a serious illness, and despite long periods of hospitalization and several operations, he became totally blind.

Returning to Biella in 1903, Rigola again took over the editorship of *Il Corriere Biellese*. He ran successfully for re-election to Parliament in 1904, but he resigned immediately, convinced that his blindness would prevent him from serving his constituency adequately. In addition to *Il Corriere Biellese*, he started a fortnightly trade union periodical, *Vita Operaia*, in 1906 to fill the gap left, so far as the Reformist trade unions were concerned, when the Secretariat of Resistance and its publication came under the control of the Revolutionary Syndicalists. When the CGL was organized he was chosen as editor of its official publication and within a few months was also named secretary of the organization.

In his earlier political activity, Rigola had been among the Intransigents

55. For biographic details on Rigola *see* his autobiography, *Rinaldo Rigola*.

within the Socialist Party and later among the Integralists. In trade union activity, however, first as secretary of the Socialist Party, and then as secretary of the CGL, he completely repudiated the possibility that trade unions could function effectively or grow strong and achieve their objectives except through primary concern with immediate problems. For Rigola, trade unions had a separate independent function from political parties, that of immediate gains for workers on their jobs. He did not reject the importance of other issues, nor the necessity to collaborate with political parties to achieve wider objectives, and at no time did he reject his own Socialist orientation, but the "bread-and-butter" problems were the main focal point of his trade union interest.

Certain conclusions followed naturally from such premises for Rigola. Strong organizations were necessary, and this meant high — or at least higher — dues to pay organizers, attract qualified leadership, and build large strike funds. More centralization of authority was necessary in the National Union to handle the calling of strikes, negotiations, and use of strike funds. Responsibility of leadership meant absolute respect for collective agreements. Strikes were only a last resort in labor disputes. Independence from political parties did not mean non-cooperation, but to Rigola it meant consistent refusal to accept deviation from trade union objectives to achieve politically dictated goals or serve political tactical advantage. His position made him a principal antagonist to the Revolutionary Syndicalists, who became his bitterest foes.

Rigola had been named to his position in the CGL on the assumption that there would be little initiative and leadership which the confederation as such would undertake. Rigola, on the other hand, grasped the opportunities of leadership and built the importance of the confederation in a manner few had anticipated. In the organization's publications, in speeches throughout the country, at meetings, conferences, and conventions of its affiliated organizations, at the confederation's congresses, in dealings with the political parties and with the government, the confederation leadership under Rigola took the initiative in implanting the basic ideas which oriented the organization.

The CGL made considerable progress until the First World War. The progress was less in dramatic membership gains — this came later, in the postwar period, under quite different circumstances — than in the strengthening and reorganization of the trade union structure and in its collective bargaining efforts. Some membership gains were made, however, and while the organization at no time during this period accounted for as many as half the organized workers in the country, it was the principal recognized representative of labor. The organized workers outside the CGL were either Revolutionary Syndicalist organizations, Catholic organizations, white-collar and government employee organizations, or independent unaffiliated local or regional groups.

The CGL at the end of its first year in 1907 had a membership of 190,422. Its strength increased steadily during the following four years and reached 383,770 in 1911. The decline to little more than 300,000 during the following year was largely due to organized withdrawal of Revolutionary Syndicalist and other affiliates (see below). The membership from then until the First World War remained approximately static. It is interesting to note, and it is symptomatic of the Rigola administration of the CGL, that membership statistics were based upon and limited to the actual number for whom per capita dues were paid to the confederation. This was, and continued to be, a rare practice in Italy. At the time it resulted on balance in an understatement of the actual strength of the CGL, since a number of affiliated organizations made a practice of paying per capita dues for far fewer than their actual members.[56] The following list gives the total CGL membership during the years 1907 to 1924:[57]

1907	190,422	1916	201,291
1908	262,006	1917	237,560
1909	307,925	1918	249,039
1910	356,420	1919	1,159,062
1911	383,770	1920	2,200,100
1912	309,671	1921	1,128,915
1913	327,312	1922	401,054
1914	320,858	1923	212,016
1915	233,863	1924	201,049

The CGL throughout its history sought to achieve a gradual centralization and an increase in its own authority. It made considerable progress, but

56. For example, before the railroad union withdrew from the GCL in 1911 it paid per capita dues for 25,000 members each year, while government statistics reported it as having 49,000 members during that period. Similarly, the seamen's union paid per capita dues for each of the years 1911–1913 for 5,000 members, while the government reported that the organization had 53,800 members. From Rigola's explanation of his report to 1914 CGL Congress in *Resoconto stenografico del IX Congresso della Resistenza, IV della Confederazione Generale del Lavoro, Mantova, 5-9 Maggio, 1914* (Milan, 1914), p. 13.

57. Rinaldo Rigola and Ludovico d'Aragona, *La Confederazione Generale del Lavoro nel Sestennio 1914–1920, Rapporto del Consiglio Direttivo al X Congresso Nazionale della Resistenza, V della Confederazione Generale del Lavoro, Livorno, 1921* (Milan, n.d.), pp. 119–121; Rinaldo Rigola, "L'Evoluzione della Confederazione del Lavoro," in the series "I Problemi del Lavoro," IV, no. 7 (new series) (September 1921), p. 23; statistics in CGL, *Battaglie Sindacali*, September 19, 1926, quoted in *Lettere ai Lavoratori*, no. 1, January 31, 1951, p. 45.

never became highly centralized. The changes effected were parallel to those of the trade union movements in other Western countries. Basically these changes were based on the trend already begun before the formation of the CGL, and centered around the increased importance given to the National Unions.

When the CGL was formed, affiliation to it was directly through the local unions, as we have seen. At the 1908 Congress the constitution was amended to strengthen the requirement of local union affiliation with appropriate Chambers of Labor and National Unions, but affiliation to CGL through local unions was still retained. As a matter of practice, however, a large proportion of the local organizations began paying their CGL per capita dues through Chambers of Labor or through National Unions. To some extent this had evolved naturally and was encouraged by CGL as an easier means of collection, since the local organizations also paid per capita to the Chambers of Labor and the National Unions to which they were affiliated. In addition, however, it also represented the deliberate effort of Chambers of Labor and National Unions — in competition with each other — to retain or build up the local unions' principal loyalties to their organizations. By 1910 only five local unions with a total of 330 members paid per capita directly to CGL rather than through the intermediate organizations.[58]

The basis of membership was changed at the 1911 Congress of the CGL held at Padua. While per capita payments to the confederation were now almost exclusively paid through Chambers of Labor and National Unions, these organizations were not officially recognized within the CGL until 1911. At the congress of that year the constitution was amended to make the Chambers of Labor and the National Unions the official affiliates of the CGL rather than the local unions.[59] Thus, while formerly local unions alone were represented officially at congresses, and the National Council was elected at the congresses, under the amended constitution National Unions and Chambers of Labor were the ones which sent delegates to congresses, and members of the National Council were named directly by these organizations. At the 1911 Congress, in fact, in an effort to

---

58. For discussion of affiliation by isolated union and by bloc, and statistics on subject, see Rigola, "L' Evoluzione," p. 23; Rigola, *Ventun mesi di vita*, pp. 39–43; R. Rigola, *La Confederazione Generale del Lavoro nel Triennio 1908–1911, Rapporto del Consiglio Direttivo all' VIII Congresso Nazionale delle Società di Resistenza aderenti alla Confederazione* (Turin, 1911), pp. 67–73; Rigola, *La Confederazione Generale del Lavoro nel Triennio 1911–1913, Rapporto del Consiglio Direttivo al IX Congresso Nazionale delle Società di Resistenza aderenti alla Confederazione* (Milan, 1914), pp. 74–78; Rigola and D'Aragona, *La Confederazione del Lavoro . . . 1914–1920,* pp. 120–121.

59. *Resoconto stenografico dell' VIII Congresso della Resistenza (III della Confederazione Generale del Lavoro), Padova, 24–28 Maggio 1911* (Turin, 1912), pp. 223–235 for discussion of constitutional amendments at the congress.

strengthen the position of the National Unions, they were given considerably more relative representation in CGL than were the Chambers of Labor. The constitutional amendments, having made it compulsory for each organization to have its affiliated local unions join the appropriate complementary organization, then gave the National Unions full representation for their members and the Chambers of Labor representation only for those members who were not represented through a National Union. This disparity in representation, however, gave rise to such strong protest that at the next congress, held in 1914, the representation of the National Unions and the Chambers of Labor at congresses and on the CGL National Council was equalized through the device of giving each organization voting strength equivalent to one half of its full membership.[60] This system was maintained until the CGL ceased to function.

There is little doubt that the National Unions through the pre-Fascist lifetime of the CGL gained considerable strength and had an increasingly dominant voice in the CGL. On the other hand, the CGL itself never became a centralized organization with very much direct authority over its affiliates. Rigola exaggerated only slightly when, at the 1921 CGL Congress he said, "The principal defect of the confederation is this: that its [National] Committee has never been and is still not even today a unitary committee. The confederation is the sum of various action organizations which have diverse needs . . . Thus the confederation, in a few words, has been until now, has been in the past and is also today more than anything else an inter-union secretariat." [61] The CGL was only one arena within which Chambers of Labor and National Unions competed for influence and vied for control over affiliated local organizations. While the arena was an increasingly important one and with time would probably have become the determining locus of authority, more important was the day-to-day competition directly between the Chambers and the National Unions with respect to authority over the local unions. That the Chambers of Labor had lost tremendously in the struggle is evidenced by the fact that the leadership of the CGL after the First World War seriously considered — and got authority from the 1921 Congress of the organization to study — the transformation of the Chambers of Labor into subsidiary branches directly responsible to the national CGL with officials named and paid by the national body.[62]

But the Chambers of Labor had not lost so much that they could not prevent this type of shift from seriously getting under way. With all the shift

60. *Resoconto stenografico del IX Congresso . . . 1914,* pp. 134–137, 191 and 201–204.

61. *Resoconto stenografico del X Congresso della Resistenza, V della Confederazione del Lavoro, Livorno, 26–27–28 Febbraio, 1–2–3 Marzo 1921* (Milan, 1922), p. 237.

62. *Resoconto stenografico del X Congresso . . . 1921,* pp. 348–355; Rigola, "L'Evoluzione," pp. 12–15.

of authority which took place from the Chambers to the National Unions and the CGL, the Chambers remained a principal focal point of loyalty to the organized Italian workers. In great part this was the reflection of the continued strong traditions of localism whose roots were so deep in Italy. In part it was the specific services rendered by the Chambers — employment offices, advice on social security, government assistance programs, workmen's compensation, educational programs, and assistance in handling grievances. The fact that the Chambers were the centers of trade union political activity and propaganda brought them in close contact with the union membership. Finally, in local negotiations and disputes, despite the efforts of many of the National Unions, it was the Chambers which, in fact, frequently furnished local leadership.

In any event, the Chambers of Labor had sufficient vitality and served an important enough local function that the CGL never succeeded in reducing their authority and power to the level the confederation sought.

The Revolutionary Syndicalists

The years 1906–1908 were stormy ones in the field of labor in Italy. The wave of organization and strikes which had swept through industry and agriculture in 1901 had spent itself rapidly as employers developed more effective defenses. Strikes in industry declined rapidly from the high point of 1042 during 1901 to 549 in 1903 and fluctuated between 631 and 628 in the succeeding years. In agriculture the variation was even greater. From the 1901 level of 629 it fell to 47 in 1903 and after rising to 208 in the following year fell again to 87 in 1905. A second wave of unrest and strikes started, however, in 1906. Strikes rose to 350 in agriculture and 1299 in industry. In the following year, they rose further to 377 in agriculture and 1891 in industry, involving 575,630 workers, 254,131 in agriculture and 321,499 in industry. By 1908, strikes declined in industry to 1459, involving 197,958 workers and in agriculture to 257 with 136,346 workers involved. This was still a relatively high level for the period, and in the remaining prewar years the number of strikes fluctuated at a lower level.

The struggle for hegemony over the workers' loyalties continued at a high pitch during the two years after the formation of CGL in 1906. To the Syndicalists of that period, the postulates of the Reformist Socialist trade unionists — strong continuing organization, responsible leadership, centralized authority, regular payment of high dues, respect for observance of labor agreements, and use of strikes only as a last resort — were all a repudiation of Revolutionary doctrine. Syndicalists earned the characterization of "cyclone unionists," a phrase which became a favorite among the workers.[63] The Syndicalists regarded strikes as skirmishes useful under any conditions

63. Rigola, *La Confederazione Generale del Lavoro . . . 1911–1913*, p. 72, footnote 1.

as preparation of the masses for the revolution. Enthusiasm was more important than organization. "Bureaucratization" was their contemptuous characterization of the CGL's attempts to foster strong trade union organization. The immediate objectives of a strike were important only for generating enthusiasm, not for gains. The French trade union movement had somewhat earlier adopted Revolutionary syndicalism as its official doctrine, but kept the general strike tactic to a theoretical level. In Italy, the general strike became a weapon practiced by the Revolutionary Syndicalists with abandon. Since strikes had intrinsic value to them, and "solidarity" strikes reflected an increased willingness of workers to sacrifice for the benefit of class interest and not just personal selfish interest, the sympathetic strike, spread over as wide an area as possible, also had intrinsic value. The common pattern thus became the individual strike followed by a general strike in the locality or province, if the individual strike was not immediately successful.

It was during this period of 1906 to 1908 that the Revolutionary Syndicalists reached their greatest strength before the First World War. They claimed approximately 200,000 workers[64] and while this claim probably was an exaggeration, they represented an acute threat to union leadership which followed the CGL orientation. The direct support which the Revolutionary Syndicalists obtained among wage earners was largely concentrated in the rural districts. In the industrial cities of the north they won relatively less following. With Parma as the heart of the movement, however, they had considerable influence and frequently attained predominance in wide areas of the Po Valley, in Emilia and Romagna. Rigola, in referring to the Syndicalist movement in his report to the 1908 CGL Congress commented,[65] "It is noteworthy that syndicalism has made progress more easily in agriculture. The industrial proletariat rejects it in a bloc. The farm laborer is still a mystic who has need to go through [the phase of] faith in miracles." Here was a basic difference between the appeal of syndicalism to the French and to the Italians. Unlike the French, the Italian industrial workers refused to accept the Syndicalist doctrine or leadership. In the rural areas, on the other hand, where large-scale use of farm labor characterized northern and north central Italy, the appeal was to groups which did not exist in any appreciable numbers in France.

The influence of the Syndicalists should not, however, be underestimated. The Syndicalist tactical approach to organization and strikes coincided with the spontaneous reactions of many workers, who lacked experience with organization, who sought dramatic answers to what appeared to them insoluble personal economic problems, and were dominated by resentment

64. *Resoconto stenografico . . . 1908*, p. 27; Rigola, *La Confederazione . . . 1911–1913*, p. 39.
65. Rigola, *Ventun mesi di vita*, p. 31.

against the existing social order. In addition, even for those who focused more directly upon their immediate economic situation and sought gradual improvement, the dramatic strike gesture and the heartwarming emotional spree of a "class solidarity" experience was more appealing than the sober preaching by the CGL-oriented leaders of discipline, restraint, responsibility, coupled with pleas for high dues and slow evolution of strong organization. The breakthrough of the trade union movement into vast new areas unleashed basic problems of trade union tactics which went beyond the questions of Syndicalist ideology as such and furnished a Herculean problem for the predominant moderate leadership within the CGL.

CGL-Socialist Party Relations

The CGL unions, in addition to contending with the generic "direct action" approach which characterized newly organized workers both in industry and in agriculture, and with the Revolutionary Syndicalist competition, also had innumerable difficulties with the Socialist Party. The Socialist Party, both nationally and in many of its local branches, looked with little favor upon CGL claims to exclusive leadership of Socialist-oriented trade unions. The Socialists were in the business of maximizing their political support; working directly with workers on their problems, even if industrial or agricultural, seemed a natural role for them to play. It was troublesome to be reminded by the CGL that local political leaders, members of Parliament, national officials of the party, were no substitute for trade union officials on matters such as collective negotiations, strike decisions, and organizational policy. In addition, it appeared to matter little to many Socialist political leaders whether local unions were Syndicalist or Federalist. They indiscriminately supported all unions and all strikes, for from a political point of view, discriminating judgments might adversely affect election support. Finally, the CGL represented a potential competitor for the loyalty of workers, which did not necessarily endear it to the Socialist politician.

The relationship between the CGL and the Socialist Party continued to be a problem throughout the lifetime of the CGL. The problem was less an attempt of the party to dominate the CGL than its failure to refrain from intervening in union business itself on a local basis — with union orientation varying with the local personalities involved — or to refuse to support any other than CGL-approved organizations and activities.

The adoption of a resolution setting up guideposts for the relationship of Socialist parties and Socialist-oriented trade union movements at the 1907 Stuttgart Congress of the Socialist International furnished a basis for attempted agreement between the two groups in Italy. In October 1907, as a result of pressure from the confederation, a conference was held among the

Directive Council of the CGL, the party leadership, and the members of the Socialist parliamentary group to work out the principles of relationship between the party and the union movement. Using the Stuttgart resolution as a basis, the CGL was able to obtain an agreement which followed its own views fairly closely. It was agreed (1) that the party and the confederation would coordinate their propaganda for the achievement of their common ideals; (2) that the leadership of economic strikes was the responsibility of the confederation and that the party had responsibility for leadership of the political movement; (3) that in strikes called by dissident organizations the party would not make appeals for solidarity if the appeal was not decided by agreement of the confederation; (4) strikes for political objectives had to be decided by common agreement.[66]

The agreement cleared the atmosphere somewhat, but as Rigola reported to the CGL Congress the following year, "If I were to affirm that this convention was respected in all its parts I would not be telling the truth."

One of the problems which concerned the CGL as a result of the Syndicalist approach to labor organization was the repeated appeals for funds made by the Syndicalist unions for subsidizing strikers. On the frequent appeals to CGL unions for general sympathy strikes in connection with Syndicalist-called stoppages, the CGL had found it possible consistently to advise its affiliates to respond in the negative. While affiliates did not always follow the advice offered by the confederation, the position of the confederation became well established as a principle despite the resultant abuse heaped by the Syndicalists upon the "traitorous" Federalists. On the other hand, the appeals for funds to support strikers were more difficult to turn down and more difficult for the CGL to control among its affiliates.

To the CGL, the accumulation of strike funds was an important objective. In the absence of such funds, appeals for contributions from other unions, while less satisfactory, was necessary. Nonetheless, the very purpose of such collections was defeated unless strikes represented only a last resort, and collections were made only for strikes having merit and justification from the point of view of the demands, the employer position, and the chances of success. The Syndicalist approach to strikes resulted in appeals for strike funds which frequently were not justified from the Federalists' point of view. Contributions for these strikes made it more difficult to finance justifiable strikes and might result in lost strikes because of lack of financial support for strikers. The appeals for funds became an everyday occurrence during these years and, in the absence of any control, was done on a free-wheeling basis among all organizations on behalf of any organization. The Socialist Party had added significantly to the irritation of the CGL by lending itself frequently to sponsorship of raising strike-relief funds in situations with which the confederation had no sympathy.

66. *Ibid.*, pp. 55, 62–63.

Rigola outlined his basic approach to organizational and strike problems at the Second CGL Congress held in 1908:[67]

1. Maintain firm the principle of organization of unions.

2. Organize on the basis of high dues and multiplicity of scope, giving to each member in proportion to his contribution — in addition to defense and conquest of class — mutual aid services, such as subsidies for unemployment, travel expenses, invalidity.

3. Continue strengthening the national industry unions, transforming the present autonomous or federated leagues [local unions] into sections of the national unions.

4. Combat *localism* without truce . . . Combat, therefore, the autonomous strikes (when these are made by the localist counter-organization), controlling the appeals for solidarity through the confederation. Substitute interunion mutualism for periodic and arbitrary appeals.

5. Promote in all ways cooperatives and the direct assumption of agricultural and industrial work.

6. Entrust the leadership of the organizations to tried personnel with the capacity of giving most ample guarantees.

At the time of the 1908 Congress some of the Revolutionary Syndicalist unions, principally the railroad unions, were still affiliated with the CGL, and the discussion revolving around the secretary's report was a lively review and evaluation of the activity and methods of the CGL. A motion approving the activity of the confederation was adopted overwhelmingly.[68]

The approach of the confederation to the calling of strikes and the responsibilities involved in disputes was best revealed in the resolution on the subject of control of appeals for strike relief funds.[69] Among other restrictions, the chambers and the federations were required to consult with the confederation before calling strikes which involved a majority or all the workers of the industry in the province or nation. Strikes called without such consultations would not be entitled to appeal for solidarity funds unless there had not been time for prior consultation, as in cases where the very existence of the organization was being defended or the worsening of labor conditions precipitated immediate action. In the latter cases consultation had to take place afterwards. To provide a continuing fund for the purpose of assistance and avoid appeals to affiliates every time a specific strike was to be subsidized, a National Resistance Fund was to be created by the con-

67. *Ibid.*, p. 33.

68. *Resoconto stenografico . . . 1908*, p. 97.

69. For stenographic record of the discussion, *see Resoconto stenografico . . . 1908*, pp. 147–217. The complete text of the resolution does not appear in the stenographic record, but is given in Rigola's report to the 1914 CGL Congress, *La Confederazione . . . 1911–1913*, pp. 43–45.

federation to which affiliated organizations were urged to contribute voluntarily on a periodic basis.

The confederation tried in the succeeding years to apply the principles established and to control appeals for assistance. Rigola, commenting to the 1914 CGL Congress on the experience of the previous six years, said:

Needless to say, the norms as in general those relating to general solidarity strikes were never strictly applied; not because they did not respond to true necessity but because it was not always possible to put up a valid dyke against the rush of sentiment and fear. Every once in a while there arose the "exceptional case" with which it was necessary to go along; every transaction was always resolved in a kind of moral complicity with the enemy, to the certain harm of the proletariat and to the progressive retardation of the organization but the situation did not permit doing differently. The confederation was consistently considered as a fund of insurance against Syndicalist disasters, like fate, to whom it is legitimate to transfer all responsibility or like the cow with a hundred udders, which must have milk for everyone and especially those to whom it does not belong.

A major subject discussed at the 1908 Congress was the question of relations with the political parties.[70] The CGL leadership desired to maintain relations with the Socialist Party for purposes which involved primarily support for specific political and legislative objectives of the CGL. They also wanted to have working relations with other parties of the Left for similar purposes. The CGL had written to the Republican Party before that party's December 1906 Congress suggesting such a relationship and while no specific formal arrangements had been made, some cooperation had been developed. In addition, of significant importance at the time for CGL, the Republican Party Congress had adopted a resolution urging trade unions led by Republicans to affiliate with the CGL and had thereby helped reverse the Republican trade unionists' attitude toward CGL when they had walked out of the first CGL Congress.[71]

The Radical Party, although having practically no trade union support, was a moderately progressive party which could be of use to CGL in its public administrative and legislative interests. As a result, the CGL leadership also had tried to develop informal relations with it. At the 1908 Congress, all three parties accepted invitations to send observers and present greetings to the congress.[72]

There is little doubt that the CGL leadership would have preferred a less

70. For other noteworthy issues discussed at the congress, see *Resoconto stenografico . . . 1908*, pp. 306–317, 317–332, 198–200, 332–339, 339–342.

71. See discussion of CGL and Republican Party actions in speech by Spinelli of Railroad Workers Union at 1908 CGL Congress, *ibid.*, p. 25.

72. *Ibid.*, pp. 285–291.

close working relationship with the Socialist Party and a free hand in developing cooperation with any parties which would agree to support CGL objectives. As Rigola put it, to the amusement of some and the anger of others at the 1908 Congress, "I am for free love; not only that, but since this labor movement is so young and so exuberant it would be a pity to force it into monogamy." He had felt impelled to preface this comment by advising against a marriage between CGL and the Socialist Party since "The moralists and the physiologists are in agreement in advising against marriages among people with common blood, since it does not respond to the precepts either of morality or of hygiene." [73]

But both the external pressures and the pressures from within CGL limited the leadership's freedom of action. The resolution recommended by the leadership to the congress was that the organization should develop relations with the "Socialist Party and any others which do not obstruct the struggle of the proletarian class and accept the program and methods of the General Confederation of Labor." While the Syndicalists with their small representation at the congress were against any political party relationships, it was evident that widespread opposition existed to the weak phrase "do not obstruct." The leadership felt compelled, before putting its report and motion to a vote, to accept an amendment which changed the phrase to "accept the class struggle." It tried to blunt the phrase as it applied to political parties by explaining that in its view the class struggle existed, whether or not acknowledged, in the economic field and that it did not, and could not, exist in the political field by the very nature of political activity.[74]

The 1908 Congress confirmed the general lines of policy developed by the CGL leadership and gave strong impetus to the self-confidence of those supporting the general policy of the organization. During the following three years, the CGL grew from 262,006 members to 383,770. In addition, collective bargaining got a stronger foothold in plants in textiles, metallurgy, ceramics, in construction, mining and agriculture.

While the educational efforts and practical policies of the CGL made progress, the forces working against the CGL orientation were strong. In the competition with the Revolutionary Syndicalist forces, the CGL organizations gained ground and the Syndicalists lost membership. The CGL affiliates, on the other hand, frequently found it necessary to make compromises in order to maintain support from workers as a militant Socialist-oriented trade union group. General strikes were still held as political protests and, in many localities, as a futile means of pressure in strikes already lost. Within the organization, in part as a reaction against what was re-

73. *Ibid.,* p. 86.
74. *Ibid.,* pp. 220–222 and 280–285.

garded as too conservative leadership, and in part as a reflection of the growth of Revolutionary factional strength within the Socialist Party, the leadership in the CGL organization found itself confronted by a growing vociferous minority of Revolutionary Socialists. Nonetheless, the leadership of the CGL and its National Federations commanded preponderant support within their organizations, and only in the Chambers of Labor did opposition groups sometimes succeed in winning control away from Reformist leadership.

CGL's relations with the Socialist Party were considerably improved during the several years after the 1908 Congress. The joint resolution of 1907 formed the basis of the relationship which was made easier by the fact that the Reformists won control in the Socialist Party in 1908 and followed a moderate policy during the next four years. There was still direct political party intervention in trade union matters in some localities, but the national party organization cooperated with CGL in attempting to minimize such occurrences. There was, moreover, cooperation between the two organizations in seeking common objectives on the political level, particularly protective labor legislation and social insurance measures. Universal suffrage was another objective on which both organizations conducted similar campaigns and claimed credit when Giolitti developed his own program in 1911. The CGL, while in fact oriented closely toward the Socialist Party, also maintained its cooperative relations with the Radical and Republican parties, although in the case of the latter party the relationship became strained as a result of a violent dispute in the Romagna area between the Socialist-oriented agricultural laborer CGL union and the Republican-oriented tenant farmer organizations. In the national election campaign of 1909 the CGL recommended to its membership that it campaign and vote for those candidates whose past performance guaranteed their support of trade union organization and supported the program of the CGL.[75] As a practical matter support went almost exclusively to the Socialist Party, although cooperation with other parties did take place in some areas.

At the 1911 CGL Congress, held at Padua in May 1911, in addition to the Revolutionary Syndicalists, the Revolutionary Socialist faction joined in the opposition, as did the Republicans.[76] The latter based their criticism principally upon the support given by CGL to the agricultural laborers' position in their dispute with tenant farmers in the Romagna area. The Revolutionaries, differing with the Syndicalists on the question of relations

75. The action taken by the CGL National Council is reported and summarized in Rigola, *La Confederazione . . . 1908–1911*, pp. 48–79.

76. For stenographic report of congress, *see Resoconto stenografico dell' VIII Congresso della Resistenza (III della Confederazione Generale del Lavoro), Padova, 24–28 Maggio 1911* (Turin, 1912).

of trade unions with political parties, voiced, however, similar criticism of the CGL tactics and policies in the trade union field. At the end of the third day the congress expressed its approval of the CGL policy orientation and the motion "applauding, the activities conducted . . . by the leadership and particularly . . . Rinaldo Rigola who was its mind and soul," received 64.2 percent of the votes at the congress. The Syndicalist motion received 29.3 percent of the votes, and the Revolutionary motion received 5.5 percent of the votes.

Extremism and the Trade Unions

New difficulties arose for the CGL during the years between its 1911 Congress and the outbreak of the First World War. Giolitti's Libyan adventure in 1912 had important repercussions by symbolizing the failure of the Reformist policy of the Socialist Party to achieve the basic reorganization of society. With the Revolutionaries' success in winning control of the party in 1912, the CGL faced new problems both in its relations with the party and in the repercussions of the new party orientation within the CGL. While these represented the more dramatic problems, there were other elements which also were important for the organization's development.

The brief economic crisis of 1908 had been overcome rapidly in Italy, and industrial expansion had renewed its rapid rate during the following several years. Following the Libyan campaign, however, there was a slowing down of economic activity which continued until the First World War. While the period was not one of depression, it was characterized by increased unemployment and pressure toward emigration. Unemployment did not reach serious national proportions, but it did create problems in a number of industries, particularly in the construction industry and in large centers. The enormous rate of emigration, which acted as a safety valve throughout the years before the First World War, reached a peak of over 800,000 in 1913. The general atmosphere of change for the better which the leadership of the CGL had helped foster became more open to question among wage earners during the 1912 to 1914 period. While wage rates and even real wages rose somewhat during these years, it would appear that the North African adventure and increased unemployment weighed heavily in countering the psychological effects of the wage trends.

The Syndicalists during this period set up a national confederation of their own, and for the first time all Syndicalists were outside the CGL. Competitive Chambers of Labor were set up by them in many centers, including Milan, Bologna, and Piacenza. During this period, although having less following than some years earlier, the Syndicalists concentrated to a greater extent in industrial centers and created problems for CGL through their activity. Rigola evaluated the Syndicalist activity of these years in his report to the CGL 1914 Congress by saying:

We do not want to attribute more importance than it merits to the fact that syndicalism has "harvested" . . . some organization here and there in our camp to enlarge its own ranks. This is without doubt one of the reasons for our lesser progress, but it would not be the greatest of evils, if the Syndicalist tactic, cyclone style, were not a psychological depressant in itself, since after a Syndicalist experiment, skepticism enters and many workers end up by not wanting to have anything to do either with *reformism* or with *syndicalism*.[77]

Within a few months after its 1911 Congress, the CGL and the Socialist Party had been confronted with the Libyan affair. The twenty-four hour general strike called for September 27 by CGL, in agreement with the party, was too late to have any effect upon the government's plans. In addition, it had not been a dramatic success so far as worker response was concerned. The CGL leadership could rightly feel that it had consistently rejected responsibility for political leadership and political change. On the other hand, as the Revolutionaries rapidly rose in strength within the party and won control of the party in 1912, they tarred the CGL orientation and tactics with the same brush as they used on their party Reformist rivals. Within the trade unions the Revolutionary strength became significant and their vociferousness in attacking the CGL leadership matched the attacks of the Syndicalists from outside the CGL.

Two weeks after the Revolutionaries had gained control of the Socialist Party in 1912 the CGL Directive Council reaffirmed its position of autonomy and cooperation with respect to the Socialist Party, adding that greater caution was now called for because of the split of the party. The CGL's announcement of its longstanding position of autonomy with respect to political parties, however, coming immediately after the Reggio Emilia Congress, had seemed a step away from pre-existing arrangements with the Socialist Party, and as in fact the orientation of the two organizations was now sharply different, the change in party leadership did have this effect.[78]

While the Revolutionaries tried hard to win support within the CGL, they never became a real threat to the leadership within federations or the confederation itself. Several Chambers of Labor, however, fell under Revolutionary control during the first year or two after their victory within the Socialist Party, the most important being the Chambers at Milan, Bologna, and Piacenza.

Milan became the principal center of public controversy among the factions, as a result of a number of circumstances. In addition to being the principal industrial center in the country, it was one of the strongest trade union centers. The Syndicalists had set up their own Chamber of Labor

77. Rigola, *La Confederazione . . . 1911–1913*, pp. 72–73.
78. *Resoconto stenografico del IX Congresso . . . 1914*, p. 121, statement by Rigola to 1914 CGL Congress, reviewing developments; *also, ibid.*, p. 67, statement by Marchetti of the intransigent faction of the CGL.

(*Unione Sindacale*) and the Revolutionaries had won control of the CGL Chamber. In addition the official Socialist Party newspaper, *Avanti,* was published in Milan and from December 1912 was edited by the then Revolutionary Socialist Benito Mussolini. Finally, the national CGL headquarters had been transferred from Turin to Milan in 1911.

A period of violent diatribes, provocation and turbulence began which made Milan the principal center of agitation and the focal point of conflict among the Syndicalists, the Socialist Party, the Revolutionary trade unionists, and the CGL.[79] The Syndicalists made progress in the area less in terms of membership than in terms of momentary following. By seizing the initiative time and again, they succeeded in setting the pace and pattern of strikes and demonstrations into which the CGL local leadership felt compelled to fit. The Revolutionary Socialist local leadership was for a time torn between its political orientation and the sobering effect of responsibility for large, well-established, strong unions. Fearful of "losing contact with the masses," worn down by the clamorous din of epithets and vituperation from the Syndicalists, the Chamber of Labor leadership gradually moved away from its position of refusing to join in Syndicalist general strikes, to separate but concurrent actions, and finally to talk of "unity of the proletarian movement."

Mussolini daily added fuel to the fires by his inflammatory articles in *Avanti* in support of the most activist position, however irresponsible.[80] He pressed the Chamber of Labor to follow the lead of the Syndicalists, he supported unity of action, he conducted a vituperative campaign against the Reformist CGL national leadership because of its lack of "Socialist militancy." In this atmosphere, violence, arrests, and bloodshed became an inevitable concomitant of the strikes and demonstrations, and themselves served the purpose, in turn, of keeping the circle of strikes and demonstrations revolving. Rigola, writing many years later, characterized the Milan situation as follows: "The political temperature gradually kept rising. The strikes and agitations for political purposes multiplied. What the party wanted was not clear. The proletariat appeared to be the victim of a neurosis, the cause of which could not be discovered. *Avanti* prognosticated the historic battle, the blood bath. The killing of proletarians served as a source for agitations. Milan had become the Barcelona of Italy." [81]

The CGL leadership, and particularly its secretary, Rigola, became a focal point of attack. The attitude of the CGL toward general strikes, incessant

79. *See* debate on this subject as it related to Milan at CGL 1914 Congress, *ibid.,* pp. 59–72, 74–76, 79–84, 119–125.

80. *La Confederazione del Lavoro* (official CGL periodical, published for a time as a weekly and later as a biweekly), VII, 228, October 1, 1914, pp. 289–291. References in the text and in footnotes to the Socialist Party official daily newspaper, *Avanti!* have omitted the exclamation point as a matter of convenience.

81. Rigola, *Rinaldo Rigola e il Movimento,* p. 201.

agitation, political use of the trade unions was well established. The general strike in connection with the Libyan affair, for which the CGL leadership had had little enthusiasm, was put under the category of an exception justified by an issue of general vital concern to the membership of the trade unions. On the other hand, neither the confederation nor the federations could control local actions. In May 1912 the CGL Directive Council had taken a major step. It had decided that membership in the *Comitato d'Azione Diretta,* the Syndicalist national coordinating body, was incompatible with membership in the CGL, since the committee "has ceased to be simply an organization of minority and has become an organization distinct and antagonistic to the confederation." [82] The Milan Socialist Party section in 1913 adopted a resolution sponsored jointly by Mussolini and Marchetti, secretary of the Milan Chamber of Labor, which postponed expulsion of members who belonged to Syndicalist trade unions since some of the members involved claimed to belong to the Syndicalist unions in order to foster "proletarian unity." [83] The action was in opposition to the policy urged by the CGL, but fit into the pattern being woven by Mussolini at the time.

An episode which brought to a climax the buffeting which Rigola and the CGL had been receiving in Milan took place in June 1913.[84] A strike had started in the automobile plants of Milan over a question of hours reduction and wage increases. As the strike continued without any concession from the automobile manufacturers, the Syndicalists moved in and promoted the spread of the strike to the entire metallurgical industry. As a result of alleged violence and disturbance, a number of strike leaders were arrested and given jail sentences.

Mussolini then took a hand as intermediary between the Syndicalists and the Chamber of Labor leadership which had until that time opposed the sympathetic strike. Mussolini succeeded in obtaining agreement between the two groups on a jointly sponsored general strike in all of Milan. Rigola had in a press interview made clear his opposition to turning economic strikes in one industry into a general strike and had characterized the widening of the automobile strike as a mistake. The reaction to Rigola's position was a new round of vituperation in *Avanti* and from the Syndicalists. Mussolini also arranged an agreement between the Syndicalists and the Chamber of Labor that Rigola would not be asked to speak at any public

82. Rigola, *La Confederazione . . . 1911–1913,* p. 87.

83. A. Angiolini and E. Ciacchi, *Socialismo e Socialisti in Italia* (Florence, 1919), vol. II, p. 1110.

84. For details of the events and their aftermath within CGL *see La Confederazione del Lavoro,* VII, 281–282 (June 16–July 1, 1913), pp. 177–178 (editorial); pp. 195–196 (description of strike events); pp. 200–204 (text of Directive Council meeting minutes); *ibid.,* VII, 288 (October 1, 1913), pp. 291–296 (text of National Council meeting minutes); *Resoconto stenografico . . . 1914,* pp. 61–62 (Marchetti); pp. 74–75 (Buozzi); pp. 123–124 (Rigola).

strike meetings. Rigola thereupon presented his resignation to the Directive Council of the CGL, explaining that he had no desire to stand in the way of unification of the trade union organizations. The Directive Council members immediately adopted a resolution supporting Rigola and offering their own resignations to the National Council. Rigola had thus forced a clear-cut issue of confidence upon the CGL highest governing body. Upholding Rigola meant a direct repudiation not only of the Revolutionaries' position within the trade unions but also of the interference of the Socialist Party represented by Mussolini in trade union affairs. The CGL National Council debated the issue on September 22, 1913 and by a vote of 210,587 to 21,105 with 11,687 abstentions adopted a resolution approving the conduct of Rigola and the Directive Council, rejecting their resignations, and calling upon all affiliated organizations strictly to observe the discipline of the CGL.

The resignation proffered by Rigola dramatized the issue of CGL relations with the Socialist Party leadership and came on the heels of two other actions taken earlier in the year which had underscored the problem. The increased agitations of the Syndicalists, and of the Revolutionaries within the CGL, had led to a considerable increase in police violence in the course of which workers had been killed from time to time. Under the prodding of Mussolini and his articles in *Avanti,* the Socialist Party called for a national general strike to dramatize the protest against police violence. The party leadership met with the CGL national officials in March 1913 to discuss the issue. The CGL leadership preferred to avoid a strike action, apparently feeling that the provocation for police violence was frequently great and that such violence was not a deliberate policy of the government. It felt compelled, however, to agree that a national general strike would be called next time a worker was killed. The CGL made the reservation that it would be committed only if a referendum among its affiliates agreed to such action.[85] While the referendum favored the proposal by a narrow margin, and the CGL National Council approved the results in April 1913, the fact that the Socialist Party had forced the hand of the confederation and the confederation's obvious lack of enthusiasm for the venture provoked discord on both sides.

A second action of the CGL which also represented a compromise with the desires of the confederation was the official position taken by the CGL toward the national political elections of 1913. The issue was discussed at the CGL National Council session of April 1913. Rigola suggested that the CGL draw up its own legislative program and support those candidates, regardless of party, who gave assurances that they would support the program. Some members of the council favored support only of Socialist Party

85. Description of meeting and text of declarations in *La Confederazione del Lavoro,* VII, 275 (March 16, 1913), p. 83.

candidates, others supported the Rigola position, while still others wanted the confederation to refrain from taking any action. A compromise was finally worked out which omitted either blanket endorsement of all Socialist candidates or the criterion of a CGL legislative program but made opposition to the Libyan affair a criterion, thereby excluding the principal leaders of the Reformist Socialist Party.[86]

As a practical matter CGL support overwhelmingly went to Socialist Party candidates. It was clear, however, that the CGL leadership and the Socialist Party orientation were far apart. Nevertheless, CGL leadership did not dare to take any drastic step in the direction of an overt break. Even when the Socialist Party failed to extend the usual official invitation to the CGL to attend the 1914 Party Congress, the CGL leadership minimized the importance of the gesture and officially accepted the explanation given by the party that since CGL could be represented under long-standing agreements between the two organizations it had not been felt necessary to extend a specific invitation.[87]

The Fourth CGL Congress held at Mantova on May 5–9, 1914, became a long series of debates between the Reformist and the Revolutionary trade unionists. While the Reformists were vigorous in their attacks upon the Revolutionaries within the CGL, they avoided any direct opposition to the Socialist Party as such. In explaining his general report to the congress, Rigola blandly said:

Review our report and you will see that during these three years, during which we have had two different directions in the Socialist Party, we have always, in the important cases, made agreements with the party, as was our duty, without regard to whether the party was Reformist or Revolutionary, because it is not up to the trade union organization to determine what orientation the party should have . . . Thus we can demonstrate that understandings, so far as they are possible, have always been made loyally, both when the party was prevalently Reformist and when it was prevalently Revolutionary. Not only that, but I could add that there was sometimes discord with the Reformist tendency, something which has not happened recently since there has been a Revolutionary directorate.[88]

He did, however, make this general criticism in his report:

The Socialist Party, taken as a whole and without distinction among factions, has a practiced organic incapacity to favor the development of a good trade union

86. Rigola, *La Confederazione . . . 1911–1913*, p. 79; *La Confederazione del Lavoro,* VII, 277 (April 16, 1913), p. 120.
87. *Resoconto stenografico . . . 1914*, pp. 96, 121.
88. *Ibid.*, p. 17.

movement. It is not against organization, certainly, but too many of its people still interpret the organization as a simple means of achieving eventual political objectives.[89]

The general policy of the organization was debated for two days. The leadership in the attack was carried mainly by Marchetti, Bombacci, and Bacci of the Labor Chambers of Milan and Ravenna. In addition to Rigola, the chief defenders of the administration's policy were the heads of various National Federations, Bruno Buozzi of the Metallurgical Workers, Argentina Altabello of the Agricultural Workers, Braga of the Bakers and Reina of the Hatworkers. It was a sign of the pressure exerted by the critics that the administration supported a confidence resolution which included a call for more intensive activity in support of the organization's stated objectives.[90]

An echo of the Socialist Party sectarianism was heard at the congress when the issue of compatibility of membership in the CGL with membership in the Masons was raised. A motion to declare such membership incompatible was defeated by a substitute motion deploring membership in the Masons as harmful to the organization.[91] Here again, while resisting the attempts of the opposition to take over the organization or have the official Socialist Party doctrine of the time adopted by the confederation, its leadership made those concessions it thought necessary to maintain unity in the organization and prevent a complete break with the Socialist Party.

The outcome of the debates at the CGL 1914 Congress was not the victory the CGL leadership felt it to be. More significant in furnishing a glimpse of the trend was the dramatic upheaval one month after the congress which has become known in Italian history as "Red Week." [92] With the background of the intense campaign carried on by the Socialists and Syndicalists to promote agitations and demonstrations against a varied assortment of grievances in the political sphere, an anti-militarist demonstration was scheduled for June 7 in various areas. Largely in the hands of the Syndicalists, Anarchists, and Republicans, the demonstration at Ancona, which had been prohibited by the government, turned into a battle between the police and the demonstrators in which three of the latter were killed.

The incident served as a spark which ignited all the resentment and will

89. Rigola, *La Confederazione . . . 1911–1913*, p. 69.

90. For text of resolution and voting *see Resoconto . . . 1914*, pp. 100 and 128–129. The resolution obtained 75 percent of the congress votes.

91. *Ibid.*, pp. 208–226.

92. For account of events *see* Angiolini and Ciacchi, *Socialismo e Socialisti*, vol. II, pp. 131–132; Filippo Meda, *Il Socialismo*, pp. 81–83; Salomone, *Italian Democracy*, pp. 60–61. For Anarchist-colored account see Armando Borghi, *L'Italia tra due Crispi* (Paris, 1924 ?), pp. 45–56.

to action which had so assiduously been cultivated by the Socialists during the previous two years and by the Syndicalist forces for many more. A general strike immediately was called at Ancona and led to further violence. This in turn led to the spread of the general strike to the rest of the country. Faithful to its agreement with the Socialist Party, the CGL proclaimed support for a general strike on June 9. The Socialist Party simultaneously did the same. *Avanti* carried the most violent calls to action and rebellion. Mussolini, as editor, supported the most extreme measures as they unfolded in the Marche and Romagna areas, where the Syndicalists, Anarchists, and Republicans combined into a fearful band of mob leadership. Communes were taken over, arsenals captured, violence became the order of the day in these areas. While the excesses were less frequent in other areas, the general strike and its accompanying demonstrations throughout the country gave Italy the appearance of a country in the midst of civil war. There was no central national coordination, there were no specific objectives, except in the Romagna and Marche area, where those leading the mobs declared the regions to be autonomous republics. The government, exercising forebearance, did not bring to bear the full weight of its police and military forces, but waited for the storm to spend itself. Nevertheless, violent clashes took place in many rural areas. On June 11 the CGL took a hand and ordered its Chambers of Labor to call off the strike by midnight. The strike gradually petered out over the next several days. Mussolini, writing in *Avanti* June 12, 1914, claimed his share of credit for the events as they spread, "We record the events with something of that legitimate pleasure which the artist must feel on contemplating his own creation. If the Italian proletariat is on its way to acquiring a new psychology, freer and more unrestrained, it is due to this newspaper. We can understand the fears of reformism and democracy faced with a situation which can only get worse with time."

The CGL action of June 11 was attacked violently as treason, as could have been expected, by Mussolini in the Socialist Party organ. A protest strike, having threatened to turn into the beginning of an insurrection, had been met with no decisive action by the Socialist Party, which was neither prepared seriously to lead an insurrection — doomed to failure in any event — nor to display the courage to call it off. The CGL leadership, assessing the situation with a better sense of responsibility, knowingly subjected itself to the aftermath of recriminations and abuse heaped upon it by the official Socialist press and other extreme elements which had taken a hand in the demonstrations. To the charges of treason made by Mussolini, Rigola commented at a meeting of the CGL National Council "We would be traitors if we had preached the revolutionary strike and then had cut it off; but no one of us had preached it and no one has been involved in this treason. A traitor is someone who says one thing in public and does something else in action; and we are not traitors." [93] The extremists like Mussolini and the other dominant Revolutionaries in the Socialist Party also felt aggrieved when the party's parliamentary group adopted a resolution written by Turati which condemned the entire affair. It affirmed that "the fundamental concept of modern international socialism . . . is not obtained through outbursts of disorganized mobs, whose failure succeeds in stirring up the most savage and stupid currents of international reaction, perpetuating the vicious circle of political sterility." [94]

The role into which the CGL had been cast, despite itself, in the Red Week situation was not a new one for the organization. It had often exposed itself to accusations of treason and abuse heaped upon it by the extremists both inside and outside its organization. The difference, however, was that in the first years of its existence it had been able to exercise the initiative in attempting to mold its organization and events to fit a pattern which it regarded to be one of progress and advantage to labor in Italian society. By contrast, Red Week was only the beginning of the turbulent era which was to follow, in which the initiative had largely passed out of the hands of the CGL.

93. Quoted from stenographic record of session in Borghi, p. 53, footnote 1.

94. Quoted in Meda, *Il Socialismo*, p. 82. Claudio Treves, the Reformist Socialist former editor of *Avanti*, also attacked the "hooliganism" of the Red Week and defended the CGL in a long article in the Socialist *Critica Sociale, idem.*

CHAPTER IV

Catholic Trade Unions Before Fascism

The Catholic social movement developed in Italy later than in most other Western countries with a significant Catholic population. Throughout the latter part of the nineteenth century the Socialists had little competition for the loyalties of the workers. As noted by Amintore Fanfani, who became a principal Christian Democratic leader and Prime Minister during the 1950's and early 1960's, "The only political group which took to heart the workers' interests in Italy before 1900 was the Socialist Party. And once the Anarchist elements were beaten, the Republicans discredited — the Catholics remained almost apart — it can be said that the Socialists had the monopoly of the impulse and the guidance of the Italian labor movement." [1]

In part the late development of an Italian Catholic social movement was a logical consequence of the late industrialization and, in turn, late Socialist development. In part, however, it resulted from the special relations between the church and the Italian state during this period. The focal point of interest and the principal preoccupation of those serving the church in Italy was the Roman question. The Italian state, having wrested control of Rome from the Pope and eliminated his temporal power over his former domains, was regarded as a usurper, and the church ordered that it be treated as such by all true believers.

Under the *non expedit* of the Vatican, Don Margotti's formula of *nè eletti, nè elettori* (neither elected nor voters) enjoined Catholics against participating in Italian national political life, although they were permitted to take an interest in local affairs. Organizational activity under the sponsorship or guidance of ecclesiastical authorities in such an atmosphere was suspected of subversive intent by the state if it overflowed beyond narrow religious limits. This, however, was not the most important deterrent. More important was the slowness in recognizing the nature of the emerging industrial society and the inapplicability of formulae better suited to previous epochs. By the time the Catholic social movement got seriously under way in Italy, the Socialist appeal had succeeded in channeling the mainstream of wage earners into its orbit in the trade unions, the political party, the cooperative movement. The new ideas which socialism offered represented, according to Professor Luigi Einaudi, the late President of Italy, "an ideal

1. Amintore Fanfani, *I problemi del lavoro in Italia prima del 1900* (Florence, 1936), p. 18.

toward which the workers felt attracted by the desire for changes and by the thirst for a new faith." [2]

The Catholic social movement and its trade union arm made significant progress through the first years of the twentieth century until the Fascist repression. In its over-all impact it strengthened the existing fabric of society during that period and contributed toward cohesiveness in a world threatened by centrifugal forces. Among the working population, however, particularly in industry, it never succeeded in diverting the loyalties and support of the predominant numbers from their various Socialist commitments.

Origins of the Catholic Movement

In Italy, in contrast with Germany and Belgium, there was little of a practical organizational nature among workers under Catholic auspices before the *Rerum Novarum* encyclical in 1891. In contrast with other countries there was also relatively less discussion and development of ideas of Christian social order during that period. The writings of such famous authorities from abroad as Monsignor Ketteler, Count De Mun, Marquis La Tour-du-Pin helped stir up interest in the new Catholic social ideas which were spreading through Catholic circles in other countries. In Italy, however, any diversion of Catholic emphasis from the Roman problem was suspect to the church authorities. In addition, the nostalgic orientation toward the ordered hierarchical medieval society and its guild structure made it difficult to break through the resistance to new ideas. Finally, the traditional attitude toward the poor was deeply felt. Arturo Carlo Jemolo, in his monumental work on church and state in Italy, says:

> The Italian Catholics were the last to join in organizing the worker forces, in studying social problems . . . There was too long a tradition of agreement between the wealthy classes and the Church . . . There was too long a tradition of teaching the necessity that the poor exist, that poverty was an indispensable element of a Christian society, assumed because the ones give proof of patience, the others of charity and all the Christian virtues, that the clergy should adapt itself and not find heterodox the doctrine which considered poverty as an eliminable evil. To admit the rights of the poor was equivalent to cutting the halo of a virtue of charity to the poor, to make it descend to the performance of a duty.[3]

It was primarily the Socialist agitations, the spread of trade union organization, which dramatically demonstrated to the church the error of leaving the workers, without a contest, in the control of forces opposed to the church.

2. Luigi Einaudi, *Le lotte del lavoro* (Turin, 1924), p. 48.
3. Arturo Carlo Jemolo, *Chiesa e Stato in Italia negli ultimi cento anni* (Rome, 1949), pp. 437–438.

As the Italian unification movement had moved forward during the 1860's, culminating in the loss of the temporal power of the church, organizations had been started under the sponsorship of the church authorities or with their support among the more active proponents of the church position. In 1865, for example, the *Associazione Cattolica Italiana per la Libertà della Chiesa in Italia* was launched with the approval and support of Pope Pius IX. It lasted no more than one year, as a result of Italian government persecution of its leadership in the territories outside Vatican control.[4] Other organizations, however, took its place. The most important was the *Società della Gioventù Cattolica Italiana* (Society of Italian Catholic Youth), formed in 1867 with a militant program of defense of the church and its faith.

The Society of Italian Catholic Youth took the initiative in 1874 in calling a congress of all Catholic organizations to discuss common problems. The idea received approval from the Vatican, and the *Opera dei Congressi* was established to arrange regular annual congresses. The congresses were primarily, and in the early years almost exclusively, concerned with problems of furthering organization and of spreading the faith. Underlying this activity and of principal importance was the Roman problem and the support which widespread organization, of whatever character, would be to the church in its relation to the Italian government.[5] As early as 1876, however, the Vatican approved the establishment of a section at the congresses called Works of Charity, which was subdivided in 1879 into Charity and Christian Economy. By 1887 the latter section adopted the name Christian Social Economy in order to reflect better its principal interests.[6]

During these early years, while interest developed in social questions, they were viewed by the mainstream of the Catholic lay movement from the traditional focus of charity and a nostalgia for medieval guild society. Nevertheless, the beginnings of organization with a social interest were evident during the 1880's. In fact at the very first congress mutual-aid organizations were recommended as desirable, "possibly modeling them after the ancient arts and crafts guilds, making the religious element predominant in them and basing them on reciprocal affection and Christian charity." [7]

4. For discussion of the origin and activities of the association *see* Fr. Francesco Olgiati, *La storia dell' azione cattolica in Italia (1864–1904)*, 2nd edition (Milan, 1922), pp. 16–21.

5. *Ibid.*, p. 18; Ernesto Vercesi, *La democrazia cristiana in Italia* (Milan, 1910), p. 9.

6. A. Toldo, *Il sindacalismo in Italia*, 2nd edition (Milan, 1953), p. 36; also, Luisa Riva Sanseverino, *Il movimento sindacale cristiano* (Rome, 1950), pp. 112–115.

7. Quoted from *Atti del I Congresso Cattolico Italiano, Venezia 12–16 Giugno 1874* (Bolongna, 1874), p. 140, in Ministero dell' Agricoltura, Industria e Commercio, Ufficio del Lavoro, *Serie B, No. 35, Le organizzazioni operaie cattoliche in Italia* (Rome, 1911), p. VII.

Nevertheless, as late as 1889 when Giuseppe Toniolo, who became in the ensuing years the moral leader of what emerged as the Christian Democratic movement, organized the *Unione Cattolica per gli Studi Sociali* (Catholic Union for Social Studies) in the Episcopate of Padua, he was looked upon with considerable diffidence in the Catholic movement since such activity might shift the principal focus of Catholics from the Roman problem. Toniolo in fact drew into his circle of disciples many of the Catholic youth who had concern for social problems and the problem of relations between the church and the Italian state. During this period, influenced by Toniolo, a group in Milan under the leadership of Father Davide Albertario, editor of *Osservatore Cattolico,* began pressing for ideas which would substitute the slogan *Preparazione nell' astensione* (preparation in abstention) for the slogan *nè eletti, nè elettori.* Out of the Toniolo and Albertario activities developed the faction of *Giovani* (Youths) who pressed for Christian Democratic ideas within the *Opera dei Congressi* during the 1890's, opposing the conservative leadership which predominated.[8]

Both the social-economic and the political areas formed the basis of the new interests among the *Giovani.* In the social-economic area, after May 1891, with the definitive pronouncements in the encyclical *Rerum Novarum,* there were few who dared voice directly their opposition to the ideas put forth at the Catholic Congresses by the *Giovani* and their moral leader, Toniolo. It was in the wider area of the political, with its inevitable impact upon the relationship of church to Italian state, that irreconcilable issues developed.

An important step forward in the economic and social area took place in 1894 when Toniolo's Catholic Union for Social Studies developed a declaration of principles and obtained acceptance of the declaration by the "Christian Social Economy" section of the Eleventh Catholic Congress held that year. It is significant that the program carried the title "Program of the Catholics in Confronting Socialism," for there was recognition, already accorded in *Rerum Novarum,* that the development of opposition to the widespread gains being made by the Socialists depended upon an alternative program and organization. The 1894 program, distinguishing Socialist "final intentions" from its causes, characterized the latter as:

the expression of real, widespread, continuing bad conditions, which in turn is the latest product of a prolonged series of violations of Christian social order founded on justice and charity. In such a case, the cause of the suffering people is the cause of the Catholics themselves, and the present restlessness of the people is one more proof of the reasonableness of their ancient protest . . . The objectives of this same agitation, insofar as they are confused with the program of

8. For account of these developments *see* Ernesto Vercesi, *Il movimento cattolico in Italia (1870–1922)* (Florence, 1923), pp. 50–73.

Socialism, while being reprovable, attest, however, that there is now no other position than either a Socialistic revolution or a social Christian restoration.[9]

What was then suggested as a Catholic alternative to the Socialist appeal was the restoration of a consciousness of Christian ethical responsibilities to individual private property, the use of small holdings and sharecropping in agriculture, profit-sharing and sale of stock to workers in industry, elimination of monopoly of credit in the hands of a few speculators in commerce. After referring in general to the need for a legislative program, it stated:

But the most solid guarantee of a restoration rests with the reconstitution of professional unions or corporations among the civic population and in the countryside, where in separate trades the large and the small would find solidarity of interests and of affection for everything which touches the common ends of civilized living and where in particular the working classes would recover tutelage and decorum. Professional unions which therefore not only have an economic scope but look toward the single result of the organic composition of society, today pulverized by a diffuse and ruined individualism . . . that if the superior classes of property owners and capitalists find it repugnant to enter into mixed organizations with the inferior classes (which represents the ideal of the organizations proposed by Catholics), in that case the Catholics would accept that the workers join in exclusively worker professional unions and proceed by way of a legal resistance in the pursuit of their own rights, without however, as a rule closing entry to welcome classes now reluctant and opposed to their organization in the future. In other words, espousing the cause of the workers, we never lose sight of the entire society and its normal balance.[9]

The declaration thus recognized the possibility of permitting organization of unions composed of workers alone rather than mixed membership of employers and workers in the same organization. Little of a practical nature was done, however, during the 1890's to implement the decision to organize. The rapid spread of the Chambers of Labor under Socialist influence, meanwhile, created increased alarm among the Catholic leadership. In 1891 the Catholic Congress, held a few months after Pope Leo XIII released the encyclical *Rerum Novarum,* adopted a resolution which in cautious language urged that the Catholic mutual-aid organizations be converted into guilds by extending their membership to include employers and workers and by gradually expanding their activity into the industrial field.[10] By the next congress held during the following year the Chamber of Labor movement was explicitly recognized as a threat, but no specific new answer to the

9. For complete text of program *see* Olgiati, *Azione Cattolica,* pp. 232–236.

10. Full text of resolution quoted in *Le organizzazioni operaie cattoliche,* p. XVI, quoted from *Atti del IX Congresso Cattolico Italiano, Vicenza, 14–17 Settembre 1891* (Bologna, 1891), p. 152.

challenge was offered. Instead the social-economic section of the congress was asked to study the problem and offer advice.[11]

By 1894, however, the second congress held that year was prepared to recommend establishment of organizations to compete with the Chambers of Labor. It recognized that the functions of "placement," "regulation of the labor market," and "protection and defense of labor" as set forth by the Chambers of Labor were desirable. On the other hand, Chambers of Labor as they functioned in Italy had "Socialist and even sometimes more or less open Masonic spirit and intentions." They claimed to exclude religious and political considerations, but were in fact "antagonistic to the Catholic religion and to the principles of its social order, organizing and educating the workers for class struggle." It was, therefore, recommended that Catholics not give their support to Chambers of Labor because of the danger to their faith and morals and that, where it was found necessary, to organize their own Chambers in accordance with the principles of *Rerum Novarum*, "to coordinate capital and labor for an identical objective of justice, peace and individual and social welfare, combating the destructive Socialist principle of class struggle." Corporations with joint employer and worker participation were still pointed to, however, as an ultimate objective.[12]

It was not until after 1898 and particularly 1900 that the Catholic movement approached the problem of worker unions in practical rather than theoretical terms.[13] Until that time mutual-aid societies remained the principal type of organization sponsored in the economic sphere. In 1883 there had been 90 societies affiliated with the Catholic Congress. By 1891 the number had increased to 274, by 1902 it had reached a total of 550, and by 1905, 763.[14] These organizations were particularly concentrated in agriculture. By comparison with the number of mutual-aid organizations then existing under the old Mazzini influence and under Socialist influence, the number of societies organized by the Catholics was relatively small. Furthermore, by the 1890's the trade unions had taken over from the mutual-aid organization as the dynamic institution which channeled active protest into effective organization.

In addition to mutual-aid organizations, the Catholic movement during the 1890's concentrated on rural cooperative credit institutions along lines

11. *Ibid.*, p. XX from *Atti del X Congresso Cattolico Italiano, Genova, 4–8 Ottobre 1892* (Venice, 1892), p. 257.

12. For text of resolution *see ibid.*, pp. XXII–XXIII, quoted from *Atti del XII Congresso Cattolico Italiano, Pavia 9–13 Settembre 1894* (Venice, 1894), p. 214.

13. *Ibid.*, p. XXVIII; Sanseverino, *Il movimento sindacale*, pp. 230–232; Vercesi, *Il movimento cattolico*, pp. 242–248.

14. Sanseverino, *Il movimento sindacale*, p. 115, quoted from *Atti e Documenti del VI Congresso Cattolico Italiano* (Bologna, 1885), p. 292; Sanseverino, *Il movimento sindacale*, p. 124, quoted from *Atti e Documenti del IX Congresso*, pp. 150–151; *Le organizzazioni operaie cattoliche*, p. XXXI, footnote 1 and p. XXXV.

promoted earlier by Leone Wollemborg of Padua and on consumer cooperatives, particularly in agriculture.

Activity in the trade union sphere was not entirely absent, however, even
during this period. According to Gnocchi-Viani, one of the principal Reformist Socialist leaders of the Chamber of Labor movement at the time,
Catholic "so-called worker associations," soon after the Chamber of Labor
movement got under way, joined the chambers and attempted to give them
a "confessional Catholic" character.[15] After these attempts had failed, special
offices were set up at Bergamo, Turin, Milan, Lodi and Bologna. These
offices, called *Segretariato del Popolo* (Secretariat of the People) apparently
had little influence among the industrial wage earners and did little serious
organizing. In the case of the Milan *Segretariato,* which was typical of the
others, a permanent committee was responsible for administration. The committee was named by the *Opera dei Congressi* and held office permanently.
Not one of the members, according to Gnocchi-Viani, was a wage earner.
The constitution set forth the purpose of the *Segretariato* as "assisting without charge persons recognized as without means, in the events of their life,
through correspondence and relations with the ecclesiastical and civil
authorities, research of documents, information on civic charity and the
means of obtaining it, professional advice by its own consultants, registration of demand and supply of labor and friendly intervention to offer
arbitration."

The effort to handle problems in industry on the basis of concepts carried
over from a pre-industrial society still handicapped those in the Catholic
movement who were concerned with competing with the Socialist-oriented
unions. Programs of the sort offered by the *Segretariato* had little appeal
to workers seeking recognition of what they regarded as their rights and
the redress of grievances. Nor was direct intervention in labor disputes always felicitous. For example, during the 1898 government repressions when
the Chamber of Labor in the principal hat manufacturing center of Monza
was shut down, the hat manufacturers repudiated the wage and hour provisions of their collective agreement. A strike started in protest which the
Segretariato for the area attempted to settle. It urged the workers to return
to work and accept lower wages with the difference to be paid by an
anonymous person who had given the *Segretariato* a fund for this purpose.
The *Segretariato* conducted an election among the striking workers which
resulted in rejection of their proposal.[16]

There are examples, however, of successful intervention in labor disputes.
At the February 1894 Catholic Congress a report on Catholic activity in the
Lombardy region cited a case in the Bergamo area, a Catholic stronghold,
against the background of Socialist activity and attempts of the diocese com-

15. Gnocchi-Viani, *Dieci anni,* pp. 24–25, 26–27.
16. *Ibid.,* p. 47.

mittee of the *Opera dei Congressi* to counteract it: "fearing a serious Socialist dispute in the Valle Seriana, where the cotton [textile] industry operated in about thirty plants with 22,000 men and women workers, the diocese committee . . . resolved to place itself at the leadership of the dispute" and after difficult negotiations with the employers obtained an hour-and-one-half reduction in the working time in the plants.[17]

Catholic Political Relations until the Gentiloni Pact

The *Giovani* faction of the *Opera dei Congressi* did not represent a single body of ideas. This was still true when it began using the designation "Christian Democracy" as its identification, a name which had already come into use in the Catholic movements of other countries. What it had in common was an interest in economic and social problems, a desire for change, and a conviction that the relations between church and state required initiative and action on the part of the Catholic movement. Toniolo, who is regarded as the first important figure in the history of the Italian Christian Democratic movement, was not interested in the practical political problems raised by others. He was more interested in economic-social problems and in the formulation of general philosophic formulae as they related to the organization of society. He has been described as representing the mystical tendency of the movement.[18] Toniolo, in his famous article on Christian Democracy, first published in 1897, defined democracy as "that civil order in which all the social forces, juridical and economic, in the fullness of their hierarchical development, cooperate *proportionately toward the common good,* redounding in its result *to the prevalent advantage of the lower classes."* [19]

A second tendency in the Christian Democracy movement of the time was represented by the energetic Father Romolo Murri. Described as representing the ascetic tendency of the movement,[20] he defined democracy in somewhat different terms from Toniolo. To him "the name democracy signified government by the people; it indicated, then, with special reference to the political condition of the people, a state of society in which the people work and negotiate in an economy of free men, and political power, entrusted directly in their hands, cannot be an instrument in the hands of a foreigner,

17. *Atti e Documenti del XI Congresso Cattolico* (Venice, 1894), p. 187 as related and quoted in Giorgio Candeloro, *Il movimento cattolico in Italia* (Rome, 1953), p. 250.

18. Beniamino Palumbo, *Il movimento democratico-cristiano in Italia* (Rome, 1950), pp. 49–50.

19. The article first appeared in the July 1897 issue of Toniolo's journal, *Rivista Internazionale di Scienze Sociali* and was reprinted many times in the succeeding years. See Olgiati, *Azione Cattolica,* pp. 247–249.

20. Palumbo, *Il movimento democratico-cristiano,* pp. 51–53.

a king or a class for the economic subjugation of the rest." [21] Murri repudiated any looking backward to a medieval guild society. He represented the most advanced wing of the movement on social questions, and on political questions went further than the others in calling for an open struggle against the state.

The third tendency of the movement was represented by Filippo Meda, leading the political-parliamentary wing.[22] Born and raised in the *bourgeois, industrial,* liberal atmosphere of Milan, his was a gradualist approach to both social and political problems with a deep consciousness of the importance of organization and of compromise. For him, in contrast to Murri, the state "could subsist very well in harmony with the Church, when its rulers will want it that way, and then it would become also an instrument of that social renovation which, guided by the Church, is prepared by evident design of Providence."

The common goal of the Christian Democrats, aside from emphasis upon social questions,[23] was toward organizing and in Albertario's phrase, "to prepare in abstention." To the staid Venetian leaders who predominated in the *Opera,* even the term Christian Democrat was anathema, let alone the social and economic program and objectives of the group. The Christian Democratic group characterized the leadership by the phrase "in Venice not even the sea moves." The Venetians accused the group, particularly Meda, of trying to force the hand of the Vatican on the question of Catholic participation in political life. After 1898, when Pope Leo XIII, in answer to a question raised by the famous French Catholic Leon Harmel, supported the concept of democracy if inspired by Christian faith,[24] the Christian Democrats in Italy were encouraged to enlarge their efforts. Milan became the center of their strength, but they gathered forces rapidly throughout the Catholic movement. By 1901 they controlled approximately 300 associations with more than 100,000 members.

The growing strength of the movement and the sharp conflict which developed within the *Opera dei Congressi* resulted in need for clarification from the Vatican. The encyclical *Rerum Novarum* had addressed itself to the Catholic approach to social questions on the basis of international Catholic concern. The encyclical *Graves de Communi re* of January 18, 1901, on the other hand, was prompted by the difficult problems arising out of the

---

21. Quoted in *ibid.,* p. 51 from Romolo Murri's *L'essenza della democrazia,* published in 1903. See also Romolo Murri, *Battaglie d'oggi, Il programma politico della democrazia cristiana* (Rome, 1901), pp. 30–34.

22. Palumbo, *Il movimento democratico-cristano,* pp. 53–54; Olgiati, *Azione Cattolica,* p. 212–219.

23. For the text of the Christian Democrats' social program of 1899, *see* Olgiati, *Azione Cattolica,* pp. 260–262.

24. Vercesi, *Il movimento cattolico,* pp. 74–76.

Italian situation and the disagreements existing within the Catholic movement of that country. The encyclical recognized the term Christian Democracy as a satisfactory one to describe the Christian social program. It distinguished Christian Democracy from social democracy by ascribing to the former an interest in bettering the "lower classes" without losing sight of the legitimate interests of the other classes and without wanting to alter the traditional regime of private property. Political content was removed from Christian Democracy. "It is not permitted to give a political meaning to Christian Democracy . . . It applies to no political formula and is intended to be able to exist with any political regime, provided the regime is not repugnant to honesty and justice." [25]

The encyclical set the limits of controversy within the Catholic movement. On social and economic matters it repudiated the position of the conservative leadership of the *Opera*. On political matters it set limits to the aggressive activity of the Christian Democrats. The encyclical had been intended to conciliate the warring factions. The Christian Democrats, however, feeling that their general position had been upheld on the broad front outside direct political questions, hailed the encyclical as a great victory for their group.[26] Pope Leo XIII had stood firm on his *non expedit*, but had reiterated and clarified his support of their social program.

At the Catholic Congress several months before *Graves de Communi re* was issued, the strength of the forces supporting concrete action in the labor field had been sufficiently great to obtain adoption of resolutions dealing with trade unions in concrete terms. These were no longer theoretical reluctant concessions to the pressing problems of organization in industry. They urged the formation of unions in industry and spelled out in realistic concrete terms the functions of such "mixed or simple" organizations: placement activities, direct intervention in obtaining labor agreements, influencing internal factory regulations, maintenance of relations with local and national government officials to influence administrative and legislative action.[27] The very success of the supporters of this position within the congress had contributed to the bitterness which led Pope Leo XIII to intervene with his encyclical.

The Christian Democrats at their Lombardy regional congress held in 1901 shortly after the pronouncement of *Graves de Communi re* underlined their position on labor matters in clear terms of confidence. In their resolutions they spoke of "recognizing the conflict and the struggle of interests and of classes in production and in public life and accepting, as the extreme

25. Sanseverino, *Il movimento sindacale*, pp. 236–239.

26. Vercesi, *Il movimento cattolico*, pp. 91–95.

27. For the text of resolutions, *see Atti del XVII Congresso Cattolico Italiano, Roma, 1–5 Settembre 1900* (Venice, 1901), pp. 134, 136, 206, quoted in *Le organizzazioni operaie cattoliche*, pp. XXVIII–XXX.

method of defending the interests of the humble, legal resistance and the strike." They pointed up their acceptance of "class organizations; simple organizations of workers." Finally, they stated their determination to challenge the Socialists in this area and to lead a movement to organize the greatest number of workers.[28]

At the 1901 Catholic Congress it became clear that while the predominant conservatives gave lip service to the new social orientation, the struggle with the Christian Democratic elements had by no means been settled. The latter, having made considerable progress in organizing associations of their own, hoped to be accepted into the *Opera* with retention of their autonomy as a bloc. When, however, the Vatican, several months after the congress, issued a new constitution for the *Opera,* the Pope had included incorporation of the Christian Democratic movement into the general organization and provided that ecclesiastical advisers named by the bishops be attached to each section. Murri, who in November 1901 had written a stirring article in his journal entitled "With Rome and For Rome, Forever," [29] immediately announced that the new constitution would not be accepted. The issue was not to become a major one, but it did start Murri on the road toward his final break with the Vatican some years later over the issue of independence from Vatican domination of the Catholic lay movement.

The gathering strength of the Christian Democrats and the evident disapproval with which the old leadership of the *Opera* viewed the social program accepted by the 1901 encyclical, led the Vatican to replace the President of the *Opera* in 1902 with someone more sympathetic to the then accepted official position.[30] This action had little effect upon the dissension within the *Opera*. At its 1903 Congress the Christian Democrats were able to gain control of the organization, but at a cost which threatened the unity of the movement.[31]

Two important events during 1903–1904 changed the course of developments in the Catholic movement for the following years. In July 1903 Pope Leo XIII died and was succeeded by Pope Pius X. Pope Leo XIII had been firm throughout his life in holding to the prohibition against Catholic participation in Italian national political life. He had also been sympathetic to the new approach to social problems. The new Pope, on the other hand, was known to feel that the *non expedit* of his predecessor should be modified as appropriate occasions arose.[32] He also, while reiterating his support for the social directives of Leo XIII, had little interest in this area, with deep

28. Sanseverino, *Il movimento sindacale,* pp. 239–240.
29. *Cultura Sociale,* November 16, 1901, p. 336, also cited in Vercesi, *Il movimento cattolico,* p. 93.
30. Olgiati, *Azione Cattolica,* pp. 275–282.
31. Sanseverino, *Il movimento sindacale,* p. 243.
32. Vercesi, *Il movimento cattolico,* p. 122.

convictions on the evils of modernism. With this situation, the Christian Democratic groups could feel encouraged in their propaganda and organizing for purposes of "preparation in abstention," but they could expect less than enthusiastic support for the social content of their political orientation.

The second event which had fundamental importance was the four days of successful national general strike in September 1904, which frightened Italian society and made revolution seem imminent. Giolitti, having shown his masterful comprehension of the forces at work in the strike situation, had dealt with it patiently and with forebearance. He then called national elections for later in the year.

By the time the national elections were called, the Catholic lay movement had had its own crisis. The Christian Democratic faction's victory at the 1903 Congress had led to increased bitterness and conflict within the *Opera*. Despite several efforts by the Pope to intervene and reduce the friction, tension had mounted almost to the breaking point. As a result, in July 1904 the Vatican ordered the dissolution of the *Opera* and the end of the congresses. Only the Second Section of the *Opera,* dealing with the economic and social organizations under Catholic sponsorship, was spared. For the rest, the various diocese and regional organizations reverted to decentralized associations under control of the appropriate church hierarchy.[33]

Against this background, the question of the Catholic position in the political elections of 1904 aroused tremendous interest. The reaction to the general strike caused fear of any forces which were regarded as Leftist and Revolutionary. Pope Pius X opened the dam. He permitted participation of Catholics in those elections where a candidate of the "forces of order" ran the danger of being defeated by a "Revolutionary." In these situations the conservative candidate could and should be supported. The specific occasion for the reversal is described as arising from the initiative of trusted friends of the Pope from the province of Bergamo. They advised the Pope that Bergamo, the stronghold of Catholic action and Catholic organization, was in danger of being won by a Radical-Freemason combination, unless the *non expedit* was relaxed. The Pope is reported to have replied, "Do, do as your conscience dictates." Whereupon one of the participants said, "Have we understood properly, Holiness? May we interpret that as 'yes'?" "Do as your conscience dictates, I repeat." [34]

The historic reversal of Vatican policy was confirmed in August 1905 in an encyclical, *Il Fermo Proposito,* repeating that the *non expedit* remained in effect except under the circumstances set out as exceptional.[35] The Christian Democratic groups had for several years been hoping — and organiz-

33. For a discussion of the immediate events leading up to the dissolution of the *Opera* and texts of the relevant documents, *see* Olgiati, *Azione Cattolica,* pp. 283–302.

34. Vercesi, *Il movimento cattolico,* p. 123; Salomone, *Italian Democracy,* pp. 36–37.

35. Sanseverino, *Il movimento sindacale,* pp. 245–246.

ing — for just such a reversal of Vatican policy, but the form the reversal took was a bitter pill for them. Their interest had been in economic and social reform upon which they had hoped to build a party which would contribute to social progress while protecting the interests of the church. In this regard they had been repudiated by the Vatican.

Ernesto Vercesi, one of the Lombardy leaders of the Christian Democratic movement who bowed to the Vatican position, nevertheless in writing the history of this period many years later commented,[36] "Once 'neither elected nor voters' was in force; now we could be *voters* for the Conservatives of the liberal *bourgeoisie* against Socialism and the revolution, but not *elected*. In order better to protect their spiritual interests Catholics had to give their votes to those Liberals who very willingly would make their own, the slogan: *To rule is well worth a mass.*"

For the most part active Catholics, including many of the Christian Democratic elements, bowed to the Vatican position. Leaders of the latter group, like Meda and others, appeared to realize the hopelessness of opposing, as Catholics, a position established by the church itself. Romolo Murri, however, reaffirming his Catholic faith and principles, established the *Lega Democratica Nazionale* (National Democratic League) in 1905 to carry on the intent of the earlier Christian Democrats. The program of the League affirmed its intention to remain faithful to democracy in helping to further the interests of wage earners and to promote Christianity as a spiritual force which opposed any form of oppression or injustice. Soon after its establishment, Pope Pius X, in a letter to the bishops of Italy, reproved the organization and prohibited priests from joining it. The organization thus became a completely lay organization. Remaining faithful to the church and its faith, and accepting the right of the church to lay down principles for the faithful to follow, it nevertheless repudiated the attempt of the church to dictate detailed tactics in the political field. It repudiated "clericalism," which it regarded as subordinating religion to politics for the purpose of protecting the political and social interests of the conservative elements in society.[37]

Murri, despite himself, found it impossible to limit his controversy with the church and carry on his activity through the League as if it were a Catholic movement with reform preoccupations in the political and social field. The church would not permit the movement sufficient latitude, nor was Murri a person of great flexibility. The dynamics of such a dispute in a country like Italy was predictable. It led eventually to his being deprived of his priesthood and being read out of the church.[38]

36. Vercesi, *Il movimento cattolico*, pp. 129, 130.

37. Palumbo, *Il movimento democratico-cristiano*, pp. 62–65.

38. For an account of the Murri movement *see ibid.*, pp. 61–92; Vercesi, *La democrazia cristiana*, pp. 33–41.

Many years later Murri acknowledged his error by pointing to the logic of the church position:

it [the church] said in substance: you declared that you wanted to reconstruct the state and society on a religious basis; at the same time you accepted religion from me and you professed obedience to me on religious matters; either, then, this religion which you accepted from me is that which you want to apply to the state and to society and then you should receive the rules from me; or there is another, and I have the right to repudiate and unmask you. An assiduous and sincere effort was made to avoid this contradiction: and it must be recognized that it was not and could not be successful.[39]

As part of the reorganization which followed the closing down of the *Opera dei Congressi* and the new Vatican position toward participation in Italian political life, Pope Pius X in 1905 issued a "Guidance to the Italian Catholic Laity." The Guidance resulted in the establishment of three independent associations, the *Unione Popolare*, which dealt primarily with moral and spiritual matters and became the forerunner of Catholic Action; the *Unione Economico-Sociale*, which directed the cooperative, mutual aid and trade union activities; and *Unione Elettorale Cattolica Italiana* which was given the function of directing the electoral activity of the Catholic laity.[40] Within a few years two additional associations were established, the *Società della Gioventù Cattolica* for the youth movement and the *Unione delle Donne Cattoliche* for the women's movement.

The *Unione Elettorale Cattolica Italiana* was used by the Vatican before the general elections of 1909 further to clarify the instructions for Catholic participation in elections. Three principal requirements were laid down for participation: (1) in the election district there had to be a militantly anti-clerical candidate who was a member of the Popular bloc (all left of center parties); (2) against such a candidate there had to be a candidate of the "forces of order" whether Catholic or not, who had to give a guarantee not to attack religion; (3) there had to be a great probability of victory for the anticlerical candidate, were the Catholic voters to abstain, while their participation had to make his defeat certain.[41] The new formula substituted for "Neither Candidates nor Voters" was *"Cattolici Deputati, non Deputati Cattolici"* (deputies who are Catholics, not Catholic deputies).

The third stage in the retreat from the universal *non expedit* policy was

39. Romolo Murri, *Dalla democrazia cristiana al Partito Popolare* (Florence, 1920), pp. 83–84, quoted in Olgiati, *Azione Cattolica*, pp. 270–271.
40. Sanseverino, *Il movimento sindacale*, pp. 246–247; Vercesi, *Il movimento cattolico*, pp. 130–131.
41. A. Schiavi, "Programmi, voti ed eletti nei comizi politici del 1909," *La Riforma Sociale* (July–August 1909), p. 388, summarized in Salomone, *Italian Democracy*, pp. 38–39.

taken before the elections of 1913. These were the first elections held after the enlarged suffrage which largely eliminated literacy requirements and tripled the voter rolls. Giolitti, as a master in political tactics and in minimizing risks, arranged for a pact with Count Gentiloni, the President of the *Unione Elettorale Cattolica* before the elections.[42] While the pact was made secretly, it became generally known before the elections, and was acknowledged by Gentiloni immediately after the elections. The pact itself was an expansion of the criteria set out in 1909. Catholics were permitted to vote for Liberal and Conservative candidates, provided the candidates accepted and observed a number of commitments including opposition to antireligious legislation, opposition to encroachment upon the jurisdiction of private schools, guarantee of the right of parents to demand religious instruction for their children in public schools, opposition to divorce laws, equal rights to economic and social organizations regardless of social or religious principles, support for gradual tax reform based upon principles of justice in social relations. The fact that the pact had been made secretly with Giolitti and his supporters caused considerable criticism and controversy. It achieved its basic objective, however, in helping to keep the Giolitti forces in control of the government in the face of a three-fold expansion of the electorate. The Gentiloni Pact, however, was by no means universally welcomed in Catholic circles.[43] It was indeed a far cry from the content and substance of political interests promoted by the Christian Democratic enthusiasts of the early years of the century.

The Vatican policy during the period before the First World War on political activity of Catholics and their participation in the elections of 1904, 1909, and 1913 had an advantage in the Italian political scene which the controversy obscured. The very fact of increased Catholic participation in the political life of the country reduced the divisive force represented by the *non expedit* policy as practiced by Pope Pius X's predecessors. With the weight of the Catholic forces thrown on the side of the "forces of order," an element of stability was added to the government during this period, putting a brake upon social reform, but enabling the government to deal more self-confidently with the growing tide of discontent from the Left. In addition, from the point of view of the Vatican, several advantages were derived. By contrast with previous governments, the governments during this period were not disposed to undertake anti-church actions and policies and the atmosphere between the government and the church consequently improved considerably, putting the Roman question further and further into the background. There were no Catholic deputies, according to the enunciated formula, that is, deputies chosen on the basis of being Catholic.

42. *Ibid.,* pp. 39–41; Jemolo, *Chiesa e Stato,* pp. 535–541.
43. Don Luigi Sturzo, *Italy and the Coming World* (New York, 1945), p. 74, unnumbered footnote.

There were, however, deputies who had been chosen as candidates from among active Catholics. These numbered two in 1905, twenty-one in 1909 and thirty-three in 1913.[44] They could be counted on to protect the interests of the church and to obtain cooperation from other deputies who owed their elections to support from Catholics.

In addition, the construction of an organization on a national basis under the *Unione Elettorale Cattolica* in every diocese in the country, and the experience gained by its activity in elections was ideal preparation for the time when a Catholic party would be launched. By contrast with the atmosphere and personalities which dominated the Christian Democratic movement when it prepared itself as a nucleus of a political party at the beginning of the century, the *Unione,* under church guidance and particularly also as a result of its basic political orientation, drew into positions of leadership and obtained experience for a group of people conservatively oriented toward social and economic problems, who accepted the tutelage of the Vatican without the reservations displayed by some of the leaders of the earlier Christian Democratic movement. The Christian Democratic elements of the Lombardy area, led by Meda, remained active in Catholic political life, and achieved positions of leadership, but the spectrum of political views represented in the movement as a whole had shifted inevitably to the right.

Emergence of Catholic Trade Unionism[45]

The emphasis on the practical problems of trade union organization after the turn of the century reflected the increased importance attached by the Catholic movement to obtaining support among wage earners and to offering practical alternatives to the Socialist trade unions. At the 1903 Catholic Congress, as described in the preceding section, the Christian Democratic forces had succeeded in gaining control of the *Opera*. At this congress the Christian Democrats' general orientation toward trade unions was adopted as the official position of the Catholic movement. The resolutions specifically acknowledged that unions combining employers and workers were not practical "under present historical conditions." It was urged that unions of workers alone be organized, that they be coordinated on provincial, regional, and national levels into federations, and that legal recognition be

44. Since the identification is not precise, estimates vary. The figures cited are from Salomone, *Italian Democracy,* pp. 37, 39, and 41.

45. Much of the material in this section has been obtained from *Le organizzazioni operaie cattoliche.* This government-sponsored study, directed by Dr. Mario Chiri, who was himself active in the Catholic movement, is a little known but invaluable basic work for the period until 1910. It is a painstaking, detailed analysis of material gathered by means of long questionnaires and correspondence among all the Catholic trade union organizations existing in Italy at the time the study was made, 1908 to 1911.

conferred upon the trade unions. It was resolved that the decision of whether an organization be made confessional should be left to prudent criteria determined according to the circumstances of time and place.[46]

As a matter of fact, the turning point in organization on the practical level had already taken place before the 1903 Congress. The ferment in the Catholic movement which resulted in the rapid spread of Christian Democratic ideas in the first three years of the twentieth century had its parallel, in minor key, in the labor field. At the 1903 Congress, it was claimed that there were already 229 Catholic local trade union organizations with approximately 70,000 members.[47] Most of these had been formed in the immediately preceding two years, a period of unusual ferment in the labor field during which the Socialist-oriented trade unions had also taken long strides forward.

The government repressions of 1898 had been extended to the Catholic lay organizations. The repressions were of short duration, as with the Socialists, and had the opposite effect from that sought by the government, since the general public reacted unfavorably to the government's actions.[48] For the first time Catholic trade unions were being formed on a widespread scale and were attempting to compete with the Socialist unions. They received a setback, however, when the Vatican closed down the *Opera* and the new policy toward political elections was developed in 1904. In the dissolution of the *Opera* the Second Section, to which social-economic organizations were affiliated, was permitted to continue its existence. Two years earlier, in 1902, the Section had set up three subsidiary federations, each with responsibility for a limited field: mutual-aid organizations, cooperatives, and "unions or leagues of resistance" (trade unions).[49] Although the ecclesiastical authorities excluded the Second Section from their dissolution order, the several years following the suppression of the *Opera* were characterized by relatively less activity and some losses in the trade union field.

When the Second Section held a general conference of its affiliates in April 1905, the number of Catholic trade unions had fallen to 195, and the mutual-aid and cooperative organizations had also suffered losses. The movement continued to lose strength until 1907 when 135 trade unions were affiliated to the Catholic organization. During the previous year the Vatican had approved a reorganization of Catholic organizations and had given encouragement to reviving Catholic efforts in this and other fields. The Second Section was replaced by the *Unione Economico-Sociale dei Cat-*

46. For the text of the resolutions *see ibid.*, pp. XXXII-XXXIV.

47. *Ibid.*, p. XXXIV; Italo Mario Sacco, *Storia del sindicalismo,* 2nd edition (Turin, 1947), p. 222.

48. Olgiati, *Azione Cattolica,* pp. 180–200.

49. *Le organizzazioni operaie cattoliche,* p. XXXV; XXXVII-XXXIX.

tolici d'Italia (Economic-Social Union for Catholics of Italy). The first general assembly of the newly reorganized *Unione,* held in March 1907, gave impetus to further organization efforts in the trade union field, as in cooperatives and mutual-aid organizations. The assembly urged organization of trade unions and, to supplement the diocese territorial subdivisions, urged that coordinating *Unioni* be formed on a provincial basis. It also decided that, where Socialist-oriented trade unions existed, competing organizations be formed, and where none existed, organizations without specifically confessional character be organized so that they could gather together all workers and represent their interests.

By 1907 the immediate reaction, confusion, and uncertainties which developed among Catholics as a result of the 1904 events had largely been overcome in the labor field. The Murri group, through its *Lega Democratica Nazionale,* focused primarily in the political field. In the labor field, however, it urged unity and political neutrality in the trade union movement. At its second congress in September 1908 it reaffirmed its position and urged its followers to join the CGL and carry into it their spiritual and social contribution.[50] The Meda and Toniolo forces of the Catholic movement which had interests in the economic and social field, however, had settled down to work within the limits set up by the Vatican. Despite the Murri position, the Catholic trade union groups were able to make some progress during the years following the 1906 reorganization. From 1910 until the First World War, however, the strength of the organizations again remained stationary.

While a federation dealing with trade union affairs had been established under the Second Section of the *Opera* as early as 1902, in the subsequent reorganizations of the Section, the federation had ceased to function. With the new vigor in trade union organization between 1907 and 1910, the need for a coordinating group dealing specifically with trade union matters became evident. As a result, in March 1909, the *Unione Economico-Sociale* issued a constitution for a *Segretariato Generale delle Unioni Professionali* (General Secretariat of the Trade Unions) to function under the former organization.[51] The secretariat was to be run by a council of five members, three elected by the affiliated unions and two named by the *Unione Economico-Sociale.* Affiliation was through the diocese union federations, except that individual unions could affiliate directly in the absence of the diocese organization.

The organization got under way in July and August 1910 when the council met for the first time and adopted regulations for the functioning of the organization, among them a provision for a full-time secretary, who

50. Palumbo, *Il movimento democratico,* pp. 74 and 90.

51. *Le organizzazioni operaie cattoliche,* p. XLV and text of constitution and its regulations at pp. 82–84.

became the principal officer of the organization. The secretariat organization remained the coordinating body of the Catholic trade unions until after the First World War. During this period it appears to have functioned with somewhat more authority over its smaller field than the national office of its counterpart, the CGL. On the whole, however, it had less authority than did any of the national offices of the post-Fascist trade union confederations.

By 1910 there were 374 Catholic local trade union organizations with a total membership of 104,600 of which 67,500 were in industry, commerce, and transportation, and 37,100 were in agriculture.[52] Two-thirds of these organizations had been formed during 1901–1902 and 1907–1909. Five had been organized before the end of the nineteenth century, the oldest two in 1894.

Of the total membership, 53.9 percent were men, 35.9 percent were women and 10.2 percent were minors. The Catholic unions had had their greatest success in the textile industry, which accounted for 41.5 percent of their membership in industry. The 33,400 members in textiles were predominantly women, who totaled 22,400, with 4800 men and 6200 minors making up the rest. The next most important industrial group organized was the clothing industry, with 5700 members of whom 3400 were women and 1500 were minors. There were 4600 employees in public service organized, 1700 workers in mining, 1500 in the construction industry, 1300 in the metallurgical and metal-mechanical industries and 1400 among woodworkers.

Membership was concentrated heavily in the Lombardy and Veneto areas, accounting for 73.5 percent of the total. The Lombardy region alone had 57,900 members or 55.3 percent and the Veneto area 17,950 or 18.2 percent. The Lombardy region had 62.5 percent of the organized Catholic workers in industry and 42.3 percent of those in agriculture. The Veneto had 16.4 percent and 21.2 percent respectively. The principal centers of Catholic strength were Milan, Bergamo, Brescia, Padua, Vicenza and Verona. Outside these two regions, the centers with the greatest strength were Ancona with 3285 agricultural union members, Ravenna with 2625 members in agriculture, Girgenti with 2721 members in agriculture and mining, and Cosenza with 2332 members, principally in agriculture.

An analysis of the constitutions of 198 Catholic trade unions made in 1910 showed that 169 were explicitly confessional in nature. The others, although recognized as Catholic unions, had, as permitted by the Catholic

52. In 1910 there was a total of 817,000 organized workers in Italy of whom 391,000 were in agriculture and 426,000 were in industry. For detailed breakdown see Ministero dell' Agricoltura, Industria e Commercio, *Supplemento al Bollettino dell' Ufficio del Lavoro, No. 12, Statistiche delle organizzazioni di lavoratori e notizie sulle organizzazioni padronali at 1° Gennaio 1910* (Rome, 1911), p. 201. The information on the Catholic unions in 1910 is from *Le organizzazioni operaie cattoliche*.

Congress resolutions of 1903 and the 1907 resolutions of the *Unione Economico-Sociale,* made no provision for the specifically religious character of their organizations. While four constitutions still permitted employers to join their organizations, none of these in fact included employers in membership. In facing the practical problems of organization, the corporativist principle of a guild society had clearly been found impractical. In general, the constitutions set out the purposes of their organizations as the protection of the economic interests of their members or of the industry, adding in many cases religious, moral and educational aspects. Class struggle was uniformly rejected in favor of collaboration and cooperation. Strikes, however, were recognized as a legitimate last resort in labor disputes.

The more pacific approach to labor relations taken by the Catholic unions is reflected in the statistics on strikes. On the basis of information furnished by the Catholic organizations existing in 1910, they had since their origin participated in a total of 114 strikes. In contrast, during the preceding five-year period, 1905–1909, there had been 6208 strikes recorded by the government.[53] On the other hand, on the basis of information published by the Italian government on strikes taking place during the period 1905 to 1910, the official 1910 study of Catholic unions concluded that in no case had it been reported that the Catholic unions or their members acted as strikebreakers. In fact, it would appear that a large number of the strikes in which they had participated were strikes called by the Socialist-oriented trade unions. To the extent that the questionnaire responses of the Catholic unions were complete, the official study could conclude that in most organizations the Catholic unionists desired greater cooperation with the Socialist-oriented trade unions, but that the latter generally rejected proffers of cooperation. The Socialist union movement was hostile toward the Catholic movement on ideological and practical grounds. Even the usually tolerant Rigola in his general report to the 1911 Congress of the CGL commented, "It is not so much the confessional label which makes us consider the Catholic organization as an enemy organization, as that this organization, both by the nature of its origin, by what it represents in fact and by the objectives toward which it is oriented, is in open antithesis to a genuine and spontaneous class movement . . . The confessional organization, like others inspired by any conservative parties, is nothing else than systematized strikebreaking." [54]

As the Catholic trade unions obtained significant membership, the coordination of the movement began to assume a traditional trade union structural pattern. Local geographic coordination more and more took place on the provincial rather than diocese level. The first national industry union

53. Quoted from official government publications in Confindustria, *Annuario di statistiche . . . 1949,* p. 381.
54. Rigola, *La Confederazione Generale del Lavoro nel triennio 1908–1911,* pp. 64–65.

was established by the Catholic movement in textiles in 1908. The *Sindacato Italiano Tessile* had some of the same difficulties in overcoming the reluctance of local organizations to join National Unions as had the earlier Socialist-oriented unions. Four years after its formation it had a membership affiliation of 5522,[55] only a small part of the textile workers organized into Catholic local unions. A second National Union was organized in the railroad industry in 1909, the *Sindacato Ferrovieri Cattolici,* which had 2714 members by 1912. Between 1911 and 1914 three additional National Unions were organized, in the metallurgical industry, among postal-telegraph personnel, and among clerical and commercial employees. By 1917 the Catholic movement had organized a total of 17 National Unions.[56] It was in its structure a fully functioning trade union movement, although it was still dependent upon and subject to the direct control of the general Catholic Action movement on a national level. The final step toward independence did not come until after the First World War.

Comparing the membership of the Catholic unions with that of the Socialist unions before the First World War, an official publication of the Italian government made the following comment:

The free leagues [Socialist trade unions] are by a great sight the most numer-out . . . the free leagues are made up predominantly of men (84.97 percent); of workers in large industry or farm day laborers (71 percent), which are the categories first and most directly opposed to the capitalistic class, and they extend above all on the plane where the first rebellions are formed and the struggles are most frequent and most bitter. The Catholic organization, instead, gathers together a greater number of women (40.71 percent); of artisans, farmers, small sharecroppers, small farm landholders (84.61 percent); middle classes most numerous in the hills and mountains for whom the formula by which the Catholic unions conduct their action can be effective: class collaboration.[57]

The Popular Party

This section will trace briefly the development of the Popular Party in the period after the First World War.[58] Its history provides background for a better understanding of the social and political climate in which the Catholic trade union movement functioned in the tragic period leading up to fascism in Italy.

After the death of Pope Pius X in 1914, his successor Pope Benedict XV

55. Ministero dell' Agricoltura, Industria e Commercio, *Supplemento al Bollettino dell' Ufficio del Lavoro, No. 15, Statistiche delle organizzazioni di lavoratori al 1° Gennaio 1912* (Rome, 1913), p. 80.

56. Sacco, *Storia del sindacalismo,* 2nd ed. (Turin, 1947), pp. 283–284.

57. *Supplemento al Bollettino . . . 1912,* p. 24.

58. For an excellent history of the party written by a leading participant, see Stefano Jacini, *Storia del Partito Popolare Italiano* (Milan, 1951).

had set out to eliminate the sharp divisions which had torn and troubled the Catholic world of affairs in Italy during the pervious years. He put the violent fight against modernism behind him. He buried the official church antagonism against the diverse Christian Democratic elements of the Catholic movement. By coordinating and centralizing the Catholic movement in 1915 and broadening its leadership to include more widely representative elements and contemporary currents of thinking, he succeeded in reunifying in substance what had become in previous years only formally and not even universally a single movement. The five general branches of the Catholic movement were coordinated under a central directive council of Catholic Action. Coordination was also reestablished on local levels through diocese councils subordinate to the national Catholic Action organization.

The end of the war presented an uncertain future for the forces represented by the church and its supporters as the rapid spread of Socialist strength and the leftward turn of Socialist orientation made the destruction of the Italian economic and political structure appear a realistic possibility. The reaction of the Catholic movement was to move principally on two fronts, the political and the trade union. On the trade union front it established the *Confederazione Italiana dei Lavoratori,* which will be discussed in the next section of this chapter. On the political front it left behind the tattered doctrine of *non expedit* and committed itself fully to participation in the political arena through the establishment of a political party.

The years of partial participation in political affairs following the first breach in the *non expedit* in 1904 had had the important effect of developing political machinery throughout the country and in forming a large group with practical experience in the tasks of organizing and leading political movements. It also had the effect of teaching its leaders the importance of unity and of developing programs which had appeal to voters. The emergence of Father Luigi Sturzo as the head of the political movement at the end of the war was a strong asset to the Catholic movement. Don Sturzo had the attributes necessary for successful leadership. His religious orthodoxy was above question. He was a passionate believer in democracy and in the need for social reform, particularly land reform and the creation of small agriculture holdings. He was an excellent administrator and organizer and had the respect of people beyond his own party.

The *Partito Popolare Italiano* was launched in January 1919 with the release of a manifesto and a twelve-point program which had been developed by Don Sturzo and a group of collaborators during the preceding months.[59] It did not have the explicit blessing of the church and was not tied to the Catholic Action organization. On the other hand, it clearly had

59. *Ibid.,* Appendix I, pp. 289–291 and pp. 20–21 for text of manifesto and program. *See also* D. Giulio De Rossi, *Il Partito Popolare* (Rome, 1919), pp. 7–11 and 13–52.

the approval of the church[60] and the month after the party was launched, the *Unione Elettorale* of Catholic Action was disbanded. Don Sturzo had made clear before the party was launched that it was to be a party free of confessional characteristics, not tied to the church, nor would it commit the church in the Italian political arena through its activities. It was to resemble the German Center Party in its relationship to the church and religion.

Its program was based on social reform, emphasizing administrative decentralization of government, protective labor legislation, legal recognition and freedom of union organization, representation of economic groups in government agencies and in Parliament, land reform, tax reform, proportional representation in political elections. Its program also contained the traditional Catholic positions on relations between church and state in the fields of education, the family, and religion.

In their first electoral contest the *Popolari* were successful beyond their most optimistic expectations: they emerged from the 1919 national elections as the second largest party in the country. Receiving 1,167,000 votes, 20.5 percent of all those cast, they elected 100 deputies to Parliament. Only the Socialists with 1,835,000 votes and 156 deputies obtained greater support.[61]

The year 1919 had been characterized by the continued upsurge of revolutionary sentiment among the Socialists and a vast expansion in their following. Italy during this and the following year seemed to many on the brink of an abyss. In 1920 the factory occupations spread throughout the country and then evaporated.

The *Partito Popolare* had been launched in part to compete against the Socialists and to offer an alternative program to the country. In large measure, however, the two parties drew their strength from different segments of the population. The Socialists predominantly depended for support upon the industrial wage earners and the agricultural farm laborers. The *Popolari* drew their greatest strength from the clerical, professional, and commercial groups in the urban centers and the small farmers in rural areas.[62] The *Popolari* tried, however, to widen their appeal and to spread their influence among those groups which were traditionally oriented toward the Socialists. In this regard they were not dramatically successful. The militant activity of leaders of the Catholic trade unions and the new party earned the party widespread support in some rural areas. Particularly in Sicily, occupation of land without sanction of law, except retroactively,

60. Vercesi, *Il movimento cattolico,* pp. 152–153. Vercesi was long a leader in the Catholic movement.
61. Istituto Centrale di Statistica e Ministero per la Costituente, *Compendio delle statistiche elettorali ialiane dal 1848 al 1943,* vol. II (Rome, 1947), tables 44 and 47, pp. 118–119 and 130–131.
62. Jacini, *Partito Popolare,* p. 281; Sturzo, *Italy and the Coming World,* pp. 79, 81, 95.

became a widespread movement under Catholic auspices. It created difficulties within the Popular Party itself, since the more conservative elements viewed such measures with severe hostility. It did, however, win for the party and the Catholic unions a respect among the rural population which gave substance to the appeals of the party for support. Outside the rural areas, except in those regions where Catholic strength had traditionally been great, the support for the *Popolari* came mainly from those seeking a moderate alternative to the threatening Socialist upsurge.

The *Popolari* continued their successes in the communal elections of 1920. They won majority control in 1650 communes out of a total of approximately 8000. The Socialists won majorities in 2162 communes, again emerging as the largest party in the country. As a result of impressive success in the national elections of the previous year and in the 1920 local elections the *Popolari* had effectively become a major factor in the national political scene.

During 1921, however, both the Socialists and the *Popolari* were put on the defensive by the rising vociferousness of the Fascist movement. The *Popolari* still showed some advances in the parliamentary elections held that year, however. For the *Popolari* the problem of the rising Fascist strength was particularly difficult. Many of those who had joined the party primarily out of anti-Socialist sentiments began finding a more congenial atmosphere among the Fascists. The right wing of the party, even among the truly Catholic elements, eventually chose cooperation rather than opposition to the Fascist party. On the Left in the party, and among the trade union elements, all-out opposition to fascism was an instinctive position reinforced by the violence of the attacks upon them from the Fascists.

For the predominant center of the party, the Fascist phenomenon presented a more difficult choice. The moderates had been responsible for participation by the *Popolari* in the governments immediately preceding Mussolini's premiership. As the Fascist movement grew more threatening, they considered the possibility of collaborating with the Socialists to oppose it. Neither they nor the Socialists could, however, bring themselves to overcome their deep-seated antagonisms and mutual distrust for each other. They were opposed to fascism and looked on with horror at its growth and menace. Yet, when Mussolini formed his first coalition government in November 1922 after having intimidated the nation into giving him power, the *Popolari* agreed to participate in the government. This represented no change of heart toward the Fascists. Although Don Sturzo himself was opposed to it, the parliamentary spokesmen for the party decided upon participation, considering it to be the only way to return the country to legality and avoid the chaos, violence, and unconstitutionality of the Fascist maneuvers.[63]

63. Jacini, *Partito Popolare,* pp. 146–150.

During the following year, although officially permitting political competition and opposition, the Fascists in fact increased their pressure and violence against their opponents. It became increasingly difficult for the *Popolari* to hold together in view of the conflicting tactical positions urged within the party. Pope Pius XI had succeeded Pope Benedict XV early in 1922 and the atmosphere in the Vatican toward the *Popolari* had changed. Pope Pius XI felt less committed to the *Popolari* than his predecessor. There were increasingly realistic reasons for the Vatican to separate itself from identification with a group as committed as were most *Popolari,* in order to attenuate the difficulties which identification might create for the church itself. Late in 1923, the *Popolari* withdrew from participation in the government but still could not bring themselves to oppose Mussolini in Parliament. They went along with a proposal by Mussolini to change the election law and do away with proportional representation, a basic tenet in the program of their party. The alternative, they felt, would have precipitated a countermove by Mussolini which would destroy even the formal pretense of constitutional government. But as this issue came to a head, Don Sturzo, who had become a center of Fascist attack and on the issue of proportional representation had been disinclined to yield, resigned as political secretary of the party to save it from embarrassment.[64]

The elections of 1924, accompanied by systematic intimidation and violence, gave the Fascists the majority they sought. The *Popolari* managed, despite the pressures, to get 645,000 votes or 9 percent of the total and to elect 40 deputies.[65] The combined opposition to the Fascists amounted to 40 percent of the total vote, a heroic achievement under the circumstances. The Matteotti assassination crystallized the all-out opposition to fascism in Parliament, and the *Popolari* participated with the other democratic forces in the Aventine experience. The fate of the *Popolari* in the succeeding years was similar to that of the other democratic forces: increasing intolerance and violence, and finally, in November 1926, the government ordered all opposition groups disbanded.

The Popular Party had had less than eight years of existence. It had launched a political movement which, side by side with the Catholic trade union movement, had acted as an important counterweight to the Socialists during the turbulent postwar years. But the centrifugal forces at work in Italian society had proved too great for the democratic institutions of Italy. The Popular Party had tried to help strengthen these institutions and was destroyed with them.

What was saved of the Catholic movement was neither in the trade union

64. Sturzo, *Italy and the Coming World,* p. 81, footnote.
65. *Compendio delle statistiche . . . 1848 al 1934,* tables 44 and 47, pp. 118–119 and 130–131.

nor political spheres. Catholic Action had become largely dormant during the years of growth of the Popular Party. The energies and leadership personnel of the Catholic movement were largely drawn into political and, to some extent, trade union activity. As the Popular Party began to decline, however, Catholic Action began to retrieve its former vigor. During 1922 and 1923 its entire structure was reorganized, with the organization subdivided into four general federations: men, youth, university students, and women. The organization's relations with the Popular Party became distant during this period and even hostile. After the demise of the Popular Party, the Catholic trade unions, and the other opposition groups in 1926 and 1927, Catholic Action was the only organization independent of the Fascist regime which was permitted to continue to function. It functioned, within its prescribed limits, throughout the period of fascism.

The Italian Confederation of Labor

In the trade union field, as in the political field, the Catholic movement committed itself fully to maximizing its influence after the First World War. This was not a new commitment. The prewar direct subordination of the trade unions to the ecclesiastically controlled Catholic Action movement and the confessional nature of the trade unions themselves were recognized, however, as a handicap in the competition with the Socialist trade unions.[66]

The step toward greater independence was taken in the trade union movement before it was taken in the political field. Upon the initiative of Giovanni Battista Valente, who headed the Economic-Social Union of Catholic Action at the time, a conference among the leadership of ten Catholic national unions and twenty-five Catholic city union centers was held in Rome during March 1918 and the decision taken to form a trade union confederation, *Confederazione Italiana dei Lavoratori*, with a Catholic orientation but with no confessional ties.[67] A National Council was set up as the governing body of the organization, composed of representatives of the National Unions and the local or provincial union centers.

The official launching of the CIL took place in September 1918 at the first meeting of the National Council. Twelve National Unions and twenty-six city or provincial union centers participated. The declaration of principles and the program adopted on that occasion became the basic documents of the organization and remained the foundation of its orientation throughout its existence.[68] The organization was declared to have a purely trade union character and to be autonomous of political parties. Accepting the ultimate objective of integral organization and representation of class in political

66. *See, for example,* Sanseverino, *Il movimento sindacale,* p. 347.

67. Sacco, *Storia del sindacalismo,* p. 223.

68. For texts of declaration of principles and program *see* G. B. Valente, *Il programma sindacale cristiano,* 3rd edition (Rome, 1921), pp. 4–14.

and economic life, it pointed out that for the present political parties and trade unions had distinct and separate roles to play. For purposes of obtaining social legislation and the political protection of the economic and moral interests of workers, however, the organization would maintain contact with parliamentary groups friendly to it. The collectivist and the capitalist concentration theses of Marxism were rejected and were characterized as anti-democratic and anti-social since in both cases it meant the proletarianization of workers. The ultimate objective, instead, was the generalization of autonomous work, the re-acquisition of property by the workers. Class struggle and the revolutionary expropriation of other classes to achieve an "absurd collectivization" was rejected. The ideological assumptions accepted by the organization pointed to collaboration of classes on the basis of reciprocal recognition of the rights and duties of each class. Without such recognition a resistance and struggle between classes would occasionally be inevitable, and for this purpose the organization should prepare itself for such measures as strikes, lockouts, reprisals and unemployment. It was declared that for the new Catholic trade union movement to remain immune from "the red and yellow degenerations, that is neither subversive nor servile," it must depend upon Catholic ideals, and thus achieve better and more equitable economic and civil conditions of life.

The program adopted at the National Council session of September 1918 listed the more specific objectives of the new organization. Among these objectives were broad social insurance measures, low cost housing, legal recognition and protection of trade unions, encouragement of collective agreements, minimum wage legislation and establishment of the eight-hour work day.

The new confederation with its young dynamic leadership gave important impetus to the Catholic trade unions. Its formal separation from Catholic Action[69] and its independence from confessional control gave it greater flexibility within the framework of a movement functioning on the basis of Catholic social doctrine. It willingly accepted the label "white unions" to differentiate itself from the Socialist Red unions, and carried on its campaigns with explicitly Catholic identification.

Like the Popular Party, the CIL went through two periods during its short existence. The first was characterized by rapid growth, positive efforts to obtain support for its general position, and direct active competition against the Socialists. The second period was a period of defense and finally of fight for existence against the Fascist onslaught.

During the two years after the war, the dynamics of upheaval and social

---

69. The Vatican formally confirmed this step after the mutual-aid and cooperative movements of Catholic Action had also formed independent confederations, by abolishing the *Unione Economico-Sociale* of Catholic Action in 1919. Sanseverino, *Il movimento sindacale,* p. 348.

ferment seemed at the time to be carrying Italy toward the possibility of a Bolshevik revolution. The white trade unionists threw themselves into the anti-Socialist struggle with vigor and energy. They offered an alternative non-revolutionary program, they opposed the political strike tactics of the Socialists, but offered support on the specific economic demands in the trade union realm itself. To the worker control of industry movement as it developed and culminated in the factory occupations of 1920, the CIL offered the alternative program of worker stock ownership, profit-sharing and share in management as a specific step in its general program of gradual elimination of wage earners and transformation of society into an "integral corporate structure" with property widely shared and representation in the economy and government on the basis of industrial classes.[70]

The CIL impact in industry, with the exception of textiles and a few centers of traditional Catholic strength, was not very great, however. CIL had actively opposed the innumerable political strikes of 1919, but played a passive role during the occupation strike movement of 1920. When Giolitti obtained the settlement of the occupation strikes, the tripartite commission he set up to develop recommendations did not include any Catholic representation. CIL protested with the support of the Popular Party, and presented its own position in a memorandum to the government on the subject of management participation. Giolitti ignored the memorandum, however, and his draft law represented a compromise between the CGL and the *Confindustria* positions.[71]

While CIL played a passive role in the occupation strike movement, its position on worker participation in industry was a basic part of the social orientation which it shared with the Popular Party. In the aftermath of the factory occupations the Confederation launched a large-scale campaign in favor of its "co-participation" position.[72] In this campaign, with its obvious political importance, it had the active cooperation of the *Popolari*. The co-operation was underscored through an agreement between the trade union movement and the party defining their general relationship and formalizing the responsibility of each to coordinate policy with the other in areas of mutual interest.[73]

70. *See, for example,* the resolution adopted at the CIL First Congress held at Pisa in March 1920, the text of which appears in the CIL's official publication, *Il Domani Sociale,* no. 13, March 28, 1920, and is reproduced in part in Sanseverino, *Il movimento sindacale,* pp. 355–356.

71. *Ibid.,* pp. 359–360. For the text of the CIL memorandum, *see* Confederazione Generale dell' Industria Italiana, *I consigli di gestione,* vol. II (Rome, 1947), document no. 5, pp. 34–40.

72. The tone and approach in its campaign can be gathered from the CIL manifesto issued on September 29, 1920. Sanseverino, *Il movimento sindacale,* p. 359.

73. Jacini, *Partito Popolare,* p. 73 and, for text of agreement, Appendix, document IV, pp. 293–294.

The CIL, despite its own efforts and the support of the Popular Party, found legitimate cause for continued complaint that the Socialist trade unions were in fact regarded as having a monopoly in the trade union field. Both the employers and their associations as well as the government, according to the complaints of CIL, generally ignored the existence of their organization. This was a principal reason why the CIL urged labor relations legislation which would guarantee minority union representation in collective bargaining and provide for such representation on the many government consultative bodies in the labor field.[74] It did not succeed in obtaining such legislation nor in making headway toward recognition in industry, except in those areas and industries where it already had significant following.

It was in agriculture that the CIL had its greatest successes. With its social orientation which favored the spread of property ownership and the elimination of the wage-earner relationship through spread of joint interest in property, its appeal in agriculture was for small-scale land ownership and the protection of tenant farmers and sharecroppers. Its strength primarily remained, still, in those rural areas where Catholic traditions were strongest, but it achieved a reputation for militancy which even the Socialists learned to respect. The occupation of large estates by landless farmers was one aspect of social upheaval in the aftermath of the war. The Catholic movement played an active role in leading such occupation movements in Sicily and in the Cremona area. It was primarily because of such activities and particularly because of the aggressive role played by the Catholic unions in the Cremona area that for a time the appellation of "White Bolshevism" was applied to the CIL agricultural activity by conservative forces even within the Popular Party.

The most famous success achieved by the Catholic unions was the result of an arbitration forced upon the large landowners of Soresina in the province of Cremona in June 1921 through large-scale agitation led by the Catholic unions and supported by the *Popolari*.[75]

The *enfant terrible* of the Popular Party, Guido Miglioli, was party leader in the province. He was on the extreme left of the party, favored cooperation with the Socialists and even signed a pact of trade union and political cooperation with the Chamber of Labor and the Socialist Party in the province which had to be repudiated by the national leadership. He was eventually expelled from the party in 1925 for his extreme positions.

The arbitrator, Professor Antonio Bianchi, an eminent agricultural specialist, made the unprecedented decision that the farm workers should have

74. *See, for example,* the report and resolution on this subject at the 1920 CIL Congress, in *Il Domani Sociale,* nos. 14–15 (April 11, 1920) and discussed in Sanseverino, *Il movimento sindacale,* pp. 357–358.

75. Jacini, *Partito Popolare,* pp. 87–90, 129, and 257.

access to the accounts of the landed estates and share in the annual profits. He even performed the unusual feat of obtaining approval for the decision from the employer representative on the tripartite arbitration commission. The award precipitated one of the most bitter reactions in Italian agriculture and was never put into practice. After failing to upset the award in the courts the landowners turned to the Fascist *squadristi* for assistance, and what they could not achieve lawfully, they achieved through violence, terror and intimidation.

The growth of CIL had been rapid in its first two years. Building upon the Catholic union base established before the war, by 1919 its membership was one-half million. By 1920–1921 it reached a membership of approximately 1,250,000. Following is the list of membership in the Italian Confederation of Labor, by National Unions, as of June 30, 1920:[76]

Sharecroppers and small tenants	741,262
Small farm owners	108,598
Farm laborers	94,961
Textile workers	131,232
Railroad workers	24,273
Metallurgical workers	15,458
Woodworkers	11,823
Construction workers	7,585
State industry workers	6,668
Postal-telegraph-telephone workers	5,980
Tram, secondary railway, inland waterway workers	5,625
Needle trades workers	4,963
Mine and quarry workers	4,882
Private clerical employees	4,825
Heliographic workers	3,641
Pawn shop workers	3,016
Paper workers	2,412
Fishermen and sailors	2,332
Leather and fur workers	2,310
Nurses	2,257
Chemical workers	2,099
Reserve noncommissioned officers	1,443
Postal lottery office workers	1,260
Private company telephone employees	1,075
Casual labor of military districts	349
Total	1,190,329

76. Reprinted in *Lettere ai Lavoratori*, no. 1 (January 31, 1952), pp. 46–47, from *Annuario Cattolico Italiano*, 1922.

As can be seen in the list above, 79.4 percent of the membership was in agriculture, and only somewhat more than one out of four members of CIL were wage earners, the others being sharecroppers, tenant farmers, and small farm owners. The principal group outside agriculture was in the textile union, with 131,200 members. Outside of textiles and agriculture, the Confederation had only 114,300 members.

In 1920 the CGL had a membership approximately twice that of CIL. The distribution of its membership was considerably different from that of CIL. CGL had 176,426 in the construction industry compared with CIL's 7585. It had 160,200 metallurgical worker members compared with 15,458 in the Catholic union and 30,000 in the woodworking industry compared with 11,823. Even in textiles, with its high proportion of women and its many plants in strongly Catholic centers, CIL's 131,232 members were less than CGL's 144,704. In agriculture, the CGL's more than three quarters of a million members were preponderantly day laborers, compared with the 94,961 agricultural workers in CIL.[77]

During CIL's first period, its period of growth, it had centralized its structure beyond the loose Confederation which had originally been established. The counterpart of the Chambers of Labor, the *Unioni del Lavoro* were established in most of the country and coordinated by the Confederation through regional confederal secretariats. In addition, specialized central secretariats were established on the confederal level to coordinate the activity of the various Federations. These secretariats functioned over broad areas, one for agriculture, one for industry, another for public service and a fourth for private and public non-manual employees.[78] The CIL was a more centralized organization than its competitor, the CGL. On the whole, however, it left considerable autonomy to its affiliated organizations.

The decline in CIL's short span of existence began in 1921 as the Fascists turned their increasing strength against all democratic forces, but with particular fury against the trade unions. In its last years, CIL was particularly fortunate in having at its head Achille Grandi, who had come to leadership through work in the textile industry. As his subsequent leadership in the post-Fascist period was to demonstrate again, he was a man of high moral principle, an able trade union leader, dedicated to the cause of democratic labor. Under his leadership the CIL offered no compromise to the Fascist

77. The CGL statistics are incomplete and understate the industry membership. The statistics are taken from the official report to the CGL 1921 Congress (Rigola and D'Aragona, *La Confederazione del Lavoro* . . . 1914–1920, p. 122 and unnumbered appendix) and only break down 1,685,976 members by industry federation, the others having paid their dues through Chambers of Labor or directly through local organizations.

78. The basic reorganization, which took place late in 1919 is described in *Il Domani Sociale*, no. 37, December 27, 1919 and summarized in Sanseverino, *Il movimento sindacale*, p. 354.

cause. But the focus of CIL inevitably changed as it was increasingly put on the defensive. Its campaign on behalf of its general positive programs and its day-to-day activity in support of immediate improvements became increasingly difficult. As discussed in the next chapter, during 1921 the atmosphere among employers had changed to one of offense against the trade unions. In addition, the decline in economic activity and increased unemployment strengthened the relative bargaining position of industry. Finally, the Fascist violence and terror and, after the March on Rome, official assaults added final misfortune to the trade unions.

The CIL, in more clear-cut fashion than the Popular Party, repudiated collaboration with the Fascists during the latter's rise to power. The opposition was conditioned somewhat by the political tactics followed by the party and the friendly relations between the two Catholic movements. Several months after Mussolini's March on Rome, the National Council reiterated its "autonomy, or better the distinction" between itself and "any political party" and repeated that "it maintains cordial contacts with the P.P.I. which, in addition to having in common the same Christian inspiration, can cooperate toward the realization of our trade union program, especially in the social legislative period." [79] More and more, however, its attention was turned to defending its very existence. The CGL ceased to be the principal enemy. Both organizations were being subjected to the same bludgeons from fascism. The CGL bore the brunt of the attacks, but the CIL was not spared. As in the political field, however, overcoming basic long-standing antagonism was a slow and difficult process; the two organizations could not establish formal cooperation until two years after Mussolini had seized power. In August 1924, two months after the Matteotti assassination, an "Inter-Confederal Committee of Trade Union Defense" was set up and met at Milan. It included the CGL, CIL, the National Syndicalist UIL and two minor organizations, the Confederation of Bank Employees and the National Union of Clerical Workers. They found no difficulty in agreeing upon resounding resolutions in defense of trade union rights and liberties. But the battle had already been lost.

The pact of Palazzo Vidoni, under which the national employers' organization, *Confindustria,* granted the Fascist syndicates a monopoly in the field of labor relations, and the 1926 legislation implementing the agreement, put an effective end to the substantive existence of free labor organizations in Italy. The CIL, like the CGL, continued to exist for a short time longer, but opposition or even independence was no longer tolerated in Italy.

79. From resolutions adopted in December 1922 by the CIL National Council and quoted in *ibid.,* pp. 365, 370.

CHAPTER V

The Rise of Fascism

The war years were years of stress in Italian society. With the outbreak of the war, the policy of neutrality announced by the government had overwhelming support in the country. Only a relatively small extreme nationalist minority had supported entry into the war on the side of Austria and Germany. The government's position that its alliance with these countries, pledging support in a defensive war, was not invoked by events leading up to the 1914 military outbreak found little dissent. On the other hand, the claims against Italy's traditional enemy, Austria, for the territories of Trieste, Istria, and the Trentino, in which a million Italians lived under Austrian rule, made the position of insisting upon a price for neutrality seem a natural one.

The democratic center of Italian politics, Republicans, Radicals, Free Masons, increasingly took up the call for Italy's intervention on the side of the Allies to help support the forces of democracy and freedom. For quite different reasons, the growing nationalist groups also took up the cry for intervention on the side of the Allies. Having given up any hope of obtaining intervention on the side of the Central Powers after the first days of the war, the nationalists supported intervention on the Allies' side to insure Italy of its "national destiny" through expansion and aggrandizement.

As the divergent but articulate propaganda for intervention spread, the government of Antonio Salandra, who owed his place to Giolitti, but had tasted the fruits of independent power, repudiated the Giolitti neutrality position by entering the war on the side of the Allies in May 1915. Salandra and his Foreign Minister, Sidney Sonnino, who was the architect of the war policy, had no particular sympathy for the democratic ideals articulated by the Allies and the democratic interventionists in Italy. They brought Italy into the war without adequate military preparation, gambling on a short war. They committed Italy to intervention in a secret treaty negotiated in London with Great Britain and France in which Trieste, Istria, the Trentino and precisely defined territory on the Dalmatian Coast, as well as an appropriate share of African spoils and increased influence in the Mediterranean, had been pledged to Italy.

The treaty did not remain secret for long. Nor did Italy's moral position improve as a result of having continued negotiations with the Central Powers for concessions as a price for remaining neutral between the time of its London pledge and its actual entry into the war a month later. The Italian

Parliament, the members of which had demonstrated their preponderant position of neutrality by their informal pledge of support for Giolitti, nevertheless was swept into support of intervention when presented with the fact of war by Salandra and Sonnino against the background of mass demonstrations and threats of violence organized by the nationalist forces under D'Annunzio.

As between the policy of "sacred egoism" followed by the government and the policy of *"parecchio"* — negotiating "quite a lot" in concessions to remain neutral — the democratic forces which had favored intervention on a less narrow nationalist basis were the least influential in the following years. The forces which had been neutralist both before and after intervention, aside from the *parecchio* supporters, were the Socialists and the Catholics. The latter groups, supported by the Vatican, opposed intervention and separated themselves from responsibility but did not attempt to interfere with the war effort itself. The Socialists ended up in the same position, but with a more vociferous verbal opposition.

At the outbreak of the war, the Socialist Party had declared for absolute neutrality and had supported antiwar demonstrations throughout the country. The CGL supported the Socialist position and joined in common manifestos and meetings.[1] Despite the repeated threats of violent reaction in the event of Italian intervention, by the time intervention had become almost certain a joint declaration by the Socialist Party and CGL admitted that they were powerless to prevent it. The declaration, issued after a conference of the two organizations held on May 16, 1915, at Bologna, which renewed their support for neutrality and asked that demonstrations be held on May 19 with "discipline, dignity and strength" against intervention, stated: "with this the Socialist Party, the proletarian organizations and the Socialist Parliamentary group, which know they cannot today be the arbiters of the capitalist world, certain of having done their duty before Italy and the International, for themselves, the country and history, will have divided and maintained separate their responsibility from that of the ruling classes." [2]

Under the formula developed by the Socialist Party Secretary Lazzari, *"nè aderire, nè sabotare,"* the party and CGL were able to get through most of the war years without more than occasional harassment and censorship. The Italian Socialist Party was the only Socialist Party among the major European belligerent countries to refrain from supporting the war. It continued to separate itself from responsibility or involvement, holding to its position of opposition without, however, creating direct practical difficulties for the war effort.

For the CGL the formula of "neither adherence nor sabotage" permitted it to play an important role in the conduct of the war on the industrial front

1. Angiolini and Ciacchi, *Socialismo e Socialisti*, pp. 1136–1139.
2. *La Confederazione del Lavoro*, IX, 327, May 16, 1915, p. 145.

while maintaining opposition to the war itself. As a means of minimizing friction on problems involving manpower shifts and industrial relations, the government set up tripartite committees of industrial mobilization, presided over by government officials and participated in by representatives of industry and of labor. The CGL furnished the labor representation and contributed substantially to the alleviation of the inevitable problems which arose in industry as a result of the war effort.[3]

The war, however, was not a very popular one in Italy, and even the initial limited enthusiasm soon dampened considerably. Instead of the quick victory on which the Italians had gambled, the war dragged on. A number of events in 1917 changed the character of the reaction to the war, the achievement of Italian objectives in it, and the nature of the postwar political problems.

During the first two years, the Socialist Party which, as has been described earlier, had come under the control of the Revolutionaries before the war, had gradually moved away from its extreme position. While maintaining its antiwar attitude, and attending the antiwar international Socialist gatherings at Zimmerwald and Kienthal in 1915 and 1916, it trimmed its sails along democratic lines during the first two years of Italy's participation in the war. In May 1917, at a conference among the Socialist Party Executive, the Socialist parliamentary group and representatives of CGL, a postwar program was worked out. It was democratic in its objectives and in its terms. While Revolutionary in its implications, it did not go further than the democratic ideas of many others who advocated reform in the postwar period. If it implied revolution, it was the peaceful democratic revolution which would have been welcomed by most of Italy. In foreign policy it sought peace without any forced annexations, with respect for the rights of nationalities; disarmament; abolition of tariff barriers and the rule of law in international relations. In domestic affairs it sought "a republican government based upon the supremacy of the people"; universal and direct suffrage; freedom of association, assembly, strikes, and propaganda; election of judicial officials; complete system of social insurance, minimum wages, collective bargaining; large public works program; and expropriation of badly cultivated land.[4]

The lengthening period of conflict, the economic disruption and privation characterized by shortages, and the fall in real wages of 27 percent by 1917 and consequent growing discontent in the country raised the credit of the Socialist Party leadership. The appeal of Pope Benedict XV to the belligerent countries calling for an end to the "useless massacre" found widespread re-

3. Rigola, *Storia,* p. 427; *La Confederazione del Lavoro,* XII, 403, July 16, 1918, p. 898.

4. Text in *Avanti,* May 15, 1917 and summarized in A. Rossi, *The Rise of Italian Fascism, 1918–1922* (London, 1938), p. 13.

sponse in the Italian public, and the Catholic press used language not dissimilar from that of the Socialists in decrying the war.[5] Desertions from the army reached a level so high and morale had sunk so low that the government undertook a campaign among its soldiers, reminiscent of ancient Roman policy, promising redistribution of land in agriculture after the war as a special appeal to them. But morale among both the civilian population and the armed forces continued to fall through the year 1917.

The Italian victory during the summer of 1917 at Gorizia lent urgency to the Austrian pleas for assistance from the Germans on the Italian front. With the collapse of the Russian armies, the Germans were able to shift seven divisions and, in combination with the Austrians, force a breach in the Alpine defenses of the Italians. The disastrous rout of the Italian armies at Caporetto during October and November was humiliating for the Italians. But it had an important galvanizing effect upon the entire nation during those weeks when it was not certain whether the troops could be re-formed and would hold along the Piave line centered at Monte Grappa. The Socialists in the more moderate wing of the party reacted patriotically, and Turati, their most prominent representative, announced in Parliament that Monte Grappa was as sacred to Socialists as to all other Italians.[6] In a similar vein the CGL official periodical wrote, "When the enemy treads on our soil we have only one duty: to resist."[7] Basically, however, although Italy improved its position on the battlefield through the summer of 1918, the aftermath of the Caporetto defeat was a heightening of dissatisfaction and discontent with the war.

Another development which profoundly affected the direction of events in Italy was the Russian revolution. To the dominant leadership in the Italian Socialist Party, the success of the Bolsheviks in Russia became the model for their orientation on the Italian scene. The fascination with successful revolution not only dominated the orientation of the leadership but it also had repercussions throughout the wage earner groups in Italy. To "do as in Russia" became a seemingly attainable objective and an automatic solution to the myriad problems which characterized the next few years. Insofar as the party was concerned, the combination of events in Italy which centered around the Caporetto disaster and the increased revulsion against the war was given focus by the Russian revolution in driving the party rapidly away from the moderate orientation of its May 1917 postwar program. In the immediate aftermath of the Caporetti defeat, Costantino Lazzari and Nicola Bombacci, the leaders of the party, were imprisoned for their insurrectionary invocations which were inspired by the Bolshevik revolution in Russia. The party activity was held in check during

5. Cecil J. S. Sprigge, *The Development of Modern Italy* (London, 1943), p. 142.
6. Sprigge, *Modern Italy*, pp. 144–145.
7. Quoted in Borghi, *L'Italia tra due Crispi*, p. 79.

the rest of the war, but its direction had been turned away from moderation.

The other event which had basic significance in 1917 was the American entry into the war. It spelled the ultimate defeat of the London Treaty objectives of the Italian government. The Wilsonian approach to the war and the peace settlement had tremendous appeal to those forces in Italy which had supported the war without accepting the "sacred egoism" doctrine of the government and the nationalists. When it became evident that the end of the war would not simply see a weakened Austrian empire, but a breakup of that empire, the strategic claims of the Italian nationalists for concessions in Dalmatia lost their validity. The emergence of the new states on the basis of nationality principles made Italy's position a sharply different one, since insisting upon territorial concessions would antagonize and create lasting resentments instead of creating friendship and cooperation with its new neighbors. The democratic interventionists arguing along these lines found themselves caught in a deadly crossfire. Ridiculed and attacked as traitors and *rinunciatari* by the nationalists, they found no support from the Catholics or Socialists, who were equally antagonistic to any groups which had favored intervention and were uninterested in assuming any positive attitudes toward the issues emerging directly out of the war.

The Italian government, insisting upon fulfillment of the London Treaty commitments, was doomed to bitter disappointment as it saw other demands met at the peace negotiations, but its own claims, beyond those based upon nationality considerations, rejected. Economic arrangements and trade concessions, which could have had basic importance for the country, were totally ignored by the Italian government, which focused alone upon the terms of the London Treaty. Nor was there any consideration given to the changed situation resulting from the creation of Yugoslavia out of former Austrian territory. The impact at home of the failure of the Italian government to obtain its objectives in the peace negotiations heightened the general attitude that the war had been useless. The Socialist and Catholic repudiation of the war effort, combined with the shrill nationalist complaints, left little room for the democratic interventionist position of Wilsonianism.

Postwar Socialism

The tragedy of the Socialist Party in the two years following the war was its inability to face the realities of the Italian political and social situation with practical goals and effective tactics. Anticipation had been widespread in Italy through the last years of the war that the Socialist Party would play a vital role in the postwar government. Had the Socialist Party accepted its role as that of a leading reform group and accepted responsibility in government, it could have achieved much of its democratic objectives as set forth in its May 1917 program. Its 1917 program was not dissimilar from that supported by widely diverse democratic groups at the end of the war.

Even the proposal of calling a constituent assembly for the purpose of reorganizing some of the institutions of government more democratically had widespread support.

The old equilibrium maintained by Giolitti among the divergent parties and factions during the prewar years had been swept away. In the first postwar elections held in 1919, the Socialist Party emerged with 1,834,000 votes (almost one third of the total votes) and 156 deputies, by far the largest party in the country. The newly formed Catholic Popular Party, as a result of its impressive showing, became the second largest party. The two parties together accounted for 53 percent of the total vote and 256 out of the total 508 members of the House of Deputies in Parliament. The rest of the votes and deputies were scattered among numerous groups of liberal, conservative, and progressive democratic elements.

The Socialists, it had been expected, would be thrust into a position of leadership and responsibility. Even the conservative forces in the country, during the immediate months after the war, had resigned themselves to this prospect. The program of the Popular Party was not significantly different from the reform program of the 1917 Socialist orientation. But if, as was probable, the basic ideological differences between the Catholics and Socialists were too great to bridge for purposes of cooperation in government, the Socialists could have found enough support among other groups in Parliament to give them leadership in government.

Long before the 1919 elections, however, it was evident that the Socialist Party had turned its back upon reform and assumption of responsibility in government. By the time the party held its congress in September 1918, as the war was drawing to a close, the swing away from a reform position was complete. The congress overwhelmingly affirmed support for extremist positions which were embodied in a program announced by the Executive Committee in December: absolute intransigence against all those who had supported the war, whatever their political orientation, and a call for the establishment of dictatorship of the proletariat as the only means of achieving Socialist objectives.[8]

In turning its back upon parliamentary and democratic means of furthering its objectives, the party precipitated grave tensions within its own orbit of influence. In January 1919 the Socialist parliamentary group repudiated the position of the party leadership. It adopted a resolution sponsored by Turati and Camillo Prampolini warning that the party position which held that a Socialist republic could be established by an act of will on the part of a minority was an illusion which would have the effect of provoking reaction and that only through reforms of an immediate nature, "can the proletariat, without deception and without illusions, really achieve

8. Sprigge, *Modern Italy*, pp. 162–163; Cannarsa, *Il socialismo*, pp. 203–204.

its own emancipation." [9] The Socialist parliamentary group was to continue predominantly reformist throughout the following years. It did not succeed in having any impact upon the party's orientation and yet felt compelled to accept the discipline imposed upon it by the party. The CGL also repudiated the Socialist Party's approach, as will be described in the next section, but also accepted continued cooperation with the party.

It has been a matter of considerable controversy whether the conditions for a successful Socialist revolution existed in Italy in 1919. Certainly there was widespread social and economic disruption. Inflation, shortages, lack of respect for existing institutions, expectation of change was widespread. Agitations, strikes, violence, were everyday occurrences. The governing forces in the community lacked self-confidence. The wage earners and peasants seemed prepared for violent change. But whether or not the Socialists could successfully have staged a revolution during the first year after the war, cannot be judged alone by such considerations. The forces for the *status quo* were also strong and could have marshalled additional support in an anti-Socialist contest well beyond those who wanted to resist any change. It is significant that during its first year of existence, the Popular Party obtained important support throughout the country on a platform of reform in direct opposition to the Socialists.

In any event, the Socialist Party, with a choice between a policy of revolution and a policy of reform, chose the verbiage of revolution and the substance of neither. Throughout 1919 and 1920 it preached revolution. In March 1919, for example, the party directorate proclaimed the imminence of a revolutionary general strike "whose organization will be made as soon as the work of organizing the proletarian and Socialist forces will give assurance of its full and complete success." [10] It incited the workers and frightened the rest of society with a steady barrage of manifestos, proclamations, speeches and agitations. It rejected the parliamentary foundations of democratic society and promised the establishment of "Soviets," "dictatorship of the proletariat," "proletarian revolution" as soon as conditions "matured" in the promised immediate future. Throughout this period, however, nothing was done by the Socialist Party actually to make any preparations for revolution. It made no attempt to clarify, in its own conception, what it meant by the slogans borrowed from the Russians, of "Soviets," and "dictatorship of the proletariat." At no time was there anything done by the party to develop its conception of how it meant to organize the society it wanted to bring about. Much more important, however, was the fact that it did nothing to prepare for seizure of power either

9. Pietro Nenni, *Storia di quattro anni (1919–1922)*, 2nd edition (Rome, 1946), pp. 12–13.
10. Nenni, *Storia di quattro anni*, p. 20.

through organization or through planning. It is little wonder that the fiery oratory and the threats of insurrection frightened the middle classes and encouraged workers to feel that they were on the brink of revolution. It is also little wonder that it was not long before a movement grown strong on the heritage of its past promise, inflated by the illusion it created among the working population of imminent miraculous liberation from the torments of existing society, began a rapid decline in strength and prestige as soon as it became clear that its will to oratory far exceeded its will to action. With the conditions of Italy at the time, and in the atmosphere of hysterical exhortations it created, the Socialists could not stand still. When they did, they found their influence waning. Despite all its thunder and bombast, the party, almost despite itself, functioned effectively during this period primarily as a machine for winning elections.

When the Socialist Party met in its first postwar congress in October 1919, on the eve of the national political elections, the "Maximalist" majority motion swept away the venerated Socialist program of 1892 as outmoded and insufficiently revolutionary. It affirmed the conviction "that the proletariat must resort to violence for defense against *bourgeoisie* violence, for the conquest of power and for the consolidation of revolutionary conquests," and establishment of the "transitory regime of the dictatorship of the entire proletariat." [11] It compromised with reality sufficiently, however, to agree to participate in the national political elections.

Filippo Turati, the veteran Socialist intellectual among the "giants" of European Socialist leaders, led the reformist forces at the congress. He made a moving plea for the democratic tradition of Italian socialism and against the verbiage of violence.[12] He incurred a strong protest in the congress when he dared suggest that "in the present Italian situation, dictatorship of the proletariat cannot be anything other than the dictatorship of some men on top of, and eventually against, the vast majority of the proletariat." On the method of violence adopted by the "Maximalists," Turati prophetically said at the congress:

But when we adopt it for miraculous Socialist improvisations, violence is nothing other than the suicide of the proletariat; it serves the interests of our adversaries . . . Today they do not take us seriously, but when they find it useful to take us seriously, our appeal to violence will be taken up by our enemies, one hundred times better armed than we, and then goodbye for a long time to Parliamentary action, goodbye to economic organizations, goodbye Socialist Party . . . To speak . . . of violence continually and then always postpone it until tomorrow is . . . the most absurd thing in this world. It only serves to arm, to rouse, to justify rather the violence of the adversary, a thousand times

11. Angiolini and Ciacchi, *Socialismo e Socialisti,* pp. 1303–1304.

12. Text of speech in Filippo Turati, *Trent' anni di Critica Sociale* (Bologna, 1921), pp. 287–340. Quoted passages are at pp. 319 and 331–332.

stronger than ours . . . This is the ultimate stupidity to which a party can come, and involves a true renunciation of any revolution.

The CGL and its Postwar Problems

Even before the war was over, the CGL found itself confronted with the problem of reconciling its own reformist views with the extremist positions of the Socialist Party. The government had announced the establishment of a Commission for the Study of Postwar Problems early in the summer of 1918 and had invited the participation of representatives of the CGL as well as Socialist Party deputies.[13] The Socialist Party, however, which had already turned its back upon its moderate program of 1917, decided against permitting any Socialist participation. The Socialist deputies, while disagreeing with the party decision, quickly fell in line. The party then sent letters to the CGL participants, which included Rigola, informing them that as members of the Socialist Party they were expected to resign from the commission and that failure to do so would be regarded as breach of discipline leading to disciplinary action. The issue was debated at a meeting of the CGL National Council on July 25. Three motions were presented and because of a split in voting by those favoring participation, the motion against participation carried, although it received only 46 percent of the votes.[14]

The decision caused an uproar in the organization.[15] The Directive Council resigned in protest, but was induced to withdraw its resignation. Rigola, who had headed the CGL since its formation, refused to go along with the others and insisted upon making effective his own resignation on September 30, 1918.[16] Thus at the opening of a crucial period in the organization's existence, CGL lost its most effective and independent-minded secretary general.[17] The independence of the CGL in its own sphere had been a basic tenet which Rigola had firmly maintained throughout his period of leadership. He had been in bad health for some years, and rather than create a continuing controversy around the circumstances of his resignation, he gave his state of health as the official reason for stepping down from his post. Rigola had offered his resignation in 1913 over a similar issue of noninterference. That he withdrew his resignation in 1913 but refused to do so in 1918 is a measure of his assessment of the chances of resisting party interference with CGL policy in the later period.

Rigola was replaced by Ludovico D'Aragona, who had served in the

13. *La Confederazione del Lavoro*, XII, 403, July 16, 1918, p. 901.
14. *Ibid.*, XII, 404, August 1, 1918, pp. 903–905, 908–909.
15. *See, for example,* lead editorial signed by Tomaso Bruno, head of the Printers' Federation in *ibid.*, XII, 405, August 16, 1918, pp. 911–912.
16. Meda, *Il Socialismo*, pp. 93–94 and footnote p. 94.
17. *Resoconto stenografico . . . 1921*, p. 21.

national office of the CGL for a number of years. D'Aragona had Rigola's complete confidence and shared Rigola's point of view both on internal CGL problems, its relations with political parties and the reformist orientation of CGL activity. In sum, the shift from Rigola to D'Aragona did not represent a change in the orientation of CGL.

Rigola's resignation dramatized the problem of relationships with the Socialist Party. The CGL National Council in September reaffirmed its independent position and authorized the negotiation of an agreement with the Socialist Party which would attempt to spell out in specific terms the spheres of independent action of the two organizations.

An agreement was reached on September 29, 1918, affirming the independence and autonomy of the two organizations in their own spheres, one in the economic and the other in the political. It then provided:[18]

1. Strikes and agitations of a national political character shall be proclaimed and directed by the directorate of the party.

2. Strikes and agitations of national economic character shall be proclaimed and directed by the Confederation.

3. Since there are questions which can be considered as predominantly political by the party directorate and as predominantly economic by the Confederation and *vice versa,* and thus give rise to . . . disputes over competence, it is agreed that whenever the Directorate is about to meet, it will transmit its own agenda to the CGL so that the latter may be aware of the subjects placed on the agenda and in a position to intervene as a matter of right, through its own representation at sessions of the Directorate. Similar arrangements shall be made for sessions of the Directive Council and the National Council of the Confederation of Labor which shall transmit its own agendas to the Directorate so that the latter, when it believes it useful and necessary, may intervene as a matter of right at the sessions of the Directive Council and the National Council.

The agreement remained in effect for four years. During these years the problem of relationship between the two organizations continued to be a controversial one and the agreement proved inadequate to solve many of the problems which arose.

The CGL was now firmly oriented toward the Socialist Party alone. Accepting political leadership from the Socialist Party at a time when the party followed policies different from those favored by the predominant CGL leadership could only be justified by a deep sense of party and proletarian solidarity, and a belief that the separation of the economic and political spheres would be furthered by the agreement. In addition, the degree of loyalty which workers displayed toward the Socialist Party and the expectations which the party had created among workers were so great that the

18. For complete text *see* Rigola and D'Aragona, *La Confederazione . . . 1914–1920,* pp. 50–51.

CGL did not feel it had a wide range of choice except to attempt to maintain as good relations as possible while attempting to protect its own autonomy and independence.

As Italy entered the postwar period it immediately became evident that the widespread nature of both economic and political discontent among wage earners would make separation of the two, even on a formal level, very difficult. By the end of the war real wages had fallen 35 percent. Shortages developed in a wide variety of consumer goods, particularly bread. Prices rose sharply. A buying spree only resulted in greater shortages and higher prices. During 1919 three separate waves of pressures developed in quick succession.

The first was a drive, immediately after the war, for the establishment of an eight-hour day in industry.[19] It was prompted in part by the long hours worked in industry during the war. More important was the fear that the demobilization of troops and the conversion of industry from war production would lead to large-scale unemployment. The eight-hour movement in Italy was, of course, not unique at the time. It had its parallel in France, Great Britain, and elsewhere. The CGL Directive Council in September 1918 adopted the eight-hour day as its most immediate postwar demand and from the time of the signing of the armistice urged all CGL affiliates to begin a campaign in their industries to obtain agreements on this subject. The CGL, in turn, took the initiative in a precedent-breaking step of attempting to arrange for negotiations with the national industrial employers' confederation, the *Confederazione Generale dell' Industria Italiana* (usually called *Confindustria*), for the purpose of reaching an all-industry agreement to establish the eight-hour day on a national scale. The negotiations did not achieve their full objective, since the employer association could not commit all of its affiliates. The atmosphere of the time, however, was such that *Confindustria* agreed in principle. Its Metallurgical Federation affiliate signed an agreement on February 20, 1919 to establish the eight-hour day in that industry, with May 1 set as the starting date in the engineering portion of the industry and August 1 for the steel industry. Other industries followed the lead of the metallurgical industry, although in some cases, as in textiles, the concession was granted very reluctantly.

The quick success of the eight-hour day movement must be attributed to the general defensive attitude of employers at the time, in their expectations of revolutionary changes to come from the Left, and the pressure of the government in favor of making concessions. The statement issued by the

19. For a good description in English of the eight-hour movement, *see* report of the European Commission of the National Industrial Conference Board (NICB), *Problems of Labor and Industry in Great Britain, France and Italy* (Boston, 1919). See also Rigola and D'Aragona, *La Confederazione . . . 1914–1920*, pp. 8–14; *Resoconto . . . 1921*, pp. 248–249; Rigola, *Storia*, pp. 438–439.

cotton textile employers' association when it agreed to the eight-hour day is worth quoting, as it gives some insight into the industrial employers' psychology during the first part of 1919. After reviewing the arguments against granting the concession, and emphasizing the disadvantageous position into which the industry would be put in competing in international markets, the statement said:

On the other hand, in view of the declaration of the representatives of the textile trade unions that . . . it is their intention to obtain by any and every method (not excluding a strike) and not later than May first, the reduction of the working week to forty-eight hours for the textile trade throughout Italy; furthermore, in view of the declaration by the representatives of the Italian General Confederation of Labor of its complete accord with the textile organizations and of its intention to support the demand for reduced hours by all means in its power (including even a general strike by all work people), the manufacturers consider it their duty, in the difficult and hazardous period through which the country is passing, not merely to avoid taking the responsibility for refusing (which in any case would fall on the other side), but even to avoid giving a pretext for disorders of incalculable extent and seriousness. Consequently, the manufacturers intend to reduce the working week, as from May first to 48 hours; but they disclaim responsibility for the results of the decreased economic activity which, in their opinion, will follow this reduction in working hours, to the detriment of both parties and of the country.[20]

While the campaign for the eight-hour day was still going on, the food shortages and the rising prices of consumer goods resulted in an increasing number of demonstrations and riots.[21] By June and early July the demonstrations and riots had spread throughout the peninsula. In the Emilia, Romagna, Tuscany, and Marche areas — the traditional areas of the extremists — insurrection appeared in full force. Warehouses, stores, even cooperatives were broken into and sacked. Government offices were occupied. At Florence the city was taken over by the insurrectional mob. General strikes at Ancona, Bologna, and as far as Palermo in Sicily closed down all activity and the mobs occupied government offices. In lesser degree riots broke out at Milan, Rome, Naples, and at other large centers. It is significant that the workers, peasants, and others involved in the rioting turned to the Chambers of Labor as the repository of their hopes for leadership and, as was frequently the case, when they declared an area to be a "soviet" they turned over authority to the Chambers.[22] Merchants frequently turned over the keys to their warehouses to the Chambers and sought protection there.

20. NICB, *Problems of Labor and Industry,* p. 167.
21. For account of this period *see* Nenni, *Storia di quattro anni,* pp. 30–32; Rossi, *Rise of Italian Fascism,* pp. 19–21; Rigola and D'Aragona, *La Confederazione . . . 1914–1920,* pp. 19–20.
22. Rigola and D'Aragona, *La Confederazione . . . 1914–1920,* p. 20.

But it had not been the Chambers of Labor which had played a leading role in instigating the riots. It had rather been the Socialist Party's repetition of revolutionary proclamations, of announcements of preparation for insurrectionary strikes, of calls to imitate the Russian revolution by establishing soviets and dictatorship of the proletariat, which had promoted revolutionary fever among the workers.

Yet, when the movement had gotten beyond the point of local incidents, when it appeared that the government forces might not be able to cope with the situation, the Socialist Party sat back and applauded, but offered no leadership or direction either back to legality or toward insurrection. Pietro Nenni, who has written a careful account of this period, has commented, "But no one put himself at the head of the masses, no one sought to give a political voice to the discontent. While the blood flowed (two dead at Florence, five at Imola, four at Taranto, one at Genoa, and so on); while the soldiers sent to repress them fraternized with the mob (at Brescia, at Sestri Ponente, at Forlì), the Directorate of the party limited itself to a stereotyped communication attesting its sympathy to the demonstrators." [23]

The government, early in July, announced a series of measures which were intended to ease the food shortage, turning over to municipal authorities the power to requisition and distribute foodstuffs. This action, combined with the lack of general focus and leadership of the demonstrations, led gradually to a return to normalcy. The CGL had sat back without intervening during the height of the rioting. On July 7, when it was evident that the Socialist Party had offered no leadership and the movement was wearing itself out, the CGL intervened, and while agreeing that exasperation with the food situation was justified, advised against being fooled by such illusory solutions as fixing prices below costs of production and recommended a series of emergency measures to the government to deal with the situation. [24]

No sooner were the food riots over when a two-day general strike closed down almost the entire economy on July 20 and 21. [25] The strike had been planned some time before by agreement of the Socialist trade unions from a number of countries meeting at Southport, England. The purpose was to protest against the intervention of the Allied armies in Russia. In Italy the announcement of the forthcoming strike had given rise to the widespread expectation that this strike was the long-promised revolutionary one which

23. Nenni, *Storia di quattro anni*, p. 31.
24. *Idem*. The Socialist Party, on the other hand, continued to condemn all such specific measures or cooperation in implementing them. See *Avanti*, July 11, 1919, quoted in A. Tasca, *Nascità e avvento del fascismo* (Florence, 1950), p. 35, footnote 41. The book is the Italian edition of Rossi's *Rise of Italian Fascism*. Rossi is a pseudonym used by Tasca. The Italian version is an enlarged edition with much valuable material in its footnotes which do not appear in the English edition.
25. Rigola and D'Aragona, *La Confederazione . . . 1914–1920*, pp. 20–22; Nenni, *Storia di Quattro Anni*, pp. 33–34; Rigola, *Storia*, p. 439.

the Socialist Party had been predicting. Despite the Socialist disclaimer that the strike was not revolutionary in intent, the fears of the government and the public had remained high. The desperate spirit of revolt, however, had been exhausted in the food riots, and the two-day strike was supported by the workers throughout the country, but in a holiday mood rather than a revolutionary one. Furthermore, the railroad union had at the last moment refused to join the strike.

The food riots and the July 20–21 strike made a deep impression in Italy. The revolutionary atmosphere which had successfully been fostered by the Socialists earlier in the year, against the background of revolutionary events in other parts of Europe — Russia, Hungary, Bavaria and elsewhere — had made it appear that Italy, too, was moving toward a Bolshevik revolution. The aimlessness and easy dissipation of the food riots and the innocuous nature of the general strike began to give courage to many that the revolution was after all not inevitable and the worker forces were not invincible.

The third wave of pressures during 1919 revolved around the question of wage increases. During the early part of 1919, when strikes had been frequent, wage concessions were made with little opposition from employers. Furthermore, the eight-hour-day drive had been given first priority. As the serious wage-increase drives got under way during the summer, however, the unions began discovering considerably more resistance from employers than they had encountered previously. The most dramatic dispute was in the metallurgical industry. Since the industry set the pace for wages in the economy and dominated the councils of the employers' association, it also set the pattern for resistance to worker demands. The metallurgical employers of Piedmont settled without a strike. The refusal of the metallurgical employers in the Lombardy, Liguria and Emilia regions, however, to grant wage concessions satisfactory to the union led to a strike in these regions in August. The strike lasted for sixty days and was settled only when the employers agreed to a settlement favorable to the workers. During August the unions in other industries also ran into greater resistance to wage demands, and strikes began in numerous industries and in various parts of the country. On the whole, however, the strikes were successful in obtaining significant wage concessions. During 1919, real wages recovered almost all the ground lost during the war and in the following year wages made further significant gains beyond the continued rise in the cost of living.

Strikes continued at an increasing level in 1920, but there was no coordination among them. They were directed not only toward wage increases, but toward a variety of objectives, many of which were of slight significance except as symptoms of unrest and, at times, irresponsible incitement. There had also been large-scale unrest in agriculture during 1919 and 1920. Occupation of land without sanction of law became a common phenomenon in some areas, sometimes led by the new Catholic political and trade union leaders. More frequently, strikes of farm workers were directed toward obtaining union recognition, shorter hours, and higher wages. Sympathy strikes were common. General local and regional strikes of sympathy were relied upon heavily for the less promising causes. During 1919 there were 1663 strikes in industry involving 1,049,000 workers with 18,888,000 days lost, and 208 strikes in agriculture involving 505,000 workers with 3,437,000 days lost. The statistics for 1920 are even higher. In industry there were 1881 strikes involving 1,268,000 workers, who lost 16,398,000 working days. In agriculture there were 189 strikes, fewer than in 1919, but more than double the number of workers were involved, 1,046,000, who lost 14,171,000 working days.

During the two years following the war the CGL underwent a phenomenal expansion. The fewer than 250,000 members which the organization had at the end of the war grew to over one million in 1919 and to 2,200,000 in 1920. The rapid expansion made impossible a continuation of the controlled, responsible activity of the prewar CGL. True, the CGL national leadership and the leadership of most of the National Federations remained moderate in their orientation, as did a large proportion of the leadership in the Chambers of Labor. But they were not wholly in control of the situation. To retain their leadership they frequently felt compelled to act more militantly than their experience would otherwise have recommended.

Although the war's end had also brought unrest and sharply increased industrial conflict to most other Western countries, in Italy there were additional elements which added to the conflict and finally contributed to the destruction of democratic institutions. On the economic side inflation and shortages, including electric power shortages, characterized early 1920, and then were abruptly reversed in the latter part of the year by a sharp downturn in the business cycle. The Socialist Party continued to refuse to permit its parliamentary representatives to cooperate in government and intensified its revolutionary *pronunziamenti*. As a British historian has described their position, "What in actual practice these preachings came to mean was not 'revolution,' but an abstention or desertion from the conduct of public affairs — the whole existing organization of the state being classified as untouchable and all civic loyalty as reaction." [26] The government, from the fall of 1919, in addition to the clamorous attacks from the nationalist Right for its inability to deliver the promised rewards of war, was subjected to the embarrassing inability to suppress D'Annunzio's continued occupation of Fiume in defiance of the government.

26. Sprigge, *Modern Italy,* p. 178.

By mid-1920 the failure of the Orlando and Nitti governments of the previous two years to cope with the situation of turmoil[27] arising from the Right and the Left resulted in the recall of that master of compromise, Giolitti, to take over the prime ministership. In a real sense this was the close of an era. It represented the recognition that the new forces unleashed after the war would not give rise to a democratically reformed society through new leadership. A return to Giolitti meant a willingness to seek the prewar methods of balance of the old leadership.

From the point of view of trade union achievements, the two years after the war were of enormous significance. The trade union movement grew to almost ten times its wartime level. After real wages had fallen in 1918 to 64.6 percent of the 1913 level, they rose to 114.4 percent in 1920, despite the five-fold rise in prices, and reached 127.0 percent in 1921. The eight-hour day had been established in most of the industry. Vacations with pay had become the rule. Grievance machinery existed for the settlement of disputes under agreements. Agreements had become almost the universal rule in industry, and in most of the important industries had been made national in scope.[28]

The Occupation Strikes

The movement to give workers some measure of participation in the management of industry was a common development in many countries after the war. The shop steward movement in Great Britain, the works council movements of Austria and Germany, represented aspirations common to workers in many countries who looked toward a change in power relations in industry after the war. In Italy the CGL had adopted this objective as part of its program and had hoped to achieve it by legislative means. Worker participation in management through stock ownership and profit participation had been a traditional part of Catholic social thinking and when the CIL was established toward the end of the war, it included this objective in its program. Despite Socialist and Popular Party support for some legislation on the subject, nothing was achieved by this means in the first years after World War I.[29]

27. The situation with respect to public security had been improved under the Nitti government. He had organized an effective new police arm, the *Guardie Regie* (Royal Guards), to supplement the *Carabinieri*. The amount of violence which characterized the period is illustrated by the calculation made by *Avanti* in its May 1, 1920 issue that from April 1919 to April 1920, 145 workers and demonstrators were killed and 444 wounded. Nenni, *Storia di quattro anni,* p. 85, footnote 2.

28. For review of collective agreement provisions, *see* Gino Olivetti, "Collective Agreements in Italy," *International Labor Review,* V, 2 (February 1922), pp. 209–228.

29. For background and discussion of developments after World War I, *see* Mario Guarnieri, *I consigi di fabbrica* (Città di Castello, 1921); Francesco Magri, *Controllo operaio e consigli d'azienda in Italia e all' estero; 1916–1947,* second edition (Milan,

It is important to differentiate between the postwar establishment of grievance committees in Italian industry and the factory council movement dramatized by the occupation strikes of September 1920. The establishment of *commissioni interne,* or grievance committees, had a history going back many years. While it had won acceptance in some plants before the war, permanent committees for the handling of grievances were still an exception. During the war the CGL had unsuccessfully urged the general acceptance of internal commissions in industry to provide for the more efficient settlement of grievances between workers and management. The government had been favorable, but had not succeeded in convincing management. In the changed atmosphere immediately after the war, however, management was more willing to make concessions to labor and this was one of the concessions granted.

The Metallurgical Workers Federation (FIOM) was the spearhead of the drive. It is interesting to note that the minority revolutionary elements in FIOM had opposed the demand for internal commissions at the FIOM Congress of November 1918 on the same ground as the Revolutionary Syndicalists before the war: that the commissions would be institutions of collaboration and that by their very nature would reduce the revolutionary ardor of the workers through the experience of cooperation. It was in the context of the debate against the revolutionary position that one must interpret the discussion of the commissions' objectives by the moderate leaders of FIOM. The FIOM General Secretary Bruno Buozzi referred to the growth of the trade unions, which, leading to discussion "not only regarding wages but the very distribution of work, tends by itself to make for sharing of the technical management of the plants between the work force and the industrialists." Colombino pointed to the educational value of experience on the commissions if eventual conquest of the plants was to prove practical. It was clear from the resolution adopted by the congress, however, that the organization was in fact seeking a grievance role for the internal commissions.[30]

Early in 1919 FIOM obtained an agreement with the Turin Automobile Employers' Association recognizing the internal commissions for the handling of grievances and internal plant labor problems. In February of the following year a similar agreement was reached with the Mechanical and Metallurgical Employers' Association in Turin. Recognition of internal

---

1947), pp. 5–103, 183–210; Confederazione Generale dell' Industria Italiana, *I consigli di gestione* (Rome, 1947), vol. II, pp. 7–10, 27–65; and M. Guarnieri and L. Colombino, *Relazione sui consigli di fabbrica, X Congresso della Resistenza, V della Confederazione Generale del Lavoro, Livorno 1921* (Milan, 1921).

30. Text of resolution in Guarnieri and Colombino, *Relazione sui consigli di Fabbrica,* p. 21.

commissions rapidly spread to other industries, and employers offered little resistance to recognition after the pattern had been set.[31]

The first attempt to set up a factory council (*Consiglio d'azienda*) with functions beyond those of the internal commissions took place in Turin during August 1919. Turin had become the center of strength of an extreme left-wing faction of the Socialist Party, which later became part of the Communist Party after it split from the Socialists in 1921.[32] The group was headed by Antonio Gramsci and published a weekly (it became a daily for a time), *Ordine Nuovo,* which was used as its principal propaganda organ. Its influence in the Turin area became dominant. It was obvious, however, that its influence in the trade union movement as a whole was not great and that FIOM, firmly in the hands of Reformist leadership, limited the group's field of operations even in the metallurgical plants in Turin. The internal commissions, controlled by the trade unions and having specific limited functions, did not furnish a convenient lever with which to broaden the group's influence.

With this background, the Revolutionaries who had opposed as reactionary any plant-worker organization in 1918 at the FIOM Congress, in 1919 became converted to the usefulness of such machinery, provided it could be freed of trade union control. The factory council movement, as promoted by the Gramsci group, became its organizational means of enlarging its influence among workers. In the propaganda on the new plant organizations, factory councils were surrounded with a mystique which was never completely consistent, but always high-sounding. Built on the foundation of the popular appeal of worker control in industry, the propaganda surrounding the council idea was widely varied in its approach: the council movement was a means of educating workers to the role they soon would have in running industry after the revolution; it was a movement to supplant the existing trade union machinery; it was a means of sharing industrial control with private management; it was a model of the soviets; and it was a means of bringing about the revolution itself.

The first factory council was established in August 1919 at the FIAT plant in Turin as a substitute for the internal commission, whose members had resigned.[33] The internal commission had been elected by members of the

31. Confederazione Generale dell' Industria Italiana, *I consigli di gestione,* vol. II, p. 8; Magri, *Controllo operaio,* p. 187; Battaglie Sindicali (replaced *La Confederazione del Lavoro* as official CGL weekly after the First World War), II, 12, March 27, 1920, pp. 3–4.

32. For an account, told from the Communist point of view, of the Turin labor developments in the postwar period, *see* volume I of autobiography by Mario Montagnana, *Ricordo di un operaio torinese,* 2 vols (Rome, 1949).

33. One of the problems which members of internal commissions faced during this period was that when they performed their duties conscientiously and sometimes settled grievances on the basis of compromise, they were repudiated by the workers

union on a plant-wide basis, was limited to trade unionists and was subject
to trade union discipline and control. The factory council was made up of
commissioners elected from each section of the plant by all workers, regardless of their union membership. The council idea was then spread to other
Turin plants where the extreme left-wing Socialists (Communists) could
control the situation. Recognition from employers was not requested, and
in practice the councils were used primarily for propaganda purposes in the
plant.

FIOM immediately took cognizance of the development and called a
conference in November 1919. Not wanting to appear opposed to worker
control of industry, but fearing the threat which the councils could represent
to the trade unions, the conference compromised and made significant concessions to the proponents of the councils. After calling attention to the
dangers to FIOM of organizations subject to the influence "of the unorganized masses" the resolution adopted at the conference agreed to:

consent to the experiment of the Factory Councils, insofar, however, as their
function is considered to be the continuation of the work of the Internal Commissions coordinated with that of the organization with whose principles it must
be inspired, be limited to the centers which have the best organized elements
and make precise their functions . . . to avoid the creation of easy illusions
among the masses which would end by having harmful repercussions upon the
class organization itself.[34]

As a result of this equivocal position, the New Order group continued its
efforts to organize factory councils in other plants of the Turin area. Gramsci
described the councils as "the elite of the new workers' state and in the
period of violent struggle, the elite of the revolutionary army"; and the
council, arising independently of the trade union, was a "true school of
reconstructive capacity of the workers," the "principal organization of
government and of worker management of production." [35] The trade union
movement as it then was organized was to become superfluous as the councils
spread, and a trade union structure would develop directly through the
coordination of the councils and be subject to the control of the councils.

In Turin, the Gramsci Communists had considerable success in establishing factory councils in various plants, although the idea did not spread
beyond Turin to any great extent. Even in Turin, however, it was not

and forced to resign. Colombino, commenting on this problem at the 1918 FIOM
Congress, said, "We have even started to doubt whether it is useful to preserve them
since when they are named, after fifteen days, the workers dismiss them accusing
them all of treason." Magri, *Controllo operaio*, pp. 186–187.

34. Guarnieri and Colombino, *Relazione sui consigli*, pp. 21–22; *Battaglie Sindacali*,
II, 12, March 27, 1920, p. 4.

35. Quoted from *Ordine Nuovo* in the pamphlet, *Le commissioni di fabbrica* by
Franco Momigliano, published by the Action Party in 1945, p. 7.

until the spring of 1920 that an attempt was made to obtain recognition from management for the councils. The council movement, as the Turin Communists oriented it, wore different faces, the political one when it described itself as the instrument of revolution and the future government of industry, and the economic one when it came around after some months to the proposition that it should be recognized by industry as co-partners in cooperative management — presumably as a down payment for revolution.[36]

The strike of April 1920 to obtain recognition for the councils was a failure. It had been precipitated by minor disputes at the FIAT's steel plant and the *Industrie Metallurgiche* plant in Turin, and was converted by the Turin Communist leadership into a general strike of all plants in Turin.[37] The issue became that of giving the factory councils authority in the plants. The employers' association welcomed the opportunity to have a showdown with the Communist firebrands and stood firm. The strike leadership then tried converting the strike into a revolutionary one and extended it to the entire Piedmont region.[38] In this area they had influence and following. Their next efforts were directed toward attempting to get the Socialist Party and the CGL, which they had up to this point ignored and ridiculed, to extend the general strike to all of Italy. The party and the CGL refused, since it was the judgment of both that a general political strike would peter out in a few days. When it became evident that the Turin strike was hopelessly lost, the CGL leadership did, however, assist the local leadership in obtaining a settlement on the basis of maintenance of pre-existing conditions and the strike was called off after ten days.

The strike settlement included acceptance of the employer association position that the factory councils would not be admitted in the plants and that institution of section commissioners was against plant regulations, although internal commissions would continue to be recognized for the exercise of their customary functions.[39] It was a complete defeat. The Turin group blamed the Socialist Party in violent language for having failed to turn the events into a national revolutionary strike and absolved themselves from responsibility in the defeat. The Socialist Party, on the other hand,

36. *See* the pamphlet *Il controllo operaio* (Milan, 1921), quoted in Ministero per la Costituente, *Atti della Commissione per lo Studio dei Problemi del Lavoro* (Rome, 1946), vol. III, p. 59.

37. For details *see Battaglie Sindacali*, II, 16, April 24, 1920, p. 1 and *ibid.*, II, 17, May 1, 1920, pp. 3–4.

38. For a good account of the strike, *see* Tasca, *Avvento del fascismo*, pp. 126–128; also *Battaglie Sindacali*, II, 17, May 1, 1920, pp. 3–4, for details of strike and CGL evaluation in article entitled "The General Confederation of Labor and the Turin Experiment — The Fallacious Turin Illusion."

39. *Atti della Commissione*, vol. III, pp. 130–131.

through its National Council and its Directorate sharply criticized its Turin branch for irresponsibility, lack of discipline and misjudging the relationship of forces in the country at the time.[40] *Avanti* also bitterly criticized the Communist leadership of the Turin party section, and described the strike action as precipitous, without preparation, without coordination and without discipline.

From the point of view of the Communists who dominated the Turin Socialist movement, the council movement was a means of getting the revolutionary objectives professed by the Socialist Party off the plane of verbiage and uncoordinated intentions, and focused on an instrument which could serve those revolutionary objectives. It also had the cardinal advantage for the Gramsci group of giving them an instrument through which they could widen their influence and by-pass the trade union and Socialist Party hierarchy. Against this background, they ascribed historical significance to the April strike, claiming they had lost in Turin, but had made the council movement and worker control of industry a national issue around which the revolution could focus.[41]

The national Socialist Party reaction had been prompted primarily by the challenge to its leadership represented by the Turin Communists. The CGL took a more serious view of the effects upon the attitude of management and non-labor groups in the community toward the strength of the trade unions and the necessity of resistance to them. D'Aragona, for example, commenting upon the strike in his report to the 1921 CGL Congress said, "This movement — Turin lockout and strike — which was turned to political ground and then carried back to the trade union arena at the end: this movement of the mob headed by elements who prided themselves for their irresponsibility toward the central organizations [Confederation and Socialist Party] in order to seek to extend it even where such extension was harmful: this movement, we say, was what encouraged the ruling class to take the offensive." [42] The strike had shown the Confederation of Industrial Employers that its determination not to concede anything further to labor and that the coordination of policy among employers for this purpose was a practical attainable objective. While the sound and fury of revolutionary doctrine still shook Italian society, the inevitability of revolution was no longer a common assumption among the leaders of industry.

By May of 1920 the CGL was already discussing the necessity of preparing for defense against the expected offensive of the employers. Yet, the most dramatic worker upheaval in the postwar years, the factory occupa-

---

40. Rigola and D'Aragona, *La Confederazione* . . . *1914–1920*, p. 69.
41. *See, for example,* article in Turin edition of *Avanti,* quoted in Rigola and D'Aragona, *La Confederazione* . . . *1914–1920*, p. 78.
42. *Ibid.*, p. 69.

tions, was already in the making.[43] A congress of FIOM drew up its demands for presentation to the metallurgical employers.[44] The demands, presented to the employers' association on June 18, included wage adjustments, cost-of-living wage bonus revision and standardization of wage scales among plants and by geographic area.[45] Neither the factory council issue nor any other issue beyond wages was raised at the time. The FIOM Congress had agreed to Buozzi's recommendation that the factory council problem be referred to the CGL for determination of policy toward it. The Revolutionary Syndicalist USI, the Catholic CIL and National Syndicalist UIL also presented demands which paralleled those of the FIOM.[46]

The employers' association decided to resist all demands from the unions and on June 22 announced its refusal to make any concessions. Buozzi and the other national FIOM leaders had found considerable reluctance on the part of the membership in many areas to support the demands if the result would be another strike. Yet they could not afford to concede defeat without a fight if they were to avoid the counteroffensive which they felt the employers' associations were preparing against them and the rest of the trade union movement.[47] They therefore sought other means of pressure as a substitute for a strike. They first ordered the workers in the industry to refuse to work overtime. As this had no effect upon the position of the employers, they first threatened and then, at a special congress of FIOM held during August 16 and 17, ordered the application of "obstructionism" in the industry starting August 19. "Obstructionism" was to be a combination of "working by the rule" and a slowdown. The union was explicit in its instructions to avoid sabotage, provocations or any aggressive actions which would precipitate individual discharges or a lockout.[48]

The workers applied their obstructionism in the plants of the entire industry. As each day passed, obstructionism began to degenerate into sabotage, despite the union's warnings. The atmosphere grew increasingly tense as the situation became more and more explosive. Against this background, the government offered its good offices to attempt to get negotia-

43. For chronicle of the events leading up to the occupation strike and the strikes themselves, *see* contemporary issues of *Battaglie Sindacali;* Rigola and D'Aragona, *La Confederazione . . . 1914–1920,* pp. 81–105; Magri, *Controllo operaio,* pp. 26–41; *Atti della Commissione,* vol. III, pp. 118–156; Nenni, *Quattro anni,* pp. 97–109; Rossi, *Rise of Italian Fascism,* pp. 75–81.

44. For official summary of congress, *see Battaglie Sindacali,* II, 22, June 5, 1920, pp. 3–4.

45. For text of FIOM demands in *ibid.,* II, 24, June 19, 1920, p. 2.

46. *Atti della Commissione,* vol. III, p. 119.

47. For Buozzi's discussion of this issue, *see Resoconto . . . 1921,* pp. 167–169.

48. Magri, *Controllo operaio,* pp. 27–29; for impact of obstruction tactic *see also Battaglie Sindacali,* II, 34, August 28, 1920, p. 1.

tions started again. The employers' refusal to make any concessions doomed the conciliation efforts. Production in the plants had fallen to 40 percent of normal.

The climax came on August 30, 1920 when the Alfa Romeo plant in Milan locked out its workers. Convinced that this was the beginning of a planned lockout by the employers throughout the industry, and fearing the consequences of another long strike, the Milan committee of FIOM ordered the workers of all Milan establishments in the industry not to abandon their work and not to leave their plants at the end of the shift. The national FIOM officials, foreseeing that their obstructionist tactics might lead to a lockout in the industry, had decided beforehand that stay-in strikes would be their counter tactic. Two hundred and eighty metallurgical establishments in Milan were thus occupied on the first day. Events rapidly outran the expectations of any of the participants. The industrialists declared a general lockout on September 1. Occupation strikes started in all plants of the industry in Turin, the center of revolutionary agitation, and then in other centers of the industry. The workers under plant committee supervision continued production within the limits of raw materials available. The occupations spread from the metallurgical industry to allied industries and plants which supplied the metallurgical industry. The strike could no longer be contained within the framework of wage issues. The workers were in control of basic industry and were trying to run it themselves. To the workers this seemed to be nothing short of the revolution itself. Publicity given to the discovery in the offices of the Milan plants during the first days of the strike of the records of systematic industrial espionage and coordinated blacklisting of trade union and political activists added dramatically to the psychological shift away from wage questions to broader issues.

The employers' association, thoroughly frightened, named a new negotiating committee and indicated willingness to make wage concessions. It was too late for wage discussions and yet it was not clear what the Socialist and CGL leaders intended. FIOM leadership, having been carried into the position of supporting the demand for worker control in their industry, soon realized that the situation was of a nature for which they could not alone assume responsibility. The CGL and the Socialist Party took over.

Giolitti saw in the occupation strikes a repetition of the 1904 strike movement. With confidence he refrained from any show of force in the industrial centers, on the assumption that the strikes would spend themselves and he would then be able to step in to achieve a satisfactory settlement. Loss of the strike might also help to chastise the Socialists enough to turn them back to constitutional means and achieve the "domestication" which he had worked on for many years before the war.

At the time, however, as the workers in the occupied plants spent their free time making weapons, the failure of the government to intervene with force furthered the conviction that a revolution was taking place.

On September 9 the Socialist Party Directorate met with the Directive Council of the CGL to debate the issue of revolution. No agreement could be reached. The party Directorate took the position that the situation was a revolutionary one, and that a successful revolution could be carried out. The CGL Directive Council, on the other hand, took the position that the issues involved were those of worker control of industry and that to carry the situation beyond this would be suicidal. The National Council of the CGL then met on September 10 further to debate the issue. Representatives of the national Socialist party and the Communists from the Turin Socialist Federation also participated in the discussions. The Turin group admitted that once the workers came out of the plants and tried to take over the city itself, they would be beaten decisively unless they could count on support from the countryside, which they admitted was unlikely.[49] And

49. Palmiro Togliatti, who later headed the Communist Party after Fascism fell, was the representative of the Turin group at the meeting. He expressed the view of the Turin Communists in support of a revolutionary solution but left responsibility for decision to the national leadership. The official stenographic summary of the meeting reports Togliatti as saying:

"The Socialist Section has put the struggle on political grounds, the trade union avenues have become more and more distant, in the Section the entire movement of defense and attack has been centralized. If there were an attack against the plants the defense is ready and would be adequate, but not an offensive. The city is surrounded by a non-Socialist zone and to find proletarian forces to help the city one would have to go as far as Veralli and Saluzzo. We want to know if a violent and insurrectional attack is to be started; we want to know what are the ends sought. You must not count on an action developed from Turin alone. We will not attack alone: to be able to attack, a simultaneous action from the countryside and above all a national action would be necessary. We want to be assured on this point because otherwise we do not want to commit our proletariat. [I] maintain that the action must be centralized in a movement of political character, the trade union and Parliamentary action should only serve as a screen."

In answer to D'Aragona's question whether Turin could defend itself, Togliatti replied, "If you give us the order to attack we will not be able to: change the conditions and we will better be able to defend ourselves. If the province cooperates the situation will change. You know the national situation, you have the elements, indicate to us what are your intentions." In response to Baldesi's question if Turin favored an economic settlement, Togliatti replied, "A static examination is not involved. You have the cards and should show them to us. In April we were better prepared than we are now. For the rest, the present situation is not one we have sought, it has been imposed. [I] maintain that the dispute cannot be defined on a trade union basis." Finally, Togliatti said in answer to Gennari's request for a definite answer on whether he favored a trade union solution, "As far as I am concerned I regard insurrectional action as better, whenever the Directorate, which has the control, tells us to." Rigola and D'Aragona, La Confederazione . . . 1914–1920, pp. 87–89. Other quotes in text are from same official summary, ibid., pp. 89–96.

Turin was the most revolutionary center in Italy. The debate went on for two days. At one point D'Aragona offered to resign and permit the Socialist Party to take over the trade union leadership of the revolution, if they were convinced of their position. The offer was not accepted by Egidio Gennari, secretary of the party, who left the decision to the CGL National Council, while urging the party's position that the situation was a revolutionary one and should be turned over to the party.

D'Aragona, in the discussion on this point said:

The Party Directorate thinks the time is ripe for a basic action, that the time is ripe for revolutionary action for the conquest of political power, for the installation of the communist society and for the dictatorship of the proletariat.

We do not believe that the time is ripe . . . we cannot accede to your ideas. We cannot accept your evaluation of the situation. You think that this is the time to begin a revolutionary action, well then, you assume the responsibility. We who do not feel able to assume this responsibility of pushing the proletariat to suicide, we tell you that we retire and submit our resignations. We feel that at this time the sacrifice of ourselves is necessary; you take the leadership of the entire movement, since you will thus be more sure of finding the General Confederation of Labor action completely in accord with your thinking and the assurance that the organization which should lead the proletariat has the same conception and the same objectives as you do . . . we will not assume the responsibility of carrying the entire proletariat to the *piazza* to have them massacred.

The vote of the National Council was 591,245 upholding the D'Aragona position and 409,569 in favor of the Socialist Party position with 93,623 abstentions. FIOM abstained from voting on the ground that it was directly involved, although Buozzi made clear he favored the D'Aragona position. The D'Aragona position, previously approved by the CGL Directive Council, provided:

that the leadership of the movement be assumed by the CGL with the assistance of the Socialist party . . . that the objective of the struggle is the recognition by employers of the principle of trade union control of the plants, intending with this to open the passage to those greater conquests which must unfailingly carry to collective management and socialization, to resolve thus in organic fashion the problems of production. Trade union control will give the working classes the possibility of preparing themselves technically and of being able to substitute . . . with its own new authority that of the employer.

Gennari pointed out that under the agreement between the two organizations, in the event of differences, as was now demonstrated by the vote of the CGL National Council, the party could assume direct responsibility for leadership of the movement and the confederation was committed not to interfere. He announced that the party did not intend to exercise this power, although the situation might change and in that case the party might do so in the future. It was only face-saving oratory. The Socialist Party had been preaching revolution without preparing for it. When confronted with a development which conceivably might be revolutionary but which the discussion of September 10 and 11 showed was doomed to failure, the party chiefs found it congenial to have the negative decision made by the trade union movement and retain their own revolutionary purity. Rossi has commented:

> After the Milan decision in favor of the Confederation viewpoint the leaders [of the party] breathed a sigh of relief. Relieved of all responsibility, they could now scream themselves hoarse about the "treason" of the General Confederation of Labor. Thus they had something to offer to the masses whom they had abandoned at the crucial moment, and were able at the same time to save face.[50]

The CGL decision and the party acceptance of the decision set the stage for the settlement of the occupations by Giolitti. He called the representatives of the employers' association, of FIOM and the CGL to a conference at Turin on September 15 where he insisted that some basis be found for agreement on worker participation in management which he maintained was justified under existing conditions. When it became evident that agreement would not be reached, he obtained agreement to a decree setting up a bipartite commission to study the problem and make recommendations for the provisions in a bill which Giolitti announced he intended under any circumstances to introduce into Parliament.[51] With Giolitti and other government officials conciliating, agreement was also reached on a wage increase to be applied to all of industry, a compromise on compensation for production during the occupations, and machinery for the settlement of cases of discipline problems on rehiring.[52] The occupation strikes continued during the period of negotiations and were not called off until the agreements had been ratified on September 22 at a special FIOM Congress and then by referendum among the FIOM membership.[53] September 27 was then set for evacuation of the plants with agreement that work would be resumed in all establishments no later than October 4.

Although the settlement involved significant economic concessions and a promise of government action on the issue of worker control, to the many who had thought that they were on the threshhold of taking power, of

50. Rossi, *Rise of Italian Fascism*, p. 70.

51. For text of decree, *see Battaglie Sindacali*, II, 37, September 20, 1920, p. 1.

52. For details of settlements which were incorporated in several documents, *see Idem* and *Atti della Commissione*, vol. III, pp. 129–130.

53. *Ibid.*, pp. 131–132; Magri, *Controllo operaio*, pp. 37–38.

"making a revolution," the settlement was regarded as a defeat. The psychology of defeat colored the workers' reaction.[54]

The end of the occupation strikes marked the beginning of large-scale reaction and the rapid growth of fascism. Employers had had a sobering experience for which they sought revenge. The middle classes, generally, sought some psychological security against working-class initiative. Insofar as the Socialists were concerned, Rossi commented, "The occupation of the factories marked the decline of the working-class movement, and the inglorious end of 'Maximalism,' though its corpse continued to litter the ground until the Fascists swept it up." Insofar as the employers' reaction is concerned, he wrote, "But the barriers between workers and employers had been broken down, and neither side could resume work on the old footing. The employers felt the occupations as a blot on their escutcheon . . . The evil spirits were to be exorcised by direct and violent action; the hour of fascism had come." [55]

Even the much-vaunted victory on worker control bore no fruit. Giolitti introduced a compromise bill in Parliament after the inevitable deadlock developed in his bipartite committee.[56] The bill got nowhere in Parliament, following Giolitti's own dismissal.

Rise of the Fascist Terror

Almost simultaneous with the end of the occupation strikes, local elections were held throughout Italy. The Socialists again demonstrated their strength by winning majority control in 2162 communes out of the total of 8000 and in 26 out of the total of 69 provincial councils.[57] It was the high-water mark of Socialist election strength and added further to the fears of the middle classes. As a practical matter, while the Socialist Party national headquarters had described the elections during the campaign as another effort to further the revolution, the local Socialists generally applied moderate and realistic leadership in municipal affairs. Nevertheless, the Socialists' strong showing at the polls encouraged further the attitude that legal means alone were not enough with which to deal with the extremist forces.

Mussolini's fascism had been only a minor, though raucous, element in the Nationalist wing of Italian politics up to this time. Indeed, Mussolini had continued to regard himself and his following as on the Revolutionary Left as long as this end of the political spectrum had seemed to offer greatest prospects for his political ambitions. He had broken with the Socialist Party

---

54. *See, for example,* Rossi, *Rise of Italian Fascism,* pp. 79–82.

55. *Ibid.,* pp. 80–81.

56. For text of Giolitti Bill and summary of various trade union and employer association positions, *see* "Workers' Control in Italy: The Government's Proposal," *International Labor Review,* I, 3 (March 1921), pp. 53–66.

57. Nenni, *Quattro anni,* p. 118.

on the issue of intervention in the war in an overnight reversal of position which won him the editorship of a new well-financed newspaper. His subsequent expulsion from the party created an unforgiving hatred of the party and its leadership. This nonetheless did not lead him to repudiate his ultra-leftist position until it became evident that the position would pay him no political dividends. The newspaper he edited, *Il Popolo d'Italia,* described itself as a Socialist paper when Mussolini founded it, reportedly with funds supplied from France. His modest following at the time was mainly made up of Socialist extremists and Revolutionary Syndicalists who for a variety of reasons shared Mussolini's position on the desirability of intervention in the war. After the war, however, Mussolini was in search of a set of popular issues and a means of tying together a following on any kind of program which would carry forward his personal political fortunes. He had sought support from the Nationalist groups immediately after the war, but had continued to be a minor figure compared with D'Annunzio. His vituperation against the *"rinunciatari"* during 1919 and his support of irridentist claims after the war had won him a place among the Nationalists. But even in this position, he hedged sufficiently not to cut all his bridges to other groups, including Giolitti.[58]

Nonetheless, on social and economic questions Mussolini continued with increasing hesitancy to support leftist policies as late as 1920. It had become evident by then that he was searching for any program, however equivocal, to gain him support. As late as the occupation strikes, when it appeared that these might lead to momentous changes, Mussolini supported them and even went so far as to swallow his pride and visit Buozzi to assure him of continued support.[59]

Mussolini had realized sooner than the Socialist leaders that their movement could not mark time indefinitely. As early as November 1919 he had written that the Socialist Party might understand the reasons for such inactivity, but the electorate would not. Either it could try winning absolute power by revolution which "would mean civil war, with the inevitable destruction of the party and the working class, and the rise of an armed dictatorship" or it could arrange for a coalition government, including other parties, based on a common program which "would lead to the fulfillment of the greatest expectation." His analysis ended with the comment, "We are loath to suggest a further possibility, deadlock in Parliament and chaos in the country." [60]

Commenting again on the Socialist position after the 1919 elections,

58. *See,* e.g., Rossi, *Rise of Italian Fascism,* pp. 84–85, on his position with reference to the Fiume issue.

59. *Ibid.,* p. 77.

60. *Popolo d'Italia,* November 22, 1919, quoted in *ibid.,* p. 53.

Mussolini three months later was convinced that the Socialists had chosen the third alternative and wrote:

The marvellous victory at the polls has simply shown up the inefficiency and weakness of the Socialists. They are impotent alike as reformers and revolutionaries. They take no action either in Parliament or in the streets. The sight of a party wearing itself out on the morrow of a great victory in a vain search for something to apply its strength to, and willing to attempt neither reform nor revolution, amuses us. This is our vengeance, and it has come sooner than we hoped.[61]

Mussolini, waiting to capitalize upon the reaction against the Socialists, however, had straddled the issue of whether riding this reaction would be best served by winning mass support to an alternative program of the Left or by throwing in his lot with the discontent on the Right. With the end of the occupation strikes, Mussolini made his choice. Retaining much of the verbiage of his revolutionary past, deliberately vague in his program, he now saw his chance of becoming the instrument and the rallying point of those forces which had had enough of legality in their opposition to the Socialists.

The months following the occupation strikes witnessed the rapid increase in strength of the Mussolini forces and widespread violence by Mussolini's swelling ranks of black-shirted bully-boys against the Socialists, the trade unions, and the cooperatives. In agriculture in north central Italy, the advances made by the trade unions and the cooperatives, and the peasant land occupations had during 1920 begun to provoke a reaction of its own. The large landowners had begun to equip themselves with mercenaries whose task was not only defense, but also threats and violence against the trade union and cooperative organizations.

The private armies in the agricultural area had grown up without help from Mussolini and his Fascist *arditi*. They were made up of youths with similar outlook, a search for adventure to substitute for the unattractiveness of adjustment back to civilian life, and an extreme nationalism. D'Annunzio, not Mussolini, was their idol. Giolitti's success toward the end of 1920, however, in obtaining a compromise settlement of the Fiume issue with Yugoslavia and in driving D'Annunzio and his "Legions" from their occupation of the territory, marked the eclipse of D'Annunzio as a political figure. The armed bands in the rural areas were thus drawn into the Fascist tide as it rose during the following year.

In the closing months of 1920 and the first part of 1921, Mussolini's movement, primarily an urban one centered in Milan, gradually acquired the support of the rural bands. Terror was common to both, however, and

61. *Popolo d'Italia,* February 26, 1920, quoted in *ibid.,* p. 53.

particularly concentrated in the rural areas of north central Italy. In increasing numbers, union headquarters were burned, union officials beaten and sometimes shot, cooperatives prevented from functioning. While Socialist Party local headquarters and officials were not spared, the greatest terror was turned upon the organizations which, while under moderate leadership, were the ones which caused economic grievances among the wealthy, particularly the landowners: the trade unions and the cooperatives.[62] In their fury, particularly in the rural areas, it was not only trade unions and cooperatives under Socialist leadership against whom violence and terror were turned, but also those under Catholic leadership. It was not only the private organizations which the Fascists attacked. As it became evident that the government would not seriously intervene to put a stop to the violence, the terror was turned against the Socialist-administered municipalities. The armed bands, adequately supplied with motorized transport, planned mobile concentration of terrorist methods in widely scattered areas. Towns were occupied, municipal officials forced to resign or were simply replaced, the population harassed, the Socialist, trade union, and cooperative headquarters destroyed, its leaders beaten, shot, or forced into hiding. In Ferrara province, where the terror was extreme during this period, the Socialists had won majority control of all twenty-one of the communes in November 1920. By April 1921 only four were still in control of the Socialists and these too were divested of their control in the ensuing months. Over and over again, the national government, when faced with Fascist violence against Socialist municipalities issued a decree dissolving the 1920 election results "in the interests of public order," thus legalizing the Fascist actions.

The national government stood idly by as the terror mounted. It would appear that Giolitti was willing to have the Socialists taught a lesson. He also was looking forward to national elections which he hoped would cut sharply into Socialist strength and give him a dependable majority in Parliament, even perhaps with the collaboration of a chastened Socialist Party. Before the war he had been accustomed to an "economical" use of violence and chicanery in the conduct of elections to insure himself adequate support. These methods had been used exclusively in the south. Now he was willing to have them tried in the north by bands led by Mussolini whom he did not regard as a serious political threat. He regarded the Fascist bands simply as "his black and tans," as he is reported to have remarked to a high British official at the time.[63]

The Fascist movement in July 1920 had 108 branches. It had increased only to 200 in October. By the end of the year, after it had begun to flourish

62. For discussion of this point, see ibid., pp. 90–96, 101–102. For discussion of the Fascist terror during this period, see ibid., pp. 105–129.

63. Sprigge, Modern Italy, pp. 190–191.

in the post-occupation strike atmosphere, there were 800 *fasci.* Two months
later there were 1000, and by November 1921 there were 2300.

At the time of the Fascist Party's congress of November 1921, the secretariat of the party made an analysis of 151,644 out of its claimed 320,000
members which sheds light on the social structure of the Fascist movement
at the time. There were 18,084 landowners, 13,878 tradesmen, 4269 manufacturers, 9981 members of learned professions, 7209 state employees, 14,988
private employees, 1680 teachers and 19,783 students. These 90,000, as Rossi
comments were the militant part of the *fasci:* the financial backers, the
leaders, and active members of the punitive expeditions. In addition there
were 36,847 agricultural laborers, mostly members of local CGL unions
forced into the *fasci* by the *squadristi* offensive, and 23,418 nonagricultural
workers, mostly from the civil service, the unemployed dock workers, and
those districts under Fascist occupation. Rossi comments, "These occupations had brought the Fascists a windfall of 138 cooperatives and 614 workers' syndicates, with 64,000 members, two-thirds of them from Emilia,
Tuscany, and Veneto. The mass of the workers in the towns and even in
the country were paralyzed and in some cases completely subjugated, but
they remained loyal to their Socialist or Catholic organizations. At the
moment the squads provided the only real driving power of the Fascist
movement." [64]

The 1921 Congresses

It was against this background that both the Socialist Party and the CGL
held their congresses at Leghorn early in 1921. The Socialist Congress was
held in January. After the occupation strikes the party had not re-examined
its position in the changed situation. It had continued its rejection of any
cooperation in the government with the same attitude of "In the present
situation, the only result of taking power would be that the present responsibilities of the *bourgeoisie* would be transferred to the Socialists." [65]
It had continued to speak of the imminence of revolution and it continued
to look to a repetition in Italy of the circumstances of the Russian revolution.
The Socialists had applied for membership in the Communist International
but had run into a basic difficulty in its relations with Moscow. The Third
International had laid down twenty-one points which affiliates were required
to accept. The Italian Socialists had had no difficulty in accepting most of
the points. The Directorate of the party by a vote of seven to five approved
the entire list unconditionally.[66] On the other hand, Giancinto Menotti

64. Rossi, *Rise of Italian Fascism,* pp. 128, 163.
65. Serrati in *Avanti,* October 20, 1920. Quoted in Rossi, *Rise of Italian Fascism,*
p. 89.
66. Nenni, *Quattro anni,* p. 115. Text of 21 points in *ibid.,* pp. 113–117.

Serrati and others in the Maximalist leadership opposed the requirements that the Reformists be expelled from the party and that the party name be changed to "Communist." *Avanti,* which was run by Serrati at the time, commented, "The conditions placed by Moscow upon our party remaining in the Third International are undoubtedly extremely grave and those who have dictated them and who have approved them entirely have given proof of not being sufficiently informed of the conditions of our party and of Italy." The refusal to expel the Reformists was put on the grounds that the Reformists had already been expelled in 1912 and those led by Turati, who had been specifically named by Moscow with Kautsky, Hillquit, Mac-Donald as prime examples of those whom it wanted expelled, were disciplined members of the party who furnished an important contribution to the strength of Italian socialism and did not represent the threat which Moscow thought they constituted by their continued membership in the party.

The Socialist Congress was focused entirely upon this issue.[67] Moscow's representative, Kabaktchiev, a Bulgarian Communist, joined with Bordiga, Lazzari, and the Gramsci group from Turin in insisting that the Reformists be expelled. The Maximalists, led by Serrati, defended the Socialist Party as orthodox in its commitments to Communist objectives and tactics, but insisted that unity of the party must be maintained. The Unitary Communists, as the Maximalist faction called itself to distinguish itself from the pure Communists of Bordiga, insisted on their position even after Kabaltchiev made clear that if their position was maintained the pure Communists would break away and form a party recognized as the only Italian Communist party by Moscow. After several days of debate, the congress voted to sustain the Maximalist thesis, by a vote of 98,028 for the majority motion, 58,783 for the Bordiga motion and 14,695 for the motion of Turati's Concentrationists, as the Reformists called themselves. There were 981 abstentions.

The Communists announced their break with the party as soon as the voting results were known and met immediately to found the Italian Communist Party. The Socialist Congress adjourned with reaffirmations of its revolutionary faith. *Avanti* announced the termination of the congress with the lead in bold-faced type, "The inexorable will of Moscow has been fulfilled. The schism has sorrowfully come, but the Italian Socialist Party continues its labors for the cause of the revolution." [68] Faced with competition on the Left from the new Communist Party, the Socialist Party continued

---

67. For stenographic account of Congress, *see Resoconto stenografico del XVII Congresso Nazionale del PSI, Livorno, Gennaio 1921* (Milan, 1921). For summary, *see* Angiolini and Ciacchi, *Socialismo e Socialisti,* pp. 1307–1312; Cannarsa, *Il socialismo,* pp. 221–230; Nenni, *Quattro anni,* pp. 110–115; Meda, *Il socialismo,* pp. 117–128.

68. *Avanti,* January 22, 1921, quoted in Cannarsa, *Il socialismo,* p. 230.

its revolutionary bombast, without re-examining its position in the light of the rising Fascist assaults upon its movement.

The CGL Congress, its first in the postwar period, was held from February 26 to March 3, 1921. D'Aragona's report to the congress on the preceding several years was a sober review of the tremendous increase in strength of the organization against a background which he recognized as increasingly menacing to it.[69] Summarizing the achievements of the CGL, he pointed to the general program of social reorganization which had been outlined by the CGL National Council of January 1919 but which had been rejected by the Socialist Party because it was directed toward reform and not revolution. D'Aragona concluded:

it would be revealing less than the truth if we sought to hide or to attentuate a fact which is moreover most evident. This: that between the minimum and maximum — between the "little or nothing" which could have been grasped from the ruling classes and the "much or all" which the Socialist Party sought with the formula of the Communist republic through the dictatorship of the proletariat; the intermediate program of the Confederation remained without effect and instead was regarded by the Maximalists with diffidence if not with disdain.

After almost two years of armistice . . . after great political and economic strikes, it must be noted that there has been effectuated neither the minimum program, nor the intermediate program, nor the maximum program.

The report, in commenting upon the April 1920 Turin strikes, and the strikes during the second half of 1920, said, "This is not the place to make recriminations: we must, however, frankly say that if certain excesses, not always spontaneous, had been avoided, perhaps the worker conquests, the workers' strength, would have been much greater today than it actually is, and the reactionary tendencies would not have assumed the proportions which they have in these recent times."

The six days of the congress were almost entirely devoted to debate on the political issues surrounding the CGL policy.[70] During the first four days, the debate revolved around the general report on CGL activity. The Communists, led by Tasca, Misiano, and Repossi, were sharply critical of the leadership's failure to take advantage of what they described as the revolutionary opportunities presented during the previous years. D'Aragona, Buozzi, Baldesi defended the position of the organization and reviewed the background of the decisions taken. The occupation strikes, and the CGL decision to lead them back to legal objectives, was a particular point of acrimonious dissension. When the confidence motion was voted upon, the leadership was upheld by a vote of 1,435,873 against 422,558 for the minority

69. Rigola and D'Aragona, *La Confederazione* . . . *1914–1920*, p. 116.
70. See *Resoconto stenografico* . . . *1921*.

motion, with 17,371 votes abstaining.[71] The wording of the majority motion reflected the fact that the CGL leadership made common cause with the Maximalists in the organization's ranks in order to oppose the Communists. It also reflected the fact that even the moderate leadership had been strongly affected by the situation as it had evolved in Italy. The resolution, in approving the activity of the organization in general, permitted some reservations. It pointed to the growth of the organization, affirmed the need to emphasize the class struggle, reviewed with pride the fact that it had been the only trade union movement in the belligerent countries to oppose the war, that its "superior" situation resulted from its class principles and its cooperation with the Socialist Party; that it had made notable economic and moral gains of a revolutionary character contributing to "the process of the dissolution of the *bourgeois* regime"; and that only the CGL had given its full commitment to the Russian revolution and the Soviet regime.

The problem of relationship with political parties was of particular interest as a consequence of the Communist split from the Socialist Party two months before. The Communists took the position that political relationships should be subordinated to international relationships and that therefore the question of CGL cooperation with political parties should be made dependent upon the decision of the Communist International on recognition of the Communist Party alone and disposition of the question of Socialist Party affiliation. The congress, however, upheld unconditional cooperation with the Socialist Party, making no provision for cooperation with the Communist Party.[72]

The political atmosphere in which the CGL functioned and its impact upon the leadership of the organization was reflected in the debate at the congress on the subject of the CGL relationships and policies toward international organizations. The CGL had affiliated with the International Federation of Trade Unions (IFTU) almost immediately after CGL was established in 1906. It had participated in the Socialist-oriented IFTU until the First World War, when the International faced a major crisis as a result of the fact that all its affiliates in the belligerent countries, with the exception of the CGL, supported the cause of their own governments despite the repeated resolutions of the IFTU in earlier years against "imperialist" wars and the international solidarity of the working class.

The CGL, like the Italian Socialist Party, was proud of the unique distinction of having withstood the national appeal for cooperation in the war and of having remained faithful to the Socialist opposition to capitalist

71. For text of majority resolution *see ibid.*, pp. 264–265; for discussion see pp. 273–292. Text of opposing resolutions at pp. 278 and 285.

72. No formal vote was taken on the resolutions, the majority resolution being approved by acclamation. *Ibid.*, p. 292.

wars. The Italian experience, the manner in which Italy had come into the war, and its objectives in the war had served to reinforce their opinion. The success of the Russian revolution had had a tremendous impact upon the thinking of all Italian Socialists, including the CGL leadership. The widespread unrest and radicalization of the population in Italy, combined with the nationalist extremism and the weakness of the government had led even those who opposed violent revolution, like D'Aragona, to feel that insurrection was imminent in Italy in 1919, though they felt it had little chance of success.[73]

Even though they began to have doubts about the imminence of revolution by the end of 1919, events in Italy did not permit the CGL leadership to relinquish the conception of class struggle and hope of replacing existing society by a Socialist reorganization of economic and political institutions. This was partly a matter of "riding the wave as if it were their own." On the other hand, they had frequently opposed excesses and had spoken up courageously in criticism of Socialist maneuvers when they had disagreed with them. A basic premise upon which they had built the CGL had been the need for disciplined membership and responsible leadership. Buozzi had expressed the approach of the CGL leadership in his report to the FIOM Congress of November 1918. He had said:

We are resolutely against the theory that the organization and the organizer must always follow the masses even if unorganized. Such a theory renders useless the organization. It serves for the formation of rebels of an hour, but never of conscious revolutionaries, to organize on an impromptu basis thousands of workers easy to lead to the slaughter, but who disband immediately as soon as the agitation for which they were associated ends. The consciousness of the masses develops and is demonstrated as a result of perfected, enlightened and disciplined activity, which only through renunciation — which is sometimes a sign of strength — knows how to conquer and conserve to prepare itself for new conquest.

He then added, "We can, however, affirm one thing with tranquil certainty: that our movement, which is the movement led by the CGL, has not occupied 'all its consciousness' with the immediate problems of today but 'wants all of Socialism.' "[74] The CGL leadership was not as radical as its declarations sometimes made it appear, but it had firm convictions on the efficacy of class struggle and the desirability of social transformation. It is symptomatic of the frame of mind of the leadership during this period that even Buozzi, in a speech in Parliament in July 1920 said, "In other words,

73. For example, *Avanti*, July 3, 1919, quoted in Nenni, *Quattro anni*, p. 30.
74. Quoted in article by Luigi Carmagnola, "Bruno Buozzi" in *Almanacco Socialista 1946* (Milan, 1946?), p. 266.

we think that countries can be better administered and better directed, when they are run by Soviets rather than Parliament." [75]

When the IFTU was reorganized after the war, the CGL felt itself bound by its previous commitment to affiliation. During the Washington Conference of 1919 called to establish the International Labor Organization, disagreements had arisen among the worker delegations which resulted in a request to the IFTU signed by Baldesi of the CGL, Ilg of Switzerland, and Prauss of Poland asking that a special conference of the organization be called. The basis of disagreement was the desire of the CGL to have the IFTU and its affiliates commit themselves to the principle of class struggle and to socialization of the means of production. Involved, too, was the desire of the CGL that the League of Nations be repudiated by the unions as an imperialist government combination and the International Labor Organization as it had been established at Washington be repudiated because of the subordinate position given worker delegations and the lack of authority of the organization. [76]

Before the IFTU Conference was held in November 1920, several developments had intervened. D'Aragona, Bianchi, and Colombino of the CGL visited Moscow as part of a larger delegation which included Socialist Party and National Cooperative League representation. The purpose of the visit, in addition to seeing the new "Socialist Fatherland," was to establish relations with the new international Communist movement. The Socialist Party was expecting to join the Third International, and the CGL representatives participated in discussions which the Third International sponsored for setting up a Red trade union international. Such was the ideological confusion of the CGL at the time that D'Aragona signed — and the CGL Directive Council later approved — a resolution which not only decided upon the establishment of a Communist trade union international, but urged the Communist minorities in trade unions to work within those unions in order to get their program accepted. [77] There had not yet been a Communist split in the Italian Socialist Party. Under these circumstances, the CGL leadership apparently felt that they were only furthering their

75. *Battaglie Sindacali,* II, 29, July 22, 1920, p. 3. Such was the spirit and confusion of the times that the March 1920 Congress of the moderate Construction Workers' Federation voted adhesion to the Third International and had to be told by the CGL that only political parties could join. Rigola and D'Aragona, *La Confederazione . . . 1914–1920,* p. 62.

76. Text in L. D'Aragona and G. Baldesi, *X Congresso della Resistenza, V della Confederazione Generale del Lavoro, Livorno 1921, Rapporti Internazionali* (Milan, 1921), pp. 6, 45–46.

77. *Ibid.,* pp. 7–9. The resolution was also signed by representatives of the Russian trade unions, the CNT of Spain, the Bulgarian and Yugoslav unions and minority union groups in France and Georgia. See also D'Aragona's report on trip and discussion by CGL Directive Council at August 24, 1920 session in *Battaglie Sindacali,* II, 35, September 4, 1920, p. 3.

own cause in common with the Russians, since they would hardly have blessed a new organization which would support a minority against their own leadership in CGL.

At the Second Congress of the Communist International the twenty-one points were adopted as conditions for affiliation, and the dispute over expulsion of Reformists from the Italian Socialist Party began. Since the CGL national leadership was all in what Moscow defined as the Reformist category, their enthusiasm for the Moscow trade union resolution soon began to diminish. An open letter to the CGL from Losovsky of the Russian trade unions, after the occupation strikes, brought into focus the differences between the Russian conception of events and that of the CGL.[78] The letter violently attacked the CGL as an organization no different from the trade union organizations of other European countries which were described as the saviors of capitalism. "Who, in Italy, hindered the revolutionary movement so brilliantly initiated? Who formed the bipartite commissions? Who sought agreement with the *bourgeoisie* and disorganized the revolutionary movement of the masses? The *duci* of the CGL. All these are facts universally known. All these are the truth, though bitter."

The letter shocked the CGL leadership into a better realization of the nature of their new international alliance. They reacted in a manner which was customary in discussions in Italian political movements but which also cut their bridges to Moscow. Their open letter of reply[79] referred to the Losovsky letter as having "given us a remarkable demonstration that in your country . . . there is very scant understanding of our political trade union movement and the Socialist spirit which animates the leaders of our principal Italian worker organization." The letter set out the CGL justification for its actions in bringing the occupation strikes to a close:

The Russian comrades should in addition take into account that not all countries are Russia and that one method alone is not indicated for all. Theory suffers the restraints of reality. The Russian comrades may be unsurpassable masters in teaching us how to govern a people which has the history, psychology, strength of sacrifice of the Russian; they cannot teach us how to handle the working masses in countries with centuries of tradition in political democracy, a psychology of their own, habits of life completely different, very different possibilities of support.

The Russian comrades can give us most valuable information on the development of the revolution in a country with a backward capitalist economy such as that of Russia, with extensive and highly productive agriculture which it has the good fortune to possess, with rich subsoil of minerals which nature has placed

78. For text of Losovsky letter, *see* D'Aragona and Baldesi, *X Congresso . . . 1921*, pp. 11–19. Also given in *Battaglie Sindacali*, II, 45, November 20, 1920, p. 1.

79. Text in D'Aragona and Baldesi, *X Congresso . . . 1921*, pp. 21–29; and in *Battaglie Sindacali*, II, 45, November 20, 1920, pp. 1–2.

at their disposition: they cannot tell us how to socialize land which must be intensively cultivated and which must be rapidly industrialized, nor how industries are made to function where the necessary raw material must all be acquired abroad.

The letter reaffirmed the CGL claim to being in the lead among trade union movements in dealing with its own problems and in supporting the Soviet Union. The CGL position at the IFTU Conference, which began shortly after the exchange of letters with Losovsky, was to press that organization toward the left.[80] The resolution adopted by the conference fell far short of the CGL desire for the rejection of the ILO, of a clear-cut statement in favor of socialization and support for bringing the Russians into the organization. It did support the "struggle against capitalism and imperialism," the "fight against militarism in all its forms" and accepted the "general strike and international boycott as a potent and effective means of struggle." [81] On this basis the CGL leadership could justify its continued affiliation with the IFTU by claiming it had pushed the organization to the left.

The CGL leadership made it appear that it was willing to put its future international relations in the hands of the Socialist Party and the Third International, and that if the International accepted the Socialists, the CGL would join the Red Trade Union International even if this was incompatible with continued membership in the IFTU. Realistically, the CGL leadership knew by the time the CGL Congress was held that there was small chance indeed that the Third International, having forced a split in the Socialist Party and backed the Communists, would also recognize the Italian Socialists. At the CGL Congress the issue of international relationships was decided in favor of the formula presented by the leadership.[82] Its careful wording reflected the complications inherent in the situation as developed by the leadership, although the intent was clear. It provided for:

(a) Unconditional adherence to the initiative for the creation of the International of Red Trade Unions, with the commitment of preserving, however, the relations which the General Confederation of Labor has with the Italian Socialist Party and provided the principle of confederal unity be recognized for Italy;

(b) Separation from the Trade Union International of Amsterdam to follow the deliberations which will be taken at the Trade Union Congress of Moscow.

80. For text of memorandum circulated by CGL to the IFTU Conference setting out its recommendations and its analysis of political problems facing the trade unions, see D'Aragona and Baldesi, X Congresso . . . 1921, pp. 31–41.
81. For text, see Resoconto stenografico . . . 1921, pp. 43–44. The CGL resolution (ibid., p. 45) arrived too late to permit its consideration.
82. For the congress' discussion of the issue, see Resoconto stenografico . . . 1921, pp. 299–348 and 355–356.

As a matter of fact, the CGL never joined the Red Trade Union International. It sent representatives to the first congress of the organization in Moscow in July 1921 and was the only West European trade union movement officially represented. The position of the Russian leadership at the congress and the attitude toward the CGL and the Socialist Party made it easy for the National Council of the CGL in November to decide to continue affiliation with the IFTU.[83]

There was surprisingly little discussion of the Fascist terror at the 1921 CGL Congress. While references were made to it, the debates were focused so exclusively upon the general political issues of the past and of future political relationships, that the subject was not treated as a separate agenda item, nor was any resolution on the subject adopted. Yet the congress took place while Fascist violence was rapidly increasing in fury. In underestimating the significance of the Fascist movement, however, the CGL shared the misconceptions of the Socialists, the other political parties and the government that this was only a temporary reaction which would have no lasting significance.

Fascism Takes Power

Giolitti dissolved Parliament in April, calling for national elections on May 15, 1921 in the midst of terrorism which he had permitted as part of his political gamble. The elections, however, did not bear out his expectations. Despite the terrorization of entire regions in north central Italy and the formation of a national bloc which combined almost all political parties except for the Socialist, Communist and Popular parties, the people continued to vote in almost the same proportion for the extreme left and the *Popolari* as in the 1919 election. The Socialists had received 1,835,000 votes in 1919, while in 1921 they received 1,631,000 with the Communists receiving 305,000. Except where the Fascist terror was greatest, the Socialists had gained votes. The total parliamentary representation was reduced, however, from 156 deputies for the Socialists in 1919 to 123 deputies for the Socialists and 15 Communist deputies. The *Popolari*, whom Giolitti had hoped to be able to ignore in Parliament after the elections, increased their total vote from 1,167,000 in 1919 to 1,347,000 and their parliamentary representation from 100 to 108.[84]

It was the Fascists who gained most in the elections as a result of Giolitti's tactics. In the 1919 national elections, when Mussolini had run a

83. Ludovico D'Aragona, *La Confederazione Generale del Lavoro negli anni 1921– 1924, Rapporto del Consiglio Direttivo all' XI Congresso Nazionale della Resistenza, VI della Confederazione del Lavoro, Milano 1924* (Milan, 1924), p. 62.

84. *Compendio delle Statistiche . . . 1848 al 1934*, vol. II, Tables 44 and 47, pp. 118–119 and 130–131.

Fascist list in Milan alone, he had received only 5000 out of the 270,000 votes cast. He had taken revenge for his humiliation by arranging for a bomb which wounded nine people to be thrown by his *arditi* at a Socialist victory parade. While he had been arrested and it was demonstrated that he was behind the affair, prosecution was not pressed.[85] In the 1920 local elections, on the basis of his 1919 experience, Mussolini refrained from putting forward any Fascist candidates. In the 1921 election, on the other hand, running candidates as part of the national bloc, the Fascists elected thirty-five deputies, with Mussolini heading the Fascist list in Milan and Bologna. The Fascist movement now had a parliamentary base in addition to its *squadristi* strong-arm units.

The CGL had taken an active part in the electoral campaign, supporting the Socialist Party candidates.[86] The organization was by now in a battered state. The Fascist violence throughout north central Italy reached its highest point of fury during the election campaign. D'Aragona later wrote:

> The electoral battle also greatly affected our organizations. There was not only a political struggle involved. It was also and above all a trade union struggle. The existence and development of our institutions were in the center of it. The electoral campaign of the Fascists developed above all against our organizations which they wanted dispersed and destroyed. The burnings and devastations were intensified. The government stood idly by, impotent or uninterested.

The economic background against which the violence took place had already put the trade unions on the defensive. The economic crisis which had begun in the latter part of 1920 spread through the economy during 1921.[87] Considerable unemployment developed in the mechanical industries, chemical industry, construction, textiles, and leather. A large proportion of plants put their workers on a part-time basis. Large-scale unemployment also developed in agriculture, hit by the industrial crisis and the sharp fall in emigration. Employers, led by the Turin industries, took the offensive against the unions. Protest strikes at the FIAT and Michelin plants were defeated; there was no face-saving for the unions. In plants where only a few months before the red flag had been raised, "undesirables" were discharged with impunity. Gradually, a campaign got under way to reduce wages in those industries hit by the depression, where the unions had traditionally been strongest. Strikes to resist the wage decreases were generally lost. The strike rate, compared with the previous year, fell sharply during 1921. The combination of economic depression and Fascist violence

85. Rossi, *Rise of Italian Fascism*, pp. 39–40 and 83.
86. D'Aragona, *La Confederazione . . . 1921–1924*, p. 49. Pp. 50–51 also give the text of the CGL election manifesto.
87. *Ibid.*, pp. 16–35; Rossi, *Rise of Italian Fascism*, p. 128.

rapidly helped to destroy many of the gains made by the unions in the early postwar years.

In June the official publication of the National Employers' Confederation could write, "Those who follow the chronicle of labor disputes and agitations will easily recognize that for some time the tendency of the masses to be agitated and demand new conditions has notably diminished. The masses are more calm: this cannot be doubted. If one excepts protest movements following conflicts with the Fascist (and therefore of a political character) few other agitations are noted." [88] The issues of the publication during the latter part of the year, however, reported increased numbers of agitations caused by worsening economic conditions in which the unions generally lost.

The Socialist Party viewed the 1921 election results as a great victory over fascism. The headlines in *Avanti* read, "The Italian proletariat has buried the Fascist reaction under an avalanche of Red posters." [89] The Fascist violence continued at a high pitch after the elections, but though the Socialists had the renewed vote of confidence from the electorate, and had emerged again as the largest party in the country, they still continued to refuse participation in national affairs. The CGL urged Socialist support for a specific governmental program of public works, minimum wages, unemployment compensation, various other economic measures and particularly urged countermeasures by the government to end violence and re-establish law and order.[90] The Socialist parliamentary group adopted a similar set of recommendations. The Socialist Party vetoed all such efforts, continuing its policy of opposition to any government. For a short moment in 1921 it relaxed its intransigent opposition sufficiently to authorize the Socialist deputies to abstain from voting in the event that a successor government to Giolitti, who had been forced to resign after the elections, would propose sincerely to follow a policy of putting an end to violence. When Bonomi, the prewar Reform Socialist leader, presented his cabinet for parliamentary approval, however, the Socialist Party lost courage and overruled the CGL and the majority of the Socialist deputies, ordering a return to the principles of opposition.[91]

Mussolini, meanwhile, having benefited from Giolitti's cooperation in the election campaign, had turned against Giolitti and joined with the Socialists, *Popolari,* and others in voting Giolitti out of office. Mussolini at this time became concerned that the widespread violence was beginning to cause a sufficiently serious reaction in the country to be dangerous for his

88. Confindustria, *L'Organizzazione Industriale,* I, 7, June 15, 1921, p. 8.
89. Rossi, *Rise of Italian Fascism,* p. 130.
90. Nenni, *Quattro anni,* pp. 142, 143, and D'Aragona, *La Confederazione . . . 1921–1924,* pp. 17–22.
91. Tasca, *Avvento del fascismo,* p. 258, footnote 21.

movement. He began to urge moderation to his following. He also agreed to a so-called pacification pact with the Socialists and the CGL in which he agreed that no more violence would take place.[92] Mussolini's gesture affected the continued violence very little. The Fascist armed bands, especially those in the agricultural areas, continued their expeditions and began denouncing Mussolini. After making the gesture of resigning from leadership of the Fascist movement, Mussolini re-established his leadership shortly afterwards by repudiating his pacific injunctions and pledges. There was no longer any pretense that Fascist terror was being used because of the Bolshevik threat.

The Bonomi government, which took office in July 1921, did little to change the atmosphere of violence which pervaded the country or to counteract the serious depression into which the economy had plunged. The unions continued their retreat before the wage-reduction campaign of the employers and the violent destruction of their headquarters by the Fascists. Through the spring and early summer attempts were made to organize armed bands of workers, *arditi del popolo,* to protect the unions and Socialist organizations against the Fascist army. But they proved no match for the Fascists and although they continued to function during the following year, they never became a coordinated effective defense instrument. The Socialist Party, in fact, in its effort to separate itself from all violence or presumed provocation officially depudiated the *arditi del popolo* movement. The Communists had denounced the Socialists for the peace pact with Mussolini, claiming there could be no conciliation with fascism. On the other hand, as Rossi has pointed out:[93]

> To them everything was fascism: the state, the *bourgeoisie,* democracy, Socialism. All these had to be fought, and it "simplified" the struggle to lump them all together . . . Actually the Communists only fought seriously against the Socialists and won their victories in attempts to outbid them. The Communist Party even opposed its members joining the *arditi del popolo,* which they denounced as a *"bourgeois* maneuver" . . . the party as such practically kept out of the fight, and by its tactics did much to help the victory of fascism.

The increasingly desperate situation in which the trade union movement found itself caused the CGL leadership to increase its pleas to the Socialist Party to change its policy and use its parliamentary strength constructively. The CGL Agricultural Federation, hardest hit of all organizations, repeatedly begged for some action to reverse the process of its extinction. The CGL Directive Council forced the calling of a National Council session of the party in January 1922, to plead for the party to authorize its parliamentary group to throw its support toward the formation of any govern-

92. For text of pact *see* D'Aragona, *La Confederazione . . . 1921–1924,* pp. 11–14.
93. Rossi, *Rise of Italian Fascism,* p. 157.

ment which would "give guarantees of restoration of elementary liberties." [94] The eloquent pleas of the trade unionists, of the political fugitives from the Fascist occupied areas of the Po Valley, and of the parliamentary group were insufficient to dissolve the myopia of the party's leadership. The decision was taken to prohibit anything more than abstention of the parliamentary group.[95] Nenni, in commenting upon the negative decision of the party leadership has written,[96] "It would be an insult to say that the leaders of the party did not participate in the anguish of these fugitives and were not conscious of the gravity of the moment. But in them doctrinairism killed action, words overcame facts, punctiliousness of factions overwhelmed sentiment."

The trade unions continued urgently to plead for a change of party policy in the following months, but of no avail. The CGL sought to widen the cooperation among the trade unions to help in the defense of its organizations. In December 1921 it formed a pact with the independent railroad and port workers federations. Two months later an Alliance of Labor was formed among the CGL, the Revolutionary Syndicalist USI, the national Syndicalist UIL, and the railroad and port workers' federations. The purpose was to attempt better to resist the Fascist violence and the employer advances against labor standards. The Alliance was able to achieve very little.[97] Its one dramatic attempt to force the formation of a government guaranteeing civil liberties at the end of July 1922 came too late to have any effect upon that problem. The general strike called by the Alliance for this purpose was supported by the workers and succeeded in shutting down all industry. After announcing that he gave the government twenty-four hours to get the strikers back to work, Mussolini at the end of that period unleashed his own forces. To the extent that they could, the Fascist syndicates supplied strikebreakers. More effective was the violence and terror used by the Blackshirts throughout the strike areas. The strikers returned to work. The strike had succeeded only in provoking a greater wave of violence against the trade union organizations. Meda, in his history of Italian socialism, commenting on the general strike, has written:[98]

but the truth is that it was the last and greatest error committed by the Socialists; they did not take into account that after so much time of preaching violence and promises and threats of the imminence of proletarian dictatorship, after so many experiments of revolutionary general strikes in 1919, 1920 and 1921, the public

94. D'Aragona, La Confederazione . . . 1921–1924, p. 84. For discussion of CGL efforts to persuade the Socialist Party see ibid., pp. 82–97.
95. See editorial, "Party and Trade Union," in Battaglie Sindacali, IV, 13, March 30, 1922, p. 1.
96. Nenni, Quattro anni, p. 182.
97. D'Aragona, La Confederazione . . . 1921–1924, pp. 109–111.
98. Meda, Il socialismo, pp. 185–186.

spirit in the country was no longer disposed to listen with faith to a language such as that which was now used to justify such a serious and perturbing action; no wonder then that the strike failed completely after twenty-four hours under the rumbling of Fascist mobilization and which broke the action and reduced it to a miserable experiment of Red proletarian weakness, begun with so much ill will and with strength too reduced to hope for anything. Therefore, it can be said that that famous general strike of August 1 did nothing else than offer proof of Socialist impotence, and prepare the events of the end of October.

The trade union movement had played its last card and lost. The Alliance fell apart.

The Bonomi government had fallen in February 1922. A political unknown of little strength, Luigi Facta, was finally tapped for office and contributed further toward the disintegration of parliamentary government. The Socialist party meanwhile was being split apart by the debate over whether it should support or collaborate in forming a government pledged to put an end to the Fascist terror. By the beginning of June a majority of the Socialist parliamentary group voted to support the formation of a government guaranteeing basic liberties, threatening to do so even at the cost of a breach of party discipline.[99] The CGL again added its support to the view of the parliamentary group and pleaded, as it had so frequently during the previous months, for a change of party policy. The party National Council decision was in the negative, combined with a threat to expel any Socialist deputy who broke party discipline.[100] The cabinet crisis which began in July finally provoked the rebellion which had so often been threatened by a majority of the Socialist deputies. Sixty Socialist deputies decided to break party discipline and support a government formed for the purpose of reestablishing order in the country. The decision, however, came too late. The *Popolari* had already turned toward the right and the other parties were not interested. Early in 1921, abstention by the Socialist deputies instead of opposition might have been enough to isolate the Fascists. By February 1922 abstention would not have been enough, but affirmative support of a government would have been necessary to help solve the crisis and obtain a return to law and order. By July 1922 even support would not have been sufficient.[101]

Mussolini, always sensitive to political currents, had commented on the June Socialist National Council discussion, "In the meantime plenty of water

99. *Battaglie Sindacali,* IV, 24, June 25, 1922, p. 3; Meda, *Il socialismo,* pp. 167–169.
100. *Ibid.,* pp. 172–175; Rossi, *Rise of Italian Fascism,* pp. 199–201; Nenni, *Quattro anni,* pp. 197–200. For summary of the stenographic record of CGL National Council debate of July 3, 1922 which resulted in motion criticizing party National Council decision, *see Battaglie Sindacali,* IV, 27–28, July 13, 1922, entire issue. For resolutions, *see ibid.,* IV, 25, June 22, 1922, pp. 1–2.
101. Nenni, *Quattro anni,* p. 210.

is flowing under the bridges of the Tiber, and it is probable that the collaboration offered by the collaborationists will soon have so diminished in
value that they will not be able to find a dog to collaborate with them." [102]

Mussolini offered Parliament during the July cabinet crisis the choice of
Fascist participation in national life through "legal conquest and saturation"
or armed revolt against "anti-Fascist reaction." Parliament muddled
through with a reorganized Facta cabinet, even weaker than his previous
one. Mussolini and his followers had begun by then to talk of a "March
on Rome" and during the succeeding months such talk increased without
provoking any reaction from the government.

The Socialists were meanwhile playing out their tragic performance. At a
congress of the party in the first days of October, three weeks before fascism
took power, almost half of its membership was expelled because of its
"collaborationist" position, that is, its insistence upon collaboration with all
democratic forces willing to oppose fascism.[103] With the split in the party,
the CGL broke its pact of alliance with the Socialists and announced its
freedom of action on the political front.[104] None of these developments
mattered any longer. The Facta government, in the face of the growing
threat of violent seizure of power by Mussolini, decided to offer up its
resignation on October 27. With the increased tension and the Fascist
militia mobilizing in earnest, however, on the following day, before the
cabinet resignation had become effective, the Facta cabinet decided to declare martial law to defend the government against the imminent "March
on Rome." The King, however, decided not to authorize the decree. On
October 29 he invited Mussolini to Rome to form a cabinet. Fascism had
come to power.

For several years the hollow formal structure of democratic government
was maintained in Italy. Mussolini's first cabinet was a coalition government
in which the Popular Party and several minor political groups participated.
It was quite clear, however, that this was a government which would not
be subject to the usual democratic parliamentary controls. The majority of
the members of Parliament played out the farce by permitting the blessing
of constitutionality to be conferred upon Mussolini's government, even as
he made quite clear in his speech before Parliament to present his cabinet
for approval, his contempt for Parliament and the constitution.[105] Full
powers to govern by decree were voted by Parliament. Theoretically,

102. Quoted from *Popolo d'Italia,* June 15, 1922 in Rossi, *Rise of Italian Fascism,*
p. 201.
103. The vote at the congress was 32,106 to 29,119. The expelled minority factions
formed their own party, the Unitary Socialist Party. Nenni, *Quattro anni,* pp. 217–
218; Cannarsa, *Il socialismo,* pp. 245–251.
104. D'Aragona, *La Confederazione . . . 1921–1924,* pp. 98–99.
105. Panfilo Gentile, *Cinquant' anni di socialismo in Italia* (Milan, 1948), pp. 166,
179–183.

opposition parties, trade unions, and the press were permitted to function. But Mussolini had his state within a state, his Fascist Blackshirts, to see that the whittling away of these liberties continued without let-up. Intimidation and violence continued to serve as Mussolini's nonofficial arm in weakening further his battered and beaten opponents.

Late in 1923 the Popular Party withdrew from the government. Mussolini then forced through Parliament a new election law which would give two-thirds of the parliamentary seats to the election list receiving the greatest number of votes, and called elections for April 1924. Mussolini had repeatedly made explicit the fact that fascism would not tolerate opposition nor subject itself to democratic control. In the Senate, in June 1923, for example, he had said, "This government is described as the destroyer of liberty. It has been too generous. But one should not abuse this generosity. If it were necessary tomorrow, I have the courage, the will and the means to be able to spill blood which I have not wanted." The following month he said in the Chamber, "We have power and we keep it. We will defend it against anyone. Here is the revolution, in this firm will to maintain power."

Mussolini got his required number of votes in the April elections. With the terror, intimidation, and violence used against all opposition parties, it is surprising that these groups got 2,500,000 votes. Of the opposition parties, the *Popolari* received the largest number, almost 650,000. The two Socialist parties and Communist party got approximately 1,000,000 votes. When the new Parliament was convened, Giacomo Matteotti, the young secretary of the *Partito Socialista Unitario,* the party formed by the moderates expelled from the Socialist Party in October 1922, had the courage displayed by few others in the Chamber. He challenged the legality of Mussolini's government. In a stirringly eloquent oration, frequently interrupted by the Mussolini followers, he reviewed the crimes of fascism and the dictatorial nature of the regime, closing with dramatic gesture in the direction of his Socialist colleagues, "And now you can prepare my funeral oration."

Ten days later Matteotti was kidnapped and murdered. The profound reaction throughout the country forced Mussolini to permit a criminal investigation to run its course. The five Fascist strong-arm men directly involved were arrested. The unrest and excitement continued as the investigation continued and stopped short only "at the door of Mussolini's private office." Mussolini felt compelled to dismiss his press officer, his private secretary, the administrative secretary of the Fascist party, his Under-Secretary of State for Internal Affairs and his Director General of Public Security.

For six months the country's reaction to the assassination created uncertainty whether Mussolini might yet be forced out of office. The opposition parties took courage in forming a challenge to the government. Shortly after the Matteotti assassination, approximately one hundred and fifty opposition deputies met and decided to withdraw from the Chamber and to meet separately as a body. The Aventine Parliament, as the group was called, proved ineffective in crystallizing any course of action. It passed its time in giving voice to sound constitutional principles, without being able to agree on any specific program to turn the events in its favor. It had counted heavily upon the King to intervene and restore constitutional government, but no action was forthcoming from the crown.

Mussolini meanwhile simply waited. By the end of the year it was evident that the opposition had lost its opportunity to act. On January 3, 1925 Mussolini took the initiative. Toward the end of December, the Aventine group had obtained the publication of a memorandum by Cesare Rossi, a Fascist official involved in the Matteotti murder. The memorandum gave details of the background of the Matteotti murder as well as many others committed by the Fascists during the preceding years. Mussolini appeared to be directly implicated and it was the hope of the Aventine deputies that he would not now be able to avoid a trial. On January 2 some of Mussolini's more moderate cabinet ministers resigned. Mussolini broke the deadlock the following day. In an address to Parliament, he belligerently asked if anyone desired to invoke impeachment proceedings. After denying any specific participation in the Matteotti assassination, he nonetheless assumed full responsibility for it and all the other acts of violence:

I declare here before this assembly and before the entire Italian people that I and I alone assume the political, moral, historical responsibility for all that has happened. If Fascism has been nothing but castor oil and truncheons and not, rather, a superb passion of all the best Italian youth, the fault is mine. If Fascism has been an association for committing crimes, then I am the head of the association and responsible. If all the violence has been the result of a specific historical, political, and moral climate, I have created the climate with my propaganda from the time of our intervention in the war until today . . . There has come the moment when one says: enough. You can be certain that within forty-eight hours of this speech the situation will be clarified in every respect.[106]

From that time on no pretense of democracy was maintained. The government gradually took on a totalitarian character. During the next two years the opposition parties were disbanded, press freedom officially abolished, the trade unions suppressed. The Fascist state was established.

The CGL had lost half its membership during 1921 and by the time Mussolini took power, its membership had been whittled down to approximately 400,000. Despite the continued difficulties, the trade unions tried to function. Increasingly, however, collective agreements were repudiated and disregarded. The Fascist syndicates had been started during the 1921–1922 period as an additional means of obtaining support for Mussolini's

106. *Ibid.*, pp. 202–203.

movement, and had been used frequently for strike-breaking purposes. By the end of 1922 they still only claimed 200,000 members, undoubtedly an exaggerated figure. During 1923 and 1924 the employer associations in some industries began to sign agreements with the Fascist syndicates, however small a proportion of the workers they represented, to the exclusion of all other unions. The electrical industry, branch line railroads, construction industry in Turin, metallurgical industry of Lombardy were among those who began setting the pattern.[107] The CGL protests were of little avail, and the weakness of the CGL unions by that time, combined with the threats of reprisals and extinction, precluded any effective strike action. On the other hand, economic recovery had begun during the middle of 1922 and rapidly gained momentum during the following several years. As a result, while wages were still cut during 1923, by 1924 they had begun to rise again. The agreements of the Fascist syndicates, however, cut into the protective standards which had been established over the years by the CGL and the other free unions.

The CGL national leadership attempted on several occasions during 1923 and 1924 to obtain commitments from Mussolini to permit trade union freedom and to cease the violence against the CGL organizations. His polite words were scant consolation for the precarious existence of the unions as nonofficial suppression continued. Ineffective as it was, only the tragic situation reached in 1924 made it possible for the CGL and the CIL to bury their ideological differences enough to form a joint Trade Union Committee, including also the UIL, Confederation of Bank Employees, and National Union of Clerical Workers. The committee drew up a joint declaration in which the organizations pledged themselves to defend and seek guarantees of trade union liberty and equal treatment of all trade union groups. Under the prevailing circumstances the committee could accomplish nothing and soon was forgotten. In its effort to stay alive, the CGL tried to avoid any political involvements and concentrated instead upon the problem of trade union rights.[108] This was, of course, impossible to achieve in view of the thoroughly Socialist orientation of its membership and leadership, and, more important, the fact that its objective of continued existence and independence depended entirely upon the political situation. The efforts at political neutrality thus took a somewhat ambiguous form. For example, in the 1924 political elections the CGL affirmed that it was "apolitical" and that therefore its members were free to follow their own consciences. It added,

107. D'Aragona, *La Confederazione . . . 1921–1924*, pp. 172–176; 206–207; 292–299.
108. *See, for example,* text of speech by D'Aragona delivered in Parliament the month after Mussolini came to power, *Battaglie Sindacali,* IV, 45, November 23, 1922, p. 1. The same issue carried text of CGL Directive Council resolution on trade union freedom.

however, that the existence of the organization depended upon the existence of civil liberties.[109] The basic fact was that the CGL could not help but be anti-Fascist and this was evident in all its activities, even when it tried to avoid flaunting its attitude toward the regime.

The CGL held its last congress in December 1924. It was a somber and depressed session.[110] None of the factions, the dominant Confederalists, the Maximalists, or the Communists, saw any hope for improvement in the immediate future. They spent most of the sessions in debates over the policy followed by the leadership and resorted to the usual invective and vituperation. It was obvious to all of them, however, that the organization had already been destroyed, and as D'Aragona had written in the conclusion of his report to the congress, "Today, democracy is suffocated; dictatorship and violence are in power. Pain and torment oppress the proletariat and the country. Liberty which appeared already securely conquered, has begun again to be an aspiration. Thought is imprisoned, the club is in style. The idea is dominated by the revolver, the brute overcomes the thinker. The intoxicating spirit of hate continues to be squeezed from the soil of Italy. Civilization appears submerged." [111]

For all practical purposes the right to strike had ceased to exist in 1925, and agreements still signed with CGL unions were a rarity. In October of that year in an agreement which became known as the Pact of Palazzo Vidoni, the General Confederation of Industry and the Confederation of Fascist Corporations agreed that the latter organization would be the exclusive representative of workers. The pact also agreed upon the suppression of the internal commissions in plants. In April 1926 a further step was taken toward confirming the suppression of free trade unions with the enactment of legislation prohibiting the right to strike. The ghost of the CGL hung on for some months more. Buozzi had replaced D'Aragona as general secretary in January 1926, but before the end of the year he was forced to flee into exile. Battista Maglione, the last secretary general, presided over the Directive Council when it decided on January 4, 1927, to confirm the fact that the confederation had ceased to exist.

The Minority Trade Union Groups

The CGL faced competition from several other trade union organizations during the postwar period, the Catholic organization *Confederazione Italiana dei Lavoratori* (CIL), the Anarcho-Revolutionary Syndicalist

109. D'Aragona, *La Confederazione . . . 1921–1924*, p. 315.

110. For stenographic record, *see Resoconto stenografico ed atti dell' XI Congresso della Resistenza, VI della Confederazione Generale del Lavoro, Milano, 10, 11, 12, 13 Dicembre 1924* (Milan, 1925).

111. D'Aragona, *La Confederazione . . . 1921–1924*, pp. 458–459.

Unione Sindacale Italiana, and the National Syndicalist *Unione Italiana del Lavoro.* The activity and organization of the CIL was discussed in the last chapter.

The Revolutionary Syndicalists, as an earlier chapter has discussed, had not followed a consistent policy toward affiliation with the CGL during the first six years after the formation of that organization. Many of the unions led by Revolutionary Syndicalists during that period constituted a minority opposition within CGL, while others were independent.[112] The Revolutionary Syndicalist-controlled Chambers of Labor of Piacenza, Mirandola, and Ferrara were affiliated with the CGL. The Chamber of Labor of Parma, the most important of the Syndicalist-controlled Chambers, was independent, as were minority organizations in many centers including Rome and Savona. The *Comitato di Azione Diretta* (Direct Action Committee) which functioned until 1912 as the coordinator of Revolutionary Syndicalist activity had no clear-cut position on the issue of affiliation with CGL and the committee itself was in fact almost exclusively a propaganda machine.

The issue had been brought to a head at a convention of the organizations belonging to the *Comitato* held at Parma on March 31, 1912. The convention provided for greater coordination and established the requirement of dues payment to the *Comitato.* The CGL reacted with the announcement that *Comitato* affiliation would from then on be regarded as inconsistent with CGL affiliation. As a result, the Revolutionary Syndicalists set up their own organization, the *Unione Sindacale Italiana,* at a congress held at Modena in November 1912. Organizations claiming a membership of 80,000 joined the new organization. The most important were the national railroad union, affiliating for 25,000 members and the Parma Chamber of Labor with 18,000 members. At the time of its December 1913 Second Congress, the USI claimed a membership of over 100,000.

The USI, unlike the CGL, had serious internal difficulties and was badly split as a result of the war. The railroad union had already disaffiliated before the war broke out in Europe. USI had joined with CGL, the railroad and seamen unions, and the Socialist Party in opposing Italy's entrance into the war.[113] On the other hand, many of USI's most prominent leaders rejected the official position of the organization and supported the war. The USI found its most important Chamber, at Parma, a center of prowar sentiment. Its Milan *Unione* also had to be expelled because of its prowar position. The Anarchists, who had joined the Revolutionary Syndicalists within the USI, increased their influence in the organization as a result of the widespread break-aways growing out of dissension over the war, but the

112. For discussion of this issue and 1912 organization developments, *see Statistica delle organizzazioni . . . 1912,* pp. 10–12.

113. Angiolini and Ciacchi, *Socialismo e Socialisti,* pp. 1139–1140, 1174–1190.

organization remained predominantly Revolutionary Syndicalist. An Anarchist, Armando Borghi, headed the organization during most of the war and postwar period.

In the immediate postwar period the USI shared in the tremendous increase in trade union membership which characterized those years. By 1919 it claimed 500,000 members. Early in 1919 the Socialist Party made unsuccessful efforts to obtain the unification of CGL and USI. The CGL was willing to admit USI organizations, but USI refused, insisting upon a reorganized movement, not absorption into the CGL.[114] The USI, with its direct action philosophy, its favorite tactics of sympathetic general strikes and demonstrations, found the atmosphere of 1919 and 1920 very congenial for its own activity. Although gradually disillusioned with the Russian revolution and the anti-libertarian nature of the Soviets and their dictatorship of the proletariat, they favored revolution and criticized the Socialists principally for their failure to translate their words into action.

As had been the case before the war, the USI had its greatest influence in the rural areas of the Po Valley, but relatively little strength in such industrial centers as Milan or Turin. As a result it played a relatively unimportant role in the great industrial disputes of the time. In the occupation strikes, for example, while it supported the occupations and criticized the CGL and Socialists for not turning the strike into a revolution, it was not invited to participate in the deliberations on the issue, nor was it influential enough to affect the outcome.[115] Its violent threats to sabotage all efforts at settlement and its continued agitations after the settlement, resulted, however, in the arrest of the entire National Council of the organization.

The trade unionists who had favored Italian participation in the war had added a strong nationalism to their Syndicalist orientation. Toward the close of the war, in May 1918, they organized a trade union center, the *Unione Italiana del Lavoro*. The UIL, in addition to the prowar Syndicalists included similar-minded Socialists and Republicans. The organization's program repudiated any relationship with political parties. It declared itself opposed to capitalism, and in favor of worker management of production, distribution, and exchange, and insofar as the nation was concerned, the working class "should not reject it, but conquer it."[116] In January 1919 it claimed 162,000 members. While it expanded considerably during the following two years, it remained approximately in the same position as the USI, a minority movement dwarfed by the CGL. During 1919 and 1920 the

114. Borghi, *L'Italia tra due Crispi*, pp. 142–143; Rigola and D'Aragona, *La Confederazione . . . 1914–1920*, p. 15. For discussions of unity during 1918, *see Confederazione del Lavoro*, XII, 411–412–413, December 16, 1918, p. 961.

115. For detailed, partisan discussion of USI position and activities during the occupation, *see* Borgi, *L'Italia tra due Crispi*, pp. 248–296, 319.

116. Sacco, *Storia del sindacalismo*, pp. 231–232, for text of program.

UIL rejected some of the more extreme activities in which the Socialists indulged, but remained a militant Left trade union group. The first postwar occupation strike was successfully led by the UIL in 1919 at a small metallurgical plant in Dalmine over the issue of half holiday on Saturday. It was the tricolor and not the red flag which the union raised over the plant during its occupation. In addition, at the victory meeting after the strike it was Mussolini who was invited to speak.[117] It will be recalled that during this period Mussolini was combining nationalism with socialism and the UIL found the combination closer to its own approach than that of the Socialist Party.

When Mussolini's fascism turned to the Right and undertook its offensive toward the end of 1920, the UIL repudiated any relationship to fascism and continued with its mildly radical program. In the process, however, it lost some of its leadership which continued the route followed by Mussolini into fascism.[118] Indeed both the UIL and USI, with their Syndicalist origins, were the organizations from which the Fascist Syndicalist leadership was heavily drawn. The organizations, however, opposed fascism, resisted its aggressions in the same manner as CGL and CIL, and were destroyed by it.

Throughout the years between the war and the complete destruction of free unions there was considerable talk of trade union unification. After the failure of the January 1919 efforts to achieve unification of the CGL and USI, the difference in approach to unification precluded any efforts from getting very far. At the 1921 CGL Congress a resolution on the subject was adopted which reflected the CGL approach: it invited the USI, the Railroad Federation, and the Seamen's Federation to join the CGL.[119] As the trade unions were placed increasingly in the position of defending their very existence, they experimented with cooperative efforts, but these were of little avail. The Labor Alliance of 1922, which brought the CGL, UIL, USI, port and railroad workers together, fell apart, as we have seen, after the July 31 general strike. The alliance of desperation among the CGL, CIL, and UIL in 1924 came so late that it could not affect the completion of the destruction of the free unions.

The Communists, who were to make so much of labor unity in the period after fascism, played an equivocal role during the crucial period of the rise of fascism. They had split the Socialist Party in January 1921 in obedience to the tactical directives of the Third International. In the trade union field, they had remained within the CGL, focusing their principal fire

---

117. Rossi, *Rise of Italian Fascism*, p. 26.

118. For example, Edmondo Rossoni, the first UIL secretary general, left the organization in 1920 to set up *sindacati economici* at Ferrara, the first nucleus of the future Fascist syndicates which Rossoni later headed. "L'Unione Italiana del Lavoro del 1918," in *Lettere ai Lavoratori*, nos. 6–7 (June–July 1952), pp. 410–411.

119. *Resoconto stenografico . . . 1921*, p. 296.

against the CGL leadership and their principal efforts were directed towards enlarging their own influence. The evaluation made by the Communists during 1921 and 1922 of the rising Fascist terror precluded any serious contribution from them either toward unity or in the fight against fascism. In April 1922 the Communist evaluation of the tragic events of those years as described in their official journal was, "If the *bourgeoisie* brings it off and white reaction strangles social democracy, it will create the most favorable conditions for its own defeat and for the victory of the revolution." [120] Even their verbal extremism in opposing fascism, and whatever meager actions they on rare occasions participated in, were tempered during that period by their concentrated criticisms of the Socialists and the CGL leadership.[121] After fascism had taken power, during the twilight years before complete suppression was imposed, the Communists made much of their desire for unity among the trade unions. The tactical line of international communism had changed. Unity of action was the order of the day. It was clear, however, from the conditions set and approach taken by the Italian Communists that unity in the terms the Communists put it was simply a propaganda position enunciated for extending their own influence inside and outside the CGL and not a practical proposal for which they sought implementation.[122]

Despite the tactics of the Communists and their efforts to widen their influence in the trade union movement, they represented less than 15 percent of the strength of the CGL at its last congress in December 1924. When the CGL leadership gave up its efforts to keep the organization alive, the Communists had control of only three minor Federations, the woodworkers, the clerical workers, and the hotel and restaurant workers.[123]

It was the shutting down of the CGL in January 1927 which gave the Communists their opportunity to lay claim to leadership of the organization which no longer could function in Italy. Accusing the CGL leadership of treason, the Communists called a secret conference of party members and sympathizers who had had influence in various Chambers of Labor and Federations in Milan on February 20, 1927. Care was taken to include representation of some Socialists who disagreed with the CGL decision of January. The Communist-sponsored conference decided to continue CGL as a clandestine organization amid clamorous condemnation of the old leadership. It mattered little that the organization in fact could not have any life of its own and that under the totalitarian conditions which prevailed, could

---

120. *Rassegna Comunista*, no. 2, April 15, 1922, p. 59, quoted in Rossi, *Rise of Italian Fascism*, p. 176.

121. D'Aragona, *La Confederazione, 1921–1924*, pp. 57–58.

122. *See, for example,* Communist-proposed resolution at 1924 CGL Congress in *Resoconto stenografico . . . 1924*, pp. 160–161, 166.

123. Giorgio Candeloro, *Il movimento sindacale in Italia* (Rome, 1950), pp. 129–131.

not even carry on any continuing clandestine activity. The Communists had succeeded, where they had failed under democratic conditions, in laying claim to the CGL organization and its tradition among the Italian workers. The appeal launched by the Milan conference of February 1927 proclaimed:

The enemies of the working class have announced with loud shouts of joy the shutting down of the General Confederation of Labor. In reality, there is involved only the desertion of some of the leaders who for a long time have been strangers to the struggles and the aspirations of the proletariat and traffickers with the enemy class. This desertion is that much more shameful since it coincided with the suppression of the proletarian parties and press and with the imprisonment and deportation of thousands of anti-Fascist workers. The National Federations, meeting in convention, give the lie to the *bourgeoisie* for their premature joy and call upon the Italian workers of all categories to gather around the glorious old General Confederation of Labor which has never been the private and transferable patrimony of any leader or any party, but has been and remains the trade union organization in Italy of the Italian proletariat open to all workers and all the political factions of the class struggle. In its offices, at last, the servants of the Blackshirts have no more posts.[124]

The mortgage was to be collected after the fall of fascism.

Buozzi, attempting to carry on in exile in France on behalf of the CGL former leadership, refused to recognize the legitimacy of the Communist maneuver. There ensued a period of rival claims to legitimacy in the use of the name of the Confederation. As the Communists went through the tactical shifts laid down in the Third International, their "CGL" followed suit. Buozzi meanwhile carried on the CGL Socialist tradition. The Communist organization, affiliated with the Red Trade Union International, became the Communist apparatus in the labor field. To the extent that clandestine activity was possible in Italy during those years, the Communists carried forward the directives which by 1929 required working within the Fascist syndical structure.[125]

After the united front tactic was decided upon by Moscow in the middle thirties, the Communists negotiated for unity with the Buozzi group in Paris. In 1936 they announced agreement upon the principle of trade union unity, which was put into practice as fascism began to crumble several years later.

124. Quoted in article by Celso Ghini in *Lavoro*, II, no. 26, June 26–July 3, 1949, p. 10.

125. *Idem;* Candeloro, *Il movimento sindacale*, pp. 130–139; Giorgio Candeloro, "Il movimento sindacale in Italia-La Lotta contro il Fascismo," *Lavoro*, IV, 42, October 13, 1951, p. 11.

CHAPTER VI

The Trade Union Movement
After Fascism

Fascism in Italy came to an inglorious end after twenty years of totalitarian rule. It was finally buried under the holocaust of a war fought on Italian soil for two years, with the destruction and dislocations which are the inevitable concomitant of warfare. The German occupation in the north with its puppet Fascist Social Republic gave the Italian people an opportunity to redeem themselves in their own esteem and that of the world through their heroic partisan underground activity.

As the reconstruction went forward in the immediate postwar years, the anticipation of social and economic renovation which had characterized the spirit of the times gradually hardened into frustration. The efforts to build a more satisfactory society within the framework of both the new democratic political institutions and the old economic institutions were a far cry from the new world which had been envisioned by the underground partisans and the majority of industrial and agricultural laborers.

After the Second World War, as in the period immediately following the First World War, the hope for change in social and economic relations evaporated when confronted with reality. The special problem faced in the forties was the strength of communism which threatened the new democratic institutions of postwar Italy. The Communist Party, long after it lost its immediate bid for power by election in 1948, continued to have the largest membership of any Communist Party in non-Soviet countries. Indeed in the national elections of 1953 and of 1958 it improved its position over that of the 1948 elections. It continued to control numerous large-scale organizations in a wide variety of fields from veterans' organizations to cooperatives, from youth organizations to sport clubs, from women's organizations to trade unions.

The trade union movement was a principal arena for the struggle between the new totalitarian forces and the democratic elements opposed to them. The Communists had early been able to gain predominance within the unified trade unions which rapidly developed after the Fascist collapse. They continued to represent the largest force after the trade unions were split into competing groups. Competing democratic organizations began to form, however, which hoped eventually to overcome worker preference for the Communist-dominated movement.

This chapter will review the development of the trade union movement in the early post-Fascist period, while the chapter following will amplify the specifically political elements which affected the character of the movement and conditioned its evolution.

The Emergence of the CGIL

Background to unity. As the fortunes of war turned against the Axis powers during 1942 and 1943, the Fascist regime in Italy increasingly faced an internal crisis of its own. Discontent began to take overt form in industrial areas of the north. During the last months of 1942 ten strikes took place, most of them in Milan and Turin. There were eleven more during the first two months of 1943. These were a prelude to the more widespread strike movement which started on March 6 at the principal FIAT plant in Turin and spread throughout Piedmont and Lombardy in the succeeding weeks. While the strike movement was broken by the middle of April and those identified as strike leaders were arrested, the strike had important repercussions. The Fascist regime felt compelled to make economic concessions to the workers in order to decrease the rising discontent. The hitherto modest anti-Fascist political underground saw its opportunity to increase the tempo of its activity and spread its influence. For the Communists, whose underground had been weak and restricted, the strike movement had offered an opportunity for extension of their influence among the industrial workers of the north and this too had important repercussions on their relative position in later years.[1]

While the regime succeeded in clamping down upon the illegal strikes in the north, its position was an increasingly serious one. With its troop commitments in other areas of Europe and its serious losses in North Africa, it was evident that Italy would be unable to defend itself against the expected Allied invasion, even with the help of the divisions the Germans had begun sending to the country. It became increasing evident, too, that the Italian population was hostile to the Axis. Discontent was rising rapidly in the army and even in the Fascist party itself. By July, when the Allied invasion of Sicily started, Mussolini felt compelled to convoke the Fascist Grand Council for the first time since 1939. The council took the situation into its own hands and voted by a two-thirds majority to have Mussolini deposed, asking the King to use his constitutional authority "to take over the actual command of all armed forces . . . and the supreme initiative of decision." [2]

1. Aldo Garosci in *Communism in Western Europe* (Ithaca, 1951), pp. 179–180, joint authors: Mario Einaudi, Jean-Marie Domenach, and Aldo Garosci.
2. For text, *see* Ivanoe Bonomi, *Diario di un anno* (*2 Giugno 1943 — 10 Giugno 1944*) (Milan, 1947), pp. 30–32. Bonomi's diary is a careful account of the developments in Rome from June 1943 to June 1944. *See also* Muriel Grindrod, *The New Italy* (London & New York, 1947), pp. 4–5. The Grindrod book is an excellent brief account of Italian developments during the period of 1943 through 1946.

On July 25 Mussolini was arrested and Marshall Pietro Badoglio was asked by the King to form a government.

The Fascist regime had ended. But Italy had begun a period of chaos and turmoil. Those involved in the high level manipulation which had resulted in Mussolini's deposition and the Badoglio government which took over from fascism were poles apart from the anti-Fascist underground forces and anti-Fascist political exiles who had plotted for years to bring about the downfall of fascism. In addition, the events of July 25 did not result in the end of the war for Italy, but only the beginning of two years of warfare on Italian soil.

The Badoglio government, during the forty-five days that it governed all Italy, continued the formal ban on political parties, although it made no serious effort to enforce it. Prohibition against the starting of new news-papers was continued, but no control was exercised over pre-existing papers, which now took on an anti-Fascist coloration. The political party ban was continued, but in semi-legality the parties opposed to fascism came out into the open, and in Rome a central committee of anti-Fascist forces was set up with representatives from the six principal parties (the Communist, Socialist, Action, Christian Democratic, Liberal and Democratic Labor), presided over by Ivanoe Bonomi, the pre-Fascist Reform Socialist leader.[3] The announcement of the signing of the armistice with the Allies on September 8 precipitated the situation which had been feared since the deposition of Mussolini. The Germans occupied Rome and rapidly took over the territories not yet occupied by the Allies. The Allies were not in a position to prevent the Germans from establishing their authority over most of Italy. The Badoglio government fled south, Mussolini was freed by the Germans and set up a new Fascist regime, the so-called Italian Social Republic at Salò, but the Germans were the effective masters and Mussolini simply their puppet.

The long period of slow gradual liberation of Italy began. In Rome the six-party committee continued to meet, underground, under Bonomi's chairmanship, as the Committee of National Liberation (CLN).[4] This was to become the central committee of the CLN's as they were established in the liberated areas of the south and in the underground of the north, although until Rome was liberated by the Allied forces in June 1944, little coordination was in fact possible.

With the background of Fascist suppression and the pressures of the period after the German occupation of Rome, it was automatically felt that cooperation among the anti-Fascist forces was necessary. As resistance developed in the north and the partisan movement became an increasingly

3. Bonomi, *Diario di un anno*, pp. 43–44.
4. *Ibid.*, p. 100.

effective force, coordination among the political groupings and among the resistance forces themselves became a primary requisite for operations. The CLN's in the north performed the coordinating function in each locality, under the general direction of the Committee of National Liberation for Northern Italy (CLNAI) in Lombardy. Most active in the underground were the Communists, Socialists, Christian Democrats, and the Action Party, who, together with the Liberals, formed the committees.

The Action Party achieved a special place for itself by virtue of its leadership of the military partisan units which it inspired. Made up mainly of intellectuals dedicated passionately to the anti-Fascist cause, the Action Party was the linear descendent of the *Giustizia e Libertà* movement organized by Nello Rosselli and others during the thirties as a republican, democratic, mildly Socialist anti-Fascist force. While the Communists excelled in their organization and influence among the industrial workers who were drawn into the resistance and looked toward domination of mass movements after the war, the Action Party militants offered selfless devotion to the cause of liberation and achieved a prestige far beyond the actual control and influence they exercised.

The underlying theme in the resistance, as in the liberated areas, was cooperation among all anti-Fascist forces for purposes of liberation and eventual reconstruction.

The trade union Pact of Rome. In the labor field unity among all trade unions in the post-Fascist era seemed a natural step. The lack of unity in the period after the First World War was blamed for failing to prevent fascism from coming to power. Cooperation among workers of different ideologies was an obvious necessity in the underground of the industrial establishments of the north. The postwar objectives of reconstruction, reinforcing democratic institutions and defending the rights of wage earners, loomed larger than the ideological and political differences which had traditionally split organized labor into competing and antagonistic groups.

The three political groups with traditional claims in the trade union sphere, the Socialists, Communists and Christian Democrats, were agreed upon the desirability of unity. The Communists had, since 1934, except for the interval of the German-Soviet pact, been following the tactic of the united front. They were committed to all-out cooperation in the war against the Axis since the German attack on Russia, and unity was a natural objective for them. The control of mass organizations was a basic tactical objective, which might afford at best a background for the establishment of a "Peoples' Democracy" and at the least give them vital influence in the life of the country. The Socialists had been committed to unity of action with the Communists on the political front since 1934, and the trade union front since 1936, except for the period of the German-Soviet pact. The Socialists confidently expected to be the largest of the three mass parties on the basis of their traditional support from wage earners. Bruno Buozzi as Socialist trade union chief was more realistic than most of the Socialist political leaders in his understanding of the Communists, but the spirit of the times and the immediate pressures of the problems which would face the new trade unions made anything other than unity in the trade union movement seem a violation of democratic expectations. The Christian Democrats in turn, with somewhat more reservation than the others, were also convinced of the desirability of trade union unity and political cooperation.

Before trade union policy became more than a theoretical exercise, a short-lived opportunity developed for testing cooperation. Marshall Badoglio's government, upon assuming office, moved in the direction of democratizing the Fascist syndicate organizations. He removed the leaders of the syndicate Federations and named anti-Fascist trade unionists of various political hues as commissioners to reorganize and run the organizations. The Italian prisons were the most fruitful source of talent for the posts. Buozzi, who had been turned over to the Italians after being arrested by the Germans in France, was among those released in the aftermath of July 25. He was named commissioner of the Fascist Confederation of Industrial Workers. By arrangement between the political factions and the government, the responsibilities were shared among the three political elements with principal claims in the labor field. Giovanni Roveda, a Communist veteran of many years in Fascist prisons, and the Christian Democrat Gioacchino Quarello were named vice commissioners under Buozzi. Similarly, Achille Grandi, the pre-Fascist head of the Catholic Textile Workers' Federation and last secretary general of the CIL, was named commissioner of the Fascist Confederation of Agricultural Workers, with a Socialist and a Communist named as vice commissioners. Each of the other syndical Confederations was handled in the same way. Buozzi headed a committee of the various commissioners to coordinate the Confederations. While the committee of anti-Fascist forces criticized the Badoglio government and condemned it both for its continued prosecution of the war on the side of the Nazis and failure to create conditions of real liberty in the country, it decided, with some hesitation, to permit Buozzi and the others to hold the commissioner posts. The posts were to be filled on the condition that democratization be permitted, the syndicates reorganized into genuine trade unions, and free elections held.[5]

During the few weeks that elapsed before the Germans occupied Rome and all north and central Italy, little was accomplished in the proposed revamping of the Fascist syndicates into democratic unions. There was too little time for the political factions among the anti-Fascist commissioners to work out arrangements for continuing cooperation. The one significant ac-

5. *Ibid.*, pp. 74–76; Giorgio Candeloro, *Il movimento sindacale in Italia* (Rome, 1950), p. 140.

complishment of the period was the negotiation of an agreement between Buozzi and Mazzini, the commissioner of the industrial employers' Confederation (*Confidustria*) providing for the re-creation of internal commissions for the handling of grievances in all industrial plants. By contrast with the selection of internal commission members before fascism, the Buozzi-Mazzini agreement provided that all workers — not only trade union members — would participate in the plant elections, and that the principle of proportional representation would be applied.[6] There was no opportunity at the time to apply the agreements signed less than ten days before the German occupation. It was recognized and applied, however, when this later became possible and, while it was modified in some respects in later years, it set the basic relationships on the plant level for industry in the postwar years.

The German occupation and the reestablishment of Fascist government in most of Italy made it clear that the trade union movement would have to be created anew, and would not be molded out of a reorganization of Fascist syndical institutions. Negotiations began in Rome under the noses of the Germans to hammer out a basis for a unified trade union movement. During the early months of 1944 an agreement was gradually worked out. The principal negotiators were Buozzi for the Socialists, Grandi for the Christian Democrats and Giuseppe Di Vittorio for the Communists. Di Vittorio, who had begun his career in the Revolutionary Syndicalist movement while he was a farm laborer in the Puglie area, had joined the Communist Party early after its establishment and had been made chief Communist trade union representative while in exile in France. Like Buozzi, he had been released from prison by the Badoglio government, having been sent there from France after the Germans had arrested him.

The agreement upon trade union unity, which became known as the Pact of Rome, was signed on June 3, 1944, on the eve of the Allied liberation of the city. By the time the pact was signed, however, an event of enormous significance for the postwar trade union movement had taken place. Buozzi had been caught by the Germans in April and was shot to death as the Germans evacuated Rome during the early days of June.[7] The Socialists thus lost their principal candidate for top leader of the trade union movement and their only labor representative who had national reputation, stature, and ability greater than any Communist labor leader, including Di Vittorio.

6. For text of agreement see Confederazione Generale dell' Industria Italiana, *I consigli di gestione,* II (Rome, 1947), 11. For English translation of text *see* Maurice F. Neufeld, *Labor Unions and National Politics in Italian Industrial Plants* (Ithaca, 1954), appendix A.

7. Bonomi, *Diario di un anno,* pp. 179 and 194.

The pact provided for the establishment of the *Confederazione Generale Italiana del Lavoro* (CGIL) as a single confederation in which the three trade union factions would participate, with single national federations, chambers of labor, and local or provincial unions. While leaving most organization problems and problems of general orientation for later decision, trade union unity was declared to be established on the basis of three principles:[8]

(a) The CGIL is founded on the principle of the fullest internal democracy. All the posts, therefore, on every level in the organization, shall be filled by election from below, respectively by the general assembly of the local union or by the assembly of regularly elected delegates. In every leadership body, from top to bottom, the proportional participation of minorities shall be assured.

(b) In all the organizations of the CGIL maximum freedom of expression must be assured to all members and reciprocal respect of every political opinion and religious faith practiced.

(c) The CGIL is independent of all political parties. It shall associate itself, whenever it is regarded as desirable, with the action of the democratic parties which are the expression of the working masses, both for the safeguarding and development of the people's liberties and for the defense of specific interests of the workers and the country.

The pact provided that each of the three factions would have equal representation in the executive bodies of the CGIL and its constituent parts, with three co-equal secretary generals directing the organization. It also set out eight immediate objectives, including promotion of organization in the liberated territories and defense of the most urgent worker interests, maximum support for the war of liberation, assistance to workers in occupied territories in support of their struggle, help in the reconstruction of the country in the spirit of full recognition of the rights of labor, and claim to all the property of the Fascist syndicates.

Early organization in the south. During the German occupation of Rome there was little coordination between the central CLN and the CLN's which sprang up in the gradually expanding liberated areas in the south. The branches of the anti-Fascist political parties which emerged and began functioning in the south reflected only generally the central leadership's thinking as it developed underground in Rome. Similarly, in the trade union field the months before the liberation of Rome were a period of chaotic organization and conflicting tendencies in the south.

As the Allies slowly progressed through Sicily and the south of Italy

8. For text of the agreement, *see La CGIL dal Patto di Roma al Congresso di Genova* (Rome, 1949), I, photostat of original text opposite pp. 32 and 33.

during 1943 and the first half of 1944, Allied military government uniformly ordered the Fascist syndicates dissolved, and established the right to set up labor organizations free of government control.[9]

During this period the quality of trade union leadership, the character of the local labor organizations, and the extent of organization were conditioned strongly by the liberation first of the backward, non-industrial areas of the south rather than the more advanced industrial north. Only in such southern areas as Sicily, Puglie, and Naples was there a pre-Fascist trade union tradition of any importance. Despite these circumstances, however, local and provincial organizations sprang up throughout the area. They were organized generally from the top down, led by men appointed by the emerging political parties or self-appointed with political party approval.

The response of the workers to union membership appeals was strongly conditioned by the twenty years of Fascist administration under which a party membership card and a Fascist syndicate membership book were almost indispensable for obtaining employment and in general for being safe from discriminatory treatment. Fascism had disappeared, but the "membership card" psychology remained, this time with respect to the new organizations which appeared to be favored by the arbiters of the new situation. In addition to this most important element, both pre-Fascist traditions where they existed and the social ferment of the postwar situation help explain the rapid growth of trade union membership. In addition, the disruptive forces of an economic and social nature which accompanied the fall of fascism in the south contributed to the process.

The trade unions which mushroomed throughout liberated Italy were in some cases organized through cooperation of the trade union elements from the three political parties — the Socialists, Communists, Christian Democrats — with claims to leadership on historical grounds. In the larger proportion of cases, however, the traditional division between "white" and "red" unions reappeared, with the Socialists and Communists cooperating in the latter organizations.

The climate of the times, from the unfavorable attitude toward dual unions held by Allied military government officials to the recognition of the basic need for cooperation in rebuilding democratic institutions, made it difficult to oppose those who favored unity in the trade union field. The negotiations toward this end, as we have seen, had started in Rome as soon as the top trade union representatives from the political parties claim-

9. General Order No. 8 in Sicily, Regional Order No. 5 for Calabria, Lucania, and Province of Salerno, followed by General Order No. 17 of January 18, 1944 and finally General Order No. 28 of July 1944 which superceded all previous orders. The Italian government decree setting forth the detailed procedures for dissolving the Fascist syndical structure was issued in November 1944. For text of decree of November 23, 1944, no. 369, *see Gazzetta Ufficiale,* December 16, 1944, no. 95.

ing a labor base returned to Rome at the time that Badoglio replaced the deposed Mussolini. With the progress of the Allied forces, however, the situation could not wait on the results of these top negotiations. Under the leadership of Dino Gentili, a self-proclaimed trade union leader of the Action Party, who returned from exile in Great Britain and appeared in Naples immediately after its liberation, an attempt was made to build a confederation which he would lead. Gentili's organization, which he called the CGL, had some success in drawing together some of the trade unions in the area.

In January 1944 a congress of the political parties making up the CLN's was held at Bari to determine their common position on the important issues of attitude toward the Badoglio government and the continuation of the monarchy. Coordination with the congress was attempted by the Rome central CLN and the Bari congress decisions were basically consistent with the Rome views, though they differed in important details. The decisions reached were that there would be no participation in the Badoglio government, that the King be urged to abdicate immediately, and that a government of the six parties be formed after the King's abdication, which would prepare the way for a constituent assembly to be elected to draft a new constitution when all Italy was liberated.[10]

Immediately following the congress a conference of trade union representatives was held on January 29 in Bari to attempt to arrange for coordination and unity among the trade unions in the south. Reflecting the six-party cooperation at the political congress and at the same time concerned with diminishing the Gentili influence, it was agreed to establish a single organization. The leadership, while predominantly Socialist, Communist, and Christian Democratic, would also include representation from the Action Party and the Liberal Party.[11] The three top positions were to be filled by Buozzi as secretary and by Roveda and Grandi as vice-secretaries, none of whom were in the south at the time. Despite the ostensible unity at the trade union conference, many of the Christian Democrats were reluctant to enter into a unified organization, and many of the "white" unions continued their separate existence. Nor had unity actually been achieved among the other trade union groups. Both the Bari and the Gentili groups claimed the right to absorb the other. In the struggle which ensued, the Christian Democrats withdrew support from the dual "unified" organizations. During February, a congress was held at Salerno by those unions subscribing to the Gentili leadership, at which officers were named and a provisional directorate was set up with a minority of places left vacant for

10. Bonomi, *Diario di un anno,* pp. 145–146.
11. *Gazzetta del Mezzogiorno* (Bari daily), February 4, 1944; *Civiltà Proletaria* (Bari Communist weekly), February 6, 1944 (I, 18); *Risorgimento* (Naples daily), January 30 and February 1, 1944 (II, 26 and 27).

those supporting the Bari group.[12] The Bari and Naples groups did not represent different political groups as much as differences in the relative importance of the position of the Communist, Socialist, and Action Party trade unionists and conflicts of personal ambitions. During March, meetings were held between the two groups and it was agreed to coordinate the two organizations, but the arrangements were unworkable from the beginning.[13]

Throughout this period, local Christian Democratic trade unionists and Christian Democratic Party officials were divided on the question of unity with other groups in the trade unions. Although some unions entered the Bari organization, most remained independent, and in February 1943 held a convention at Salerno to establish a confederation which assumed the same name as had been used by the Catholic unions before fascism — *Confederazione Italiana del Lavoro*.[14]

The CGIL takes over. The signing of the Pact of Rome clarified the confused organizational picture in the south. As a political agreement reached by the authorized trade union representatives of the national Socialist, Communist, and Christian Democratic parties, it was regarded as superseding all previous arrangements. The three political groups, having agreed upon equal representation and power within the CGIL for each other, relegated to a minor role all other political groups in the trade union field, but urged them to join in the organization.

The Action Party group, and particularly its principal trade union representative, Gentili, had been ambitious in its plans for leadership in the trade union field. It was evident, however, that the Action Party had little direct influence among workers in the south and Gentili had maintained his position largely through cooperation from representatives of the Communist and to some extent the Socialist parties who were inclined to freewheel in the absence of effective party coordination before the liberation of Rome. The Pact of Rome and the subsequent actions of the groups which signed it, eliminated the influence of the Action Party in the trade unions within a matter of months.

Two weeks after the Rome agreement, Di Vittoro in an interview during a trip to Naples underlined the significance of the pact. In answer to a question regarding the organizations which had already been set up in the south, he said that the pact was a result of consultation on the national level of the trade union factions and that all others would simply have to fit into the new organization.[15]

The immediate task of the new organization in achieving effective unity

---

12. *Risorgimento,* February 20 and 23, 1944 (II, 44 and 46).

13. For details of arrangements *see L'Italia del Popolo* (Bari weekly), March 23, 1944 (II, 13), and *Civltà Proletaria,* March 26, 1944 (II, 25).

14. A. Toldo, *Il sindacalismo in Italia,* 2nd ed. (Milan, 1953), p. 79.

15. *Risorgimento,* June 16, 1944 (II, 144).

was twofold. There was little problem with the groups adhering to the Bari organization. The Action Party group was of little consequence, and the Socialist and Communist leadership which controlled the organization accepted the Rome decision enthusiastically. On the other hand, it was necessary to convince the independent Christian Democratic CIL to disband and have its affiliates merged into the new organization. At the same time, the implementation of the Pact of Rome on a practical level also necessitated isolating Gentili. His influence in the Naples organization had to be reduced to the point that his refusal to accept the decisions of the Rome Pact would not prevent its implementation in the Naples area.

The task of bringing the Christian Democrats into the new CGIL was handled by Grandi. He brought to his task not only his unequalled reputation as the most prominent and best of the trade union officials produced by Christian Democracy, but also the national support of his party.[16] At a conference in Naples during July, Grandi obtained a pledge from the leaders of the CIL that they would disband the organization and recommend support of the pact to the CIL affiliates.[17] While the actual merger depended upon agreement on representation, this did not become a serious problem since the Communists and Socialists were willing to share equal representation and responsibility with the Christian Democrats.

The coordinating of the Naples organization into the CGIL was primarily a task of getting the Communists and Socialists in the organization to accept the decision of their national leadership. Gentili had already been hedged in by these political groups during the few months before the Pact of Rome. When he opposed the pact, he was isolated from his supporters in the other parties and his influence rapidly destroyed. During August 1944, first the Naples Chamber of Labor voted affiliation to the CGIL, then the council of the Naples local unions followed suit, and finally a conference of the Gentili-sponsored CGL urged its affiliated organizations to join the CGIL.[18]

Sufficient progress had been made in the establishment of a single unified organization for the calling of a conference of the CGIL in Rome on September 15–16, 1944, to prepare for a full congress of the organization.[19] The conference coincided with a visit of British and American trade union

16. The party decision was confirmed by its National Council early in September 1944 and the party pledged itself to make "every effort that unity becomes general and operative." Complete text in *Indirizzi Politico-Sociali della Democrazia Cristiana. Voti e Risoluzioni del Consiglio Nazionale, della Direzione e delle Commissioni di Studio* (Rome, 1945), p. 11.

17. *Civiltà Proletaria*, July 30, 1944 (II, 43).

18. *La Voce* (Naples daily, published jointly by Socialist and Communist parties) August 13, 26, and 29, 1944 (I, 6, 17, 19).

19. A stenographic record of the conference is published in *La CGIL dal Patto di Roma*, vol. I, pp. 17–59.

representatives and a representative of the International Federation of Trade Unions, the IFTU. These representatives were invited to attend the conference and actively participated in the proceedings. The foreign trade union representatives were Luigi Antonini for the AFL, George Baldanzi for the CIO, Will Lawther and Thomas O'Brien for the TUC, and Walter Schevenels of the IFTU. Schevenels presided at the conference.

In addition to the national secretaries and the members of the executive body, approximately 100 representatives of 25 Chambers of Labor and 9 provincial Christian union offices attended. At the suggestion of the foreign delegation, the conference devoted most of its time to a discussion of the principles upon which unity could be maintained within the CGIL. The discussion covered the problems of relations with political parties and the desirability of trade union independence, but did not get into any of the problems of basic differences in trade union orientation among the Christian Democrats, Communists, and Socialists. The conference thus represented no point of major conflict. Gentili, who had requested the right to present his point of view, was denied admittance to the conference despite the attitude of the foreign delegation that he should at least be permitted to speak. On the basis of a report by Di Vittorio, who spoke for the CGIL secretariat, a concluding resolution was adopted which urged that elections be held within three months after the establishment of any organization, that national industry unions be set up by calling national congresses of representatives from the local unions in each industry, and proclaimed the independence of the CGIL from all political parties. The declaration ignored the realities of the political struggle which was inevitable in the organization and was hailed at the conference as a guarantee of the sincerity of the parties establishing the movement.[20]

The CGIL and the Naples Congress. By the time the CGIL held its organization congress at Naples from January 28 to February 1, 1945, the pattern of immediate postwar trade unionism was discernible.

The economic situation was desperate in liberated Italy. The widespread disruption of transportation and communications, the large-scale destruction of the very limited existing industrial capacity, lack of raw material and power, food shortages in urban centers, widespread black markets, a rapidly increasing inflation, all contributed to a chaotic situation.

Delicate political problems made for even greater difficulty. The immediate one was the question of the relations between the Italian government and

20. The foreign observers, who favored unity, were favorably impressed both with the conference and what they saw of the Italian trade union situation. See article by Will Lawther, "What I Saw of Italy in Process of Liberation" in *Daily Telegraph* (London) September 28, 1944 and "Supplementary Report by Luigi Antonini" in pamphlet *Italian Labor Today,* American Federation of Labor (October 1944), pp. 11–18. The text of the joint statement of the foreign delegations is printed in *ibid.,* pp. 5–6, and in *The Manchester Guardian,* September 28, 1944.

Allied military government. The Allies maintained complete control of areas in the vicinity of the battlefront. The other areas after liberation were gradually turned over to the jurisdiction of the Italian government, although policies of the government remained subject to Allied veto. Difficulties arose frequently as a result of lack of clear-cut jurisdiction and different policies followed on occasion by the Italians, the military commands and Allied military government and the Allied Control Commission on wage control, prices, requisitioning, mobilization, and rationing.

The more general political problem in Italy at the time was the groping efforts to find a responsible government to reflect the political climate in a country which had had no free elections for more than twenty years.[21] The unexpectedly long gap between the German occupation of Rome in September 1943 and its liberation by the Allies in June 1944 was a period of frustration and increasing bitterness. The six parties in the anti-Fascist combination, functioning at times separately and at times through the CLN's, were increasingly critical of the Badoglio government of technicians which did little even within the limits set by the Allies. Political support in the country was distributed among the six parties, although the proportions were not known. The Socialist, Communist, and Christian Democratic parties, the latter as successor to the pre-Fascist Popular Party, claimed the largest support as mass parties. The Action Party, despite its heroic contribution in the resistance, was not regarded by the other parties as having a potential mass following after the war. The Liberals and the Labor Democrats were regarded as minor parties with important pre-Fascist personalities but little general following.[22]

The Badoglio government could claim no popular political support and Badoglio had pledged that he would resign upon the liberation of Rome when new men would become available. As time went on, however, efforts to include the six parties in government increased since it became clear that something had to be done without waiting for the liberation of Rome. An impasse was reached, however, on the issue of abdication. While negotiations went forward to obtain the King's abdication in favor of the Crown Prince and the Christian Democrats, Liberals and Labor Democrats indicated willingness to participate in a Badoglio government after abdication, the Socialist, Communist, and Action parties refused to participate unless the institutional question itself was faced on a more satisfactory basis.

The arrival of Palmiro Togliatti at the end of March 1944 in Naples from his long exile in the Soviet Union broke the deadlock. As a high functionary

21. Grindrod, *The New Italy*, pp. 18–27, and Bonomi, *Diario di un anno*, pp. 95–200 for review of political developments during the period.

22. For a brief description of the six parties, *see* Muriel Grindrod, *The New Italy*, pp. 22 and 34–41, and H. Stewart Hughes, *The United States and Italy* (Cambridge, Mass., 1953), pp. 124 and 128.

of the Comintern for many years and as the Italian Communist spokesman in Russia, he returned as the authentic Moscow-endorsed leader of Italian communism. He reversed the position of the Communists overnight and agreed to participate in a Badoglio government without even insisting upon immediate adbication of the King in favor of the Crown Prince. The Socialist and Action parties, finding that they were isolated, felt compelled to reverse their positions. On April 12 the King announced that he would retire when the Allies entered Rome, and on April 20 Badoglio was able to form a government which included the six parties. Two months later, with the liberation of Rome, the King retired, his place being taken by Crown Prince Umberto with the title of Lieutenant General. The Badoglio government was replaced with a government headed by Bonomi with equal representation by the six parties. The Bonomi cabinet lasted until November 1944. Although the immediate cause of its collapse was dissatisfaction with the government's purge methods and failure to push reconstruction faster, the underlying reason was disagreement among the parties, especially on the issue of the role of the CLN's. The Socialists and the Action Party refused to participate in the new cabinet organized by Bonomi because of the British veto against the naming of the eminent anti-Fascist Count Carlo Sforza as Foreign Minister. Bonomi thereupon divided the cabinet posts equally among the four remaining parties. The second Bonomi government remained in office, without great achievement, until the north was liberated in May 1945.

The Communist Party, under Togliatti's leadership, had as its basic objective during this period the laying of the groundwork for what it hoped would make possible the development of a "peoples' democracy" and give it effective control on the pattern then being evolved for east European countries.[23] The immediate objectives were to participate in government, whatever the political combination, and if possible obtain key posts; to become a mass party identified with the Italian pre-Fascist working class traditions and with patriotic national objectives; and to build strong mass organizations, particularly in the labor field, which it could control and use in its struggle for power. On the government level, while the party participated in government continuously from April 1944 to the end of May 1947, it never succeeded in obtaining the key posts of Interior, Defense or Foreign Affairs. In the earlier period of its participation, in 1944 and 1945, its policy was one of extreme moderation, aimed toward bringing about elections, ending the war rapidly, obtaining a peace treaty and the withdrawal of the Allied troops. In the liberation struggle, the prominent role played by the Communists in the underground permitted identification with the national interest in dramatic fashion. It also afforded an effective opportunity for

23. Garosci in *Communism in Western Europe*, pp. 183–185.

building mass support and for training a vastly expanded party leadership elite.

The creation and control of a large trade union movement was one of the most important immediate Communist objectives. Whatever the intentions of the other groups participating in the creation of the CGIL, the Communists made political orientation of the trade unions unavoidable. There were other considerations, as well, which pushed CGIL in the direction of politics. During this period, with a war-disrupted economy, the government and Allied controls which affected directly the economic interests of wage earners, it was understandable that the trade unions would focus their attention on political party support.

Each of the three "mass" parties had an important interest in furthering its ideology, if not its party influence within the CGIL. The Christian Democrats were particularly conscious of the danger of cooperation with the Communists within the trade unions. On the other hand, they felt they had more to gain than lose through participation in a unified movement. Representative of the Christian Democratic thinking on this issue at the time was the statement of an important spokesman:

There was . . . considered the great possibilities which were offered to the Catholics: to penetrate in the midst of the masses, particularly the workers, among whom the Marxist conceptions had penetrated most profoundly . . . to convince them that in the social doctrine and action of the Catholics they would find protection less illusory and closer to their own interests . . . To this is added, finally, the overriding requirements of Christian Democracy, expression of the Catholics in the political field, which proclaimed itself as a great party, to have influence and a connection, even if limited, over the entire trade union movement, instead of control of only a part of it, leaving to the other political parties the uncontested and uncontestable domination over a large part, if not over the greatest part, of the working class.[24]

The Socialists during this early period were a rather confused group. It is doubtful that even if Buozzi had still been alive, he could have given purpose to the essentially heterogeneous grouping within the Socialist Party. From the early days after the liberation began, the party and its trade union counterpart within the CGIL were torn apart by factions ranging from those who wanted to combine the party with the Communists to those who after the fall of fascism regarded the Communists as the principal danger to the country.

Both the Christian Democrats and the Socialists, particularly the latter, seemed only dimly aware that a struggle for control was inevitable in the

24. Leopoldo Rubinacci, *Ordinamenti sindacali,* no. 2 of *Quaderni Sociali* series of the Instituto Cattolico di Attività Sociale (Rome, 1947), p. 28.

CGIL. In any event, they neither had the resources in trained manpower, the organization, nor the singlemindedness to offer effective competition to the Communists. At the time of the establishment of the CGIL, the Communists already had a leadership tempered by many years of conspiracy and illegal underground activity. In addition, the liberation struggle going on in the north during 1944 and early 1945 was providing the Communists with further opportunity to perfect their organization and develop leadership elements. In their drive for the control of the CGIL they brought discipline, experienced leadership, ample financial resources, organizational drive, and a singleness of purpose which were largely lacking in the other groups.

The Communists had a difficult and challenging assignment during this period. On the one hand, their tactics dictated following a policy which was made to appear patriotic, non-revolutionary and essentially conservative. Cooperation with the Allies in finishing the war, cooperation in reconstruction, cooperation in re-creating "democratic capitalist" institutions, cooperation within the government — a government of any character — made the Communists in Italy at the time sound like a party somewhat to the right of the Christian Democrats. On the other hand, their objective was also to build a mass party and above all to win control of the trade union apparatus. A more detailed analysis of Communist policy and tactics in the trade unions is discussed in the next chapter. For the present, an indication of their success is the fact that by the time the CGIL held its congress in Naples in January 1945, over 40 percent of the delegates supported the Communists.

The Naples Congress itself, however, was not made a test of strength of the political groups.[25] Quite the contrary. It had been called as the first congress of the unified trade union movement from all liberated Italy, and unity was the main theme of the sessions. All groups, and particularly the Communists, leaned over backward in their efforts to show that the CGIL was to be nonpartisan and avoid ideological conflict. In the functioning of the organization, the national office was to continue on the basis of equal distribution of positions and power among the three principal political groups. There was not even any defined division of responsibility made among the three secretary generals, to avoid giving one a more important responsibility than another.

The Naples Congress was attended by 322 delegates from 43 of the liberated provinces representing 1,035,000 organized workers. The organization claimed 1,300,000 members in liberated Italy, although it had collected its share of dues from only 275,000 members.[26] At Naples as at the Rome Conference in September, 1943, Di Vittorio was without doubt the dominating figure. Despite the theoretical equality with the other two secretary

25. For stenographic record of the congress, see La CGIL dal Patto di Roma, vol. I, pp. 95–243.

26. Ibid., pp. 95, 102, 112, 180 and 207.

generals he had already taken over effective leadership of the national office through a combination of ability, party machine, and dominating personality. He leaned over backwards, however, at the congress to avoid giving offense to the Socialists and Christian Democrats. He paid homage to the contribution which the latter would make within the CGIL and in his general report, as well as during the discussion, he stressed unity not only as the best defense of the workers' interests but as a condition of stability of Italian democracy. It was he, however, who set the tone of the congress and ably dominated the proceedings.

The congress appeared at the time as an impressive demonstration of the wide area of agreement on trade union issues among the various political factions of the CGIL. No competing conflicting resolutions were brought to a vote and unanimity was maintained throughout. The congress reaffirmed the agreement that CGIL would be non-party but that it would be political in the sense that it would concern itself with the broad problems of democracy and liberty as they arose on the political horizon. Di Vittorio even claimed that the nonpartisan unified character of the CGIL would prevent the "mass" parties from drifting too far apart.[27]

The congress approved a provisional constitution, and while urging elections among all its affiliates, also urged single election lists agreed upon by all factions, thus in fact maintaining the principle of equal sharing of responsibility in leadership among the three political factions. It was recommended, however, that Chambers of Labor place responsibility for execution of decisions in the hands of one of the three secretaries. On the national level, provision was made for enlargement of the CGIL executive bodies when the north would be liberated to permit representation from that area.

The congress also reviewed the economic problems with which the CGIL was concerned. Di Vittorio reported a number of accomplishments of the organization in the trade union field. The Buozzi-Mazzini agreement was being applied in all plants of liberated Italy through the election of plant grievance committees. A cost-of-living indemnity had been extended to all workers and the size of the end-of-year bonus had been increased to the equivalent of one month's wages. Pensions of retired workers had been increased.

Among the immediate demands set forth by the congress were wage increases and the establishment of an automatic cost-of-living wage adjustment system, as the CGIL had already demanded in a memorandum to the employers' confederation and the government in December 1944. The congress also offered CGIL support of wage increases for government employees. It expressed interest in the problems of the agricultural population by pledging support in obtaining better contracts for sharecroppers and tenant farmers and by supporting a program of land reform while promis-

27. *Ibid.*, pp. 106–107.

ing protection to those who occupied the unutilized land of large land-holders. On a general level it committed itself actively to campaign against the black market and to work for the reconstruction of the country while demanding a direct role in the reconstruction planning. Finally, the congress unanimously recommended that monopolistic industries and those plants controlled by the *Instituto per la Recostruzione Industriale* (IRI), the government-owned industrial holding corporation, be nationalized.[28]

An interesting aspect of the early period in the reconstruction of the trade union movement had been the fact that the provincial Chamber of Labor structure of the pre-Fascist period had spontaneously been reconstituted and had frequently been the starting point in setting up a trade union movement from the top down. Few National Federations (National Unions) had, however, been set up. At the time of the Naples Congress only four National Federations had been established: among agricultural workers, railroad workers, post office and telegraph workers and bank employees. As a result of the interest of the national CGIL officials, concurrent with the Naples Congress, conferences were held at which National Federations were set up among workers in the metallurgical industry, in textiles, chemicals, road transport, amusements, bakeries, printing, and among miners, street car workers, and school teachers.[29]

Consolidation and Growth

The trade unions in the north. Northern Italy has been the area of greatest industrial development and of greatest progress in modernization of agriculture. Without the north, Italy would be a backward, underdeveloped, semicolonial type of area. Yet from the time of the German occupation of Rome until more than a year and half later, at the end of April 1945, the two areas were sealed off from each other into two separate economic, political, and military territories.

The trade union traditions in Italy were basically traditions of the north, both in industry and in agriculture. Most of the trade union leadership had come from the north. It was felt at the time of the Naples CGIL Congress that when the north would be liberated, the character, orientation, and activity of the trade union movement would be sharply affected. As a matter of fact, relatively little of a basic nature changed after liberation. The reasons lie in the character of the developments in the north before liberation and of the trade union movement in general.

Even before the Allied invasion of Italy there had been an increasing amount of organization by underground anti-Fascist parties in the north. The March 1943 strike movement in Turin, which had spread to other northern industrial areas, is claimed to have been sufficiently general to have

28. *Ibid.*, pp. 108–120 and 232–237.
29. Candeloro, *Il movimento sindacale*, pp. 150–151.

paralyzed war production.[30] During the Badoglio "45 days" period, the anti-Fascist groups had begun to form in the open, but were forced to go underground again when the Germans occupied the country. The resistance movement grew rapidly during the rest of 1943, and in 1944 Committees of National Liberation sprang up throughout the north. Tens of thousands of partisans operated in the hills. Groups were organized principally by the Action, Communist, Socialist and Christian Democratic parties, and to a minor extent by the Liberals. The CLN's, in which the five anti-Fascist parties cooperated, directed and coordinated the activity. The Democratic Labor party did not exist in the north. At Milan, CLNAI was organized as the principal coordinating committee for underground activity in the north and controlled the funds supplied from Rome through a representative of the *Credito Italiano*. Arms and supplies were obtained through captured German equipment and, in the later period, also from Allied sources.[31] The partisan movement was gradually welded into an effective and efficient fighting machine.[32]

Partisan committees were set up in industry including management representatives in those cases where management was regarded as trustworthy. The committees organized slowdowns of production destined for the German war machine, disrupted deliveries, and in general attempted to minimize the contribution of Italian industry to the Axis war effort. Typically, the labor groups in which Socialists, Communists, and Christian Democrats cooperated, which had begun the work of democratic reorganization of the Fascist syndicates during the Badoglio forty-five-day period, transformed themselves into clandestine resistance centers. These centers were tightened up and functioned in factories and workshops, fomenting strikes, spreading propaganda, and organizing sabotage. The centers were coordinated into a structure which became the Chamber of Labor after liberation. In the period immediately before liberation, the vital task of the committees had been to prevent the destruction or the removal of plant machinery by the Germans, a task in which they were remarkably successful.

When the liberation of the north was completed in April 1945, all the

30. Candeloro, *Il movimento sindacale*, p. 138. The CGIL boasted in a message to British and American workers on September 16, 1944, at the time of its first conference, "Fascism was not beaten either by the King or Badoglio or by the vote of the Supreme Fascist Council. Fascism was beaten by the combined blows of the Allied military force and of the rising popular opposition inside [the country] which had its highest and most efficacious expression in the general strike of March 1943 which paralyzed for about two weeks the war industry of north Italy." *La CGIL dal Patto di Roma*, I, 58.

31. Leo Valiani, *Tutte le strade conducano a Roma* (Florence, 1947), gives a good account of this period.

32. Field Marshall Alexander is reported to have described the Italian partisan movement as the best in Europe after Tito's. W. Hilton Young, *The Italian Left* (New York and London, 1949), p. 178.

apparatus of a trade union movement emerged overnight. Within a few days after liberation in Genoa the Chamber of Labor was already functioning and concerning itself with trade union questions. On May 3, 1945, it announced:

> All collective agreements formulated before the liberation will have full effect in the manner most favorable to the workers . . . In order to avoid false and prejudicial interpretations of working conditions, no dismissal of personnel will be consented to before an agreement is reached with the new union.

The power of the Chamber of Labor at the time was such that the announcement was in fact observed in industry.[33]

The spirit of cooperation and of common enterprise among wage earners in industry made unity in the trade union field a perfectly natural phenomenon. The revolts in the northern cities which helped rout the Fascist and German armies as the Allies approached these areas led to a period of purging from public life and from industry those who had served the Fascists and the Germans. Much more than in the south, the development of the partisan movement had created a social ferment and revolutionary spirit which pervaded the population in the north. It was to be expected that as a result widespread expectations for fundamental change and improvement had been built up which under the best of circumstances could not have been met by the realities of postwar Italian life. The Communists shrewdly built on this spirit and channeled it into identification with their own massively expanded apparatus.

The trade unions in the north were quickly coordinated into the CGIL. The process presented little difficulty, since contact had been maintained by the CGIL with the clandestine labor organizations throughout 1944 until the liberation of the north was completed. Furthermore, the national political commitments for unity on a tripartite basis had already been the practice underground for almost two years.

On June 24 to 26, 1945, a meeting was held between the Chambers of Labor in the north and the national officials of the CGIL. The conference confirmed the action already taken individually by the Chambers of Labor to affiliate with the CGIL. It also elected twenty-one representatives to fill the places on the national Directive Council left open for the unions in the north at the time of the Naples Congress. A resolution was adopted urging continuation of the freeze on employment to prevent aggravation of the unemployment problem; coordinated activity of all Chambers of Labor to seek lowering of the cost of living; action to adjust wages to increased cost of living; improvement in conditions of sharecroppers by increasing their share of the product; and nationalization of key industries.[34]

33. *Il Lavoro Nuovo* (Genoa), May 4, 1945; *L'Unità* (Genoa), May 4, 1945.

34. The text of the final resolution of the conference is given in *La CGIL dal Patto di Roma*, vol. I, pp. 249–254.

The end of hostilities in Italy tripled the size of the CGIL, and brought into its ranks overnight hundreds of thousands of industrial workers to balance the predominantly agricultural and white-collar character of the membership in south Italy. Yet, there was no basic change in composition of leadership or its orientation. The reasons are, in part, political. The same political combinations functioning in the government and in the CGIL before liberation of the north functioned in the partisan and in the underground trade union apparatus. The leadership in the CGIL had in a sense already discounted the liberation since it was a leadership named from political parties which made their choice from among their ranks, regardless of whether the individuals had been in exile, were available in the south or had to be brought through the lines from the north. Finally, the basic economic problems faced by Italy throughout 1944 to 1947 raised the same type of problems for the trade unions both in the north and south: skyrocketing prices, pressing shortages in consumer goods, large-scale unemployment, the need for reconstruction.

Economic problems. The economic problems facing the Italian people were overwhelming throughout the immediate postwar period. War damages suffered by Italy have variously been estimated to have been from six to twelve billion dollars. Physical destruction was enormous. Of the approximately 33,600,000 room units existing at the beginning of the war, 1,878,000 were destroyed, 1,132,000 heavily damaged and 3,379,000 slightly damaged. Damage to the railroad system reduced its capacity by 30 percent below prewar levels. No more than one-eighth of the tonnage of Italy's merchant marine was left. Damage to industrial plant and equipment was approximately 25 percent of prewar capacity, despite the heroic successful efforts in the north to prevent German destruction and removal of industry. Shortages of fuel and raw materials contributed further to the difficulties, and actual production in 1944 was only 36 percent of the 1938 level, falling to 23 percent in 1945.[35] In agriculture, war dislocation and lack of fertilizers and machinery, coupled with a severe drought in 1945 reduced cereal production to 55 percent of its prewar average. It has been estimated by the United Nations Relief and Rehabilitation Administration (UNRRA) that food consumption of the nonagricultural population averaged approximately 1550 calories per head per day in 1945.[36]

Without the assistance given first by Allied military sources, particularly the United States, and then by UNRRA, the position of the Italian population would have been even more serious than it was during this period. Even the 1550 calory level had been reached only because foodstuff shipments by the United States government and UNRRA reached three times

35. Bruno Foa, *Monetary Reconstruction in Italy* (New York, 1949), pp. 22–26.
36. United Nations Relief and Rehabilitation Administration, *Economic Recovery in the Countries Assisted by UNRRA* (Washington, September 1946), p. 124.

the level of prewar cereal imports. In such a situation, with controls placed by the government on distribution, prices, and wages, little alternative remained to a trade union organization, whatever its inclinations, than to act essentially as a political pressure group rather than as an "industrial relations" organization.

Trade union growth and Communist consolidation. The liberation of the north had been followed in June 1945 by the organization of a government headed by Ferruccio Parri, Action Party leader of the underground forces in the north. Parri's government, in which all six parties participated, had the difficult task of reintegrating the north with the rest of the country, and starting the slow process of reconstruction and recovery. In the disagreements which developed very soon among the parties, the Parri leadership was quickly sacrificed and his government resigned in November 1945. Alcide De Gasperi, leader of the Christian Democrats, succeeded Parri to the premiership, with a reorganized cabinet which included the same political party participation.

The De Gasperi assumption of leadership in government in December 1945 marked the beginning of Christian Democratic predominance in the country. De Gasperi himself headed the government for more than seven years with a display of remarkable ability in maintaining political balance and in devotion to the construction of democratic government institutions. For eighteen months after he took office, through three cabinet reorganizations, he held together within his cabinet the increasingly divergent forces of the Christian Democrats, Socialists, and Communists. Deterioration of East-West relations and the consequent policies of the Communists and Nenni Socialists in Italy finally made continuation of the coalition impossible. At the end of May 1947 De Gasperi successfully reorganized his government and excluded the two parties from office.

During the spring of 1946 the first free elections were held in Italy in more than twenty years. During March and April municipal elections were held throughout the country. From among the 5596 communes in which elections were held at that time, the Communists and Socialists together won a majority in 1976 communes and each won a majority alone in 140 additional communes. The Christian Democrats won in 1907 communes, the other parties and party combinations won in the remaining 1433 communes.

The national elections of June 2, 1946, at which a constituent assembly was elected for the drafting of a new constitution, confirmed the general distribution of strength of the political parties as shown in the municipal elections. The three "mass" parties emerged by far the largest in the country, with the Christian Democratic party winning the greatest support, almost as large as the combined strength of the Communists and their Socialist allies. The Christian Democrats obtained 35.2 percent of the vote, with the Socialists receiving 20.7 percent and the Communists 19.0 percent. On the other hand, the Action Party received only 1.5 percent of the vote and the Republican Party 4.4 percent.[37]

The Communists and their Socialist allies participated in the government during the two years after the cessation of hostilities, and made a considerable contribution toward reconstruction and recovery in the economy and toward development of democratic forms and institutions on the political front. The period was a painful one in the accomplishment of the enormous tasks confronting the nation, and the Communists took full advantage of the situation in playing the role, simultaneous with participation in government, of chief critics and rallying point of the discontent which manifested itself, especially among wage earners. While production was slowly raised in the postwar years, it did not reach its prewar level until 1950, and during the period of 1946 and 1947 was between one half and three-quarters of the prewar figure.[38] Unemployment and underemployment were high and took on the chronic pattern which characterized the economy in succeeding years. Inflation, which had assumed major proportions through the war, took on a more and more serious aspect during the two years following the war. Wholesale prices, using 1938 as 100, were 858 in 1944, 2884 in 1946 and 5159 in 1947, reaching their peak in September 1947 at 6202.[39] Cost of living, using 1938 as 100, stood at 2823 in 1946 and 4575 in 1947 reaching its peak in September 1947 at 5331.[40]

It was against this background that the trade union movement grew rapidly, and the Communists found little effective opposition to their domination of the CGIL. There was a tremendous amount of agitation and a high rate of labor disputes and strikes. The strikes were essentially demonstrations to create pressure on the government or on both the national employers' confederation and the government, rather than to test the bargaining power of labor against management in particular plants or industries. Short stoppages were the typical pattern. In addition, strikes as essentially political demonstrations generally embraced geographic areas rather than the plant or industry. The most frequent demands in these disputes, aside from wage increases, were to block discharges, protest skyrocketing prices, demand expanded public works, insist upon punishment of ex-Fascists and demand land redistribution in agriculture.

37. Istituto Centrale di Statistica, *Annuario statistico italiano, 1944–1948,* series V, vol. I (Rome, 1949), table 156, pp. 152–153.

38. Confindustria has estimated the 1946 level as 48.0 percent of the 1938 industrial production level and 1947 as 63.0 percent, later raising the latter estimate to 77.0 percent. Confederazione Generale dell' Industria Italiana, *Annuario 1948* (Rome, 1948), p. 40 and *Annuario 1952* (Rome, 1952), p. 42.

39. Confindustria, *Annuario di statistiche del lavoro 1949,* tables 156 and 158, pp. 232–233.

40. *Ibid.,* table 145, p. 219.

Agreements reached in May and June 1945 between the Chamber of Labor of Milan and the provincial employers' association temporarily prohibited all discharges, raised wages, and tied them to cost-of-living fluctuations. The Allied military authorities had ordered the agreements cancelled as contrary to sound policy, but were forced to reverse themselves when the other northern Chambers of Labor pressed the same issues and pressures became too great to resist.[41] The settlements were of short duration and the same issues continued to be a source of major difficulty during the following two years.

No doubt the turbulent round of strikes, agitations, and demonstrations of the period of late 1945 and early 1946 was largely the natural aftermath of the war. On the other hand, it is clear that the Communists succeeded in building their strength within the CGIL through their ability to make themselves the effective spokesmen for the problems then facing wage earners. By January 1946, the National Council of the Christian Democratic Party, though reaffirming its support of trade union unity, criticized the Communists for promoting a "state of permanent agitation among the workers against their real interests" and invited the Christian trade union faction in the CGIL to watch "that the policy of the trade union follow the enunciated principles and in full independence of private interests of parties and be directed, in the present circumstances, toward facing the economic recovery of the country, which alone can give real benefits to the workers and is the indispensable premise to the further conquests by the workers."[42]

The Communists built their strength rapidly within the CGIL. In the north, at the time of liberation, they were already significantly stronger than either the Socialists or the Christian Democrats in the trade unions. By the end of 1945 they were already reaching the point of majority control. In Turin province, for example, the Communists received 58.8 percent of the votes in the provincial metal workers' union election compared with 31.1 percent for the Socialists and 6.8 percent for the Christian Democrats. In the same province, the Communists received 50.1 percent of the vote among the chemical workers while the Socialists received 25.0 percent and the Christian Democrats 7.8 percent.

By 1946 the CGIL was effectively under Communist control. The Communists obviously had the initiative, they had placed their people in strategic positions throughout the organization, they had won the confidence of the CGIL following in larger measure than had the competing factions. Nonetheless, during 1946 they refrained from pressing their advantage over the other factions to the point of developing too much controversy within the

41. Confederazione Generale dell' Industria Italiana, *Un anno di trattative sindacali, note e documenti* (Rome, December 1946), pp. 7–8 and 33.

42. Quoted in Confindustria, *Notiziario,* III, 2 (January 20, 1946), p. 9. The CGIL secretariat issued a statement denying the accusation. *Idem.*

organization. On the political side they agreed that the CGIL refrain from taking a position in the municipal and constituent assembly elections. While the CGIL supported the republic against the monarchy in the referendum held on the subject on June 2,[43] this was not a controversial issue within the organization, since all factions favored the republic. The issue of the republic, indeed, was made a major CGIL theme at the time, and it was indicative of the role the CGIL had assumed in its relation to society and the government, that it announced a national cessation of work for twenty-four hours to celebrate the republican victory, giving the government in effect the choice of declaring the day a national holiday or having the republic come into being while a general strike was in progress. The government ratified the CGIL decision by declaring the day a national holiday.[44] In general, however, the Communist CGIL leadership pursued the tactic of surface cooperation with the Socialists and Christian Democrats.

On economic issues and in labor matters, they pressed hard and outbid the competing factions in their efforts to channel worker loyalties in their direction. The first official disagreement within the CGIL developed over wage policy in July 1946.[45] All three factions agreed upon the desirability of negotiating an adequate arrangement for automatic wage adjustments to compensate for cost-of-living changes. A difference arose, however, between the Communists and Socialists, on the one hand, and the Christian Democrats on the other at a CGIL Directive Council session concerning the extent to which, as the Christian Democrats argued, limits should be set on further demands for wage increases beyond the sliding-scale arrangements, in the light of the inflationary situation and the precarious state of economic reconstruction and recovery. For the first time an issue was permitted to be decided by a vote instead of working out a unanimous decision. The Communists and Socialists outvoted the Christian Democrats, and the CGIL negotiations which followed with *Confindustria* were on the basis of both cost-of-living and general wage adjustments.

The Christian Democrats had had little expectation of predominant influence in the unified CGIL in the light of the historical, traditional attachments of wage earners in the pre-Fascist trade union movement. They had, however, evolved a cohesive faction which functioned as a unit and presented a distinctive competitive element to the workers as an alternative to the Communist predominance in the organization.

43. The results of the referendum were 12,718,641 for a republic and 10,718,502 for continuation of the monarchy. Istituto Centrale di Statistica, *Annuario 1944–1948*, pp. 154–155.

44. Vittorio Gorresio, *I moribondi di Montecitorio* (Milan, 1947), pp. 45–46.

45. Confederazione Generale dell' Industria Italiana, *Un anno*, pp. 80–83, reproduces article from *L'Unità*, July 16, 1946, which gives full summary of positions taken by each faction at CGIL Directive Council session, and pp. 83–86 gives text of final resolution adopted at the session.

Confidence had been placed primarily in the Socialists as a counter-force to the Communists in the unified trade union organization. It was found early after liberation, however, that the Socialists frequently had little more in common than their party label. Under such circumstances, it is not surprising that the label itself in time was torn into pieces. Views varied from the desire to unite organically with the Communists — a position encouraged by the Communists in the early years — to a desire to make common cause with the Communists on an autonomous party basis, to sharply anti-Communist moderate Social Democratic positions. When it became evident that the forces under Pietro Nenni, who favored unreserved Communist cooperation, would be predominant in the party, a series of splits away from the party developed. The first of these, led by Giuseppe Saragat, took place in January 1947 and resulted in the formation of a moderate Socialist Party, *Partito Socialista dei Lavoratori Italiani* (PSLI), a party which did not succeed in building significant strength, however, in the labor field.

While most Socialist trade union officials were to the right of the official Socialist position of complete cooperation with the Communists, very few supported PSLI. The Socialists were never a well-knit group and frequently worked at cross purposes within the CGIL. Officially, however, they cooperated closely with the Communists in accordance with the policy of their party, which had control over their appointment and removal. In addition, the highest Socialist official in the CGIL, Oreste Lizzadri, was of left-wing conviction whose energies seemed more directed toward frustrating his more moderate Socialist trade union colleagues than competing with the Communists. Even the replacement of Lizzadri by the more moderate Fernando Santi in 1947 helped little, since Santi permitted himself to be dominated on the one hand by Di Vittorio and on the other hand by his fear of being isolated from the left-wing forces which controlled his party.

Collective bargaining and national agreements. The dramatic day-to-day events during the early postwar years frequently obscured the pattern of collective bargaining and agreements which extended throughout industry. The Fascist regime, after destroying the democratic trade union movement, had created a syndicate structure on a national scale under control of the Fascist Party. Brushing aside the collective agreements of the preceding period, the Fascists had created on a vastly expanded scale through their controlled monopoly unions and employer associations, a collective agreement structure, in substance used as a gigantic apparatus to serve the interests of the regime. The system of all-industry national agreements and national industry agreements, for example, served as a convenient mechanism for applying the deflationary policies of the government through wage reductions written into the agreements.

The abolition of the Fascist unions and Fascist industrial relations legislation by Allied Military Government directives and Italian government decrees did not extend to the Fascist collective agreements. The latter were permitted to remain in force until replaced by agreements negotiated by the new trade unions. The result was a ready-made highly centralized collective bargaining structure covering all of industry which was taken over and continued by CGIL and *Confindustria*.

The centralized agreement structure was suitable for the realities of the immediate post-Fascist period. The CGIL, built from the top down, had developed large-scale membership in remarkably little time, but the chaotic economic situation, the absence of well-organized local unions or experienced leadership in many areas and the political balance of control in the trade union movement as a whole favored centralized handling of collective agreements.

Nor were the employer groups opposed to a continuation of the national system of bargaining. With the traditional habits of business sharpened by twenty years of fascism, competition on the level of wages was regarded as undesirable, and anything other than the codification of standards for labor on a national industry basis was viewed as anarchy. In addition, it was recognized that while the formal structure was continued from the Fascist period, the substantive nature of bargaining had completely changed with the change in regime. Under these new circumstances, it was felt that the national leadership in the trade unions would represent a more "responsible" view than would the local membership pressures resulting from the political atmosphere of the time.

Finally, the wild inflationary situation of the immediate postwar period favored the continuation of national bargaining. The government found the task of watching and supervising wage movements much easier under the circumstances. The trade union movement with its "class justice" orientation regarded uniform wage movements under central control as an easier way of applying its own policies. Employer organizations, for motivations not dissimilar from those of the trade unions, followed the same logic.

National all-industry agreements between CGIL and *Confindustria* became the major level of negotiations. The standards fixed in these agreements were then applied in the individual national industry agreements. On the crucial question of wages, the pattern was set by the national all-industry agreements — called inter-Confederal agreements — which set wage rates in four basic skill classifications and established a sliding scale cost-of-living allowance for the entire country with zonal differentials. While individual industry agreements and sometimes even provincial agreements set specific wage scales, it was the inter-Confederal agreements which set wage policy for all industry. In the same fashion, it was through all-industry inter-Confederal agreements that such major subjects as lay-off policy was handled, grievance procedure settled, and vacation policy and end-of-year bonus policy negotiated. The national industry "category" agreements sometimes improved upon the standards fixed by the inter-Confederal agreements although the pressure within *Confindustria* was against such variation.

Strains in CGIL Unity

The Florence Congress of 1947. The organizational activity of the CGIL and its aggressive defense of the wage earners had notable success in building the strength of the organization. By the time the CGIL had its first unified national congress in June 1947 at Florence, it claimed a membership of 5,735,000.[46] The Communists had already succeeded, in fact, in winning control of the organization and, early in 1947 in anticipation of the CGIL Congress, moved to scuttle the formality of equality of representation among the three major factions. They took the position that responsibility in leadership should be in proportion to actual support from membership. The result was a storm of protest from the Christian Democratic and PSLI trade unionists.

Typical of the justification given by the Communists for their position was the statement of Roveda, secretary of the Turin Labor Chamber and of the National Metallurgical Workers Federation (FIOM): "The abandonment of the equality among Communists, Socialists, and Demo-Christians, besides meaning the abandonment of an equivocation justified only by circumstances, will result in a specification of respective responsibilities and, consequently, in an undoubted improvement in the activity of the organization."[47] Di Vittorio described it as "nothing other than the application of the Unity Pact of Rome."[48]

The Christian Democrats and PSLI were in the difficult position of seeming to be against applying formal internal democracy in the CGIL. Giovanni Rapelli, who had replaced Grandi as Christian Democratic secretary of the CGIL upon the latter's death on September 28, 1946, complained that with the application of proportional representation, the strongest party would control the organization and he was generally pessimistic about continued trade union unity.[49] The PSLI Social Democrats described the suggestion of the Communists as a threat to trade union unity and complained that proportional representation would mean the domination by political leaders of one party over workers of other parties. It was clear that the Communists would carry their position in the CGIL, and that the Nenni Socialists of PSI would support them.

The bitter, acrimonious atmosphere within the trade union movement did not originate with this issue, however. This represented, rather, the

46. *La CGIL dal patto di Roma,* vol. III, p. 346.
47. *La Nuova Stampa* (Turin daily), February 14, 1947.
48. *L'Unità* (Rome daily), February 12, 1947.
49. *Il Popolo* (Rome daily), March 1, 1947.

culmination of innumerable issues growing out of the Communist initiative in running the CGIL even while the tripartite façade of equality still existed. Basically, the issue was one which could not be solved by agreement. The Communists, although supporting recovery and reconstruction of the economy, were at the same time aggressively acting as spokesman for the protection of the rights of wage earners. In practice, they followed the trade union tactic of offering initiative, leadership, and organization for the achievement of this end. Their principal goal in this period had been to capture control of the CGIL. They succeeded, and the opposition groups had not as a practical matter offered very stiff competition.

The Florence Congress of the CGIL, postponed several times through early 1947, was held during June 1 to 7.[50] The basic issues threatening the unity of the organization were not faced. The congress represented a landmark in that it closed the epoch during which unity was regarded as possible and desirable by the non-Communist groups.

The Communists had 57.8 percent of the voting strength at the congress. The PSI, which supported the Communists on all issues of significance, represented 22.6 percent of the delegation strength. The Christian Democrats had 13.4 percent of the votes, while the PSLI and the Republicans had 2.2 percent and 2.0 percent respectively.[51]

The general resolution on trade union policy, organization, and orientation was a compromise worked out by the principal factions.[52] A compromise was also worked out on the representation issue. The tripartite secretary arrangement was changed, with Di Vittorio becoming responsible secretary general, and one secretary each chosen by the Communists, Socialists, and Christian Democrats.[53] All groups repeatedly pledged their loyalty to the unity principle and little of the bitter feelings among the delegates was permitted to come out in the open.

The one issue around which a major controversy developed was the article in the CGIL constitution referring to political activity of the organization. The Christian Democrats insisted on elimination of the article which asserted that while the organization would maintain independence from political parties, it would take positions on issues of interest to all workers. The compromise proposal offered by the Communists modified the article to

50. *La CGIL dal Patto di Roma,* vol. III, is the stenographic report of the congress. It also reproduces the texts of the general motions presented by each of the political factions in the CGIL.

51. *Ibid.,* p. 346.

52. *Ibid.,* pp. 348–353.

53. The Secretariat, including six vice-secretaries, had the following political composition: 3 Communists, 3 Socialists (PSI), 2 Christian Democrats, 1 PSLI, and 1 Republican. The Directive Council had 38 Communists, 19 Socialists, 11 Christian Democrats, 2 Republicans, 2 PSLI, 1 Action Party, 1 Anarcho-Syndicalist and 1 Independent. *Ibid.,* pp. 367–368.

require a 75 percent favorable vote in the executive body of the organization before the CGIL would intervene in political matters. The compromise was rejected, however, by the Christian Democrats, but was adopted despite their dissent.[54] The wording in the constitution actually mattered little, since Communist control in the organization insured that their policies would be followed and the political situation in the years after the Florence Congress allowed the Communists to use the CGIL for their own purposes.

The Communist offensive. The political character of the CGIL leadership had been an important element in keeping unity in the organization, so long as the three major political parties retained joint responsibility in government. This had been true even while the relations of the parties had deteriorated through 1946 and early 1947. The reorganization of the cabinet within a few days of the CGIL Florence Congress changed this atmosphere completely. De Gasperi eliminated the Communists and Socialists from their ministries, and set up a cabinet of Christian Democratic, technical and independent personalities. He later widened the cabinet with representatives of the Republican, Liberal, and PSLI groups.[55] The principal objective was announced to be the handling of the problem of inflation. The well-known liberal economist, Professor Luigi Einaudi, was given responsibility for coordinating all government economic policy.

The summer and fall of 1947 witnessed a drastic change in the economic and trade union atmosphere of the country. The government, under Luigi Einaudi's inspiration, inaugurated a deflationary program which, combined with longer-run economic forces already at work in the economy, bore fruit by the fall in reversing the wildly inflationary situation which had continued until that time. On the trade union side politics and particularly the Communist political position dominated the scene. It had been feared by many that the exclusion of the Communists and Nenni Socialists from the government would lead to a determined effort by these groups to create demonstrations, strikes, violence on a scale sufficiently large to prove to the government that without these groups inside the government, public order could not be maintained. Actually, nothing of the sort happened. Uncertainty and confusion characterized the Communist position during the summer months. The same strikes for wage increases and the same demonstrations against the high cost of living took place in no higher order of magnitude than before the tripartite government coalition had broken up.

The increase in agitations, strike activity, and general trade union militancy developed some months after the new government had been in office. The establishment of the Cominform and the new international Communist line, following on the heels of the all-out declaration of war

54. For discussion of this issue at the congress and text of articles, *see Ibid.,* pp 118–119, 134–136, 175–177, 201, 270, 316–317, 337–338, 341–344, 363.

55. *See* Leo Valiani, *L'avvento di De Gasperi* (Turin, 1949), pp. 102–128.

against the Marshall Plan, started the Communist apparatus in Italy on its new line, as in other western European countries.

A large-scale campaign of economic disruption got under way during the fall. It was able to feed on the immediate effects of the deflationary government policy — a drop in producton and an increase in the already large-scale unemployment. But the Italian CGIL Communist leaders did not, as the Communists did in France, try an all-out national general strike. A more diversified set of techniques for disruption of the economy was used in a series of short stoppages, slow-downs, and general strikes affecting different areas and sectors of the economy in rotation, gradually encompassing the entire country. A great wave of strikes characterized the labor scene during the winter of 1947. But the Communist objectives were not achieved. Although the economy was hurt, it suffered no serious setback. Politically, the government was able to maintain its position without concessions to the Communists. The basic effects were felt in the trade unions. The CGIL was weakened and was pushed further along the road toward a split. As in France, the Communist labor offensive of the winter of 1947 spelled the end of trade union unity. Unlike France, however, the actual splitting up of the organization did not start until some months afterwards.

During the winter of 1947–1948, Christian Democratic and PSLI officials frequently voted against the majority strike decisions in the executive bodies of the unions. Accusations, recriminations, and sharp controversies were carried on in the press between the Communist and the Christian Democratic trade union leaders. The most notable of these cases involved a general strike in Rome in December 1947 during which the Christian Democrats not only voted against calling the strike, but urged workers to refrain from striking. The issue over which the strike was called involved the CGIL demand for increased public works to alleviate the growing unemployment problem.[56] The political nature of the strike was underlined by the fact that immediately before the strike started the government had committed itself to the expenditure of an amount close to that demanded by the trade unions. The Communists insisted on going through with the strike anyhow.

The Christian Democratic faction thereupon urged workers to disregard the strike call. The situation led to a sharp controversy in the National

56. CGIL, *Notiziario*, I, 17, December 20, 1947, pp. 3–4; *Il Corriere della Sera* (Milan daily), December 9, 10, 11, 12 and 13, 1947; *Il Popolo*, December 9, 10, 11, 12 and 13, 1947; *L'Unità*, December 9, 10, 11, 12 and 13, 1947. The Christian faction distributed a leaflet on the eve of the strike calling on the workers to disregard the strike call ". . . Do not concede to political imposition. By reporting for work you defend your liberty and concretely contribute to that productive recovery which alone can resolve the problems of labor and reconstruction." Quoted in G. B. Bozzola, "Cinque anni di sindacalismo communista in Italia," *Realtà Sociale d'Oggi* (Milan), VI, new series, 2 (February 1951), p. 107.

Directive Committee of the CGIL. The Christian Democrats, PSLI, and Republicans had earlier decided that since the strike weapon was being abused by the Communists, referenda should be held before strikes were called.[57] The minority defended this thesis at the Directive Committee meeting and the Christian Democrats justified their position in the Rome strike on the basis of its political nature. Di Vittorio, on the other hand, accused the Christian Democrats of strikebreaking and of breaching the principles of trade union discipline.

The most extreme view of the Communists was expressed by Renato Bittosi, one of the CGIL national secretaries, and reflected the attitude of some among the Communists that trade union unity was already a thing of the past. "At the Confederal Directive Committee which will soon be held at Bologna, we Communist trade union leaders will raise the problem of belonging to the CGIL of those who in violation of the decision of the majority encourage or take part in strikebreaking. The Christian faction should know that in CGIL we Communists will not tolerate this fifth column." [58]

Di Vittorio proposed a set of rules which would permit making public the views of minorities on CGIL decisions by attaching a summary of such views at the end of official CGIL announcements of policy decisions. Minorities, however, would be required to maintain union discipline, abide by majority decisions and refrain from attempting to undercut them.[59] When these proposals were rejected by the Christian Democrats,[60] it was decided to circulate the proposed rules to all provincial organizations for discussion and expression of views. Since the rules represented a plausible position so long as trade union unity was maintained, the Communists made the most of the position of the Christian Democrats to propagandize in the provincial organizations in their own favor. The rules were, in fact, adopted at the CGIL Directive Committee session of February 24–25, 1948 with the Christian Democrats abstaining and the Republicans and right-wing Socialists approving with reservations. The Christian Democratic position was based on the claim that the new rule modified the Pact of Rome and the constitution of the organization and that it was, therefore, an issue properly handled at the congress of the CGIL.[61]

57. For discussion of this issue, *see, for example, Quotidiano* (Rome daily), December 18, 1947; *Umanità* (Milan daily), December 18, 1947; *Il Popolo,* December 28, 1947; *L'Avanti* (Rome daily), December 17, 1947; *L'Unità,* December 27, 1947.

58. *L'Unità,* December 16, 1947.

59. Report of meeting and text of rules given in CGIL *Notiziario,* I, 18, December 30, 1947, pp. 4–5.

60. For text of Christian faction's position, *see Il Popolo,* January 21, 1948, p. 1.

61. CGIL, *Notiziario,* II, 6, March 1, 1948, pp. 141–143. For summary of views of Pastore for Christian Democrats, Canini for PSLI and Parri for Republicans, quoted from their newspaper statements, see, ACLI publication, *Informazioni Sindacali,* II, 1 (January 1948), p. 37.

The April 18, 1948 national elections. The strained relations between the Communist-PSI combination and the minority groups in the CGIL were accentuated during the early months of 1948 as the campaign for the first parliamentary elections under the new constitution was bitterly fought out. The Nenni Socialists (PSI) presented a common list of candidates with the Communists under the banner of a "Democratic Popular Front." The Saragat Socialists (PSLI) made common cause with another Socialist breakaway group under the leadership of Ivan Matteo Lombardo and Ignazio Silone. The Christian Democrats, however, became the rallying point of the anti-Communists. The Communists had made such impressive progress in organization and influence that it was feared the elections might carry them to power in combination with their Socialist allies, or make effective government impossible without them. The campaign was thus regarded to be of vital importance, reflected in the intensity and determination with which it was conducted. The East-West conflict had focused world attention upon the Italian election, coming as it did after the Communists' winter offensive against the western European economies, with its background of Soviet rejection of cooperation in further reconstruction in Europe and of the establishment of the Cominform. The Communist coup in Czechoslovakia shortly before the Italian elections heightened the significance of the elections in the minds of Italians and the western world generally, and may have had some immediately negative effects upon the fortunes of the Communists in Italy.

The elections, held on April 18, 1948, gave an unequivocal answer to the Communist bid for power. As the only "mass" party outside the Communist front, the Christian Democrats had become the rallying point of those opposed to the Communists. They received 12,708,263 votes or 48.5 percent of the total cast, and obtained a clear majority in the Chamber of Deputies, electing 306 deputies of a total chamber of 574. The Communist front obtained, however, a substantial proportion of the vote, 8,137,468, or 31.0 percent of the total. The Socialists were clearly shown to be the junior partners in the front, receiving 53 seats compared with 131 received by the Communists. If one uses first preferences marked on the common lists of the front as a criterion, the Communists received about 5 million votes or 18.7 percent while the Socialists received the remaining 12.3 percent. The Democratic Socialist combination received 1,856,287 votes or 7.1 percent of the total and elected 33 deputies. The Republicans, with 651,394 votes, or 2.5 percent of the total elected 10 deputies. The Liberals elected 15 deputies, the Monarchists 13 and the remaining 14 deputies were elected from among various rightist groups, principally the neo-Fascist Italian Social Movement (MSI) which had received 527,039 votes or 2.0 percent of the total.[62]

62. Istituto Centrale di Statistica, *Annuario 1944–1948,* table 160, pp. 158–159 and *I deputati e senatori del primo parlamento repubblicano* (Rome, 1949), p. 75. For

During the election campaign the dissensions and strains within the CGIL were greatly increased. Many of the CGIL leaders were candidates for election to Parliament and each of the factions had an obvious important political stake in the elections. The organization officially took no position,[63] but the Communists, with their complete control of CGIL machinery, used the organization to further their campaign propaganda. The CGIL official weekly, *Il Lavoro*, for example, was used consistently to popularize the propaganda themes of the Democratic Popular Front and to put the Christian Democratic position in an unfavorable light. While Giulio Pastore, who had replaced Rapelli as head of the CGIL Christian Democratic faction in 1947, protested, it had little effect.[64]

The Democratic Alliance of June 1948. In the aftermath of the political elections, which assured the possibility of stable democratic government for a five-year period, the lines between the factions within the CGIL were more tightly drawn than ever. The Christian Democrats on the political level could govern if need be by themselves, but preferred the cooperation and participation of the minor democratic parties, the Liberals, the Republicans, and the Democratic Socialists. De Gasperi led the government again and remained the undisputed leader of the party throughout the following five years. He offered political stability and a firm democratic orientation, although he promoted little of an affirmative nature in the economic and organizational sense to win back to the center parties the support given to the extreme left. Immediately following the 1948 elections, the atmosphere was one of democratic victory and assurance that the Communists no longer represented an immediate threat.

It was in this atmosphere that the democratic elements within the CGIL began to prepare for their exodus from the organization. In June the Christian Democratic, Republican and PSLI leaders of the CGIL set up an "Alliance for the Unity and Independence of the Trade Unions." They denied the accusations of the CGIL majority that they were maneuvering toward splitting the organization.[65] The program they adopted on June 17 was directed toward obtaining greater democracy and tolerance for minority views in the CGIL.[66] They obviously could have had no expectations that

---

Communist-Socialist vote breakdown analysis see *Orientamenti* (monthly PSI bulletin), new series, no. 7–9 (March–May 1949), p. 95.

63. The CGIL had in fact sent a circular to all National Federations and Chambers of Labor (Circular No. 293) on February 13, 1948 warning against permitting the organization to get directly involved in the election campaign and urging that where union officials of different factions might be running against each other as candidates for Parliament, attacks be avoided which might have repercussions upon the CGIL. CGIL, *Notiziario*, II, 5, February 20, 1948, p. 116.

64. *See* his letter to the editor of *Lavoro* printed in *Il Popolo*, March 28, 1948.

65. *Lavoro* (official CGIL weekly), I, 17, June 23, 1948.

66. For text of declaration *see Informazioni Sindacali*, II, 6 (June 1948), pp. 70–75.

in the situation as it existed on the political and trade union levels at the time, unity in the trade unions could be preserved. On the other hand, the theme of unity had been given such unanimous support in the process of rebuilding the trade union movement and making it a powerful institution, that unity had become a symbol with a force of its own. Before breaking away from the unified organization, even though politically the organization now principally served Communist tactical purposes, a period of preparation was required in the view of the minority groups.

The alliance was intended to serve this purpose of psychological preparation for breaking unity and affording a rallying point for maximizing the strength of the democratic groups. Developments thwarted this purpose. Within a month the chain of events unleashed by the attempted assassination of the Communist leader, Togliatti, resulted in the first break in trade union unity. The democratic elements left the CGIL not in a coordinated, organized fashion but in a series of splits which made the process of building democratic unionism in opposition to CGIL a more difficult and painful process.

The Democratic break-aways. The Christian Democratic faction was the first to break away from the CGIL. It left within a month after the formation of the alliance, without consulting its Republican and Democratic Socialist colleagues. The attempted assassination of Togliatti on July 14, 1948 and its consequences led directly to the break. The attempted assassination was an individual act of a Rightist student, who shot Togliatti as he was leaving the Parliament building in Rome. Togliatti was seriously wounded and for a time his life hung in the balance. The immediate reaction throughout the country was a shutdown of all economic activity through a general strike with insurrectional overtones. Many plants in the north were occupied by the workers, with red flags raised on the roofs, in some instances municipal buildings were occupied, and throughout that day the government was uncertain whether it was faced with a full-scale insurrection. By the time the Executive Committee of the CGIL met at 6 P.M. on the day of the attempted assassination to declare a national strike, the order was superfluous. The declaration approved by the Executive Committee set no time limit on the strike and encouraged fears that the strike was part of a Communist insurrection by such statements as "The Italian General Confederation of Labor, in proclaiming its solemn protest, affirms that the present government, because of the policy it follows, does not guarantee the liberty and peaceful cohabitation of all the citizens in the framework of democratic and republican law."[67]

Actually, it would appear that the Communists had no intention at the time of attempting an insurrection, but that during the first day its primary concern was to get control over a movement which was partly spontaneous,

67. Text of declaration in CGIL, *Notiziario,* II, 20, July 20, 1948, p. 507.

partly the result of over-zealousness by its local leaders and was from their point of view completely out of hand.[68] In addition, once the movement came under their central control, its purpose became one of limited demonstration of strength in their protest against government policies.

The government felt compelled to act as though it were faced with insurrection. Troops were called up. The Minister of Interior, Mario Scelba, mobilized the police forces throughout the country. The government carefully refrained from taking direct action against the Communist Party or the CGIL, but demonstrated its readiness to cope with the situation as events would require. Its statement to the people was an appeal for termination of the strike, and a condemnation of the strike action.[69] The coolheadedness of the government during the first day of the strike saved the country from bloodshed.

At the time of the CGIL Executive Committee meeting on July 14, the Christian Democratic members voiced concern over the situation. Whether they actually voted against the general strike motion became a matter of controversy later, but it appears that in the confused atmosphere of the meeting no formal vote was taken.[70] The Republican representative on the committee, Enrico Parri, had urged that the strike be limited to twenty-four hours and while the PSLI representative was not at the meeting, the Central Trade Union Committee of that party took a similar position.

On July 15, as the strike entered its second day, the eleven Christian Democratic members of the CGIL Directive Committee sent a statement to national CGIL headquarters threatening to leave the organization unless the strike were called off by the end of the day. The Christian Democrats meanwhile did not attend the Executive Committee meeting scheduled for that night. The Executive Committee meeting of July 15 was held against the background of the Christian Democratic faction's threat and the government's announcement that it would take appropriate action directly against the CGIL unless the strike were called off. The Executive Committee decided that the strike would be terminated by noon, July 16. The Christian Democratic trade union faction met that same night. At the close of its meeting, Giulio Pastore announced that since no reply had been received to the letter sent to the "Social-Communist leaders of the CGIL," his group was sending instructions to Christian Democratic workers throughout Italy to resume work in the morning.

The first split had taken place. The Christian Democratic national CGIL officials no longer attended meetings of the CGIL executive bodies. On July

68. *See, for example,* Vittorio Gorresio's analysis of the situation in his *I carissimi nemici* (Milan, 1949), pp. 275–289.

69. *Informazioni Sindacali,* II, 7 (July 1948), p. 39.

70. CGIL, *Notiziario,* II, 20, July 20, 1948, pp. 508–510; *Informazioni Sindacali,* II, 7 (July 1948), p. 38, 39–40.

22, the National Council of ACLI, the organization which had been established for worker education and assistance purposes by the Catholics in 1945 and had been the nucleus around which the CGIL Christian Democratic faction of CGIL had been built,[71] declared "that the recent general strike, having destroyed the Pact of Rome, and violated the spirit and letter of the statute, has produced a definitive and irreparable rupture in trade union unity," and that as a result the Christian faction "cannot consider the breaking of such unity, since one cannot destroy what is already destroyed but must only formally recognize it." The statement concluded by announcing that the Christian trade union faction would organize a democratic trade union organization.[72] The Christian Democratic party also announced its support of the position taken by the Christian Democratic trade union leaders.[73]

Formation of LCGIL. The CGIL Executive Committee announced on July 20 that the Christian Democrats by their actions had put themselves outside the organization. A circular was sent to all Chambers of Labor and National Federations ordering that all those agreeing with or supporting the ACLI motion should automatically be deprived of their positions in the CGIL and its subdivisions.[74]

The Republican and PSLI trade unionists, taken by surprise by the Christian Democratic action and resentful of the failure to coordinate with them, had meanwhile decided to remain in the CGIL. The PSLI trade unionists urged instead that a congress of the CGIL be called to re-examine the basis for genuinely nonpolitical party trade union orientation.[75] At the national conference of PSLI trade union officials held in Milan during August, this position was confirmed, but came to nothing when the PSI trade union faction refused its support, committing itself to continued cooperation with the Communists.[76] The Republicans and Democratic Socialists damned both the Communists and Christian Democrats as having been responsible for the conditions creating the split. Giovanni Canini, the principal PSLI representative in CGIL, in a speech at the August 21–23 PSLI Trade Union Conference characterized the situation before the split as one in which

71. The eleven Christian Democratic members of the CGIL Directive Committee were also members of the ACLI National Council. For a discussion of ACLI, *see* next chapter.

72. *Informazioni Sindacali,* II, 7 (July 1948), pp. 42–43.

73. *Ibid.,* p. 53.

74. CGIL, *Notiziario,* II, 21, July 30, 1948, p. 537. *Informazioni Sindacali,* II, 7 (July 1948), p. 44.

75. *La Voce Republicana* (Rome daily), July 24, 1948; *Battaglie Sindacali* (fortnightly of the Ufficio Sindacale Centrale of PSLI, using same name as pre-fascist CGL weekly), Milan, II 4, July 31, 1948; *L'Umanità,* July 28, 1948.

76. *Battaglie Sindacali,* II, 16, August 31, 1948; *ibid.,* II, 17, September 15, 1948; *Informazioni Sindacali,* II, 8–9 (August–September 1948), pp. 49–50 for text of resolution.

the Communists followed a constant policy of agitation and the Christian Democrats followed a constant defense of the government. The Republican trade union faction at its convention on September 24–26, 1948, declared in a resolution that the Communists and the Christian Democratic trade union factions provoked the split of the CGIL for party purposes and not for the necessity of the defense of the interests of the working class.[77]

The Christian Democratic trade union group at a meeting of all its former CGIL officials held on July 31 and August 1 agreed to give responsibility to its eleven leaders who had been members of the CGIL Directive Committee for coordinating the effort to mobilize as many members of the CGIL as possible to leave the organization.[78] Calling itself the Christian Trade Union Faction (CSC) the group proceeded to organize, in effect, into a new trade union organization leaning heavily for support upon the ACLI. Instead of setting up formal organization immediately, however, it was decided first to obtain the endorsement of a congress of ACLI. Also left for ACLI Congress approval was the position advocated by the top Catholic trade unionists that the organization be established along non-confessional lines open to all democratic groups. It was natural for the ACLI to be called upon in this fashion since it had functioned as the cohesive force for the Catholic faction within CGIL. The ACLI Congress was held on September 15 to 18.[79] It overwhelmingly approved the establishment of an organization along the lines recommended by the Catholic trade union leaders.[80]

A constituent convention was then called on October 16 to 18, 1948, at which the *Libera Confederazione Generale Italiana del Lavoro,* the Free Italian General Confederation of Labor (LCGIL), was formally established with Giulio Pastore as secretary general.[81]

The CGIL reacted violently to the establishment of LCGIL, attacking it largely upon the basis that LCGIL was a plot of the Christian Democratic government and of employers to split and weaken the trade union movement. The propaganda of the Communists also lumped the split with their attacks upon the European Recovery Program as an imperialist venture of the United States. The CGIL, in an effort to belittle the effect of the split, tried to give the impression that a significant part of the Christian Demo-

77. *Ibid.,* pp. 51–52; *Battaglie Sindacali,* II, 16, August 31, 1948.

78. *Informazioni Sindacali,* II, 8–9 (August–September 1948), p. 19; *Il Popolo,* August 8, 1948.

79. *Le ACLI,* fortnightly bulletin of ACLI, III, 12, August 15, 1948, p. 1.

80. The text of the final resolution of the ACLI Congress on the subject of trade unions is given in *Informazioni Sindacali,* II, 8–9 (August–September 1948), pp. 47–48. See also, *Le ACLI,* III, 14, September 20, 1948, p. 3.

81. *Informazioni Sindacali,* II, 10 (October 1948), pp. 41–42 and *ibid.,* II, 11–12 (November–December 1948), pp. 51–52; also *Bollettino d'Informazioni Sindacali* (official periodical of LCGIL and, from May 1950, of CISL), I, 1, December 20, 1948.

cratic faction had not followed the Pastore group out of the organization. A Social Christian Trade Union faction was set up within the CGIL and given considerable publicity by the organization. The faction was led by a handful of minor figures who had practically no following.[82] While the CGIL for a time threatened to sue the LCGIL for taking a name so similar to its own, the issue was raised only for propaganda purposes. On one significant matter the CGIL proved conciliatory. At the end of July the Christian Democratic faction leaders had started a court action to obtain division of the assets of the CGIL on the grounds that since the Pact of Rome had been broken, the organization as set up in that pact no longer existed. A compromise agreement was reached in which the CGIL agreed to pay twenty-three million lire in settlement of all claims against itself and its affiliates.[83]

In its early organizational stages the already existing structure of ACLI was of great assistance to LCGIL, and ACLI activists were urged by their organization to help in building the organization.[84] During the months following its establishment the LCGIL built its structure of National Unions and provincial equivalents of Chambers of Labor. By the beginning of 1949 it had a membership estimated at over 600,000, drawn almost exclusively from those who had supported the Christian Democratic faction in the CGIL.

Organization of FIL. The Republicans and Democratic Socialists meanwhile found their position increasingly difficult within the CGIL. As the relations between the western countries and the Soviet Union deteriorated and as the Communist parties of western Europe increasingly sharpened their position against "class collaboration" and against "American imperialism," the CGIL became more and more directly used as a political instrument, conceding little to the non-Communist minority elements within the organization. The exodus of the Christian Democrats had removed the only significant anti-Communist opposition. In power terms, the PSLI and Republicans represented little more than about 4 percent of the organization's membership. Given the Communist line of the moment, and the relative weakness of the minority groups, the CGIL leadership apparently felt keeping the minorities from splitting away was not worth any concessions.

During April a much publicized Labor Constituent Assembly was held after months of preliminary negotiations. The assembly was to study the

82. CGIL, *Notiziario*, II, 25, September 10, 1948, p. 651; *ibid.*, II, 27, September 30, 1948, p. 690; *ibid.*, II, 28, October 10, 1948, pp. 705–706.
83. *Ibid.*, II, 21, July 30, 1948, pp. 538–539; *ibid.*, II, 23–24, August 30, 1948, pp. 605–606; II, 31, November 10, 1948, p. 790. *Informazioni Sindacali*, II, 7 (July 1948), pp. 50–51. The courts refused to accept any further claims after the settlement was made. *See* e.g., CGIL, *Notiziario*, II, 29, October 20, 1948, pp. 740–743.
84. *See, for example,* "Compiti attuali" in *Le ACLI*, III, 14, September 20, 1948, p. 3.

problems relating to the creation of a democratic unified trade union movement. While the LCGIL refused to participate in the assembly, a few dissident Christian Democratic trade union leaders of the LCGIL attended.
Most of the attendance was from among PSLI and Republican and dissident PSI trade unionists and representatives of some white-collar employee National Unions which had left CGIL and had remained autonomous.
The assembly, despite much oratory, accomplished little. Its one decision
was to call for the establishment of a "study and propaganda committee"
to create "the preliminary conditions for . . . a consultation of all the elements of labor." [85]

While the PSLI and Republicans desired to leave the CGIL during the
early months of 1949, they realized their weakness as a trade union force,
and feared that if they joined in the LCGIL they would be lost as an unimportant minority group. Basically, their reluctance to join in the LCGIL
also stemmed from their attitude that anti-clerical traditions were strong
among the workers in many of the industrial areas and that the LCGIL
would be regarded as dominated by the Christian Democrats even if they
joined the organization. As a result, as they moved toward a break from
CGIL, they planned to set up a third organization which would attempt to
build up strength rapidly and would only then merge with the LCGIL.

An episode which hastened the split from the CGIL and dramatized the
non-democratic orientation of Communist leadership occurred at Molinella
on May 17. The PSLI faction had earlier won a majority in the communal
Chamber of Labor — possibly the only such situation in Italy. When the
PSLI majority took office, however, the Communists organized an assault
upon the offices and took them over after considerable violence during which
a woman was shot to death and thirty to forty workers were wounded.[86]

On May 24 a meeting of the PSLI Trade Union Council adopted a resolution to abandon the CGIL. The decision was approved by the party directorate two days later.[87] The Republican trade unionist leaders, on the basis
of the results of a referendum held among their following, voted on May 22,
1949 to leave the CGIL. A meeting of the two groups was then held on June
4 and a new organization, *Federazione Italiana del Lavoro,* the Federation
of Italian Workers (FIL), was set up. Enrico Parri and Giovanni Canini,
the leaders of the Republican and PSLI trade unionists were jointly named
as the national secretaries of the new organization.[88]

85. *Il Lavoro Italiano* (independent weekly, which became official UIL periodical
from February 1950), Rome, I, 1, May 27, 1949; *L'Umanità,* April 12, 1949, p. 1. For
critical comments by Pastore, see, LCGIL, *Conquiste del Lavoro,* II, 17, May 1, 1949,
p. 1.

86. *L'Umanità,* May 18, 1949.

87. *Battaglie Sindacali,* III, 7, May 24, 1949; *Informazioni Sindacali,* III, 5 (May
1949), pp. 301–302; *L'Umanità,* May 25, 1949.

88. *L'Umanità,* June 4, 1949.

The CGIL reaction to the latest defections from its ranks was characterized by Di Vittorio in an editorial in the Communist daily, *L'Unità*, entitled "Useless Betrayal." "Antonini, Dubinsky and the State Department can be satisfied — their orders have been followed to the letter . . . We assure the naive that *nothing at all will happen* . . . Parri's and Canini's activities, since they are without power or ability, will not exert the least influence on the situation." [89]

The autonomous Socialists. There were other officials of the CGIL who left the organization at approximately the same time as the Republicans and PSLI. A group of Socialist trade unionists at the PSI Congress of May 11–15, 1949 had attacked the policy of the party favoring cooperation with the Communists, taking the position that such cooperation had paralyzed all Socialist initiative in the CGIL. When the congress reaffirmed its position of close collaboration with the Communists, this "autonomous" Socialist trade union group left the party in the split which Romita precipitated at the time. The group included two National vice-secretaries of the CGIL and the Socialist national secretaries of the chemical, textile, and metal workers' Federations. The Socialist national secretary of the Farmworkers' Union, who had resigned from his position and left CGIL some months before also became part of this group.

The group had earlier negotiated with PSLI trade unionists to leave the CGIL together. In fact, conversations between the trade unionists as well as conversations directed toward political unification between the political representatives of the two groups were going on when, without warning to the "autonomists," the decision to leave CGIL was taken by the PSLI group. The day before the decision discussions had taken place regarding the transformation of the PSLI national convention into a congress for Socialist unification of the ex-PSI forces. The immediate reaction was a statement by Romita, one of the ex-PSI political leaders, that the decision "seriously compromises the deliberations of yesterday evening and prejudices in a serious manner achievement of Socialist unification . . . [we] propose to remain within the CGIL to work in a democratic and unitary manner, at least as long as the possibility exists." The group had no intention of remaining in the CGIL, but the PSLI action had removed the possibility of a combined walkout and reduced the possibility of the "autonomists" joining in FIL. Two underlying issues appear to have been the question of allocation of positions in the new organization to be formed and refusal of the "autonomists" to accept commitments in advance that the new organization would fuse with LCGIL.

At a meeting of the Directive Committee of the CGIL on June 13, the Socialist CGIL secretary, Santi, obtained the removal of Dalla Chiesa and Bulleri, the two autonomous Socialist CGIL vice-secretaries, on the grounds

89. *L'Unità* (Rome), June 9, 1949.

that they had left PSI and that they had been proposed originally for their positions by the PSI faction at the Florence Congress of CGIL.[90] Within a short time all the "autonomous" Socialist trade union leaders were outside the CGIL.

Unification negotiations — formation of CISL. Pastore had announced on behalf of LCGIL long before the CGIL split of May–June 1949, that his organization was open to any democratic groups breaking away from CGIL. FIL announced at the time of its organization on June 4 "that FIL intends to work for the unity of the world of labor through the unification of all those trade union forces which follow the same objectives of independence and democracy of the trade union." [91] Negotiations between the two organizations got under way officially early in August.[92] It was agreed that for immediate trade union issues FIL and LCGIL would exchange views before taking positions and that a continuing committee would be set up to consider the problems of unifying the two organizations. Several white-collar unions which had left the CGIL and had remained autonomous were encouraged to participate in the unification discussions. As the negotiations proceeded, efforts were made to include the "autonomous" Socialists. These efforts failed, however, and plans for unification proceeded without them.

During September it was agreed in principle that unification should take place as soon as national congresses of the two organizations could be held to approve such action.[93] During the fall and early winter, however, bitter polemics developed between those who favored unification and those who opposed it. There was little problem within the LCGIL. While there were some dissenting voices principally that of Guiseppe Rapelli and his followers, the Congress of LCGIL held on November 4 to 7, authorized the General Council of the organization to proceed to make arrangements for the unification.[94] The problem of unification arose mainly within FIL and with the "autonomous" Socialists. Few of the leaders of FIL were, in fact, anxious to proceed to unification immediately. The pressure of events and finances, however, was such as to quiet their reservations. While they claimed to have organized 400,000 workers by the end of 1949, it is doubtful that

90. CGIL, *Notiziario*, III, 17, June 20, 1949, p. 642; *Lavoro*, II, 25, June 19–25, 1949.

91. *Notiziario Sindacale* (official FIL monthly), I, 3-4 (September–October 1949), p. 7.

92. *Bollettino d'Informazioni Sindacali*, II, 16, August 31, 1949, p. 3. *Conquiste del Lavoro* (official weekly of LCGIL and, from May 1950, of CISL), II, 32, August 14, 1949; *Notiziario Sindacale* I, 1–2 (July–August 1949), pp. 10–11.

93. *Bollettino d'Informazioni Sindacali*, II, 19, October 15, 1949, p. 9; *Conquiste del Lavoro*, II, 37, September 25, 1949. For text of agreement setting forth principles of unification, *see Conquiste del Lavoro*, III, 4, January 29, 1950.

94. The LCGIL general council took final action on unification on February 16, 1950. *Conquiste del Lavoro*, III, 8, February 26, 1950, p. 1.

they achieved a following as great as the strength of the Republican and PSLI faction at the 1947 CGIL Congress, which had been approximately 190,000. They had from the start been handicapped by the accusation that they were committed in advance, as a result of pressure from American trade unions, to unification with LCGIL by the end of the year.[95]

Considerable opposition to unification existed within FIL as well as from the Republican Party. In fact, when Parri and A. Claudio Rocchi, the principal Republican trade unionists in FIL, committed themselves to unification despite the party's opposition, they were expelled from the party.[96] Parri and Rocchi pointed to their position as a demonstration of their political independence and their exclusive concern with trade union matters. The party, on the other hand, in support of its position, pointed to its referendum among Republican workers and the opposition of most Republican trade unionists to unification. The party, after unification, also claimed that most Republican workers did not follow Parri and Rocchi into the unified organization.

The "autonomous" Socialists had negotiated with FIL to enter that organization after its formation, but broke off when it was clear that the leaders of FIL were irrevocably committed to immediate unification with LCGIL and were not willing to assign to the "autonomists" a sufficient number of positions to permit them effectively to influence the unification policy.[97] The aftermath was an exchange of recriminations which led to complete breaking off of relations between the two groups.[98]

As FIL prepared for its congress which was to decide the unification question, its top leadership became concerned with the rising opposition to the unification already decided upon by them. The Milan FIL provincial union chamber even initiated a periodical and launched a manifesto in opposition to unification, which was circulated to other FIL affiliates. The national FIL leadership took the position that opposition to the national office position was sabotage of the organization, and appointed commissioners to take over the offices from operating officials who opposed unification in a number of smaller provincial centers, including Reggio Calabria, La Spezia, Parma, and Bari. In the large centers, such as Milan and Rome, where the majority was against unification, the FIL leadership did not dare apply similar tactics. As a result of these developments, by the time the FIL Congress was held early in February 1950, the organization had in fact already been split. Most groups opposing unification, having been treated

95. For FIL position and defense of its policies, *see* FIL, *La nostra battaglia per i lavoratori, congresso nazionale, Napoli, 5–6, Febbraio 1950, relazione della segreteria* (Rome, n.d.), especially pp. 3–12 and 57–60.

96. *L'Umanità*, December 15, 1949; *Cronache Sociali*, June 1, 1950, p. 84.

97. *Panorama Socialista* (Rome weekly of L'Unificazione Socialista group), new series, no. 1, October 5, 1949.

98. *See, for example,* FIL, *La nostra battaglia*, pp. 7–8, 11.

as though opposition to unification was a breach of organizational discipline, chose not to send representatives to the congress. The congress overwhelmingly approved unification with the LCGIL.[99] It is doubtful, however, whether much more than half of the FIL membership entered the new unified organization.

The actual unification was a piecemeal affair which proceeded during March and April in the various provincial and industry unions. The official establishment of the new national organization took place on April 30. The new organization called itself the *Confederazione Italiana Sindacati Lavoratori*, Italian Confederation of Trade Unions (CISL). It claimed a membership of between 1,500,000 and 1,600,000, which in the tradition of postwar Italian trade unionism was no doubt exaggerated. To help overcome the identification of the new organization in the minds of many workers as a Catholic trade union, the LCGIL leadership had made concessions on a generous scale to representation claims of FIL and the autonomous national white collar unions on the executive bodies of CISL. These national unions, which had been much publicized as a significant element in the unification, in fact split three ways. Some members went back to CGIL — which had previously urged its supporters in these organizations to remain inside unless unification was attempted. Others eventually joined the new organization, UIL. Only a part went into CISL.

Pastore became secretary general, but of the four national secretaries, only one was a Christian Democrat, Luigi Morelli. The others were Canini, Parri, and Consoni, the latter representing the autonomous national unions. The Christian Democrats did not take an absolute majority of the seats on the Executive Committee.

Despite the allocation of positions, however, the former LCGIL leadership ran the new organization. This was inevitable in the light of the relative quality of leadership and the relative membership strength brought to the CISL by LCGIL. It is doubtful whether the membership brought to CISL by FIL and the autonomous unions accounted for as much as 15 percent of its strength. The membership growth of CISL during its first years was modest. It made no appreciable inroads into the CGIL membership, although the latter organization did lose strength in some industrial areas while gaining strength in some southern agricultural areas. In this early period, CISL seemed still to be regarded as a Catholic organization and seemed identified in the minds of workers with the Christian Democratic government.

Establishment of UIL

The "autonomous" Socialist trade unionists and the groups within FIL which had opposed unification, set up a third labor confederation, the

99. *L'Unione dei Lavoratori* (official weekly of FIL), II, 5, February 5, 1950.

Unione Italiana del Lavoro, the Italian Union of Labor (UIL) on March 5, 1950. It had few funds and could not afford any ambitious organizational campaign. It was handicapped at the same time by a less concrete but important basic problem. Through 1948 and the first half of 1949 many workers within the ranks of CGIL had increasingly become disillusioned with the Communist leadership's use of the organization as a political instrument. They stayed in CGIL, by and large, rather than join LCGIL because of their attitude that on immediate job problems the CGIL offered them more militant leadership and effective protection. At the time of the establishment of FIL, that organization had expected to capitalize upon the situation by offering a militant alternative to what it regarded as the excesses of CGIL and the timidity of LCGIL. It lost whatever potential it had for separate appeal by committing itself almost immediately to unification with LCGIL. In addition, through the rest of the year, the polemics, the accusations, and recriminations between those who wanted unification and those who opposed it created a situation of further distrust by the workers. The result was that those organized workers who might under other circumstances have left the organization stayed in CGIL or dropped out of the trade union movement entirely, presumably as repelled by the spectacle of Socialist and Republican squabbling as by Communist excesses. During this period, the "autonomous" trade union leaders, though out of the CGIL, set up no organization of their own. With their reputation as energetic organizers, leaving key positions in the CGIL, they had confidently expected to carry significant numbers out of the organization. Instead, for almost nine months, they offered no alternative organization to workers.

This combination of factors had destroyed, at least for the time, the possibility of promoting a dramatic widespread exodus from the CGIL into a new organization, whatever its appeal on militant non-Communist grounds might be. The psychological time for capitalizing on disaffection had passed. The result was that UIL got off to a slow start and though it made progress during the latter part of 1950, its membership level remained modest. While it claimed approximately 400,000 members at the end of 1950,[100] the figure, like most trade union membership figures in Italy, was no doubt greatly exaggerated.

An element which must also be taken into account was the fact that relations between UIL and CISL were sharply hostile and criticism was directed more frequently at each other than at the CGIL. After its formation, UIL had invited both CISL and CGIL to meet with it to discuss the possibility of cooperating on specific trade union issues when agreement was found to exist among the three organizations. It was not planned that any continuing machinery be set up for cooperation, however. The CGIL agreed

100. *Il Lavoro Italiano,* III, 1, January 6, 1951, p. 1.

to such a meeting, but the CISL refused and instead attacked UIL for playing into the hands of the Communists.[101] This led to a series of acrimonious exchanges which rebounded to the advantage of neither organization.

The situation in 1950. While the splits away from CGIL were taking place, the atmosphere and relative bargaining position between management and labor was radically different from the atmosphere prevailing during the early years after the fall of fascism. There were three basic changes which had occurred: (1) the Communists, particularly after the general elections of April 18, 1948, were no longer regarded as an immediate threat to the fundamental political, economic, and social institutions of the country; (2) the success of the deflationary policy during the latter part of 1947 had resulted first in reduced production and then in the stabilization of the economy at a low level of production with large-scale unemployment. While the general production level did rise slowly through 1949 and 1950, heavy industry remained at a low level of activity and large-scale layoffs in these industries continued through 1950; (3) the CGIL policy of "permanent agitation," combined with the increasingly open use of the CGIL as a direct political tool, not only had split the labor movement into three competing groups, but had also resulted in hundreds of thousands of workers dropping their membership in trade unions altogether.

All these elements had contributed to the strengthening of the bargaining power of management and the employer associations. Although the CGIL could deliver far less to its membership than previously, nonetheless it had managed to maintain the initiative in the labor field. The principal concern of workers had become the fear of lay-offs and need for employment. The CGIL made these matters the principal economic issues around which it centered its activities during 1950. Such activities took both a general and a specific form. Its specific form was intransigent opposition to lay-offs, particularly in heavy industry. In a number of instances during 1950 the CGIL dramatized its position through worker occupation and expulsion of management from plants which were for a time operated by the workers alone. Its general form was a much publicized national economic expansion plan, its *piano del lavoro,* which it developed and dramatized as the only method of maximizing employment.

The CGIL's national economic plan became, in fact, its principal economic propaganda weapon during 1950 to counteract the unfavorable publicity CGIL was getting in its specifically political activity. The plan and the campaign in support of it were announced at the congress of the CGIL in October 1949. Regional meetings were held during the ensuing months leading up to a national conference held at Rome in February 1950. The planning of the session and the dramatization of the issues involved were

101. UIL, *Relazione presentata al primo congresso nazionale dell' Unione Italiana del Lavoro, Roma, 6–7–8 Decembre 1953* (Rome, n.d.), p. 29.

sufficiently successful that the Rome conference was attended by economic and political figures from all political parties as well as by several Ministers in the government. It was first-page news throughout the country. The plan itself was not oriented toward revolutionizing the economy, but was largely a Keynesian type of approach to the problem of increasing production and employment opportunities.[102] It mattered little to the CGIL that technical aspects of the plan were faulty. What was important was its propagandistic success. The CGIL staged another national conference on the plan during June in Milan and managed to keep it in the public eye throughout the year.[103]

The CGIL support among wage earners, however, was not uniformly favorable. Despite its opposition to the Atlantic Pact and landing of arms in Italy, arms were landed without incident and protest demonstrations were largely disregarded. The demonstrations called to protest General Eisenhower's visit to Italy in January were also far from successful. The CGIL had become one of the principal instruments in the "peace" campaign of the Communists and on this issue it had considerable more success in its petition campaigns.

The increased opposition of government and management to CGIL initiatives did not necessarily reduce worker support of CGIL, as such opposition served as a double-edged sword. It lessened support of the organization among more timid groups of workers. But among workers who had a traditional distrust of government and an active resentment against management, the CGIL capitalized upon the government's and management's attitudes in strengthening its claim to being a militant defender of workers' rights.

An element which also affected the situation through 1949 and early 1950 was a series of violent clashes between worker demonstrators and police in which a number of workers were killed and wounded. The CGIL used these incidents as focal points for protest demonstration strikes of national scope.[104] Response to strike calls of this character, as to those of an economic character, were generally much more favorable than those specifically identified as political.

Trade Union Competition

The period of dramatic shifts and reorganizations during 1948 to 1950 was followed by several years of imperceptible change and seemingly relative stability in the distribution of trade union forces. Basic changes were

102. See CGIL, *Il piano del lavoro* (Rome, 1950), the stenographic record of the February 18–20, 1950 Rome Conference.
103. Giuseppe Di Vittorio, *Comincia la lotta per il piano del lavoro* (Rome, 1950).
104. CGIL, *Da Melissa a Modena* (Rome, 1950).

occurring, but they were not of the dramatic order of earlier years. Nor did the latter years witness a state of flux among trade union membership which had potentially existed earlier. The distribution of membership among the three trade union organizations, according to their own claims at the end of 1950, was 5,000,000 in CGIL, 1,500,000 in CISL and 400,000 in UIL.[105] During the following years the membership claims, although consistently exaggerated, indicated the trend in relative strength among the organizations. CGIL claimed 4,938,000 members at the time of its congress in November–December 1952.[106] and 4,625,000 at the end of 1954.[107] CISL claimed 1,812,000 members at the time of its congress in November 1951[108] and approximately two million members at the end of 1954. UIL claimed approximately one half million at the time of its December 1953 congress and the same number for the following year.

There were many encouraging signs in the economy during the early 1950's. Industrial production began increasing at a relatively high rate. The increased level of industrial production had only modest impact upon the welfare of the wage-earner population, however. Real wages for employed workers rose somewhat during the period, but unemployment remained at the same level as it had been since 1948, approximately two million. More basically, the structure of the economy was still characterized by a high degree of rigidity and monopolization.

The April 1948 election had represented a turning point in the postwar Italian scene. The Christian Democrats had a safe majority of their own in Parliament, and on most issues of importance could count on the smaller center parties, the Republicans, Liberals, and PSLI. The government, despite the opposition of the Communists and Nenni Socialists, had obtained parliamentary support for international commitments which placed Italy firmly within the Atlantic community and the western democratic defensive alliance. Within the country, the security forces had gradually

105. Confederazione Generale dell' Industria Italiana, *Annuario di statistiche del lavoro. Supplemento 1950* (Rome, 1951), tables 232–234, pp. 266–268. The tables give a breakdown of membership by industry, using data furnished by each organization for its own membership.

106. CGIL, *Notiziario*, VI, 23–24, December 15–December 31, 1952, p. 694. The same figure was claimed as membership at the end of the year. *Lavoro*, VI, 5, February 1, 1953, p. 11.

107. *Lavoro*, VIII, 5, January 30, 1955, p. 23. CGIL claimed that the statistics from 1952 onward were not entirely comparable with earlier figures, since in certain fields it encouraged its members to join, instead, autonomous organizations such as elementary school teachers, insurance agents, Association of Southern Farmers, Association of Employees of Agrarian Consorzi. *Idem* and CGIL, *Notiziario*, VI, 23–24, December 15–December 31, 1952, p. 679.

108. CISL, *Primo congresso nazionale, relazione della segreteria confederale, Napoli, 11–14 November, 1951* (Rome, n.d.), p. 11.

been built up to the point of eliminating a large part of the terror which the Communists had been able to maintain in some areas and of rendering hopeless any internal insurrection. On the other hand, in the economic and social sphere, the government had failed to offer bold leadership and had even failed effectively to capitalize on those basic programs of reform which it did institute, such as its historic land reform program.

The communal elections of 1951 and 1952 were a preview of the national parliamentary elections of 1953. In the communal elections, while the Communists with their Socialist allies lost control of some large municipalities in the north, they received a larger proportion of the vote than in the 1948 national elections. For the country as a whole, the center coalition lost both to the left and to the extreme right. The Communist-Socialist combination received 33.1 percent of the votes, and the Monarchist-neo-Fascist combination received 9.9 percent. The center parties received approximately half the total vote. The election results reflected the miscalculation of the character of Communist strength in the country, the deep-seated dissatisfactions which existed among the population, and the Communist ingenuity in maintaining itself and its multitude of satellite and controlled organizations as the rallying points of discontent.

The 1953 national elections confirmed the strength shown earlier by the Communists and ended the secure majority held by the Christian Democrats since 1948. The Christian Democratic party and its allies in their search for democratic government stability had pushed a law through Parliament before the elections which gave any political combination receiving more than 50 percent of the popular vote a premium of seats in Parliament. An uproar was raised throughout the country over the issue, both while it was before Parliament and during the election campaign. Labeled the *legge truffa* (swindle law) and reminiscent of a similar measure applied by Mussolini to insure preponderance for the Fascists in 1924, the law appeared to have succeeded only in increasing discontent with the center parties. The law, in fact, was not applied after the elections because of the political difficulties it would have created in the country.

In the elections the Christian Democratic party received 40.1 percent of the votes, compared with 48.5 percent it had received in 1948. The small center parties lost even more heavily. The Social Democrats, who had unified the various PSI break-away groups, first into two parties and in 1951 into one — the *Partito Social-Democratico Italiano* (PSDI) — received 4.5 percent. A dissident Socialist group which subsequently joined the PSDI received 0.8 percent, the Liberal party received 3.0 percent and the Republicans, 1.6 percent. The Communists and Nenni Socialists, running in a common front, had maintained their separate party identities in the election and in combination had received 35.4 percent of the total vote compared with 31.0 percent in 1948. The Communists received 22.6 percent and the Socialists 12.8 percent.[109]

The months following the June 1953 election represented a high point for Communist political propaganda initiative in the country, almost comparable to 1947–1948. The Christian Democrats no longer had a majority of their own in Parliament. While the four center parties together did have a majority, it was a precarious one. Furthermore, the election results created a situation of uncertainty and instability which was reflected within the center parties themselves. The Republicans felt that they had been repudiated as a national party and should therefore not participate in government.

More important was the attitude of PSDI and its general secretary, Saragat. In his view the policy of his party had been repudiated and only a weaning away of PSI from the Communists could offer hope of stable democracy in Italy. For more than six months Italy gave the impression of being unable to find a government with sufficient political support to govern the country. De Gasperi tried to form a government and failed. After others had similarly been unable to obtain majority parliamentary support, Pella, a right-of-center Christian Democrat, succeeded in forming a government in September. He succeeded, however, only on the basis that his was a nonpolitical caretaker cabinet, and at the end of the year when it appeared that his government might begin moving away from its caretaker character, he was defeated in Parliament. A long crisis developed, actually a continuation of the same political stalemate existing since the June 1953 elections. In February 1954, Mario Scelba, who as Minister of Interior during most of De Gasperi's tenure in office had been responsible for building the police forces as an effective security bulwark against Communism, succeeded in breaking the deadlock. He turned his back firmly upon the efforts implicit in Fanfani's attempt to form a government with rightist support in the preceding month. He worked out an agreement for government participation by the PSDI, which had realized by then the futility of its efforts to induce Nenni to break with the Communists. The Liberals also joined the government and the Republicans supported it in Parliament, although they continued their refusal to participate. Scelba made his alliances on the basis of sharing authority as well as responsibility with the minor parties. The latter had had enough of responsibility without authority under De Gasperi governments, and committed themselves to share responsibility with Scelba only after obtaining concrete assurances on the government's program.

During the months of government stalemate in 1953, the Communists had done their best to promote the atmosphere which had existed before the 1948 elections. They hammered away at the claims that stable government was impossible in Italy without their leadership, that the country could not

109. Istituto Centrale di Statistica, *Annuario statistico italiano, 1958* (Rome, 1959), table 160, p. 143.

obtain the reforms and the protection of national interests from the weak political combinations which would follow from the elections, and that in any event, Communist political ascendency was assured.

Scelba, who for many years had been identified by the Communists as a principal enemy in his role of Minister of Interior and unequivocal anti-Communist, set out his government program in terms of social and economic reform combined with a program of eliminating the privileges enjoyed by the Communists beyond the requirements of law. His achievements in the economic and social field were modest during his first year in office, and the implementation of his anti-Communist measures had little direct effect upon Communist strength. On the other hand, he demonstrated that effective government was still possible in the parliamentary situation resulting from the 1953 elections, that measures could be taken against the Communist organizations without violent reaction, and that Italian democracy could still function despite the threat from the political extremes. In the new atmosphere, the fortunes of the Communists ebbed significantly in 1954 and 1955, although they continued to represent a massive threat with wide popular support.

CISL builds its organization. The CISL, as conceived by those responsible for its creation, undertook to build a new type of unionism different from the Communist-controlled CGIL and from the Italian trade unions of the past which traditionally had had a specifically ideological orientation and close working relations with one or another political party. As a movement it considered its orientation to be exclusively one of democratic trade unionism with a focus similar to that of other European democratic trade union movements. Compelled to contend with the basic problem of overcoming Communist hegemony of the bulk of the workers, its reaction to competition from other non-Communist trade unionism was one of intolerance. It would not agree to the legitimacy of more than one democratic trade union movement in the face of Communist competition. This was especially sharp during the first years after its formation. CISL had been established as the combination of non-Communist trade union forces opposing CGIL. Yet, not all trade unionists had accepted the unification, and UIL had been formed out of those who refused to enter the new organization. The very existence of UIL, with its reliance upon the traditional Italian trade union pattern, represented a challenge to the CISL approach. As a result of this attitude and the UIL attitude that UIL represented the democratic Socialist trade union traditions while CISL was largely a Christian Democratic trade union movement, the first years after the formation of both organizations were characterized by sharp antagonisms and reciprocal public attacks and criticisms.

During this period CISL faced difficult problems both in evolving its own orientation and in its efforts to enlarge its influence among wage earners.

As has already been described, the principal elements forming the organization had been the Catholic faction of CGIL which had formed the LCGIL in 1948. While the former LCGIL leadership shared positions with those joining in CISL from FIL, it retained principal authority on all levels of the new organization. Furthermore, since it had had enough of factionalism in CGIL, and insisted that political partisanship must be avoided, the organization prohibited the formation of factions within its own ranks. The leadership, while not repudiating its own personal Catholic orientation, was committed to nonpartisan administration of the trade unions. The general secretary of CISL, Giulio Pastore, having come from the Catholic movement and having been head of ACLI, had acquired his postwar trade union experience in CGIL and then as head of LCGIL. His strength of character, his dedication toward building his organization and his devotion toward the enunciated principles of CISL, combined with his sense of internal organization, gave him undisputed leadership in the organization, and the character of CISL through the years increasingly bore the stamp of his personality and orientation.

The very nature of CISL's approach, however, presented considerable difficulties particularly in its early years. As an organization based upon principles of responsibility toward the community as a whole and not only toward the narrow immediate interests of its membership, it conditioned its policies to the economic and political scene which sometimes seemed to set narrow limits to its militancy. In the economic sphere, for example, as an alternative to CGIL demands for general wage increases, it emphasized the necessity of increased productivity and production, stability of the economy, and relationship of wage movements to these factors. It urged redistribution of the national income both through government measures and collective bargaining, but resisted the temptation to support indiscriminate wage demands made by CGIL. Thus, for example, when the economic repercussions of the Korean War and the European defense reaction to the Soviet threat to be felt seriously in Italy through price rises and food shortages, CISL early in 1951 developed a general economic program which it urged upon the Italian government. The program included setting up priorities in use of raw materials and in investments, encouragement and direction of investments, stabilization of prices, and efforts to increase productivity. On this basis, CISL offered to forego demands for general wage increases or increases not related to "effective increases in the productivity of labor." [110]

In the political sphere, CISL was forced to include in its area of concern

110. *Memoria sulla congiuntura economica presentata al consiglio generale* (*Bari, 4–5–6 Gennaio 1951*), n.d. The CISL pamphlet *Il metodo della CISL, I lavoratori difendono l'Italia, L'Italia difenda i lavoratori,* published as number 2 in its series, "*Documenti*" (Rome, 1951) in addition to reproducing the text, pp. 3–43, has the text of a series of follow-up documents on the issue.

the stability of democratic government, given its basic concern with the preservation of democracy. In the unstable political situation in Italy, CISL felt compelled to take into account the potential political repercussions of its trade union policy decisions. While CISL's consistent position in defense of democratic institutions over the years worked in its favor as dissillusion-ment with Communist policy and tactics grew, its interpretation of its re-sponsibilities sometimes carried it into unpopular tactical positions which appeared to be dictated simply by a desire to avoid embarrassment to the government.

An example of this situation was the railroad strike of January 13, 1953. A long-standing dispute over wage increases in which the government had made no satisfactory offer of settlement had resulted in a decision by the CISL, UIL, and CGIL railroad unions and several autonomous unions in the industry to call a twenty-four-hour national general strike on the rail-roads. The De Gasperi government faced an internal crisis on the issue of wage concessions which might have increased the difficulties the govern-ment expected to have in obtaining approval in Parliament of its electoral reform law. Rather than further such a crisis, CISL called off its participa-tion on the eve of the strike as a result of an appeal from De Gasperi and vague promises of future action.[111] CISL suffered the consequences within a few weeks, when it lost heavily to the CGIL in elections held among railroad personnel for selection of representatives to the council of railroad administration.[112]

In general, the repudiation of the CGIL tactics of constant agitation, of intransigent rigidity in its demands, of unequivocal militancy in support of any popular issue among wage earners, made CISL appear on many occa-sions to be less concerned with the immediate interests of workers than was CGIL. For example, it was willing to compromise with employers in mass lay-off situations by contrast with the CGIL uniform position of un-compromising opposition. It refused to support strikes until all other means of settlement had failed, by contrast with CGIL policy which regarded strikes as tactical weapons serving primarily political causes. In general, its more moderate use of pressure tactics made CISL's immediate task of win-ning worker confidence a difficult one, although the CGIL tactics over time proved disadvantageous to it as its constant agitations bore little immediate fruit.

111. *Conquiste del Lavoro,* VI, 2, January 25, 1953, pp. 1–2; *ibid.,* VI, 3, Febru-ary 8, 1953, pp. 1–2; *Bollettino d'Informazioni Sindacali,* VI, 3, February 15, 1953, p. 103; CGIL *Lavoro,* VI, 7, February 15, 1953, p. 7; Sindacato Ferrovieri Italiani, *Bol-lettino Sindacale,* no. 12 (December 1952), pp. 493–494; *ibid.,* no. 1, January 1953, pp. 1–3; *ibid.,* no. 2, February 1953, pp. 33–36; *Il Lavoro Italiano,* V, 11, March 16, 1953, pp. 1 and 4.
112. *Rinascità* (PCI official monthly), X, 1 (January 1953), p. 61.

CISL also had to contend with another aspect of workers' reactions. The Italian workers sought an organization which would demonstrate its willingness and ability to obtain concessions for them. At the same time they viewed these matters against the background of traditional ideological attachments which had their roots deep in working-class traditions. CISL was led predominately by Catholic leaders and its effort to establish itself as a nonpartisan democratic trade union had to contend with the fact that the bulk of wage earners accepted Socialist traditions and viewed Catholic leadership of a trade union movement as a stamp characterizing the organization as clerical. It was difficult for workers to accept at face value the announced character of CISL as a nonpartisan organization, and the label of "Christian" was one which workers applied to the organization either in support of it, as did the workers in some areas who traditionally accepted a Christian social orientation, or in criticizing it, as did the bulk of workers who accepted a generic Socialist ideology and regarded Christian leadership in the trade union sphere with suspicion.

A further element which increased the difficulties for CISL was the fact that the aftermath of economic stabilization and gradual economic expansion, the post-1948 political atmosphere and the splitting up of the trade union movement had strengthened the position of industry. *Confindustria* and its members were little interested in improving industrial relations through enlightened policies of concessions and better personnel policies. Employers generally made concessions only when forced to do so, and they regarded personnel matters less as a vital function to create a better productive atmosphere in their plants than as an unavoidable but bothersome task. In such an atmosphere, the extremist generally found more fertile ground among wage earners than did the defender of reasonableness.

Despite these difficulties, however, CISL made progress, particularly after the re-establishment of a relatively stable center government in 1954. In the economic sphere CISL recognized that its role as a trade union required an interest in the broad economic policies followed by the government and the economy. Mass lay-off problems could not always be satisfactorily solved on the plant level, reduction in unemployment could not be accomplished through collective bargaining alone, real wage levels depended on elements outside the wage agreements made with *Confindustria*. General economic and social problems, tax policy, investment policy, trade policy, antimonopoly policy, reforms in many aspects of the industrial, commercial, and agricultural sectors of the economy became focal points of interest to CISL as it gradually evolved a sense of its own potential role.

UIL Seeks Recognition. The UIL during its first few years had a difficult time. The fluidity which had characterized the 1948–1949 period had already passed when UIL was organized in March 1950. It lacked resources to establish offices immediately throughout the country or to undertake large-scale organizing campaigns. Aside from the hostility of the CGIL, which was inevitable, it was regarded by CISL and its supporters as an usurper on the trade union scene. UIL justified its own independent organization on the grounds that its frankly democratic Socialist orientation was the only appeal which eventually could win the workers with strong Socialist traditions away from CGIL. It characterized CISL's claim to nonpartisanship as only tactical propaganda and unconvincing to workers. In reviewing the reasons for the establishment of UIL, the UIL National Secretariat general report to the first national congress of the organization held in December 1953 stated:

There undoubtedly existed and still exists among the Italian working masses consciousness of the harm which the subordination of trade union organizations to the interests of a totalitarian state brings to the cause of proletarian emancipation. Nevertheless, in an economic-social situation such as prevails in our country, the working class could not but be suspicious of those whom developments made to appear as sharing the social conceptions expressed by a government and by an order of society substantially hostile to it. Thus, placed before the alternative between a trade union, democratic in appearance, dominated by confessional and pro-government factions and a trade union appearing to expound the vital needs and the aspirations for profound social change in the country, the workers, perhaps even those who had already abandoned the CGIL independently of the Christian Democrats, would have chosen the CGIL and ended by returning to it.[113]

Characteristic of the sharp tone taken by UIL in its early years in evaluating the CISL unification, was the references to it by Italo Viglianesi, the young energetic head of UIL in his review of UIL's first ten months' activities:

The UIL was born as a result of the will of young men, rebelling against the calculations and interested advice of "well wishers," against the allurements of certain promises of comfortable living, against the astuteness of certain old schemers adept at the formula of the carrot and the stick, of the promise and the ransom.
The UIL was born out of the slaughter of FIL, dissolved among the corruptions and the most bestial extortions, intimidations, the coronation of about one year of marketing in trade unionists, in positions, in funds, in careers.[114]

UIL remained under pressure from the time it was organized to yield the democratic trade union field to CISL and either disband or unify with the latter organization. CISL had for more than a year succeeded in preventing

113. Unione Italiana del Lavoro, *Relazione presentata al primo congresso*, p. 28.
114. *Il Lavoro Italiano*, III, 1, January 6, 1951, p. 1.

UIL from being admitted to the International Confederation of Free Trade Unions (ICFTU). In its effort to obtain recognition of its legitimacy, membership in the ICFTU was an important issue for UIL and it had filed its application for admission immediately after its formation. Because of CISL opposition, seconded by the American Federation of Labor, which strongly supported the proposition that CGIL could most effectively be opposed only by a single unified democratic trade union movement, the ICFTU delayed admitting UIL until the end of 1951. The admission of UIL to the ICFTU had little impact upon the relationship between the two Italian organizations, although the increased moral position of UIL by virtue of international labor recognition, modified CISL's position of wanting UIL disbandment, in the direction of a desire for unification. A joint appeal by the AFL and CIO in May 1952 for the two Italian organizations to work together and eventually unify had no effect. UIL expressed willingness to establish cooperative arrangements with CISL on trade union and other issues but rejected unification, except as a long-term objective. CISL, on the other hand, insisted upon immediate unification, rejecting any other collaboration except if directly related to unification. The result was another round of polemics.[115]

In February 1953 the secretary general and president of the ICFTU succeeded in obtaining agreement between the two organizations for a continuing cooperative arrangement under which consultation would take place on common issues and cooperative action would be taken where agreement was found possible.[116] By this time it had become evident that UIL would not agree to unification nor disappear from the scene. CISL, therefore, submitted to the agreement urged by the international organization. As a practical matter, the agreement had little impact since the consultative machinery never functioned. In the fall of 1954 a joint committee of CISL and UIL was established, as a result of further ICFTU efforts to promote cooperation.[117] For a time there was hope that cooperation and joint consultations might develop on a continuing basis. For the first time in the aftermath of the joint success in negotiating the *conglobamento* agreement, which is discussed in the next section, the organizations referred to each other in friendly terms. Viglianesi, for example, early in December 1954, spoke of "the democratic organizations UIL and CISL." Similarly, Pastore

115. For text of AFL–CIO statement and CISL reply, *see Bollettino d'Informazioni Sindacali,* V, 14, July 31, 1952, pp. 3–5. For UIL reply, see *Il Lavoro Italiano,* IV, 29, July 21, 1952. See also, Canini article in *La Giustizia,* August 31, 1952 and UIL reply reproduced in UIL *News Letter,* September 1, 1952.

116. For text of agreement, *see Conquiste del Lavoro,* VI, 5, March 8, 1953, p. 7. UIL's executive committee approved the agreement on February 20 (*Il Lavoro Italiano,* V, 9, March 2, 1953, p. 1) and CISL's general council approved during its February 24–26 session (*Bollettino d'Informazioni Sindacali,* VI, 5, March 15, 1953, p. 6).

117. *Conquiste del Lavoro,* VII, 40, October 16, 1954, p. 1.

in his New Year's press conference referred to the "democratic sister organization UIL." [118] The thaw did not last, however, and relations fluctuated in
the following years depending upon the pressure of issues and organizational interests.

During its early years UIL displayed a durability which disappointed its
critics on the Italian labor scene. It was not forced to disband or unify with
CISL because of its lack of material resources nor did it change its basic
orientation. On the other hand, it had no dramatic successes, growing only
very slowly and remaining far smaller than CISL both in membership and
in the support it won in plant grievance committee elections.

UIL attempted to function in the tradition of the Reformist Socialist CGL
of the pre-Fascist period. It welcomed support from the Social Democratic
and Republican parties, while repudiating political party influences on the
organization and its policies. It opposed CGIL efforts to use the trade union
movement for Communist political objectives and took positions supporting
the democratic orientation of Italy's foreign policy. While supporting the
government on specific issues, it generally was critical of the slow progress
of economic and social reform instituted in the country and was critical of
the government for failing to undertake basic reform programs.[119] To the
extent that circumstances would gradually loosen the ties of workers to
CGIL and make them seek alternative organization within the traditions of
worker organizations, UIL hoped that it would be regarded as the logical
alternative to CGIL. It meanwhile attempted to build its reputation as a
militant democratic Socialist-oriented movement.

CGIL and the competitor organizations. The CGIL continued to dominate the labor scene, despite trade union competition after the splits. Its
exploitation of the labor situation for the Communist Party represented a
complicated problem of balance for the leadership. To maintain its position
of dominance it continued to function in a manner which would make possible its claim to being the only dependable protector of workers' interests.
It pressed hard for wage increases whenever the opportunity presented itself. During 1951 and 1952, when CISL opposed general wage increases in
the name of economic stability, CGIL demanded a 20 percent general wage
adjustment and built up considerable agitation on the subject. When it appeared, however, that the only concessions which *Confindustria* would agree
to were increases in family allowances as demanded by CISL and supported
by UIL — although UIL had earlier demanded a general wage increase —
CGIL went along and agreed to a settlement on that basis. Its agreement,
however, was followed by sharp criticism of *Confindustria* for its low-wage

118. *Il Lavoro Italiano,* VI, 48, December 6, 1954; *Conquiste del Lavoro,* VII, 50,
December 25, 1954, p. 1.

119. UIL, *Relazione . . . 1953,* pp. 29–46; Viglianesi March 1953 press statement in
Il Lavoro Italiano, V, 10, March 9, 1953, pp. 1 and 5.

policy and of the competing trade unions for their lack of militancy in protection of labor's interest. A new wage-increase drive was gotten under way
by CGIL almost immediately.

CGIL was the most articulate defender of job protection in industry when
a round of mass lay-offs took place in metallurgical and textile plants during
1952. It did not resort to the tactic of the occupation strike very frequently,
as it had in similar situations two years before, since it apparently felt that
the advantages of the tactic had temporarily been worn out. On the other
hand, it was more rigid than its competitor organizations in opposing lay-
offs, and promoted demonstrations, strikes, sympathetic stoppages to dramatize its position.

Throughout these years it attempted to promote common action among
the three trade union groups. If successful in achieving unity of action, as
it frequently was, it was confident that it could dominate the situation and
appear as the promoter of unity, better to defend the workers. If unsuccessful, it attacked the other organizations as lacking in militancy and as "lackeys"
of the employers and the government. Unity of action played an important
part in the CGIL and the Communist tactical objectives during these years.
The reaction of both UIL and CISL affiliates varied with the issues and they
tried to limit their joint action with CGIL to exclusively economic issues,
on which no other alternative to unity appeared effective against employer
opposition. Even under these circumstances CISL was considerably more
reluctant to be drawn into unity of action than was UIL.

CGIL, on a general economic level, continued to present its national economic plan, its *piano del lavoro,* as the only means of obtaining an expanding economy, breaking up monopolies, achieving full employment, and
raising living standards. During the years following the launching of the
plan, it continued, with occasional modifications, to be the symbol toward
which CGIL pointed as proof that only it — and any parties supporting its
plan — had any interest in economic expansion and full employment.

These policies and activities were the consistent pattern by which CGIL
tried to win support from wage earners on the basis of gaining and defending immediate economic interests. The CGIL maintained that existing
society offered no adequate solution to the problems of employment and
higher living standards. Consistent with the Communist Party's own strategy, while presenting the Soviet Union as the symbol of the "Workers'
Fatherland" where problems of the wage earner had been solved, it was
deliberately vague about its ultimate objectives in the Italian situation. It
was scornful of the pre-Fascist Reformist Socialists, assigning blame to
them for the successful rise of fascism. On the other hand, it exploited the
generic, vague Socialist orientation of wage earners and attempted to have
itself identified — together with the Communist and Nenni Socialist parties
which supported it — as the only creditable purveyors of effective Socialist

traditions. It repeatedly claimed for itself the role of true defender of the constitution and of the national interest. It was in these terms that it criticized lay-offs, unemployment, low living standards. It was also in these terms that CGIL tied the economic problems of Italy to its criticism of the government's domestic economic policies and, above all, the government's policies of acceptance of foreign aid, commitments for Western defense, armament program and acceptance of United States off-shore procurement contracts. The latter policies were made a particular focus of attack as part of CGIL's participation in the Moscow peace campaigns, and CGIL played a prominent role in the attempt to depict Western defense efforts as the basic threat to peace and Italy's participation in them as a suicidal policy contrary to national interests.

The CGIL was on the whole successful, particularly in the early years after the splits, in maintaining overwhelming predominance in the trade union field. It succeeded in doing so despite the increasing hesitancy with which it was followed on specifically political issues. The numerous demonstrations, agitations and work stoppages it sponsored in protest against the first unloading of arms in Italy in 1950, the Italian visit of the NATO Commander in early 1951, consideration of EDC by the government in 1954 and the successor Western European Union arrangements in 1954 and 1955, received increasingly less support among wage earners.

On the other hand, on economic issues CGIL continued to obtain overwhelming support for some years after the splits. Its practice of gearing its tactics in economic issues to its political objectives gradually contributed to some loss of support even on the economic issues. Agitations and strikes sponsored by CGIL on economic issues, for example, sharply increased early in 1953 because the government was attempting to obtain approval in Parliament for a new electoral law opposed by the Communists and Nenni Socialists, and during early 1954 because Scelba upon taking office proposed a domestic program which challenged the Communists and a foreign policy of continued support of the Western Alliance. The CGIL and Communists had learned that their most effective political manipulation of CGIL was through the trade union weapon of economic agitation.

It was not popular repudiation of the Communists and Nenni Socialists, as testified to by the June 1953 election results, which explained the decreased support of CGIL. It was primarily a combination of other elements which began to play a part. The state of constant agitation and emotional turbulence which the CGIL maintained from 1950 through 1953, was by 1954 — as it had become earlier in 1948 and 1949 — more of a strain than many wage earners cared to support. In addition, despite the stiffened attitude of *Confindustria* and its affiliates toward the trade unions, real wages had risen somewhat during the period. Despite the continued high level of unemployment, employed workers were earning more in industry than ever before. Finally, the competitor trade unions, despite their lack of dramatic successes during this period, had demonstrated their durability, had built up their machinery of organization and increasingly attempted to take the initiative on trade union issues.

Following the national elections in 1953 and the uncertainties of the political situation which followed, the Communists had attempted to create an atmosphere in the country conducive to their being drawn into the government or of demonstrating that political stability was impossible without them. It was during this period that two national general strikes in industry, participated in by all three trade union Confederations, added to the impression that moderation had failed. The strike issue was a wage consolidation program on which *Confindustria* refused to negotiate. After the 1952 family-allowance agreement, another wage adjustment drive had gotten under way. UIL had urged during the negotiations leading to the 1952 settlement that there be a *conglobamento* (consolidation) of several allowances into the base pay, the most important being the cost-of-living allowance. Since these allowances had over time become a significant proportion of earnings, in some cases exceeding the base pay, the desirability of consolidation had been conceded as a matter of principle by all groups including *Confindustria*. UIL combined its *conglobamento* demand into a general 10 percent package wage demand after the family-allowance settlement. CISL, too, made *conglobamento* its principal demand with differentiated wage adjustments tied to wage consolidation. CGIL also added *conglobamento* to its 20 percent general wage adjustment demand, which it subsequently scaled down to 15 percent. *Confindustria,* while not rejecting in principle the desirability of consolidation of the wage elements, refused to negotiate on the issue. Its position was prompted by the fact that the consolidation even at best would result in an increased total wage bill because of increased social security payments and minor wage-rate adjustments required to maintain wage differentials.

By the summer of 1953 the unions were convinced that only strike action would force *Confindustria* to negotiate on the issue. As a result a forty-eight-hour national general strike was called by the three union organizations during September which shut down all industry. Failure of *Confindustria* to modify its position led to a second general strike in December. The two strikes, coming at a time when the possibility of a stable center government seemed to have been destroyed by the 1953 elections and demonstrating the dramatic effectiveness of a strike call in shutting down all industry, added to the atmosphere that the Communists were attempting to promote: that they were an indispensable force for governing the country. While CGIL had lost some strength during the preceding years, during the latter part of 1953 it again seemed on the march.

The strikes of 1953, however, represented a significant turning point.

CISL had consistently taken the position that it was not following CGIL lead, but was willing to stage simultaneous strike action when it judged the situation on its own merits to warrant such action. In fact CISL had taken the initiative in deciding to call the September strike and had been followed by the other organizations. In the strike movements themselves, however, CGIL with its much larger machine had given the impression of leadership and, of equal importance, such strikes fit well into the tactics promoted by the organization.

It was CISL, however, which took the initiative on the political and economic fronts in a manner which assisted in reversing the political tendencies of the previous months. In December 1953 it made a dramatic, thoughtful appeal to the center parties for cooperation in establishing a center government with a program of democratic reforms. It repudiated any Christian Democratic combination with the Right as dangerous to Italian democracy. Pastore refused to accept the proffered Ministry of Labor post in the cabinet Fanfani unsuccessfully attempted to set up in January 1954. This refusal underscored Pastore's personal commitments and, more important, the skepticism with which CISL viewed efforts to establish a government dependent upon Right support. The successful formation of the Scelba government in February based upon the Center formula helped the democratic trade unions, although only incidentally because of CISL's advocacy of this formula, a position shared by UIL. More important was the fact that the government stood for acceleration of reforms, defense of democratic institutions, and unequivocal opposition to the Communists, and succeeded in demonstrating that stable government committed to democracy was still possible after the 1953 elections. CISL moved more actively into the political arena during 1954. In the 1953 elections twenty-four members of Parliament had been elected from among CISL ranks: twenty-three deputies and one senator. All were elected on Christian Democratic auspices, except for one Social Democratic deputy. The group became a coherent vocal faction during 1954 in sponsoring and supporting measures of special interest to labor. In the Christian Democratic Party Congress of June 1954, CISL had its own organized faction, bidding for recognition and for acceptance of a pro-labor program. While it was only a relatively small faction at the congress, it received a respectful hearing and obtained important representation in the party governing bodies. In addition, the loss of strength of the Right within the party and the victory at is congress of a center-left program added prestige to CISL which went beyond CISL's direct accomplishments at the congress.

CISL also took the initiative on the economic front in 1954 and in combination with UIL for the first time succeeded in isolating CGIL in a national labor dispute. In the aftermath of the December 1953 general strike, in its determination to avoid repetition of joint national strikes and their interunion repercussions, CISL attempted to get negotiations with *Confindustria* started through the intercession of the government. UIL judged the efforts to be premature and joined with CGIL during the first two months of 1954 in a round of provincial and individual industry strikes further to pressure *Confindustria* into negotiating. When *Confindustria* in meetings with the government and then with CISL showed willingness to begin negotiations, UIL and CGIL joined in the negotiations. CGIL, after briefly participating in the negotiations, however, walked out, claiming that *Confindustria* was offering no concessions despite the view of the other organizations that negotiations were not hopeless. CGIL then embarked on a series of agitations, strikes, and demonstrations to bring pressure to bear on *Confindustria* and to get favorable settlements from individual employers.

CISL and UIL meanwhile continued their negotiations with *Confindustria* and in June reached an agreement providing for *conglobamento* in all industries. The agreement resulted in a total addition to the annual industry wage bill estimated at eighty billion lire or 5 percent of the existing payrolls. For the first time since the trade union splits, *Confindustria* signed a national agreement without CGIL. This represented a signal victory for CISL and UIL. CGIL had apparently misjudged the situation. In its confidence that it represented preponderant power in the labor field, it had assumed that *Confindustria* would not dare sign an agreement without its participation. Nor was CGIL's position improved by the political motivations which appeared to have prompted its tactics. The CGIL break-off of negotiations appeared prompted less by trade union considerations than by Communist tactical considerations in the domestic political and international spheres. On the international level agitations were regarded as desirable at the time to fight acceptance of the European Defense Community. In the domestic political sphere the Scelba government was destroying the psychological advantages previously enjoyed by the Communists by advocating economic reform policies. In addition, the government was threatening to move directly against the Communists in such areas as employment in government agencies, their monopoly of trade with East European countries and the use of the former Fascist buildings which Communist-controlled organizations, and particularly the CGIL, occupied. Agitations and strikes to embarrass and destroy confidence in the Scelba government were, therefore, desirable from the Communist viewpoint. These considerations were permitted to outweigh the trade union considerations within the CGIL. As a practical matter the CGIL and Communist Party neither succeeded in their political objectives, nor had they correctly estimated the trade union situation. While CGIL loudly proclaimed the *conglobamento* agreement as an employer-imposed fraud, it did not dare commit itself too far in a campaign against it in view of the concessions workers had obtained under it. CGIL attempted to save face by claiming credit for wage concessions in individual industry agreements negotiated by all three trade union groups during the following year. As a practical matter, however, CGIL had been forced to accept the *conglobamento* agreement signed by CISL and UIL.

The combination of political and economic developments described above, against the background of general economic improvement and effective stability offered by the Scelba government, resulted in important shifts in the trade union scene during the following year. CGIL lost significantly in the Internal Commission elections during late 1954 and in 1955. CISL and UIL increased the tempo of their organizing activities. While large-scale membership shifts did not take place, the non-Communist unions, with their relatively better mutual relationship, were able to win support in increasing measure as organizations which could function effectively in defense of worker interests and obtain respectful hearings from employers and the government. The most dramatic success of the non-Communist unions in 1955 was in the internal commission elections at the FIAT plants. Traditionally, the FIAT workers have been the most radical and disciplined workers in Italian industry. For some years CGIL had received approximately 65 percent of the votes in the annual internal commission elections with CISL receiving approximately 25 per cent and UIL 10 percent. In the March 1955 elections CGIL lost its majority, receiving 36 percent of the vote. CISL received approximately 41 percent and UIL 23 percent.

Despite the losses suffered by CGIL during 1954 and 1955, it remained by far the largest trade union organization. It could no longer pretend, however, to hold monopoly in the labor field. The increased amount of self-criticism and criticism from the Communist Party in late 1954 and in 1955 was an indication of the loss of confidence felt by the organization and those who controlled it.

CHAPTER VII

The Communists and the Trade Unions

The extraordinary growth and continued impressive strength of the Communist Party was the basic landmark on the labor scene in the first decade after the fall of fascism. Its major achievement of obtaining rapid predominance in the trade union field through direct control of the CGIL was a cornerstone of that strength.

In later years, the Communist apparatus which had been built so rapidly was put on the defensive and lost much of the initiative it had exercised in the 1940's. As an election machine and in terms of popular electoral support, however, it continued to show extraordinary strength. While it had received approximately five million votes in the national political election of 1948, its popular vote rose to 6,122,000 in 1953 and, in 1958 to 6,704,000, representing in the later two elections 22.6 percent and 22.7 percent of the total national vote. Yet, as discussed in the next chapter, the tide had turned against the Communists and this became most evident in the trade union field, where for some years CGIL significantly lost support to its competitor organizations.

Before proceeding with the developments in the fifties, however, a review of the reasons for early Communist predominance and the relationships of other political parties, particularly the Socialists, to this phenomenon may help in an understanding of the earlier period.

Basis of Communist Strength

In 1950, the Communist Party boasted a membership of over 2,560,000, including 465,000 in its youth organization.[1] Its apparatus reached out into all parts of the country through its 95 territorial federations which in turn were broken down into communal, zonal, and sectional organizations and finally into cells. In a strongly Communist province like Bologna, the party claimed that there were 221 party sections and 4436 cells in 1949.[2] For the country as a whole, the party claimed there were more than 63,000 cells in 1950 and of the 8000 communes in the country only 1478 of the smallest did not have party sections.[3] In addition, the party controlled organizations

1. Celso Ghini, "Osservazioni sul partito, le sezioni e le cellule," *Rinascita,* VII, 10 (October 1950), pp. 460–461.
2. Comitato Regionale Emiliano PCI, *Le organizzazioni clericali in Emilia* (Bologna, 1950), p. 52.
3. Ghini, "Osservazioni sul partito, . . ." *Rinascita,* pp. 459–460.

in a bewildering variety of fields, from sport clubs to peace organizations, from cinema clubs to cooperatives. Above all, it controlled the CGIL.

All this had been rapidly achieved in a brief period of years, even months in some cases, and by 1948 the Communists had succeeded so well that it appeared to many at the time of the national election campaign that year that they might actually come to power by ballot in Italy. While the succeeding years witnessed first a halting of the Communist advance and then a slow rolling back of their strength, they still represented a very formidable force.

In those early years of reconstruction of the institutions, the free political organizations, and the devastated economy of the country, the Communists succeeded in getting as far as they did for a combination of reasons: the confusion of the times, the single-mindedness of their purpose, and the default in effective competition from the Socialists.

To an impressive degree the Communists successfully arrogated to themselves the important symbols to which wide segments of the population, and particularly, wage earners, were attached. The Communists during much of the Fascist period had maintained an underground apparatus in Italy. While this was true of other groups as well, the Communists exploited their record far better than others. In this they were assisted by the fact that the Fascist regime had identified all opposition as Communist and communism had been equated with anti-fascism among large sections of the population.

In similar fashion the Communists successfully exploited their record in the active partisan resistance after the Allied invasion. Their contribution had indeed been a significant one, and they pressed their advantage by identifying their record in the resistance with the national democratic objectives and by bidding for the leadership to which this was presumed to entitle them.

During the resistance period, as the movement had gradually been co-ordinated, the Communists had been among those who had pushed hardest for inclusion of all non-Fascist groups in the Committees of National Liberation. They pushed this type of national front and simultaneously used it to maximize their own strength and recruit as broad a leadership for the party as possible from among the thousands of young men and women who entered the movement.[4] A large part of the middle and lower leadership of the party was recruited from the more active elements of the resistance who joined the party as a further step toward what they became convinced would be the true liberation of their country. Exploiting fully the contribution they were making, the Communists identified the resistance movement

4. Togliatti's instruction of June 6, 1944 to Communist Party members in the German-occupied regions set forth the general tactics to be followed. For text *see* Palmiro Togliatti, *Per la salvezza del nostro paese* (Rome, 1944), pp. 156–158.

as much as possible with their own party and assiduously went about maximizing their own organizational gains. After the war they continued to capitalize upon and exploit the role they had played.

In addition, the Communists reached back to the pre-Fascist traditions which had popular appeal among the underprivileged in industry and in agriculture, and in large measure successfully arrogated these traditions to themselves, primarily at the expense of the Socialists. The diverse and even inconsistent revolutionary traditions which were still alive among industrial and agricultural workers were assiduously identified with the Communists and the organizations they controlled. Nothing but scorn was heaped upon the Socialist reformism of pre-Fascist Italy. On the other hand, they claimed as their own the more dramatic and glorious episodes in modern Italian social movements. In 1948, for example, when a Social Democratic trade union leader criticized excesses on the part of the CGIL and asked that the organization "return the masses of workers to the road of traditional unionism" the official organ of the CGIL, *Lavoro*, wrote:

What does he mean by traditional unionism? The insurrections against the flour milling taxes, the Sicilian *fasci*, the barricades of the Milanese workers in 1896, the tremendous strikes of the farm laborers of the Po Valley, Red Week, the factory council movement at Turin, and other heroic examples of combat which have been conducted by the workers for eighty years to restrain the greediness of the employer class and alleviate the exploitation to which they have been subjected? [5]

For a large proportion of the industrial workers and the farm populace the Communist Party and its controlled organizations became the special instrument both for the protection of their rights and the ultimate creation of a little understood social order which they felt would make life more just and tolerable. Even while the Communists worked within the government toward establishing the parliamentary democratic structure of postwar Italy, they also concentrated their efforts upon establishing the claim that social justice was their unique mission.

The Communists outbid the other parties in invoking democratic symbolism in support of their cause. Through the years 1944 to 1946 this was an easy thing for them to do. The international East-West relations by and large had not yet forced unpopular objectives upon them. In fact, moderation was the keynote they stressed. Condemnation of fascism and its heritages, eulogizing by contrast democratic institutions, constructing democratic trade unions free of government domination, these were the popular themes of the day. And the Communists, busily building their organizations within this framework, were the ones who were the most articulate. Hundreds of

5. *Lavoro*, I, 37, December 6, 1948, p. 1.

thousands who were sincerely interested in these objectives were drawn into the Communist movement and, through the indoctrination and atmosphere to which they were subjected in party cells and party work, became loyal party members.

It is true that the Communists did not, even in this period, follow the spirit of the democracy with which they tried to identify themselves, but the times were turbulent and the popular pressures great. For example, Ruggero Grieco, a leading Communist, was reported to have incited farm laborers in southern Italy to occupy land, with the exhortation, "Accomplish the land reforms yourselves. Afterwards, you can be sure, the jurists will come to explain to us in exact terms what has happened." [6] But land reform was an issue on which Italian governments had defaulted for almost a century and few of the underprivileged blamed the Communists for inciting the land-hungry southerners to occupy land on the great estates in the area.

Most broadly, the Communists during the early period identified themselves with the national aims of the community as much as possible. When Togliatti returned from his Russian exile in 1944 he dramatically reversed the previous position of the party and agreed to participate in the government under the monarchy. The more moderate parties which until then had withheld support from any government under a monarchy tainted so heavily with fascism were forced to follow suit. The Communists subordinated all public problems to carrying forward the war and the reconstruction of the country. That the Communist position on the war effort was determined by Russian and not Italian considerations was not an impressive argument at the time. During the years that they participated in the government, they never tired of repeating the theme of national unity and reconstruction of the country, although their actions outside the government increasingly belied their pronouncements.

Furthermore, the activities of the Communists in the industrial sectors of the economy during the early postwar period gave them added prestige. The Communists had been in the forefront of those organizing the workers in the north before liberation to prevent the destruction of the industrial apparatus. After liberation they concentrated their effort within the *Consigli di Gestione* (Joint Management Councils) machinery in helping to get production started again. The industrial workers' contributions along these lines were significant and heroic and the Communists managed to be in the forefront of the effort. They were able to claim with considerable justice that they were working in the national interest and in the immediate interest of the community as a whole. But they were also working successfully to dominate the council machinery.

The social ferment unleashed as a result of the fall of fascism was an ideal situation in which the Communists could operate. The fact that on a

6. Vittorio Gorresio, *I carissimi nemici* (Milan, 1949), p. 211.

national level the Communists were following policies far from revolutionary was of little restraining influence upon the local organizations in sponsoring popular causes. One of the basic tenets in Communist tactics, that as the "vanguard of the proletariat" they must be at the head of every agitation, every protest movement, every mass demonstration, was applied consistently and with important success. It does not appear to be completely accurate, as some claimed in Italy at the time, that the Communists were solely responsible for the "state of permanent agitation." There was sufficient spontaneous sentiment in the population for redress of grievances of an economic, social, and political nature to make easy the creation of an apparent "state of permanent agitation."

The Communists, however, whether promoting a particular situation from its origin or not, made it their business not only to lead such movements, but as much as possible to institutionalize them into organizations under their control. It was irrelevant to them that specific movements might be for objectives apparently inconsistent with commitments they had made within the government. They made popular causes their own. They were against inflation and helped organize committees throughout the country to assist in enforcing price controls, but they were also at the head of movements for wage increases. They were for balanced government budgets, but they led demonstrations for larger public works programs. They were for complete separation of church and state, but their favorable vote in the Constitutent Assembly made possible the ratification by the postwar government of the 1929 Lateran treaties. They encouraged increased productivity and on the plant level they worked through joint management councils to solve production bottleneck problems, but were also intransigently opposed to the dismissal of surplus workers. The popular issues of the day, in the chaotic situation which existed, were ideal for their purposes and they made the most of the opportunities.

Of fundamental importance was the fact that the Communists knew what they wanted, had a program of organization, and concentrated upon organizational objectives in a fashion which was tragically lacking among the Socialists and to some degree among the Christian Democrats. Mention has already been made of the organizational concentration of the Communist party during the resistance. This continued after the war. Funds never seemed to be lacking — an important advantage which the Socialists did not have. The Communists concentrated principally on the selection and training of leadership and directed a significant part of the energy of their organization toward this end. Party leadership schools operated on a national, regional, provincial, and local level. The selection and training processes were a basic part of the Communists' operations. The other parties, organized on more traditional and looser lines, paid little attention to such matters. Statistics are not available for earlier years, but it was claimed for the party that during 1948 20,000 leaders from various levels in the hierarchy went through party schools. An additional 3,700 took correspondence courses from national headquarters.[7]

The party built upon a hard core of leaders on the national level who had been tempered by twenty years of dedication to the Communist cause both in exile and in the underground or Fascist prisons. It drew heavily upon the ranks of its recruits, first in the partisan movements and then in the trade union movement. The complex apparatus built by the zealots of the old guard in a short time was a remarkable achievement. The rapidity with which the Communist Party was turned into a mass party precluded the possibility of building a monolithic structure immediately. The process of consolidation and leadership training, however, continued to be given high priority and a kind of concentrated attention which is completely foreign to democratic parties.

So long as the Communists maintained the initiative and grew as a force in the country, bandwagon support was forthcoming. For some years after the war, communism looked to many in Italy as the "wave of the future." Many joined the movement as insurance against the day when the Communists might come to power. Among the wealthy this insurance more often took the form of heavy contributions to "just causes." Among other groups, particularly among workers, party membership had assumed more immediate importance than simply insurance for the future. Protection on the job, selection for filling limited job opportunities, avoiding social ostracism were more important than the cost of the party membership book. The party, of course, was very much aware of the process. It encouraged the atmosphere in which these reactions flourished, and what is equally important, proceeded through good works and indoctrination to turn reluctant recruits into dependable party workers.

Intimidation also played a part in the spread of Communist influence. It was not unusual during the early days after liberation that physical intimidation of management helped end a labor dispute promptly. There are undocumented claims that employers in many instances paid funds into the Communist Party or into some more congenial front organization in an effort to buy labor peace. But intimidation in labor disputes was not a creation of the Communist Party. It was part of the spirit of the times which was exploited ruthlessly and effectively by the party. More significant was the intimidation, varying from subtle to brutal, exercised among large groups of workers in heavily industrialized areas such as the Milan suburb, Sesto San Giovanni, and in the farm areas of Emilia. As late as 1950, after the Communists on a national scale had ceased to be an immediate threat,

7. For an interesting description of the operation of the central party school, methods of selection, courses followed and training given, see Mario Spinella, "La scuola centrale del partito," *Rinascita,* V, 8 (August 1948), pp. 324–325.

it was dangerous for non-Communist trade union organizers to venture into many of the rural areas of the province of Bologna or Reggio Emilia. This area had richly earned the name of the "triangle of death" as a result of the zealousness of the Communists in protecting the "Faith" and in keeping out the "Infidel." The surge toward the Communist movement was great, but intimidation helped considerably in keeping people on the "path of righteousness."

The party exacted a heavy contribution from its membership in time, energy, and discipline, and in their hands a position and title were useful psychological compensations. The importance of "belonging" and particularly of holding a title is a consideration which has better been recognized by authoritarian than by democratic movements. The Fascists had used the technique extensively. So did the Communists in Italy, as elsewhere. To large numbers of Italian workers, resentful of their lack of economic security, their low living standards, their feeling of not belonging or having a stake in the community, such emoluments as the Communist party offered, whatever the other motivations for participation in the Communist movement, had vital importance as a binding force.

The official party estimate in 1949 was that 450,000 members or about 20 percent of the entire membership held office on one or another level in the party, ranging from membership on the central committee to cell committeeman or group head.[8]

The hierarchy of the Communist Party, with its numerous layers, was only one part of the Communist machinery. The party provided positions in trade unions, cooperatives, Communist-controlled communal and provincial government administrations, factory internal commissions, labor management councils, ex-partisan, women's, youth, peace, cultural, and recreational associations and multitudinous other organizations either controlled by the party or in which the party had strong representation. The web woven by the Communists throughout the life of the Italian community withstood the efforts at containment made by other community groups. The area of greatest importance both to the Communists as well as to the community as a whole in this conflict was the trade unions. It was here that the Communists concentrated their greatest efforts and remained most successful.

Communist Domination of the CGIL

Within the trade union movement, the Communist success in dominating the CGIL machinery in a very short time was based on the combination of the same factors explaining the important growth of the party. In its very inception, the CGIL had been a creature of political decisions. The Pact of

8. Celso Ghini, "La composizione sociale del partito," *Rinascita*, VI, 3 (March 1949), p. 133.

Rome was negotiated and implemented by the trade union specialists assigned by the three political parties involved. The principal representatives of two of the groups, Buozzi for the Socialists and Grandi for the Christian Democrats, were indeed men of great stature and experience as trade unionists and had appeared confident that they could avoid political domination of the CGIL. Buozzi, who was almost inevitably slated to head the trade union movement, was the only person who might have matched Di Vittorio in the qualities of leadership necessary to compete within CGIL. Buozzi, however, was killed as Rome was liberated. The question of control of the trade union movement at the time was no doubt too complex to have rested upon the abilities, however great, of one man. The loss of Buozzi, however, was a severe blow to the Socialists.

Only the Communists consistently pursued their goal of domination. The entire atmosphere of trade union leadership rested upon political decisions. The movement's structure was built from the top downward. The basic decision in creating a unified movement was a political decision. Yet, to an astonishing extent, the non-Communists appeared to ignore the fact that under the circumstances a struggle for power over the organization was inevitable. But it was not the Communist party alone which used the method of party determination of trade union leadership responsibility. During the period of initial organization, no pretense was made in CGIL about the selection of national or provincial officials. They were appointed by the political parties on an equal basis.

Even after elections were instituted, however, the story was not significantly different. The appointed officials were simply elected if they continued to have the support of their political party. In addition, while the national CGIL had urged union elections as soon as possible, it also urged that single slates of candidates be presented on the basis of agreement among the political factions. This was, in fact, the universal practice during most of the period of unity within the CGIL. Trade union officials continued to feel more responsible to their political group than to the membership in the organization. Their appointments in the final analysis depended upon continued confidence from their political group much more than it did from the union membership. In this regard all three of the major political factions were essentially the same. The difference was the greater care with which the Communists made their selections, the stricter standards required by them, the greater attention paid to this problem and the greater readiness to make changes whenever the Communist party decided such changes were desirable. Above all, however, the difference was the absence of a strategy for domination by the other groups.

This was not a situation which gradually disappeared. As late as 1948, for example, the national CGIL circularized its affiliated organizations, reminding them that no one should assume leadership posts just because he belonged to the majority faction, but that he must first be elected.[9] This was really not a complaint against the practice but a plea for preservation of the showcase democratic formalities.

How strongly the political ties were felt is illustrated as late as February 1949 in the case of the resignation of the Socialist trade unionist Gianni Cella from his position as national secretary of the CGIL Farm Laborers' Union. His letter of resignation explained that the Communist policies within the union made it impossible for him to agree to continue in office and asked that a substitute be named as soon as possible. The letter was not addressed to any CGIL body but to the National Directive Council of the Socialist Party (PSI).[10]

The Communists reached far beyond the trade unions and the plant internal commissions in building their influence among industrial wage earners. As mentioned in the last section, one of the instruments which came into their hands in the early postwar period was the management participation councils. As in the period following the First World War, the worker participation-in-management movement itself came to nothing in a relatively short time but stirred up considerable controversy. Mussolini had tried to bolster his captive Republic of Salò through announcement of a series of measures of a social character, few of which he could implement. One of these was provision in November 1943 for the establishment of *Consigli di Gestione* — Joint Management Councils — in all industrial establishments. These *Consigli,* with worker representation, were to share in the management of industry.

In the industrial north during the period of clandestine activity before liberation, the *Consigli* idea was taken over both as an instrument for plant actions to hamper the German war effort and as a pattern for participation in management after the war. While the CLNAI immediately after liberation announced that the councils should be set up throughout industry, neither Allied Military Government nor the Italian government gave them official blessing. In the atmosphere immediately after liberation, the councils were accepted in many establishments and with CGIL enthusiastically supporting the effort, by 1946 it was claimed that there were as many as 500 councils. During 1945 and 1946 coordinating machinery was gradually established on local, regional, industry, and national levels. Despite steady efforts during the first years after the war, however, proposals making councils compulsory in industry failed to get sufficient support to be enacted into law. Most councils early came under Communist control, and the coordinating machinery became an important instrument in their hands for information gathering and propaganda. National congresses of the councils were held

9. CGIL Circular No. 314 of June 5, 1948, text in CGIL, *Notiziario,* II, 16, June 1, 1948, p. 401.
10. Text of letter in *Battaglie Sindacali,* III, 3–4, February 15–28, 1949.

in October 1946 and November 1947 with considerable fanfare. Nevertheless, despite the useful contribution made by many of the councils in helping to get production started again immediately after liberation, recognition was gradually withdrawn from the councils as employers began to recover their self-confidence.[11] Loss of recognition, however, was not permitted necessarily to end the life of the councils during the late 1940's. The CGIL and particularly the Communists found them too useful a propaganda instrument. Even after most of the councils had disappeared by the early 1950's, the national and regional council committees still were actively used by the Communists in connection with their opposition to lay-offs in industry and the publicity for their *piano del lavoro*.

The Socialist Party's Orientation

The tragedy of the Socialist forces in the immediate post-Fascist years was their inability to capitalize upon the situation in Italy in a way which might have given them a predominant role in the political and trade union life of the nation. Such predominance had been their expectation during the early days following Mussolini's downfall. In 1943 the Socialist Party boasted "Completing the work of *Risorgimento*, the Socialist Party made of oppressed, exploited, starved plebeians, a proletariat prepared to offer its own candidacy for power, in the interest of the national collectivity . . . The Socialist Party intends to develop with all means the class struggle of the exploited against the exploiters in order to lead the proletariat to the conquest of power." [12] In the same declaration, however, the party held that the way to success was through unity of the proletariat achieved by eventual fusion between the Socialists and Communists and announced that a new unity of action pact had been made with the Communists:

Aware of the irresistible strength which the working class will carry as a result of its unity, the Socialist Party intends to achieve the fusion of the Socialists and Communists into a single party on the basis of a clear understanding of the revolutionary purpose of the proletarian movement. To prepare the way toward the achievement of unity and to coordinate the directives in the political and trade union camps, the Italian Socialist Party has concluded a unity of action pact with the Communist Party.

The two parties operating in exile out of Paris had made a cooperation pact in August 1934 which was followed in a short time in other countries with similar "Popular Front" arrangements in accordance with the new

11. Confederazione Generale dell' Industria Italiana, *I consigli di gestione,* 2 vols. (Rome, 1947); Confederazione Generale dell' Industria Italiana, Labor Management Councils in Italy (Rome, 1951).

12. In "Political Declaration of the Socialist Party" released in Rome on August 25, 1943. Text in *La politica del Partito Socialista (dall'Agosto 1943 all'Aprile 1945),* "Avanti!" (Rome, 1945), quotations at pp. 44–45, 50, 53–55.

international Communist line of the time. The Italian agreement, like the others, was broken when the Communists followed the new line resulting from the Soviet-German pact of August 1939. The 1943 unity of action pact went far beyond the arrangements in the 1934 agreement or the de facto cooperation since the German attack on Russia in 1941. It said, in part:

. . . firmly resolved to realize in Italy the political unity of the working class . . . convinced that the path leading to organic unity is that of unity of action which puts to the best the ideas, methods and men . . .

Agree among themselves:

(1) to create a permanent committee of unity of action which will elaborate a common platform of battle for the Socialists and Communists;

(2) to promote at the base the common work of the militants of the two parties in the camp of the armed struggle of the people against . . . Hitlerism and . . . fascism;

(3) to entrust to a special committee the study of the solution of all trade union problems so that the Socialists and Communists can proceed closely united in the class struggle; to associate efforts . . . against any attempt directed toward placing responsibility for the Fascist regime upon the people . . .

. . . the two parties recognize in the Soviet Union the vanguard of the labor movement and the surest ally of the people in their struggle against the reactionary and imperialist forces, for independence and liberty, and place complete confidence upon the solidarity of the [British] Labor Party, of the Anglo-American worker organizations and the Communist and Socialist parties throughout the world.

The top officials of the party, and particularly Pietro Nenni, the secretary general, were convinced that the failure of the resistance to the rise of fascism in the early twenties was due to the division of the working class into conflicting and divergent groups. Unity of the "working class parties" was regarded as indispensable for the defeat of anti-democratic forces and for the eventual success of socialism. This position was not taken without some reservations, which were, however, lost sight of in the official party position as time went on. For example, the basic issue of complete subservience to the immediate interests of the Soviet Union's foreign policy was a subject of discussion and criticism by the Socialist Party in April 1944 when Togliatti returned to Italy after his long exile in Moscow and overnight reversed the Communist position on the monarchy issue. This issue had been made a paramount one by the Socialists, who regarded the monarchy as so compromised with fascism that it would be unable to continue after the fall of fascism. The agreement of the Communists to enter the government forced a reversal of position by the Socialists as well as the Action Party which had taken the same position as the Socialists. The

Executive Committee of the Socialist Party criticized the Communist position on the grounds that it was prompted by the Communists' complete subservience to Russian foreign policy:

The question of the autonomy of the working class of individual nations with regard to the foreign policy of the Soviet Union has given rise to frequent crises in the unity of action and to many discussions. This has also been represented in the recent crisis of Naples in a most disagreeable form . . . [we have] the constant conviction that when the existence of Russia is menaced, the working class must subordinate all to its defense. But this criterion does not imply a permanent identification between its own requirements and the policy of the Soviet Union . . . We reject the Trotskyite thesis of a world revolution which must exclude Russian needs and which speaks of revolution betrayed every time Russia refuses to risk its own destiny in an adventure by running to the aid of this or that revolutionary movement (for example, China in 1926–27) and the contrary thesis, which subordinates the proletarian policy in all countries to the momentary and contingent interests of Soviet diplomacy (for example, the position of the Third International in September 1939) . . . The gymnastic of turnabouts does not suit the hygiene of unity of action and the Socialists cannot accept the method which consists in substituting orders from above for the experience from below.[13]

The unity of action agreement remained and was honored by the Socialists, however. It also withstood the disagreement with the Communists over participation in the second Bonomi cabinet in December 1944. By the time the first post-Fascist Socialist Party congress was held in April 1946, the experience of working with the Communists had crystallized sharply divergent views within the party. The balance at the congress was such, in fact, that the question of fusion with the Communists was not made an issue, with even the Left elements in their resolution reaffirming "the necessity for the autonomy and independence of the Party" and declaring that "There does not exist a question of fusion of the two Parties, but only a question of unity of the working class." [14] This resolution received a plurality of 46 percent while the Right and Center motions received 11 percent and 40 percent respectively. As a result of the congress and the national elections during the following month, a new pact was made with

13. See, for example, the Socialist statements of October 1943 and February 3, 1944, ibid., pp. 59–60, 67, 72–73, 90–93.
14. Cannarsa, Il socialismo, p. 291. The Central Committee for North Italy of the Socialist Party, meeting secretly in Milan on November 19, 1944 had already expressed some reservation concerning fusion when it declared, "The single party of the proletariat is still not an immediate possibility at present: it is an end to be achieved through a fusion of elements and values, not through a simple summation of forces." La politica del Partito Socialista, p. 136.

the Communists in October 1946 which set forth a program of immediate public policy objectives, but contained phrases like "in their full independence and autonomy" in referring to the inter-party relationships.[15]

At the congress the basic divergence of views within the Socialist Party had been highlighted in the debate led by Giuseppe Saragat on behalf of the democratic Socialists. The keynote was expressed by Saragat:

it is a camouflage of facts to present Communism as converted to the democratic concept of western Socialism when everything in its organizational structure, in its policy and in its mentality cries out to the contrary. Democracy has become a word with manifold meanings; and among these there is also what the old language of men define with the opposite term: dictatorship. But whoever has the instinct of liberty cannot fool himself. And the workers do not fool themselves when, faced with the two Parties, they make a solemn choice, even when vulgar spirits have tried to deprive this choice of meaning and present it as something of little significance.

On the subject of fusion, Saragat set the basic theme by saying:

Fusion, as it is conceived today, is not animated by a true desire of unity of the working class but by the will to take control of it, to orient it in accordance with particular interests. The Communists start from the illusion that this policy will create a band of protection to save Russia and they do not realize that instead they create a terrible shirt of Esau on the democratic forces of the West, the only forces which can avoid war.[16]

The situation within the Socialist Party still seemed sufficiently fluid at the 1946 Congress to leave open the possibility of a shift of orientation. By January 1947, however, Saragat and others who shared his views were convinced their cause was hopelessly lost within the party. They broke away from the party and set up a new Social-Democratic-oriented party, the *Partito Socialista dei Lavoratori Italiani* (PSLI). There followed additional organized defections in 1948 and in 1949. The party thus was left without serious challenge in the hands of those who favored close collaboration with the Communists, although both the Socialists and the Communists had ceased even to speak of organic unification by the end of 1948. The Communist motivation probably was the recognition that a separate Socialist party with close ties and a program largely indistinguishable from the Com-

15. Cannarsa, *Il socialismo*, pp. 291, 294–295.

16. Text of speech printed as pamphlet, Giuseppe Saragat, *Socialismo democratico e socialismo totalitario — Per la autonomia del Partito Socialista, Discorso pronunciato il 13 Aprile 1946 al congresso nazionale socialista di Firenze* (Milan, 1946), quotations from pp. 23 and 25.

munists served their purposes better than a fusion of the two groups, both because of the further splits which this would provoke and the more limited appeal it would represent.

On the other hand, reservations about the closeness of collaboration with the Communists continued to exist among significant numbers in the party. At the January 1948 congress of the Socialists one third of the delegates opposed a single voting list with the Communists for the April national elections, although less than 1 percent voted direct criticism of the party leadership.[17] While the June 1948 congress resulted in a compromise position, it basically continued the pro-Communist orientation which was confirmed at the May 1949 congress and again at the 1951 congress.[18]

There was no complete identification of Socialist Party orientation with the Communist Party on all issues. On the other hand in those years there was little of importance in policy to differentiate the two groups. For several years after 1949 the two groups were drawn increasingly close together. On the level of appeals for support it was the Communist Party which was at considerable advantage over its Socialist collaborators for reasons already discussed. The poor showing of the Socialists in the joint election effort of 1948, for example, led to a sneering and deprecating attitude on the part of the Communists which the Socialists condemned but about which they did nothing. During these years, it became increasingly difficult for the Socialists to assert any real independence, even as the Communists increasingly treated them as captive junior partners. Their official basic orientation made them a prisoner of the ideological strait jacket into which they had squirmed with a substantial assist from the Communists.

Socialists in CGIL

Given the official orientation of the Socialist Party, it is not surprising that it came out second best, by far, in the leadership competition with the Communists in the trade unions. The Party's selection of Oreste Lizzadri as principal Socialist representative in the CGIL was a particularly unhappy choice. Lizzadri's primary interest was political, of the fusion Socialist stripe, rather than trade union. While he had held minor trade union posts before fascism, he had been secretary of the Socialist Party for southern Italy until the liberation of Rome. Lacking interest in competing against the Communists, he did little to weld the Socialist trade union leadership into a

17. In the 1946 elections, while campaigning in a united front, the two parties had separate lists of candidates. The minority at the 1948 congress favored the same procedure for the elections of that year, while the majority favored the Communist suggestion of single lists. Cannarsa, *Il socialismo*, pp. 308, 328–334. *Orientamenti*, new series, no. 7–9 (March–May 1949), pp. 3–7, 66–69, 77–79.

18. Resolution texts in Arnaldo Forlani, *Il PSI di fronte al comunismo dal 1945 al 1956* (Rome, 1956), pp. 81–83.

cohesive group within the CGIL. In fact, his performance at the Naples January 1945 CGIL Congress finally precipitated a revolt among the generally moderate Socialists who were among the most important trade union leaders. The latter group, led by Arturo Chiari, Giovanni Cannini, Vasco Cesari, Luigi Fabbri, and Eugenio Laricchiuta forced the Socialist Party at a special meeting of the Party's Executive Board in February 1945 to promise to replace Lizzadri after the liberation of the north and to establish a special trade union office at national party headquarters.

Lizzadri was as a matter of fact not replaced until the CGIL Florence Congress in June 1947. Fernando Santi, an experienced trade unionist and moderate Socialist from Milan was named to replace him, largely as a result of the pressure of the Socialist trade union officials upon the Party's officials. But even if Santi had had the possibility of following other than a pro-Communist line in the CGIL and building Socialist trade union strength on a basis other than fusion Socialist, this was minimized by the Party leaders who tried to isolate him by putting Lizzadri on the Party's Executive Committee in charge of labor policy and putting Elia Bucci, another fusion-oriented Socialist, into the job of CGIL vice-secretary. The moderate Socialist trade union officials who had hoped to form a circle of experienced trade unionists around Santi to help him build up Socialist trade union strength, were thus frustrated in their effort. Santi, in fact, offered little leadership for the building up of independent Socialist strength in CGIL in the following years. He was kept as senior Socialist secretary of CGIL, but because of his moderate personal views was in fact effectively isolated from genuine responsibility in the organization.

The Socialist Party through most of the early postwar period was thus concerned with the problem of its internal struggle over political orientation in the trade union field. Since a large proportion of the Socialist trade union officials were moderate Socialists, the Party worked at cross purposes. It tried in much less than energetic fashion, on the one hand, to build its trade union strength and, on the other, in contradiction of the first purpose, tried to isolate or eliminate the moderate Socialists who were sometimes among the most able organizers. Basically these latter efforts resulted in nullifying the reality of an independent Socialist alternative to Communist domination of the CGIL.

The Socialist Party power over Socialist representation in the CGIL was such that at no time could the Socialist trade union officials act in contradiction to the general policy of the party on the issue of relations with the Communists and remain in office for long. The case of Cella's resignation from the Farm Workers' Union has already been cited as has the case of the Autonomous Socialists in 1949. Many moderate Socialist union officials finally dropped out of the trade union movement entirely; others were removed from office and consequently left trade union activity. By the time the Socialist defections from CGIL began in 1949, only a small part of the moderate Socialist trade union officials were still left in the organization and only a part of these followed either the PSLI or Autonomist factions out of CGIL. Those remaining in CGIL had become so much prisoners, both psychologically and materially, of the PSI trade union apparatus, that they remained in PSI and followed PSI policy in the CGIL.

In the early days after the fall of fascism, the interest in building Socialist trade union strength had stemmed from the natural desire of the Socialists to see their political orientation have strong influence in CGIL. There were many both inside the movement and outside, including American trade unionists with an interest in Italian labor affairs, who were conscious of the importance of democratic Socialist strength as an alternative to eventual Communist domination of the organization. They realized that simply to rely passively upon the normal evolution of events in CGIL would lead to the victory of the best organized minority; that the Communists would take over the organization unless other groups were sufficiently aggressive and well organized to compete successfully for eventual control in the organization. The action taken in support of this position, however, was far less than what was obviously required. In fact, little organized activity took place outside the official PSI machinery. The PSI itself established a trade union office to guide the Socialist policy in the trade unions and to help enlarge Socialist trade union influence. Keeping the Socialist trade unionists loyal to the pro-Communist orientation of the Party appeared, however, to be its principal concern. Eventually, when the Communists felt it necessary to tighten their political grip on the reins of the CGIL, the 1949 CGIL Congress dutifully elected Agostino Novella, who had been in charge of trade union affairs at Communist party headquarters, and Cacciatore, who had held a similar post at Socialist headquarters, as national secretaries — the former placed in charge of organization problems and the latter in charge of press and propaganda.

At no time did the Socialists have the material means to compete with the Communists. In the early period, when most work had to be done on a volunteer basis in CGIL, the discrepancy in resources and its consequences for the relative position of Socialist and Communist trade union officials were crucial. In subsequent years, when CGIL payroll was an assured one, the dispenser of funds was the Communist machine, which by then was entrenched in the leadership of the CGIL.

The Party position on trade union policy was followed in general by the Socialist trade union officials. Despite Party efforts, however, there remained a greater reluctance among the trade unionists to follow close pro-Communist policies than in the party itself. For example, the Party leadership in July 1948, after the Christian Democratic split from CGIL, sponsored a four-day session to discuss trade union affairs. Its declaration on trade union policy after giving the usual lip service to the principle "that today more than ever the CGIL has the task of following a labor union policy free from any [political] party mortgage or dependence, a labor union policy which is not factional but of unity," went to say:

The labor union organization must withdraw from the suggestion of a practice of diffuse agitations and strikes without a coordinated vision and with the practical result of wasting its strength, in order instead to gather its energies and concentrate them opportunely with maximum vigor on the specific objectives offering possibility of success both in the area of immediate demands as well as those relating to economic policy and particularly relating to our productive structure and structure of foreign trade in relationship to lay-offs, to investment policy, to the Marshall Plan and to the bonds interposed by the latter upon our exports; in this action nothing must be neglected which tends to individualize and block instead of unifying the sectors of interest in occasional conflict among themselves present in the employer bloc . . . The PSI calls attention to the fact that today more than ever the plan of a Socialist labor union policy coincides with that of the reconstruction of our country on popular bases and outside the control and domination of our own and foreign capitalists.[19]

At the September 1948 conference of Socialist trade union officials, which was the follow-up to the Party's labor conference of the previous July, a general resolution was adopted which dutifully affirmed the "absolute necessity of a unitary labor union action." It added, however, that "collaboration in the unitary organizations must be founded upon a frank and democratic presentation of respective points of view with full respect for minorities in the reaching of common decisions and with absolute loyal discipline in the execution of the decisions themselves." Significantly it stated that "it is desirable that in the labor union and factory elections, the [Socialist] faction itself should proceed to form Socialist slates," adding, however, that the slates should be "open, whenever it appears possible and useful, to all those who are specifically disposed to adhere and fight for the achievement of the objectives fixed in the Socialist program."

The role of Socialist trade union officials of both moderate convictions and even of pro-Communist orientation was not a happy one within the CGIL, particularly after the break-aways of 1949. Both because of the splits and because of the increasingly direct use of CGIL for Communist Party tactical purposes, the Communists attempted to keep Socialist officials in their cooperating positions, but, except for the most trusted pro-Communists, gradually succeeded in isolating them from the membership and removing any genuine organizational responsibility from among their duties.

19. *Orientamenti,* new series, nos. 7–9 (March–May 1949), pp. 14–16, 19–21.

Catholic Labor Activity

The Catholic trade union tradition, while firmly established, had been too limited in its geographic and industrial roots to offer the Christian Democrats the realistic expectation that they could become the majority element in the new trade union movement when it emerged after fascism. The opportunities offered them by unity in CGIL were, as we have seen, to avoid being isolated and to have the long-term possibility of widening their influence.

The background against which the trade union activity of Christian Democracy evolved is important to review as part of the climate of clerical and anti-clerical orientation which is so widespread on the Italian scene.

Mention has already been made of the special circumstances in which the lay activities of the Catholic church take place in Italy. In addition to the fact that the population is almost exclusively Catholic, the location of the Vatican has through the centuries made the church much more concerned with private and public secular affairs in Italy than elsewhere. At the same time, the very proximity of the seat of church authority, its armed conflict to protect its temporal power against those who pressed for unification of Italy during the last century, its refusal to recognize for almost three quarters of a century the Italian right to a large part of central Italy because of church claims upon the territory, the anti-clerical propaganda of the Socialists, and the impression in general that the church has been aligned with those forces opposing social and economic change, has created antagonistic attitudes which are sharper and more widespread than is generally realized outside Italy. On the other hand, its hold over the activities in the lives of large numbers, particularly in some rural areas, also goes beyond the usual experience of people in other countries.

The manifestations of the church's extra-ecclesiastical interest after fascism took numerous institutional forms, many of them traditional in Italy as elsewhere. Beyond the hierarchy and the direct influence of the church itself, the principal organization directly under church tutelage was Catholic Action (*Azione Cattolica*), which at the time had its constitution determined by the Vatican, its top policy board composed of an Episcopal Commission of six bishops and archbishops, its national lay officers named by the Vatican, and its diocese and parish lay officials by the appropriate bishop (although some members of its executive bodies were elected). Catholic Action had been permitted to function during the Fascist period and was reorganized and expanded after the war. It continued, however, as an all-purpose organization broken down into four general national organizations, each of which had branches throughout the country. The four organizations — for adult men, adult women, male youth and female youth — in turn had organized numerous special purpose organizations, from sport clubs to organizations of jurists. In addition to the four organizations, there was also a University Federation, a Teachers' Movement and a University Graduate Movement. The central Catholic Action headquarters also had press offices, a Secretariat for Morality, a Catholic Education Office, a Catholic Motion Picture Center, Catholic Theatre Center, Catholic Radio Center, and a Catholic Institute of Social Activity. Each of these offices had its own branches in the various federations and in the local organizations to carry on press, propaganda, and educational activities. All organizations on every level had ecclesiastical advisers. The multitudinous organizations which made up Catholic Action were concerned with almost all problems relating to public and private affairs of a personal, social, recreational, educational, professional, and political nature.

On the exclusively political side, the Christian Democratic Party represented Catholic principles. The party had no direct relationship with the church, but was led by devout Catholics whose leadership on such issues as relationship between church and state and the role of the church in such matters as education, marriage, the family, was unquestioned in the party. The De Gasperi leadership, however, was firmly oriented toward complete independence of the party from the church and dedicated toward preventing issues of relationship of church and state from becoming a basis of controversy and therefore of division in Italian society. Within the party, however, there was considerable variation in position on economic and social questions. A left minority, for example, was led by Dossetti, Fanfani, and other former university professors who in the late 1940's and early 1950's urged the use of fiscal policy, agricultural reform and encouragement of an active investment policy as a means of meeting Italy's economic problems. Unlike the Popular Party of the pre-Fascist period, the Christian Democratic Party was not at the time a party of wide social and economic reform, although its political pronouncements in the early post-Fascist period were couched in radical-sounding terms, as were those of almost all parties in western European countries in the immediate postwar period. As the party became the principal rallying point for anti-Communism beginning in 1947, it attracted widely diverse elements to whom the religious aspect of the party was only remotely incidental to its importance as the special instrument of the anti-Communist forces. The dominant leadership, however, remained in the hands of the De Gasperi group which leaned heavily for support upon the conservative elements in the party.

Both Catholic Action and the Christian Democratic Party represented continuations of similar institutions which had existed before Fascism. There were two innovations in Catholic secular organizations in the post-Fascist period, however, both in the labor field. The first was the agreement to have a unified trade union movement in which the Catholic elements would join as equal partners with the Socialists and Communists and no longer have a trade union movement of their own. Second, largely as a consequence of the first, ACLI, the Christian Associations of Italian Workers (*Associazioni Cristiane dei Lavoratori Italiani*) was organized in August 1944 to operate as a workers' educational, cultural, recreational, and assistance organization.

ACLI was organized in recognition of the fact that Catholic training and education among workers could not effectively be done directly by a general purpose organization like Catholic Action, nor could it be carried forward through trade unions organized together with Socialists and Communists. It was also recognized that only through an organization like ACLI could Catholic strength within CGIL be maximized. The organization, with ecclesiastical advisers on each level, was set up along lines parallel to the structure of trade unions with national industry organizations, each broken down by provinces, communes, local groups, and plant centers. In addition, the general ACLI organization had a regional, diocese, communal, and parochial structure.

While ACLI as such was not identical with the Catholic faction within CGIL during the period of trade union unity, there was close identity between the two, both through overlapping of leadership and membership and by close personal and working relationships. After the Catholic faction split from CGIL in 1948, in a decision which appeared in advance to have the sanction of the Vatican, ACLI made facilities available to help organize the workers away from CGIL.

In a speech to representatives of ACLI, who had gathered in Rome for a national conference, Pope Pius XII, as reported in *Osservatore Romano* of July 1, 1948, would seem to have given his approval in characteristic diplomatic and indirect language:

What should one think of the exclusion of a worker from work, because he is not a person pleasing to the trade union, of forced work stoppages for achieving political aims, of straying into many other erroneous by-ways, which lead far from the true welfare and the much invoked unity of the working class?

One has true unity only if the honest scope of the workers' movement is recognized, at least in its natural foundations. We had in mind this essential point when in our discourse of March 11, 1945, we spoke of the relations of ACLI with the unified trade union. That was and is an experiment which shows to what extreme limit the Catholic workers have gone in their willingness to collaborate. You, beloved sons, have given manifest proof of this willingness, because in the trade union as such you see a solid support of the economic society of our times, recognized more than once by the social doctrine of the Church.

But if the present form of the trade union should come to endanger the true scope of the movement of the workers, then the ACLI would certainly have the vigilance and action which the gravity of the case would require. Truly there are involved today important decisions and reforms in the national economy, in the face of which a class struggle based upon distrust and hatred would succeed in compromising the trade union idea, if not in leading it directly to ruin. Therefore, you must make Christian principles definitely prevail in the trade union; then it will prosper to the advantage of the workers and of all the Italian people.

The Pope in his address to Italian workers in March 11, 1945, in giving his blessing to ACLI and describing them as "principally cells of the modern Christian apostolate," had warned of the limits to cooperation of the Catholics in the unified CGIL:

This [unity] presupposes, as a fundamental condition, that the trade union is kept within the limits of its principal purpose, which is to represent and defend the interests of workers in their labor contracts. In this function the trade union naturally exercises influence over politics and public opinion. But it cannot exceed this limit without seriously prejudicing its own cause. If ever the trade union, as such, by virtue of political and economic evolution, should assume, as has happened elsewhere, what would amount to a patronage or a right to dispose fully of the worker, of his strength and of his means, the very notion of the trade union, which is a union having for its purpose one's own assistance and defense, would be either altered or destroyed.

By agreement with the Catholic trade unionists, ACLI advanced the date of its congress to September 1948 and there confirmed the decision that a separate trade union movement should be established. With little dissent, it was agreed that the new trade union movement should be non-confessional and open to all democratic elements. Just as ACLI had geared its machinery in the early post-Fascist period to get workers to join CGIL as part of the Catholic faction and to obtain appropriate representation,[20] so it now turned to the task of getting its own members and other workers to join the newly formed LCGIL.[21] It continued, however, to perform its other educational, assistance, and recreational activity as before. ACLI also continued to perform the function of spiritual guidance to Catholic workers in the new free trade unions as they had previously in CGIL. For example, Mgr. Luigi Civardi, chief ecclesiastical adviser to ACLI, sent a circular to all ACLI ecclesiastical advisers soon after the setting up of LCGIL; he said in part:

20. The original ACLI Constitution listed as one of its principal purposes to "obtain the active participation of its members in the life of the unified trade union." *Le Associazioni Cristiane Lavoratori Italiani* (Rome, 1945?), pp. 21–22. In speaking of the formation of Chambers of Labor and tri-party representation, the pamphlet said, "It should be done in such a way that there is always also a secretary designated by the ACLI." *Ibid.*, pp. 24–25.

21. *See, for example,* article entitled "Compiti attuali" in *Le ACLI,* III, 14, September 14, 1948, p. 3. Also ACLI pamphlet, *Fondamento e finalità delle ACLI* (Milan, 1949), p. 15.

The new "Free Trade Unions," in which all our ACLI members should join, also welcome many other workers who are not part of our associations, and who have however a Christian conscience. These trade unions . . . do not have nor can they have an ecclesiastical adviser.

This being the case, the ACLI advisers should consider themselves in fact as the spiritual advisers of the trade unionists and of the Christian workers who belong to free trade unions which are religiously neutral. They shall also be called to take advantage of the spiritual benefit of the formative activity, of the religious ceremonies, which we will have occasion to participate in.[22]

With the establishment of LCGIL, however, ACLI temporarily lost a great deal of its drive and there were even for a time some within the organization who felt that the establishment of LCGIL made the continued existence of ACLI superfluous. The attitude had become sufficiently widespread that in September 1949 the Vatican felt it necessary to assure the organization of its continued importance. Since it was envisioned that the new trade union organization was to be religiously neutral and genuinely independent, the traditional function of ACLI remained for ACLI to perform. The Secretariat of State of the Vatican sent a letter of September 15, 1949, to the head of ACLI which was given considerable publicity. It said in part:

Since recent events in the field of organization of labor have given rise in some circles to perplexity and uncertainty concerning the functions of ACLI and their relations with other related associations, so that its existence and function have almost been made superfluous, His Holiness, always paternally concerned with the turbulent problems of the working class, desires to make known, through me . . . His illuminating expectation and comforting word.

Well known to his Holiness is the precious contribution which the ACLI . . . have carried to the cause of the Gospel and to reinforcing the piety and faith in this painful postwar period as well as to the formation of a Christian worker conscience, to the affirmation of just aspirations of the workers, to a strong and ordered tutelage of their many interests, to the assistance of their multiple necessities and to the very creation of free trade unions, distinct from themselves . . .

There thus remains sanctioned the indisputable desirability of the permanence and of the mission of the ACLI . . . If on the one hand the Associations of Catholic Action marshall their members in strict adherence to the hierarchy of the church, and on the other hand, the trade unions look to the defense of the economic and professional interests of the working class, the ACLI can claim for themselves the greatest and most arduous duty of regrouping, in the most extensive numbers possible, every kind of worker to revive and reinforce in them the conviction that "in the application of the doctrine of Christianity in accordance with the teaching of the Church" is "the foundation and the condition of

22. *Le ACLI,* IV, 1, January 1, 1949, p. 4.

a renovated social order in which there is assured according to justice the recognition of the rights and the satisfaction of the material and spiritual needs of the workers" (Article 1 of ACLI Constitution) . . .

The ACLI will continue with the unanimous and generous support of the Clergy and of Catholic laity to carry on their multiple and beneficial action.[23]

The support given by ACLI first to LCGIL and then to CISL[24] was only part of the effort of Catholics to win support for and strengthen the trade union organizations. The general vice-president of Catholic Action, Luigi Gedda, had organized civic committees in February 1948 to support the Christian Democratic Party in the April elections of that year. These committees, headed by a national committee of which Gedda was president, were set up in each diocese and in each parish with representatives of Catholic Action, ACLI, and the Christian Democratic Party. Through their press offices and their psychological offices they had done an extremely energetic job during the election campaign. The committees were continued after the election and late in 1948 made the trade union field their principal field of endeavor. Under the slogan of "As in March and April for the political victory so in November and December for the trade union victory," the 20,000 civic committees throughout the country were mobilized to try to get workers to join the new trade union movement.[25]

The campaign was organized through mobilization not only of the forces directly under control of the organizations within the committees, but the committees tried to obtain active support from the clergy. The church was sufficiently concerned in the issue, particularly in the light of the Communist strength in CGIL, to give its direct support to the new trade union organization.[26]

The basic theoretical orientation of traditional Catholic social doctrine in the trade union field had rapidly been diluted by the realities of the situation in postwar Italy. In an early period, there had been frequent references to viewing the trade union as having the same status for workers as municipalities have for citizens; that all workers automatically become members and automatically be required to pay dues, that the union be

23. *Le ACLI*, IV, 10, October 1, 1949, p. 3.

24. ACLI continued to take positions with regard to basic trade union matters. For example, during the LCGIL–FIL negotiations regarding unification, the National Council of ACLI gave approval to unification by confirming the continued validity of the resolution adopted by the ACLI congress of September 1948 which had approved the concept of unity of all democratic trade union forces. See *Le ACLI*, IV, 10, October 1, 1949, p. 4.

25. *See, for example,* the National Civic Committee pamphlet, *Il Movimento Sindacale* (Rome, 1948?).

26. *See, for example,* proclamation issued by bishops and archbishops of the Emilia region in February 1949, *Informazioni Sindacali*, III, 2 (February 1949), p. 138.

given special legal status and that differences among workers and their factional representatives be threshed out within the organization itself, that collective agreements be extended to all industry and be made legally binding.[27] There was still a good deal of the nostalgic hangover from medieval guild thinking. The Catholics did, however, obtain sufficient support from the Socialists and Communists to have written into the Italian Constitution that legislation should provide for unified trade union representation in collective bargaining negotiations and for the extension of the collective agreement to the entire industry.[28] However, the strength of the Communists in the trade union field, combined with renewed contact with trade unions outside of Italy, rapidly modified the guild notions and eventually eliminated them from trade union thinking.

The Christian Democratic Party had played an important role in the formative period of the CGIL. Unlike the Socialist and Communist parties, however, it did not afterward remain the organization through which policy and administration had been funneled for the Christian trade union faction. With the CGIL Christian faction, it was most directly ACLI, with very remotely Catholic Action and ultimately, in a most general sense, the church hierarchy and the Vatican in the background. Since, however, all Catholic organizations, including the Catholic trade unionists, had common popular identification with the Christian Democratic Party, the trade unionists had the difficult problem of differentiating themselves in the public mind from the accusation of subservience to Christian Democratic government.

Evolution in LCGIL-CISL Policy

Even while the three-party government was still in office until 1947, their position of moderation on the wage question, which coincided with the position of the Christian Democratic Party, put the Catholic trade unionists in an unfavorable competitive position in CGIL. Their position toward the agitations and strikes of 1947–1948 also was made to appear conditioned by pro-government considerations. When LCGIL was established, its policy in general appeared to be to avoid direct criticism of government and its eco-

27. *See, for example,* statements in first circular issued by Christian Democratic Party on August 28, 1944 in *Il programma del Partito Democratico Cristiano, voti e risoluzioni del consiglio nazionale, della direzione e delle commissioni di studio* (Rome, 1945), p. 64. Also editorial by Giulio Pastore in *Il Popolo,* March 3, 1945. Compare with declaration by pre-Fascist Popular Party in D. Giulio De Rossi, *Il Partito Popolare Italiano* (Rome, 1919), pp. 20–21.

28. As discussed in the next chapter, no labor law has yet been enacted, however, to implement the constitutional provision, except the 1959 law which empowers the government to extend an agreement to cover non-signatories in the area or industry within the scope of the agreement.

nomic and social policies.[29] It was driven, in fact, by its opposition to the CGIL tactics into a position which made it appear that it opposed all mili tant unionism. On wage questions it offered little active competition to the CGIL in its early months. On the question of a general economy-wide wage increase in February 1949, it referred to "the illusory nature of an indis criminate wage increase which, among other things cannot but aggravate the already insupportable conditions of life of those deprived of income and those with fixed incomes." [30] This may have coincided with what was con sidered good economics, but it did not increase the organization's attraction among workers. Even on the question of a wage increase for one industry the metallurgical industry, the LCGIL early in 1949 took the unpopular side of the issue and the LCGIL metallurgical union carried on a campaign among the workers to show the bad effects which a wage increase demanded by the CGIL would have.[31] It favored, instead, the extension of the in dividual piece rate system whenever possible.[32]

The LCGIL justified its general position by pointing to its claim that it was building a new unionism whose fundamental principles included "abandonment of demagogy, actual respect for obligations assumed, maxi mum good faith and loyalty in discussions and, above all, never forgetting that the interests of the working classes are closely related to the moral and economic reconstruction of the country." [33] Such valid principles were, how ever, less appealing to workers than the concrete promises and activities of the CGIL at the time.

The LCGIL leadership gradually went through an evolution in its think ing and orientation on wage and other economic problems and early in 1950 explicitly criticized the government for its economic policy. From that time on, as discussed elsewhere, LCGIL and then CISL developed a series of initiatives on wage and other economic issues to command respect among wage earners and gradually put CGIL on the defensive. The merging of

29. For example, in a press interview on October 23, 1948 and in a press conference on November 14, 1948, Pastore went into detail concerning the LCGIL program and the serious economic situation. On the latter subject, he commented upon its causes its problems and its possible remedies, without mentioning the government or govern ment policy. For texts of interview and press conference, see *Bollettino d'Informazioni Sindacali,* I, 1, December 20, 1948, pp. 8–11.

30. From text of resolution of executive committee session February 23, 1949, given in *Bollettino d'Informazioni Sindacali,* II, 4 February 28, 1949, pp. 9–10; the basi decision had earlier been taken by the LCGIL general council on January 28–30. See *ibid.,* pp. 3–6 and *Conquiste del Lavoro,* II, 5, February 6, 1949.

31. The Metallurgical Union issued a pamphlet on the subject. *See Conquiste de Lavoro,* II, 13, April 3, 1949. *See also* editorial in LCGIL official publication (*ibid.* II, 5, February 6, 1949) by Sabatini, secretary general of the Metallurgical Union.

32. *See, for example,* editorial, *Conquiste del Lavoro,* II, 18, March 13, 1949.

33. From editorial by Luigi Morelli, national secretary LCGIL, in *Conquiste de Lavoro,* II, 20, May 20, 1949.

FIL and LCGIL changed the dominant LCGIL leadership very little in CISL. New names — without great influence or authority — were simply added. The national leadership, in which Pastore had no serious competition in his authority, more consistently emphasized the basic problems facing wage earners, particularly the problem of unemployment. It was led both by the situation itself and the competition with CGIL to become more specifically concerned with and articulate on the subject of the failure of the government's policies to ease the unemployment situation.

It is of interest that the more provocative and critical position taken by CISL after its first months of existence was probably little related to the influx of Social Democratic and Republican elements into the merged organization. More important was Pastore's increased willingness to co-operate with the left-wing *Dossettiani* within the Christian Democratic Party. While the *Dossettiani* were a relatively small minority in the party, they commanded respect beyond their small following. Recognition of the mutual advantage accruing from cooperation between the two groups formed the basic attraction, although there was no explicit understanding, nor did Pastore shut himself off from the other elements in the party. The inter-relationship, however, gave the trade union movement more active organized support in the party. At the same time, CISL itself developed greater independence in its party relationships.

Social Democrats' Role in Trade Unions

The Saragat Socialist Party (PSLI), from the time it was organized in January 1947 to the time it merged with the Unitary Socialist Party (PSU) in April 1951 into the Social Democratic Party (PSDI), did not succeed in having a major influence in the trade union field. In fact, its influence was a gradually diminishing one during that period. At the CGIL Congress in June 1947 its trade union group received 2.2 percent of the total votes at the congress, less than one-tenth as much support as received by the PSI faction.[34] When the PSLI faction of CGIL, together with the Republican faction, broke away from CGIL and formed FIL in May 1949, it did not succeed in getting all its followers out of the CGIL.[35] Finally, when FIL and LCGIL combined into CISL, some of the PSLI membership balked at the combination and followed UIL.

Part of the explanation can be found in the difficult alternatives with which the PSLI trade unionists were faced and the indecisive manner in which they made their choices. At the time that the Christian Democrats

34. *La CGIL dal patto di Roma,* vol. III, p. 346.
35. The largest bloc of PSLI supporters who remained in CGIL were members of the Electrical Workers' Federation. Headed by Vasco Cesari, a PSLI member, the union remained intact within CGIL. At the Federation's national congress in March 1949, the PSLI faction had received 20,910 votes, equivalent to 39.3 percent of the total votes. *Battaglie Sindacali,* III, 5, March 16–31, 1949.

left the CGIL, the PSLI group, because of the circumstances of the split found it difficult to do other than remain in the CGIL. Furthermore, the PSLI faction felt, erroneously as it turned out, that they would be able to increase their strength by an active policy of opposition within the CGIL.

As a result, when a faction caucus was held several days after the Christian breakaway, it was decided to stay in CGIL, while criticizing the Communist abuse of their control of the organization. To set up safeguards against abuses, it was urged that a special congress of CGIL be called to review the problem and establish the organization as "completely free, autonomous and independent of the various political factions." [36] The following month a national conference of the faction confirmed the decision of the caucus and elaborated on the constitutional changes it desired to push for at the special CGIL congress it hoped would be held. An appeal was also made to the PSI faction to join with it in support of its demands within the organization.[37]

The PSI faction refused to cooperate. Nothing came of the demand for a special CGIL congress. The PSLI trade unionists did little in actual fact to strengthen their support in the CGIL, but continued to attack the Communists and also the LCGIL when it was set up. At its national congress in January 1949, PSLI condemned both CGIL and LCGIL on the grounds that one was bound to the Communists and the other to Catholic Action, but took no position on the question of its members leaving CGIL, saying only that PSLI had the responsibility of leading labor once again to "its rightful ground." When, in May of that year, the PSLI trade union leadership and then the Party Directorate voted for a break-away from CGIL, it had in fact done little to lay the groundwork for a new organization. FIL, the organization it set up in cooperation with the Republicans, represented for the most part a structure with little major worker support. Plunging immediately into negotiations with LCGIL for the establishment of a joint organization, FIL found, when unification was formally achieved, that it could not even carry all its modest membership into the new organization. PSLI itself, torn by the issues of participation in the government and unification efforts with the Socialist Unitary and Autonomist Socialist groups, was equivocal on the subject of trade union unification because of the divergent pressures within the party. Even after the FIL Congress in February 1950, the party leadership issued a statement which gave little clear-cut guidance to its membership, although seeming to favor unification.[38]

The PSLI trade union leadership which entered CISL received positions of honor in the organization, but lacked any real responsibility or power. The problem of the PSLI trade union policy was demonstrated some

36. *Battaglie Sindacali*, II, 14, July 31, 1948.
37. *Battaglie Sindacali*, II, 16, August 31, 1948.
38. *L'Unione dei Lavoratori*, II, 8, March 1, 1950.

months after the establishment of CISL, when even while the PSLI trade union leaders in CISL attacked UIL, the head of their party visited UIL national headquarters with appropriate publicity and wished the organization success.

Autonomous Socialist Trade Unionists

Amid the pressures which were directed during the last half of 1949 toward the immediate unification of all non-Communist trade union forces, the Autonomous Socialist trade unionists held out and spurred an opposition movement. The logic of immediately having a single organization oppose the CGIL and thereby concentrate the forces opposed to Communist-controlled trade unions was denied by the group. It was not opposed to unification in the long run. It maintained, however, that while unification of the non-Communists forces was desirable eventually, it would be self-defeating if entered into immediately.

The basis for this position was the claim that in the ideologically drenched atmosphere in labor circles at the time, the immediate task of organizing workers away from CGIL could best be achieved by appealing, separately, to the traditional ideologies among wage earners, Catholic and Socialist. Only through militant trade unionism combined with such ideological appeals could success be achieved, they claimed. They acknowledged the desirability of eliminating the specific political content of trade unionism as urged by LCGIL, but claimed that this could be done only after a process of using the ideological reactions of workers to win them into non-Communist unions and demonstrating that these unions could work together and be militant at the same time. For the time, they felt that LCGIL and later CISL were in any event identified by workers as Christian Democratic and to pretend otherwise was to be unrealistic and base one's analysis on illusions.

Those arguing for immediate unification claimed that only a new kind of unionism could succeed in overcoming Communist domination in the trade union field: a non-ideological unionism which would on the basis of its trade union activity alone convince workers that they had more to gain from such a union movement than from CGIL. As already discussed in the previous chapter, the wide divergence in positions resulted in bitterness between those holding the two points of view and prevented any continuing cooperation between the CISL and UIL.

The Republican Trade Union Role

The Republican trade union group at no time represented an important national force in CGIL. At the 1947 CGIL Congress it garnered barely 2 percent of the votes. The Republicans had largely been ignored in the initial reestablishment of trade union organizations after fascism. They were given positions in subordinate capacities when the CGIL trade union hierarchy was set up. Only in certain localities did they have significant strength, mainly in the Romagna area, the heart of traditional republicanism in Italy.

The Republican Party, as well as the Republican trade union leaders, were strong in their denunciation of political party control in trade union affairs. They could easily afford to be, in their position of hopeless minority. The irony of their position, however, was the fact that the Republican Party was the only party which by virtue of circumstances felt compelled at the time of the splits and reorganization to expel national trade union officials for refusing to accept party policy on trade union affairs. The Parri and Rocchi expulsions, growing out of the support given by these trade union leaders to the unification of FIL with LCGIL, has been discussed in the previous chapter. The Republican Party in its 1948 and 1949 congresses had strongly condemned party interference in trade union affairs,[39] yet it invited "the Republican wage earners to maintain the autonomy of FIL and reject every proposal for fusion with any other trade union confederation." [40]

That the Republican Party should have taken a position on an important trade union issue was as natural in the Italian political traditions as it was for it earlier to have condemned political party interference in trade union affairs.[41] The party was convinced of the validity of the same general line of reasoning as that followed by the Autonomous Socialists. In addition, it claimed that the referendum held among its trade union members earlier in 1949 meant that a new referendum was required to justify any new policy. Finally, despite its willingness to share responsibility in the predominantly Christian Democratic government, its traditional distrust of clericalism manifested itself on trade union questions concerning relations with LCGIL.

The divergent views of the party and the two top Republican trade unionists represented an unusual test of worker reaction under the circumstances. It would be a mistake, however, to regard the fact that most Republican trade union members appeared to follow the recommendation of the party rather than that of the top Republican trade union officials as a test of the relative strength of political party and trade union allegiances. This consideration no doubt was present, but only to a relatively minor extent. It was rather a reflection of the fact that most Republican trade union members at the time found the party's analysis of the trade union situation more congenial than that of Parri and Rocchi.

The early postwar period had been one of fluidity because of the need to

39. Relevant portions of resolutions quoted by Parri in article in *L'Unione dei Lavoratori*, I, 11, December 21, 1949.

40. Quoted by Rocchi in article in *L'Unione dei Lavoratori*, I, 9, December 7, 1949.

41. In addition to the articles referred to above by Parri and Rocchi, as well as other declarations made by them, FIL itself condemned the Republican Party position in December 1949. See *L'Unione dei Lavoratori*, I, 10, December 14, 1949.

build entirely new political and institutional arrangements after fascism had been swept away. Just as during the comparable period after the First World War, there had been the widely held expectation that radical social and economic transformation would accompany the reconstruction of the country. Yet these expectations in the later period went unfulfilled, as they had in the earlier period. The political and institutional arrangements built after fascism, new as they were and democratic as they were, served mainly, in this regard, to confirm the continuity of the economic and social structure. Again, as in the earlier period, the political balance and the character of the political forces as they emerged permitted no wide enough consensus in the population to achieve more than an unstable equilibrium, which left large segments of society frustrated in their long time aspirations and their hopes for the postwar period.

As in the earlier period, it was the balance of left extremist forces and of conservative forces which permitted no real maneuverability to those who sought social and economic reforms within the framework of the new democratic institutions. The conservative forces had been on the Italian scene in their traditionally entrenched positions of social and economic importance for long enough and had had enough experience in Italy's turbulent history to have found it possible to adapt rapidly as power forces within the new institutions. It was on the extreme left that the new political phenomenon, the Communist Party, represented a new element on the political and labor scene. It was in combination with a mid-century version of a Maximalist Socialist Party firmly allied to it, that the Communist Party played its role of trumpeter of revolution.

Principally, and dramatically, the Communists had built themselves into the political and labor scene with a rapidity and in a manner which went far beyond any comparable efforts in the past. This chapter has set out the factors which affected the outcome of the Communist efforts both in terms of the party and its domination of the trade union movement as well as the complex of relationships of other parties and groupings to the competitive situation on the labor scene. The next chapter returns to the unfolding of events during the 1950's as the Communist tide receded modestly in the stormy evolution of Italian labor.

CHAPTER VIII

Trade Unionism in the Fifties

While it remained the largest trade union organization during the decade of the fifties, CGIL's position for much of the period was a defensive one. It could no longer consistently set the tone or maintain the initiative in the labor field. It sustained important losses in membership and in the Internal Commission plant elections. It was forced to review its own position toward organization and bargaining problems in the light of the orientation and approach of the CISL and the competition from both CISL and UIL. Finally, it faced important adverse repercussions from international developments such as the Soviet suppression of the Hungarian revolt, as well as significant internal strains resulting from the increasingly differentiated relationship between the Communists and the Nenni Socialists. Nonetheless, by the end of the decade and the beginning of the sixties it had made adjustments to the new competitive situation sufficiently well to begin to make a modest recovery.

The economic expansion during the 1950's in Italy exceeded any past period in its history and compared favorably with that of other European countries. As discussed in Chapter I, gross national product (at constant prices) expanded at an annual compound rate of 6.2 percent from 1949 to 1953, slowing down somewhat during the next four years to 5.4 percent. Industrial production expanded at a compound annual rate of 10.1 percent from 1949 to 1953 and 8.1 percent during the following four years.[1] The economic recession which adversely affected all European countries during 1958 and early 1959 slowed down the Italian economy less than the others. Industrial production in Italy was 3.6 percent higher in 1958 than the pre-recession year 1957.[2] By the latter half of 1959 Italy was again in the midst of a rapid economic expansion with its gross national product and its industrial production rising at a higher rate than before the 1958 slowdown. Industrial production was 10.5 percent higher in 1959 than during the previous year and in 1960 rose by 15.2 percent.[3] By 1961 industrial production was 97 percent higher than it had been only eight years before. Gross na-

1. United Nations Economic Commission for Europe, *Economic Survey of Europe in 1957* (Geneva, 1958), chapter II, p. 3.
2. Computed from United Nations Economic Commission for Europe, *Economic Bulletin for Europe,* vol. 12, no. 1 (Geneva, June 1960), table 13, p. 27.
3. Computed from Organization for European Economic Cooperation, *Twelfth Annual Economic Review September 1961* (Paris 1961), table 8, p. 150.

ional product (at constant prices) rose by 6.8 percent in 1960 and 6.7 percent
n 1961.[4]

During the decade of the fifties industrial expansion largely took place
through capital investment and increased productivity. The United Nations
Economic Commission for Europe commented in 1961 that compared with
other European countries "employment increased least in relation to output
n Italy, where the very rapid rate of industrial expansion during the present
boom has only moderately relieved the problem of unemployment."[5] Employment did increase in industry, however, and in the large industrial centers of the north labor shortages, particularly among the skilled trades,
became an important limiting factor for industrial expansion by 1961. Nevertheless unemployment in many areas persisted, although the amount was
 matter of controversy because of two widely divergent official sets of
statistics regularly released by the Italian government.[6]

The problem of the south remained. Very significant progress was made
through a large-scale land reform and economic development program, but
the road remained a long one. As a whole, the South remained an underdeveloped area of widespread poverty and large-scale underemployment, estimated to be as high as 65 percent,[7] characterized its agricultural economy.
The enormous gap between north and south continued to increase, since the
remarkable pace of industrial advances in the north overshadowed the
significant gains made in the south.

In the unprecedented expansion which characterized the industrial sector
of the economy, wage earners received less than their proportionate share
of economic improvement. Nevertheless, the industrial workers' wage level
showed progress. Wages rose by 27.9 percent during the six years of 1953
through 1959, and in the latter year were 56.3 percent higher than in 1948.
While cost-of-living increases ate away most of this improvement, real wages

4. New York *Times* (International Edition), January 15, 1962, page 13.
5. United Nations Economic Commission for Europe, *Economic Survey of Europe
1960* (Geneva, 1961), chapter I, p. 9.
6. A principal explanation given for the significantly lower industrial expansion
in 1961 compared with the previous years was skilled labor shortages. New York *Times*
(International Edition), January 15, 1962, page 13. The unemployment statistics released by the Ministry of Labor are based upon registrations at government employment offices and are much higher than the estimates made by the Central Institute
of Statistics, based upon labor force sample surveys. The former statistics continued
to find a level of approximately 1.5 million unemployed in 1960, while the latter estimated a level less than half that large. For discussion of the statistics and the technical
differences between the two series *see* Cesare Vannutelli, *Labor in Italy in the "Sixties"*,
p. 4–7, reprinted from Banco di Roma, *Review of the Economic Conditions in Italy*
(Rome), XV, no. 1 (January 1961).
7. United Nations Economic Commission for Europe, *Economic Survey of Europe
1959* (Geneva, 1960), part I, chapter VIII, p. 5, footnote 8,

in 1959 were 8.5 percent higher than six years before and 13.6 percent higher than in 1948.[8]

Meanwhile, in the four-year period of 1953 to 1957 alone, per capita national income in constant prices had risen by 18.9 percent (and by 32.5 percent between 1951 and 1957).[9] During the period 1952 through 1958 private consumption expenditures rose 27.9 percent,[10] and again by 11.8 percent during the following two years.[11]

Nenni Socialists and Autonomy

While the Italian economy expanded rapidly but left unresolved many of its basic structural problems, the political situation evolved in confused fashion without resolving the problem of instability which had characterized the immediately preceding period. For the parties of the Left it was a period of confused maneuvering with uncertain potential consequences for the country. International developments and particularly Soviet policy had a strong impact on the domestic tactical positions of the extreme Left.

After Stalin's death, in the period between 1953 and 1956, the "easing of tensions" in the cold war and the promotion of the Soviet version of "coexistence," had taken concrete form in a number of ways. An armistice was achieved in Korea. The Indo-Chinese war was wound up through partition. The Soviet Union finally agreed to an Austrian peace treaty. It was decided by the Soviet Union that the Communist heresy of Titoism should not prevent the normalization of relations with Yugoslavia. A summit meeting with the western powers and the Soviet Union at Geneva for a very brief period created the illusion of improved relations.

The Italian Communist Party under this new Soviet policy found itself in a more comfortable position than during the late forties and early fifties. It was less constrained to take positions inconsistent with Italy's national interests as during the earlier years. The sweet tune of reasonableness, played with relish by Togliatti, emphasized during these years the advantages for Italy of neutralism in international affairs. With the difficulties in forming a stable government in the period after the 1953 national political elections, Togliatti hinted that for the "modest" price of a neutralist commitment, the Communists would give their support to any government.

It was the Nenni Socialists, however, who took the lead in much more

8. Computed from Confindustria, *Rassegna di statistiche del lavoro*, XII, 2 (March–April 1960), table VI, 2, p. 160.

9. Computed from data of Istituto Centrale di Statistica and based upon CISL, *Reddito, occupazione, produttività e salari in Italia dal 1953 al 1958* (Rome, 1959), table 3, p. 9.

10. Computed from United Nations, *Yearbook of National Accounts Statistics 1959* (New York, 1960), table 1, p. 128.

11. Computed from Organization for European Economic Cooperation, *Twelfth Annual . . . 1961*, table 5, p. 148.

explicit fashion. As discussed in a previous chapter, the PSDI under Saragat had reacted to its losses in the 1953 election by refusing for a time to resume cooperation in a predominately Christian Democratic government. Saragat during this period encouraged the exploration of the possibility of including the Nenni Socialists in a government majority. The Nenni Socialists, who had done well in the election campaign with their slogans of a "Socialist alternative" and the necessity of Socialist "dialogue with the Catholics" transformed their emphasis to the necessity of an "opening to the Left." The lesson to be drawn from the election results, according to this position, was that only cooperation with the Left on the part of the Christian Democrats could offer stable government, solve the economic and social problems facing the country, and satisfy the preferences of the electorate as shown in the election results.[12] In the election the PSI had perceptibly loosened its ironclad bonds with the Communist Party by campaigning on the basis of unity with the Communists, but maintaining its own identifiable slates of candidates on separate lists. During the immediately ensuing period, nonetheless, no doubt was left that the Nenni Socialists would not permit a split between themselves and the Communists.

A general declaration to this effect by the Central Committee of PSI shortly after the election, however, did not stop the speculation in other political parties concerning the possibility of such a split. The declaration had stated:

> The June 7 vote has posed the necessity and the concrete possibility of a new policy and a new majority, capable of interpreting the popular aspirations for peace, for democratic development and for social progress. To achieve this policy, an essential condition is the unity of all the Socialists in the PSI and the unity of the parties of the working class as a function of a steadily widening democratic unity in the struggle for peace, liberty, and independence, and for work and revival.

To set at rest any further speculation on the subject, Nenni stated in his report to the November 1953 Central Committee meeting of his Party, "No tactical motives will ever induce us to sacrifice the unitary policy which constitutes the fundamental acquisition of twenty years of struggle and experience."

At the same time, Nenni reflected the resentment he felt at the attitude expressed by many that his Party was so mortgaged to the Communists that the limits of his position were set by the Communists. He thundered within a month after the elections, "When one talks of a Communist veto to our opening to the Center and of the Center toward us, or of permission which our party is supposed to have to seek, one argues on the basis of data,

---

12. *See, for example,* PSI Directorate resolution and Central Committee resolutions of June 30, 1953, texts quoted in Forlani, *Il PSI di Fronte al Comunismo,* pp. 116–117.

prompted by the usual anti-Communist idiocy, which are absolutely contrary to the truth." [13]

It soon became clear to Saragat and his Party as well as to the Christian Democrats that an "opening to the Left" in the terms posed by Nenni was impossible of achievement without foregoing most of their own fundamental positions. As we have seen, by February 1954 the Center coalition had been reconstituted under Scelba, with Saragat as Deputy Prime Minister. The very nature of the combination — required for a Center coalition majority in Parliament — was a highly unstable one. The Christian Democrats were an extremely heterogeneous coalition themselves, and while the control of the Party moved toward the left, the wide diversity of political views and particularly of economic and social positions represented an extremely broad spectrum. The Center coalition, furthermore, included the Liberal Party as well as the Republicans and the Social Democrats, and while the three agreed upon fundamental political and foreign policy issues, the Liberals were poles apart from the other two parties on economic and social policies. The result was growing frustration with the compromises and divisions which made decisive action impossible. The Scelba government lasted some seventeen months, and was replaced by the Segni government in the summer of 1955. The Segni government, in turn, exhausted the possibilities of compromise and was replaced in May 1957 by the Zoli government, which functioned primarily as a caretaker administration in preparation for the national political elections scheduled for the following year.

The posing of the question of an "opening to the Left" in the aftermath of the disappointments of the 1953 elections only foreshadowed the concentration upon this issue during the following years. It presented a very attractive appeal to a wide group in the Christian Democratic Party and particularly in PSDI. If the PSI could be broken away from its alliance with the Communists and enter into cooperation with the traditional democratic forces within the Christian Democratic Party and with the PSDI, it was reasoned, a policy of economic and social reform could be put into effect, government stability could be maintained, and the support of large groups of disaffected wage earners and rural population could be won over to democratic institutions. Italy might in this fashion finally achieve a democratic unity which had been conspicuously lacking over the previous years.

Within the Nenni Party considerable ferment appeared to be developing around the issue of autonomy from the Communists. The obvious bonds between them were gradually loosened during this period. The repercussions of the secret Khrushchev criticism of Stalin at the Twentieth Congress of the Soviet Union's Communist Party was important in this regard. After the

13. *Ibid.*, p. 118.

publicity given to the Khrushchev report in the West the Italian Communist Party for a very brief time admitted that something fundamental in the Soviet institutions themselves could alone offer an explanation for the phenomenon of Stalinism and its success in implanting itself upon the Soviet Union. The Party returned to orthodoxy after only a short spell. The PSI and particularly Nenni himself were more consistent. They regarded the admissions as reflecting fundamental requirements for changes in the Soviet Union.

Review of the Soviet experience opened by the Twentieth Congress and the debate of the Khrushchev report demonstrates that the values of freedom are indissoluble from Socialism and that even if limited by force of events or the errors of men, break out in the end as essential forces. The review cannot be exhausted with the condemnation of the degenerations of power brought on under Stalin's leadership, it cannot stop with a return to collegial leadership, it cannot be satisfied with rehabilitations and more tolerant methods. It must be identified with the political organization of power, it must transfuse the principles of freedom into the institutions, into the methods of government, into the practices, give wide democratic guarantees to the citizens in their relations with the state.[14]

The articulated divergence between the two extreme Left Italian parties was widened further as a result of the Hungarian revolution and its suppression. The Italian Communist Party, more than the Communist parties of other Western European countries and particularly that of France, had welcomed the "several roads to socialism" theme of the Twentieth Congress of the Soviet Union's Communist Party. It had welcomed the Gomulka regime in Poland after the Poznan riots as a desirable application of "de-Stalinization." It also welcomed the revolution in Hungary in its early days as a desirable step in the direction pointed to by the Twentieth Congress. Only with the intervention of Soviet troops did the Communists in Italy find themselves in the embarrassing position of doing an about-face and justifying the intervention in terms of the official Soviet Union explanation, that the revolution had been taken over and led by "reactionary elements."

Within a month of the suppression of the Hungarian revolt, the Italian Communist Party at its Eighth Congress reflected both its "several roads to socialism" emphasis as well as its acceptance of the Russian position on the necessity of Soviet intervention in Hungary:[15]

14. From resolution adopted by PSI directorate on July 5, 1956, quoted in *Avanti,* July 6, 1956.
15. *The Eighth Congress of the Italian Communist Party, Rome, December 8–14, 1956,* published by Foreign Section of Italian Communist Party (Rome n.d.), pp. 31–32.

Recent experience teaches us that whenever the orientation of the Twentieth Congress was welcomed — as in Poland — it made possible the consolidation of the unity of the Party and the majority of the people around the new policy.

Wherever this was not done, wherever the Party did not know how to place itself in the lead and organically direct the process of renewal, a tragic and disastrous situation was met with, as in Hungary.

In studying these events, what should be borne in mind on the one hand, are the erroneous policies that made them possible, in the first place the insufficiency of the search for a national development of socialism and also the slavish imitation of the Soviet model, which determined a profound division in the Party, the government and the people; and on the other hand, the presence and the organized activity of the internal and foreign class enemy.

Considering the point the situation had reached, Soviet intervention was a painful necessity, but it could not and ought not to have been avoided if it meant failing to live up to the principles of proletarian internationalism, if it meant preventing the creation, in the heart of Europe, of a situation fraught with peril for peace; the advent of the most reactionary forces in Hungary would have again thrown the people under oppression, impeding it for a long time from being able to take up once more the construction of a socialist society.

The PSI on the other hand condemned the Soviet intervention in Hungary and criticized the position adopted by the Italian Communist Party. At its congress held during February 1957, the Party Directorate reported its position to the congress. Commenting on the Twentieth Congress and the Polish and Hungarian developments, the report stated:[16]

We are thus analyzing not only the errors or crimes of men but the ideology and the system . . . Freedom of opinion, of press, of organization, of strike, of elections are not *bourgeois* or proletarian, but are conquests of universal values to be defended always and in every case . . . There is need to reaffirm the permanent value of democracy without which everything is corrupted in arbitrariness and tyranny, even the institutions resulting from the proletarian revolutions of our century . . . The PSI has rejected the indiscriminate accusation of counter-revolutionaries and Fascists launched by the Communists against the workers and students of Budapest, who were Communists in their majority . . . The PSI has condemned the Soviet intervention and occupation as contrary to the fundamental principles of the independence of peoples and of proletarian internationalism.

Before the Hungarian affair, in the spring of 1956, an apparently logical step toward a policy of "opening to the Left" came to the fore on the Italian political scene: the proposal to seek reunification of the Socialist forces,

16. PSI, *Partito Socialista Italiano, 32° Congresso Nazionale* (Milan–Rome, 1957), pp. 29–32.

through a merger of PSI and PSDI. Some of the PSDI leadership and particularly Saragat were deeply concerned that merger of the Social Democrats with the Nenni Socialists would carry them back to the intolerable situation from which they had escaped only by splitting the Socialist movement almost ten years earlier. They were not convinced that Nenni was prepared to turn his back on the pro-Communist positions he had so faithfully held for so long. Nor were they convinced that he could carry his Party with him even if he were prepared to break with his past commitments. Finally, they feared that their own position of firm commitment to the West on foreign policy issues would be gravely compromised as a result of such a merger.

The popular appeal for Socialist reunification, however, constituted a pressure which was difficult to ignore and both Nenni and Saragat issued pronouncements during the summer of 1956 which made both appear interested in progressing in this direction. Saragat and Nenni held a much publicized, but "secret" meeting on August 25 at Pralognan in France, where Nenni had been vacationing. The Socialist International sent the French Socialist leader Pierre Commin to Italy at the end of August to explore the possibilities of reunification. While each of the two Italian leaders emphasized different issues, both appeared to be seeking to minimize their differences. Saragat emphasized democratic values on the national and international level, while Nenni emphasized the need to end the division of the world into two military blocs and to end the divisions in the trade union sphere. The question of relations with the Communists remained fundamental. It was regarded as a hopeful sign when Nenni refused to permit his parliamentary group to go along with the Communist deputies in demanding the convocation of Parliament to discuss the French-British intervention at Suez.[17]

Two weeks later, however, on October 5, to the surprise and anger of Saragat and his Social Democrats, the PSI leadership signed a new unity of action pact with the Communist Party. The operative part of the pact read, "The two parties are in agreement that the changed situation involves, for both parties, forms of collaboration different from those established by the unity of action pact of 1946. Consequently they decided to assure the development of relations between Socialists and Communists through consultations at the center and in the local organizations for the examination of problems of fundamental interest to the working class and for action common to all workers." [18]

It has been reported that Nenni had been put into a minority position at a meeting of the PSI Directive Committee where a resolution had been adopted calling for a "search for new forms of relations with the Com-

17. *Le Figaro* (Paris), September 15–16, 1956.
18. For full text *see* Forlani, *Il PSI*, p. 143.

munist Party." Togliatti reportedly immediately jumped into the situation and negotiated the new pact with the PSI secretariat.[19] Under other circumstances the wording of the new pact might have been welcomed as a sign that greater autonomy than had previously existed would be practiced by the Socialists in relation to the Communists. Under the circumstances of active efforts to move the PSI and PSDI closer together, it could only be taken as an underscoring of fundamental differences between the two Socialist parties. The PSDI immediately condemned the PSI action and in a resolution of its Directive Committee on October 9 pointed to the impossibility of serious negotiations toward Socialist unity except on the basis of "acceptance of democracy as a permanent value and as [the basis of] the internal organization of the Party, the fixing of a foreign policy within the framework of solidarity among the democratic countries of the West and the exclusion of any formula of Popular Front, both during election campaigns and for the formation of a government." [20]

Nenni minimized the importance of the pact with the Communists and emphasized the problem of winning over his Party to his own position of autonomy. Nevertheless, the momentum which had been generated during the previous months in the direction of Socialist unification was halted.

Nenni's continuing difficulties within his own Party were demonstrated shortly afterward at the PSI Congress held at Venice. By the time the congress was held in February 1957, the Hungarian affair had appeared to have driven a further wedge between the Socialists and the Communists. Nenni was able to obtain overwhelming support for his position on the issue at the congress. Yet, before closing, the congress elected a central committee, a majority of whom were not sympathetic to Nenni nor to his autonomous position.[21] Nenni was being served warning by the various opposition groups within his Party and particularly by the professional apparatus of the Party that they had little sympathy for a truly autonomous position which would carry them far from their traditional relationships. Nevertheless, Nenni was prevailed upon to remain head of the Party after the warning had thus been administered.

Little of a dramatic nature developed during the following year in the relations among the parties of the Left. The question of Socialist reunification remained, but little took place. Within the PSDI, sentiment continued to be strong for exploring more energetically the possibilities of Socialist unification. The appeal of a reunited Socialist movement which could sharply shift the balance in Italian politics and through participation in

19. See, for example, Le Monde (Paris), October 7, 1956.
20. Le Monde, October 11, 1956.
21. For the official reports to the congress, stenographic summary of discussion, texts of resolutions adopted, and results of Central Committee election see Partito Socialista Italiano, 32° Congresso Nazionale.

government impose a social reform policy was a strong one within the ranks of the Social Democrats. At the October 1957 Congress of PSDI, the Left factions of Matteotti and Zagari received 43.5 percent of the vote, but Saragat retained control of the Central Committee when his Center faction received 48.3 percent support, and the Right faction of Simonini and Rossi, which received 8.2 percent, supported him.[22]

Communists Seek Initiative

The PSI relations with the Communist Party appeared to be cooling off and the parties appeared slowly to be drifting apart after the 1957 PSI Congress. Nenni worked within his own Party against strong opposition to improve his personal position. The national political election campaign in 1958, however, pressed all parties into active competition for support among the electorate. PSDI had freed itself of commitments to the government when the Zoli government had been formed the previous year, and as the election drew near, was involved in a series of polemical exchanges with the PSI over issues of democracy, neutralism, and relations with the Communists. The PSI, in turn, went out of its way to establish a sharp differentiation between itself and the Social Democrats, offering itself as the only legitimate Socialist Party with promise of achievement in the field of social reorganization.

The Communist Party also began a controversy with PSI by accusing it of adopting ambiguous positions and of failing to stand forthrightly in support of what it called "Socialist positions." Nenni struck back by reviving the differences between the two parties in their evaluation of the Twentieth Congress and of Hungary:

We do not claim that the only road to socialism is that of democracy in all circumstances of place, atmosphere and time, but in Italy, yes, in the West, yes . . . We do not accept the principle of the *Etat-Guide* . . . The country needs a party like ours which does not feel obliged to obtain a guarantee, permission or a delegation from anyone. There are various ways of conceiving of exercise of power and of the relations between socialism and democracy, between socialism and freedom. The Twentieth Congress seemed to provide a bridge. Later developments have revived dissensions. These have not been eliminated, but have been aggravated by the success of force and the return to sectarianism, dogmatism, and servility.[23]

The Communists did not pursue the controversy during the remaining days of the election campaign, in the apparent belief that this type of dialogue would win them no votes.

The election, held on May 25, 1958, left the country with the same basic

22. *Le Monde,* October 22, 1957.
23. *Le Monde,* May 9, 1958.

distribution of strength so far as Center government was concerned.[24] The principal losses in the elections were among the Right and extreme Right parties. The Monarchists, who had split since the 1953 election, fell from 6.9 percent of the total votes to 4.8 percent and the neo-Fascist MSI fell from 5.8 percent to 4.8 percent. The two Monarchist groups elected a total of 25 deputies, compared with the 40 they had held in the previous parliament, while the MSI was reduced from 29 to 24. While the Christian Democrats increased their popular vote by more than one and one half million, receiving 42.4 percent of the total vote and 273 deputies, they again remained dependent upon the support of other parties to obtain a majority among the 596 deputies for the formation of a government. The smaller Center parties moved in opposite directions. The Liberal Party gained some additional popular support and increased its representation to 17 from its previous level of 14. The Republican Party, in combination with the Radical Party, lost some of its previous support but increased its representation from five to six. The Social Democrats increased their popular support by almost 10 percent, receiving 4.5 percent of the total vote and 22 seats, an increase of three. Their total vote of 1,345,497 was still well below the 1,858,346 votes (7.1 percent of total) which they had received in 1948 when they had obtained 33 seats. The popular vote had increased almost 3,300,000 or 12.5 percent since 1948.

The Communists did surprisingly well in view of the repercussions in Italy of the Hungarian affair, the PSI developments, and the prosperity of the economy. While their percentage of the total vote was almost stationary — they received 22.7 percent compared with 22.6 percent in 1953 — their actual vote of 6,704,454 was 582,532 higher than in 1953. During the period immediately following Hungary, the Party had been thrown into a crisis. A wave of resignations by a number of important nationally known figures had been the dramatic manifestation of a more general crisis in the Party. The Communists, on the basis of their own figures, had lost one half million members in the three years after 1954, when they had claimed 2,300,000 membership. By 1958, however, the Party apparatus had been reorganized and consolidated and functioned as an effective electoral machine. The traditional deep-seated disaffection with existing society, the resentments and frustrations felt by broad sectors of the population, helped maintain Communist electoral support. While the Communists lost some support in the industrial north, they more than made up for these losses in the backward rural south.

The election results gave the Nenni Socialists a much stronger position than they had had previously. Their popular vote of 4,206,726 was about 750,000 (21.5 percent) higher than it had been in 1953. Their relative vote

24. Official election results for 1958 and previous elections given in table 160 of Istituto Centrale di Statistica, *Annuario statistico italiano 1958* (Rome, 1959), p. 143.

was 14.2 percent of the total votes cast compared with 12.8 percent in 1953, and they increased their representation in the Chamber of Deputies by 9 seats to a total of 84. While they still had far fewer seats than the Communists, who won 140 (a loss of 3 since 1953), they had increased their popular appeal through their looser ties with the Communists, their vague autonomous position and their criticisms of Center government, the Communists and the Social Democrats.

As the efforts got under way to seek the formation of a new government following the elections, Togliatti reflected the Communist concern with any formula which would isolate them from the Nenni Socialists. He appealed for unity of "all democratic and anti-Fascist forces, beginning with all the parties of the working class." Underscoring his claim on behalf of the Communists, he warned that "without the Communists or against them no work of political or social renewal of our country can be accomplished." [25]

Nenni, on the other hand, claimed a great victory in the election. He made ambiguous pronouncements which gave no indication of willingness to break completely with the Communists nor did he clearly set forth his position on the issues which the democratic parties considered crucial. Saragat was prompted to characterize Nenni's ambiguous position by asking whether Nenni would claim "that he has both a full wine cask and a drunken wife." [26]

The election results had improved the position of the Christian Democratic Party, but it remained dependent upon support from others in forming a government. In this situation, the "opening to the Left" formula was regarded by a great many as fundamentally desirable and by as many others as catastrophic. Even those who were favorably disposed to such a step, however, hesitated to press the issue under the continued ambiguous positions taken by Nenni. As a result, the government which was formed during the summer of 1958 was headed by Fanfani with the support and participation of the Center-Left parties. It was pledged to a program of social reform and was consequently welcomed by the non-Communist trade unions. The expectation that the government would "do something" about economic and social reform was sufficiently strongly felt that Giulio Pastore, who had headed CISL since its formation, agreed to leave his organization and accept a position in Fanfani's cabinet. Pastore became Minister in charge of economic development of the south.

The Fanfani government lasted only six months. During its short tenure it was subjected to violent attacks from the Communists, the CGIL, and also the Nenni Socialists when it began a program of cutting down the extra-legal privileges enjoyed by the Communist Party and organizations

25. Quoted in article by Saragat, *La Giustizia* (Rome), May 29, 1958.
26. *Idem.*

such as the CGIL which were controlled by it. More important was the opposition within the Christian Democratic Party and from the Liberal Party to the programs of social reform proposed by the government. It was this opposition which brought down the Fanfani government in January 1959. The basic instability resulting from the need for support from groups which held such widely divergent economic and social positions as the Social Democrats and Liberals, combined with the wide spectrum of differences within the loose confines of the Christian Democratic label, continued to plague the architects of Center government. The Segni government which followed Fanfani veered toward the Right for its support and lasted one year. One of the longest government crises in the postwar period followed. For seventy-one days efforts were made to patch together a government. None of the well-worn formulae could be sufficiently refurbished to obtain majority support for a Center government. As a result, the Christian Democratic leader, Tambroni, found himself taking office in April 1960, almost against his will, with the votes of the neo-Fascist MSI giving him the margin necessary for majority.

The Tambroni government lasted only three months. The revulsion of the democratic parties against permitting neo-Fascists to play a role in public life and hold the fate of a government in their hands was the basic cause of its fall. The more dramatic considerations were the strikes and riots which were led and exploited by the Communists and assisted by the Nenni Socialists, playing the role the Communists particularly relished, that of defenders of democracy against the threat of fascism. The dramatic riots were begun by demonstrations on June 30 in Genoa to protest the holding of a congress of the MSI. The demonstration was sponsored by the CGIL with the active assistance of the Communist and Socialist Parties, and when the police attempted to keep the demonstration within reasonable bounds, rioting ensued. That the police could hardly be described as vengeful is amply shown by the figures of those hurt and wounded released by the CGIL itself: 162 police and 20 demonstrators.[27]

In their enthusiasm for exploiting a popular issue and their search for martyrs, the CGIL, the Communists, and the Socialists followed the Genoa demonstration with others in a number of cities. They were successful in obtaining their martyrs. The demonstration in Rome had not received police authorization and when an attempt was made to disperse the gathering crowd, rioting began which resulted in the wounding of a number of demonstrators. The demonstration at Reggio Emilia, however, was the one which gave its sponsors dramatic symbols for their cause: five demonstrators were killed in the violence between the police and the crowd.

27. *Lavoro*, XIII, 28, July 10, 1960, pp. 1 and 5–7; *Lavoro*, XIII, 29, July 17, 1960, pp. 3–11; *Rassegna Sindacale* (official CGIL monthly), 31–32 (July–August 1960), 1509–1518.

The MSI had long since cancelled its congress at Genoa, after the government refused to guarantee the safety of delegates immediately following the Genoa demonstrations. The second round of demonstrations had found their excuse in an all-out attack against the "Fascist-supported" government and its "Fascist police methods." The deaths at Reggio Emilia became the basis for a CGIL call for a twelve-hour general strike on July 8 throughout the country. The strike call was condemned by the non-Communist trade unions which from the time of the Genoa demonstrations had described the Communist tactic to be exploitation of popular antipathy for the neo-Fascists and a search for martyrs further to dramatize their efforts.[28]

The general strike call was far from a great success, but it was sufficiently impressive in some centers for the CGIL to claim an overwhelming victory. The demonstrations concurrent with the strike resulted in further violence in a number of cities and the death of a demonstrator at Palermo and one at Catania.

Political "Opening to Left" Considered

The demonstrations and rioting dramatized for the Social Democrats and the other Center-Left parties that they had little alternative but to work together in government. Their falling out had given rise to a situation lending itself naturally to exploitation by the Communists. The Nenni Socialists had shown that they could not resist joining with the Communists on as popular an exploitable theme as alleged anti-Fascism. Yet they too appeared sobered by their experience in the early July riots. Their determination to remain the junior partners of the Communists within CGIL, which had spearheaded the Communist performance, did not seem to be modified. There nonetheless was a further gesture of Socialist autonomy on the parliamentary level. After the July riots the Center-Left political parties agreed upon the replacement of the Tambroni government with one to be headed by Fanfani. The new government, like the Fanfani government in 1958, pledged itself to a more active policy of social reform. The Nenni Socialists for the first time separated themselves from the Communists by abstaining rather than voting against the Fanfani government's investiture.

The Communist-sponsored demonstrations in the summer of 1960 had been interpreted by some as a manifestation of new Soviet tactics following the U-2 incident and Khrushchev's torpedoing of the summit meeting in Paris. But the logic of the domestic situation and the Communist Party's problems in Italy offered sufficient background to explain the tactics followed by the Communists. The Communists appeared for some time to be concentrating upon avoiding isolation and seeking issues on which they could demonstrate their concern with democracy. At the ninth congress of

28. *Conquiste del Lavoro*, XIV, 28, July 10, 1960, pp. 1–3; *ibid.*, XIV, 30, July 24, 1960, p. 3; *Il Lavoro Italiano*, XII, 29, July 19, 1960, p. 1.

their Party held at the end of January 1960 these had been principal themes. Togliatti had emphasized them in his report to the congress and had urged that the Party must demonstrate to all that:

the face of arrogance and intolerance is not ours, but that of our enemies. We must make it understood that we do not want to remove anything from democracy, but rather that we want to add many things . . . The best guarantees which we give are in our very commitment to establish today a great alliance of social forces belonging to diverse fields . . . not alliances of convenience . . . What is involved is reciprocal help that these groups of citizens must give each other to resolve vital questions.[29]

In the situation of the moment, an unpopular government embarrassingly requiring the votes of neo-Fascists to remain in office was an irresistible target for the Communists to attack through dramatic action which might draw in the Nenni Socialists and others who could not resist the siren call of the nostalgic spirit of the Resistance. The Communists may have failed to reverse the basic tendencies leading away from their Party. But the adventure had been a signal opportunity for them since it had dramatically put them and the CGIL in the position of claiming before the workers and the public generally that they were defenders of the democratic order.

When the Fanfani government took office in the summer of 1960, the sobering experience of the months before appeared to give new determination to keep a Center government in office on a more stable basis. But the Nenni question remained. It had tempting potential. If the PSI could be included within the range of parties playing the democratic parliamentary political game according to the rules, and if it could be trusted to refrain from pulling Italy out of its firm Western commitments, the stability of government could be assured and a march forward could be undertaken along the road of social and economic reforms. It might also dramatically reverse the considerations which gave the Communists their continued support. Many political figures hoped that this would become a possibility. Some of the political opposition to the election of Gronchi as President of the Republic several years before had been based upon his apparent desire to see such an evolution. Fanfani and others prominent in the Christian Democratic Party reputedly shared Gronchi's views. For a large part of the PSDI the favorable considerations operated with even more force than for others. Reunification of Socialist forces would place them in the middle of the political arena with sufficient strength to direct the course of government policies on fundamental matters in equal combination with the Christian Democrats.

There were strong forces in the Christian Democratic Party in addition

29. Quoted in Livis Longo, "In Margine al IX Congresso del PCI," *Quaderni di Azione Sociale* (official ACLI monthly), XI, 1 (January 1960), pp. 54–55.

to the parties with right-of-center orientation which viewed with jaundiced eye any evolution in this direction, both as a practical matter and as a matter of principle. Many, however, including most of those sympathetic to the objective of such reorganization, feared that the price exacted would inevitably be too high. Nenni remained basically neutralist in his position on foreign affairs. While he no longer argued for repudiation of Italian commitments in NATO and other Western arrangements, he did maintain that Italy's continued participation should be used to further a neutralist Europe within such arrangements. It was not at all certain, furthermore, that an evolution in Soviet policy might not draw Nenni back to the position of solidarity with world communism he had held for many of the postwar years. Even more basic was the question raised by some — whether the Nenni Trojan horse was not custom-built for the conveyance of the Communists on the Italian scene.

Within the domestic political arena, the participation of the PSI in the Communist-sponsored demonstrations of July 1960 was far from reassuring on the score of Socialist autonomy. Equally important and significant was the firm insistence of PSI and Nenni himself that he would never "split the working class" and that CGIL must therefore continue to be the trade union organization to which the Socialists would remain committed, until replaced by an organization reuniting all labor. The Nenni Socialist position in CGIL will be treated in the next section. What appears clear is that continued commitment to unity with the Communists in a trade union organization thoroughly in Communist hands made it difficult for many to have confidence in Nenni and his Socialists as a completely autonomous political force.

CGIL Suffers Reversals

The dramatic reversal of trade union support at the important FIAT plants in 1955 which was followed by similar although less dramatic reversals elsewhere during that year has already been referred to in a previous chapter. Actually, in less publicized fashion, the CGIL had shown some losses in plant elections during the years before the 1955 FIAT fiasco. On the basis of CGIL's own compilation of Internal Commission election results, it had received 71.3 percent of votes cast in elections during 1953 and 68.3 percent in 1954.[30] In the light of CGIL's claims after the 1955 plant elections that CGIL losses were the result of employer intimidation, it is interesting that Di Vittorio commented upon the elections held during 1954 at a press conference at the end of that year:

30. Maurice F. Neufeld, *Appunti sul funzionamento delle commissioni interne* (*Estratto da "Il Diritto del Lavoro"* — 1956, no. 6), table 1, opposite p. 16. The CGIL based its figures in 1953 upon results from 3780 plants with 904,233 valid votes cast and in 1954 on 3462 plants with 950,002 valid votes.

We do not deny that CISL had some successes nor do we claim that all these are due to employer pressure in favor of its lists. The true successes of CISL, however, are not obtained at the expense of CGIL. They are due to the fact that greater activity of CISL in the plants has permitted it to get to vote — and sometimes even to get them to adhere to a new trade union — a certain number of less advanced workers who, through apathy, had not been organized and had not even participated in elections.[31]

As the process of reversals quickened during the first half of 1955, highlighted by the FIAT election, however, CGIL felt compelled to argue publicly that employer pressure, prompted in many cases by pressure from the United States using off-shore procurement contracts as a weapon, alone accounted for the reversals.

In the plants where the employer pressure did not make itself felt (but these plants are unfortunately exceptions) and even in all those where employer pressure has not gone beyond certain limits, the positions of last year have remained approximately unchanged, while in almost all the plants where employers have resorted to every means, legal and illegal, moral and material, to assure the victory of CISL and UIL, the break-away organizations have seen their own ratio increase appreciably at the expense of the unitary organization . . . Temporary hiring . . . mass discharge of the best CGIL activists . . . threats of closing down entire plants . . . intimidation of older workers . . . downgrading . . . assignment to heavy work . . . creation of special departments . . . to which are assigned the "unfaithful" or "dangerous" elements . . . threats of discharge . . . accompanied by promises of premiums, individual or group increases.[32]

There is little doubt that management efforts in many industrial establishments had been directed toward the weakening of CGIL. This was particularly true in some of the largest establishments including FIAT. There were, however, other factors which played a fundamental role. Even so far as employer pressures are concerned, the CGIL had to a surprising extent ignored or downgraded their importance in reacting to specific situations. *Confindustria* and the three major trade union confederations had signed an agreement in May 1953 replacing the 1947 agreement on

31. Quoted in *Confederazione Italiana Sindacati Lavoratori, 2° Congresso Nazionale, Roma 22–27 Aprile, 1955, Relazione della Segreteria Confederale* (Rome, 1955), p. 63.

32. Mario Montagnana, "Risultati e insegnamenti delle elezioni per le commissioni interne," *Rinascita*, XII, May 5, 1955, pp. 347–348. For detailed position of CGIL and its accusations against management and CISL and UIL *see* text of Di Vittorio report to CGIL Directive Committee session of April 1955 in Giuseppe Di Vittorio, *L'Unità dei lavoratori* (Rome, 1957), pp. 145–157.

Internal Commissions.[33] The negotiations had extended over years and it was a reflection of the generally weakened position of the trade union movement that the new arrangement loosened considerably the language covering the protections offered the Internal Commissions in industrial plants. It is surprising that CGIL agreed to the modifications, particularly those in Article 10 which dealt with time off for Internal Commission members to perform their responsibilities. CGIL had been the principal defender of the Commissions and had the most to lose from modifications. The timing of the agreement, one month before the national political elections, gave rise to some speculation that the Communist Party in its effort to improve its chances of obtaining cooperation among wide sectors of the electorate had chosen this means of demonstrating its cooperative reasonableness.[34]

FIAT had taken the initiative in the summer of 1953 in interpreting the new agreement to mean that it was no longer bound by past practice on time off for Commission members, and cancelled all such previous arrangements. CGIL protested the FIAT decision but took no action to prevent its application. As a result, other employers took similar steps and the limitation rapidly became generalized in industry.

CGIL similarly showed a singular lack of militancy in protesting against discharges, transfers and discriminations against its activists and its representatives on Internal Commissions, which developed as a second stage of the employer offensive. The General Report to the February 1956 CGIL Congress claimed that 674 members of Internal Commissions, 1128 activists and "thousands of workers" had been discharged during 1955 alone because of their CGIL activity, or, as the report more elegantly put it, "because they refused to renounce their dignity as workers, because they did not bow before the *padrone*." [35] Yet, except on a verbal level, little active protest of an important nature was developed by CGIL in the plants to oppose the employer offensive. The campaign against the European Defense Community arrangements was given far more importance by the CGIL at the time.

When, at the national conference of the Communist Party in January

33. For translations of texts of both the new agreement and the one it replaced, *see* Maurice F. Neufeld, *Labor Unions and National Politics in Italian Industrial Plants,* Institute of International Industrial and Labor Relations (Ithaca, 1954), appendix 2, pp. 111–119 and appendix 5, pp. 127–135.

34. Giorgio Galli, "La CGIL paga il prezzo dell' accordo 8 Maggio 1953," *Il Mercurio,* II, 24, June 11, 1955, pp. 8–9. Galli's thesis is that the Internal Commission electoral losses of 1955 were the eventual price paid by CGIL for its politically dictated signature to the 1953 agreement.

35. *Una economia del lavoro contro l'economia dei monopoli, Relazione al IX Congresso della CGIL dei Segretari Confederali S. Pessi e F. Santi, Quaderni CGIL 4* (Rome, 1956), pp. 18–19.

1955, the problem of the employer offensive was raised and it was urged that an all-out fight "for freedom in the factories" be launched, Togliatti is reported to have replied, "The essential thing today is the fight against the imperialist war-mongers. This is the theme of the Party, and no question can be posed separately from this."[36] With this order of priorities, three months later, when the Party had gathered sixteen million signatures on a petition demanding that the atomic bomb be outlawed, a majority of workers at FIAT had turned their backs upon the CGIL. The focus of Communist interest at FIAT had for many years been to keep it as a stronghold of political support. When, as early as 1950, the CGIL appeared to be locally concentrating too exclusively upon economic and trade union issues, Togliatti is reported to have told the Turin Communist Directive Committee, "does there not exist here a weakening of our influence not as a fighting organization but as a Socialist organization? . . . Even recruitment should not be made exclusively on economic trade union bases. The handling of problems opens the road for us, but the action of conquest . . . should be an action of ideological conquest . . . Do not pose only problems of trade union character, but also problems of general propaganda."[37]

Of increasing eventual importance for its trade union support was the neglect by the CGIL of plant level problems in all their aspects, concentrating instead upon international political obectives woven into national level labor issues around which massive campaigns, manifestations and strikes on a national scale could be staged. Such a focus inevitably involved in some measure a price in the amount of support within individual plants. The employer offensive of 1954–1955 pushed in the same direction with some success. Workers were not as willing to join in protesting discriminatory practices against CGIL as they might have some years before. Management's actions might earlier have boomeranged badly. They did not in 1955. Furthermore, the very weakness of CGIL's response made workers even less enthusiastic about an organization which seemed unable and frequently unwilling to protect its own people.

CISL Plant Level Policies

To make matters worse for CGIL, it did not have the trade union field to itself. In the competition for support among wage earners, CISL had begun in 1952 and 1953 to enunciate a new approach to collective bargaining and organization in an effort to reach more effectively the very area in which CGIL appeared weakest. In a general way at its Bari session in 1952 and in more precise fashion at Ladispoli in February 1953, the CISL General Council spelled out a new approach to collective bargaining

36. Claire Sterling, "The Crucial Hour for Italian Democracy," *The Reporter* (New York), June 2, 1955, p. 12.

37. *Il Popolo,* May 16, 1950.

agreements.[38] It took the position that plant level agreements must be sought as a supplement to the national industry level agreements if the worker in individual plants was to have any influence upon his own wage level beyond the basic minimum established in the national agreements. The differentiation of wage levels adapted to the situation in individual companies and plants had remained almost exclusively in the hands of management. CISL by its policy decision made a bid for the development of collective bargaining at the company or plant level. The logical complement necessary to achieve this objective was the development of a plant level trade union structure which had existed only in vestigal form among many of the trade union organizations, and in 1954 CISL took the decision to emphasize the development of such a structure.

The CISL undertaking was a formidable one, and in the next few years was only very modestly successful in limited areas. The establishment of a trade union structure on the level of the plant and the encouragement of decentralized bargaining required a body of trained trade union officials and activists which simply did not exist. Only by an ambitious and energetic program of worker education and training did CISL over the years begin to fill the gap.

Fundamentally, the employers and their association, *Confindustria,* opposed strenuously any effort at plant level bargaining. They opposed even more strenuously any recognition of the trade union on the plant level. CISL efforts in the year following its 1953 decision were mainly educational, propagandistic, and organizational rather than productive of collective agreements. This very process, however, placed them in a position of bidding for worker support in concrete terms on issues arising within the plants.

CGIL's reaction to CISL's new approach was highly critical and antagonistic. The new bargaining approach was described as an effort to fragment the working class, to develop a new corporativism and basically to serve the interests of the employers. The criticisms were used as an additional club by CGIL with which to beat CISL as an organization attempting to destroy the traditions of class solidarity and playing the game of the employers.

By early 1955, however, CGIL was beginning to have second thoughts on the subject. The comment of Di Vittorio at his press conference at the end of 1954, quoted earlier, implicitly conceded that CISL appeared to be making progress in its new approach. A turnabout on such an issue was a painful process for CGIL, however. At its Directive Committee session in April 1955, with the FIAT election disaster looming large over the horizon, CGIL took

38. "La politica salariale della CISL," *Bollettino di Studi e di Statistiche* (official CISL monthly), no. 11 (November 1955), pp. 405–426; CISL, *Il sindacato e l'organizzazzione di fabbrica, Quaderni di Studi e Documentazioni,* no. 1 (1955), pp. 62–74; CISL *2° Congresso Nazionale,* pp. 136–141.

a first feeble step in this direction by deciding that the situation "required a trade union policy articulated on the level of the plant, group or sector." [39] During 1955, however, CGIL remained in fact sharply hostile to the new plant level focus.[40] Only gradually did it overcome its deeply ingrained ideological prejudices and come grudgingly to the position of agreeing to the desirability of handling individual plant level wage situations pragmatically as trade union business. At its congress in February 1956, the CGIL took a second reluctant step along this road. In the general report to the congress, it was admitted that "Too often our economic policy demands and our wage demands have remained unrelated, so that in some cases the economic positions were reduced to propaganda positions for the outside covering our deficiencies in the plant level struggles." [41] An attempt was made to draw a sharp distinction between the CISL approach and that proposed by CGIL. It was claimed that the former was oriented simply toward the sharing of some part of increased productivity, while CGIL would remain firmly oriented toward the criteria of the workers' needs and their efforts.

Actually, in the following few years, CGIL began concentrating to a greater extent upon its organization on the plant level, but did not emphasize particularly the matter of plant level bargaining. It continued to accuse CISL of attempting to lead away from national level collective agreements, which CGIL regarded as the basic framework of protection to workers. It also became increasingly involved in polemics with CISL over the question of the relative role of the trade union and the Internal Commission within the plant. The subject will be treated more fully later, but basically as a reflection of the policy of encouragement of unity of action and the blurring of distinctions between separate trade unions, CGIL forcefully supported the maintenance and strengthening of the role of the Internal Commissions. For exactly opposite reasons CISL opposed any strengthening of the Internal Commissions and looked toward a gradual evolution in the direction of implanting and expanding the role of the trade union as such within the plants.

This was an interesting reversal of positions for the organizations. After the trade union break-aways, CGIL had decided at its congress in 1949 to concentrate upon the promotion of plant trade union committees made up of its activists inside the plant to act as agents for the union in promoting the trade union and political objectives of CGIL among the workers. The effort was prompted by the new situation of competitive unionism and the heavier concentration by the Communists upon purely political objectives. In 1951 the CGIL plant committees had come under attack from CISL and

39. *Una economia del lavoro,* pp. 73–74.
40. Conversations with the author in Rome during June–July 1955.
41. *Una economia del lavoro,* pp. 57, 74–77.

UIL as well as from the general press as clandestine instruments for developing political agitation and undermining the Internal Commissions. CGIL had defended the committees as a desirable means of giving plant level existence to the trade union and denied that they impinged upon the responsibilities of the Internal Commissions.[42]

During the mid-fifties the positions pressed by CISL were an advantage to it in its competition against CGIL. During the four years from May 1953 to May 1957 there were 748 plant or company agreements signed involving approximately 400,000 workers in 569 plants, according to a compilation made by CISL.[43] More than half the workers involved were in the 194 plants covered by 287 agreements in the metal-mechanical industry. Other industries prominently represented were chemical, textiles, and public services. The subjects covered were primarily plant minimum wage scales (30 percent), production or productivity bonuses (20 percent) and other types of bonuses or indemnities (28 percent).

These agreements followed no uniform pattern so far as negotiation or signature were concerned. *Confindustria* opposition remained strong to such agreements and particularly to the recognition of the union in the plant. As a result, when agreements were entered into by management they were frequently signed with the Internal Commission even though in many of these cases they had been negotiated with trade union representatives. According to the CISL compilation, 41 percent of the agreements were signed with the Internal Commission, 10 percent were signed with only the CISL members of the Internal Commission, 23 percent were signed with a CISL union alone and 26 percent were signed with both CISL and other trade unions. The CISL data do not identify the other organizations other than to comment that many of the agreements included in the 26 percent were signed by CISL and UIL alone.

UIL during this period was much less enthusiastic than CISL about a plant level agreement policy, reflecting its much weaker structure on local levels and its smaller resources for pursuing such a policy. It too, however, developed a local leadership training program and stressed the building of plant level union organization to attempt to meet the new situation.

No doubt many of the agreements simply confirmed decisions management planned unilaterally in any event, but in most cases the agreements represented specific guarantees and all at the least had symbolic importance. To the extent that they represented favored treatment of CISL as against CGIL, they did not necessarily build credit among the workers for CISL.

42. *Lavoro*, IV, 43, October 10, 1951, p. 2; *ibid.*, V, 2, January 12, 1952, p. 4.

43. CISL, *Il sindacato democratico per lo sviluppo della società italiana ed europea, Relazione della Segreteria Confederale al 3° Congresso Nazionale, Roma, 19–22 Marzo, 1959* (Rome, 1959), pp. 295–303; *Politica Sindacale* (official CISL bi-monthly), II, 3 (June 1959), pp. 297–298.

As with more direct anti-CGIL action by management, however, the mood among wage earners was such that strong reactions did not take place. As a result, CISL was given the opportunity to capitalize upon these situations to the extent that it was able over time to demonstrate that it could also develop effective militant positions and action when appropriate occasions arose.

Communists and their "Transmission Belt"

The buffeting to which CGIL was subjected on the industrial front and from its competitor organizations had put it increasingly on the defensive between 1954 and 1956. As an immediate reaction to the dramatic reversals it suffered in plant elections in 1955, it began a series of reorganizations in its affiliated organizations, particularly in the metallurgical industry where its losses had been greatest. The top officials of the Metallurgical Workers' Federation, including its secretary general, Renato Bitossi, were removed and transferred. The Confederation temporarily appointed Agostino Novella general secretary. Novella had years before been assigned from the Communist Party to national CGIL headquarters as trusted watchdog for the Party. Fernando Foa was sent in as his deputy and was counted on to develop a program and effect a reorganization of policy, tactics, and organization within the limits set by Novella. Foa, who had come to the Nenni Socialist Party from the Action Party and had performed brilliantly as assistant confederal secretary in charge of economic policy for CGIL, had gradually broadened his activity as he demonstrated his reliability, ability, and resourcefulness.

CGIL, however, was also beginning to feel the effects of Nenni's moving away from complete identity of the PSI with the Communist Party and of the increasing discussion both within and outside the Socialist movement of the possibilities of Socialist reunification. The Socialists within the CGIL had long since lost genuine authority and during the "Frontist" period of Communist-Socialist relations, particularly following the split of the democratic groups from CGIL, neither had the bargaining power nor the inclination to challenge the Communists even on day-to-day matters, let alone on major issues. The Socialist trade union officials in CGIL remained firmly committed to remain in CGIL, but the loosened ties between the two political parties made them more conscious of their own identities and therefore encouraged them to speak up more freely within the CGIL councils in criticism of positions too blatantly dictated by the Communist Party.

As a result of the combination of pressures both inside but particularly outside the organization, the CGIL leadership and the Communist Party felt compelled to go through a showcase cleansing of methods relating to domination of trade union affairs by the Party. Since the CGIL had for years been held up before the public by its critics as nothing more than a "transmission belt" for Communist policies, the Communists beat their breasts in self-criticism and promised it would be no more. The Communist Party Congress late in 1956 was the occasion for the performance. Coming as it did after the Soviet Union's Communist Party's Twentieth Congress, with its "roads to socialism" theme and its Stalin revelations — although right on the heels of Soviet intervention in Hungary — the Italian Communist Party apparently felt it could afford the luxury of such discussion.

Di Vittorio, as head of the CGIL and member of the Party's Political Bureau, played the role of innovator. At the Party congress he announced:

> We must liquidate definitely the famous theory of the transmission belt . . . The liquidation of the theory . . . is justified by the fact that at present there are several workers' parties which exercise an influence over the different strata of organized workers. The trade unions, therefore, to be unitary cannot be the transmission belt of any party. I propose that this principle be affirmed clearly . . . and that all the Communists of Italy be pledged to observe it scrupulously. We are, together with our Socialist comrades, the principal promoters of trade union unity. We must therefore always be conscious that any interference of the Party . . . in the trade union constitutes an attack against its unity. This principle is valid also for the trade union militants who must not be removed from their posts because of the requirements of the Party. This will permit greater stability and a higher level of training of the trade union militants.[44]

The theses of the congress dutifully registered the identical theme:

> To be considered profoundly erroneous and harmful . . . is the habit of attributing to Party organizations the execution of tasks which belong to the mass organizations, each of which has its specific field of action and ought to have its own internal autonomous and democratic functioning. The basic task of the Communists in the trade union field is to win all the workers over to a unitary policy and to the life and action of the trade union. The Communists that militate in the trade unions must not form into groups in order to obtain positions of leadership and control or prepare beforehand the decisions that are to be taken within the trade union organizations . . . The Communists advocate and defend the complete autonomy of the trade unions . . . The Communists affirm that it is not possible in Italy, today, to limit and deaden the function of the trade union to that of a simple "transmission belt" for this or that party. The relations between the workers' parties and the trade unions belong to the internal dialectics of the workers' movement and cannot constrain the trade unions to a position of subordination. This does not mean, however, that the trade union movement ought to keep itself imprisoned in a barren and corporative exclusiveness, in an apolitical "neutrality," taking over the equivocal and

44. Giuseppe Di Vittorio, *L'Unità dei lavoratori*, pp. 180–181.

anachronistic ideology of "pure trade unionism." This is contrary . . . to the whole history of the Italian workers' movement.[45]

These declarations and resolutions changed little of substance in the relationship between the Communist Party and CGIL. They reflected, however, the increasing pressure of opinion and events upon the organizations. The Party congress had taken place within a month of the Soviet suppression of the Hungarian revolution and had not yet felt the full brunt of criticisms resulting from it. CGIL even more than the Communist Party, however, was shaken by the repercussions of the Soviet action in Hungary since it was under heavy pressure already from other fronts.

Hungary and Aftermath

In the post-Twentieth Congress atmosphere, the CGIL followed the lead of the Communist Party in its favorable attitude and comments on the Polish riots and the Gomulka government. Similarly, the issue of its official publication, Lavoro, which appeared after the beginning of the Hungarian revolution but before the Soviet intervention, carried a long account commenting favorably upon the actions of the revolutionaries.[46] Di Vittorio in a public statement also justified the rebellion as a revolt of workers against tyrannical practices.[47] Soviet intervention immediately forced a switch. Embarrassing though it was, Di Vittorio justified the Soviet action as a necessary liberating move.

For the CGIL itself the problem was more difficult in view of the Socialist condemnation of the Russian action. CGIL felt compelled suddenly to discover the virtues of silence. At its Directive Committee session of November 20, the issue was resolved in a declaration that "it is not compulsory that the trade union organization always take a position on national or international questions or developments of a purely political character . . . If differences develop among groups or factions within the organization, each group may wish to make its own position known within the limits set by the requirements of protecting trade union unity." [48]

Striking a posture of neutrality was not enough to save CGIL in the following months from a wave of resignations among its officials on all levels among those belonging both to the Communist and the Socialist parties. In some cases members switched to UIL — particularly those who

45. The Eighth Congress, pp. 91–93.
46. Lavoro, IX, 44, November 4, 1956, pp. 5–6.
47. For comments upon Di Vittorio's statement and his later reversal see Il Lavoro Italiano, VIII, 44, November 12, 1956, pp. 1–2.
48. "La politica della CGIL dal IV al V Congresso" (entire issue), Rassegna Sindacale, no. 28 (April 1960), pp. 17–19. The French CGT also felt compelled to take a similar position of neutrality.

were members of PSI — and some to CISL. The Communist general secretary and Socialist national secretary of the Commercial Workers' Federation, for example, resigned from the CGIL (and from their parties) to join UIL.[49] When two secretaries of the Genoa Chamber of Labor resigned and joined UIL, but failed to resign from the PSI, the Party expelled them. Despite its weaving on the issue of autonomy, PSI insisted upon disciplined acceptance by its membership of continued affiliation to CGIL.

CISL also got an influx of former CGIL militants.[50] A great many of those who left CGIL, however, simply dropped out of the trade union movement. On the basis of its own claims, unreliable as they are, the CGIL admitted that membership fell from a level of 4,622,000 at the end of 1955 to 4,078,000 at the end of 1957 and fell another 400,000 during 1958.[51]

Both the CISL and UIL reacted strongly to the Soviet intervention in Hungary and demonstrated a rare degree of cooperation by issuing joint declarations and promoting joint demonstrations throughout the country.[52] Such cooperation was only of a transitory nature, however, and only signaled one of the crests in the waves marking the relationship between the two organizations.

Trade Union Reunification Proposals

Socialist autonomy tendencies, discussion of opening to the Left and of Socialist reunification and the repercussions of international Communist developments pushed to the fore discussion of different forms of reunification or reorganization of the trade union movement. For Nenni, either because he sincerely opposed the further splitting of the trade union movement as a violation of his ideological article of faith concerning working class unity, or because he feared that he could not carry his own Socialist ranks along with him and would doom his party to minor importance among workers, there was no equivocation in his position that the Socialists must remain within CGIL. Within the framework of his evolving political objectives, reunification of the entire trade union movement became the formula pressed by him and his followers. This position, which he set forth after his meeting with Saragat in August 1956, remained the policy of PSI

49. *Il Lavoro Italiano*, IX, 8, February 19, 1957, pp. 1 and 4.

50. *See, for example, Conquiste del Lavoro*, X, 14, April 6, 1957, p. 1 and X, 21, June 1, 1957, p. 1.

51. *Lavoro*, XIII, 3, January 17, 1960, p. 5 for 1957 and 1958 figures. The figures for 1955 given in CGIL, *Discorsi e documenti del IV Congresso della CGIL, Quaderni CGIL 5* (Rome, 1956), p. 114.

52. *Conquiste del Lavoro*, IX, 42, November 3, 1956, pp. 1 and 4, and *ibid.*, IX, 43, November 10, 1956, pp. 1 and 4; *Il Lavoro Italiano*, VIII, 44, November 12, 1956, pp. 1–2.

throughout the following years, reinforced at two conferences of his trade union followers.[53]

The Communists in turn stepped up what had consistently been their position, that only a unified trade union movement would be able adequately to represent wage earners in their struggles on the economic front. It had been the consistent judgment of the Communists that they could continue to dominate any combination, just as they had before the trade union splits in the late forties. But in the middle fifties there was a greater emphasis in Communist tactics upon efforts at broad combinations of political forces. In addition, the trade union organizations competing against CGIL had greatly increased their relative importance. Reunification could no longer be conceived of in terms of offering a place in CGIL to those who had earlier left it. Furthermore, the PSI position on the political front offered for the time the distant but potential risk that its trade unionists conceivably might pull out of CGIL if Nenni really did opt for autonomy and carried the day. Under these circumstances, even if the Communists had not been enthusiastic about the choice, agreement to push for reunification on a basis other than CGIL had to be agreed upon with the Nenni Socialists in order to attempt to seal off such a possibility of a split.

As early as the beginning of 1955, Di Vittorio began urging that the strengthening of the workers' position required the establishment of a cartel among the three principal trade union confederations, to work together on those issues upon which they could agree.[54] This represented a retreat from the monopoly claims by CGIL of earlier years. But it offered too little reassurance of a new position to the PSI.

It was early in September 1956, as the Socialist reunification talks reached a first crescendo, that a new position was enunciated. The position was first announced, not by an official body of CGIL, but by Fernando Santi, the Socialist CGIL assistant general secretary and Novella, the Communist Party apparatus "boss" of CGIL, both speaking at a public meeting at Bologna. Ten days later the Secretariat and the next month the Executive Committee of CGIL made the new position their own: the CGIL was willing to disband in favor of a new confederation gathering together all trade union elements; trade union unification must have neither conquerors nor conquered, but must be the common victory of all.[55]

53. Nenni's announcement after his meeting with Saragat referred to the need for a common commitment "to end all trade union division, so damaging to the interests of workers, and promote unity of trade union action of all workers for purposes of constituting a unitary, autonomous and independent trade union of which CGIL represents the natural democratic base." *Azione Sociale* (official ACLI weekly), VIII, 38, September 23, 1956, p. 1.

54. See, *for example,* Di Vittorio's contribution in *I sindacati in Italia, Saggi di G. Di Vittorio, G. Pastore, I. Viglianesi, G. Rapelli, F. Santi, E. Parri, G. Canini* (Bari, 1955), pp. 9–114.

55. "La politica della CGIL dal IV al V Congresso," pp. 10–11.

As was entirely predictable to the Communists and the Nenni Socialists, both the CISL and the UIL turned down the proferred offer in unequivocal terms. Each of the two organizations, however, used the occasion to set forth its different reorganization plans for the trade union movement. The CISL General Council, meeting a few days after the CGIL's Executive had made its announcement, pledged its organization to work toward the unification of all democratic trade unions — CISL, UIL, and autonomous organizations. Among the principles it set forth as a basis for such unification was (1) faithfulness to a policy of gradual transformation of the economic system, (2) progressive acquisition of responsibility by the trade unions and their collaboration with other democratic forces to stimulate social progress, (3) commitment of the trade unions to consider political and economic freedom to be indivisible and to fight against all dictatorships, (4) rigorous defense of the autonomy of the trade unions and rejection of Communist ideology as irreconcilable with democracy and the interests of the workers.[56]

The UIL position had been set out in detail by Viglianesi a month before and was confirmed by the UIL Directive Council in the context of the CGIL announcements within a few days of the CISL pronouncement. The UIL had justified its separate existence from its inception by its claim that only a democratic Socialist-oriented organization could fill a gap left by the Communist CGIL and what it claimed to be the Catholic identified CISL, and that eventually such an organization would become the principal point of attraction away from CGIL. The Socialist political reunification talks were thus regarded by UIL as offering it a major natural opportunity. What was needed was a democratic Socialist-oriented trade union organization — free from party domination — and the natural step for the Nenni Socialists if they were serious about autonomy and Socialist reunification was to leave the CGIL and join with UIL.[57] It was this position which UIL offered in opposition to the CGIL and to the CISL proposals.

There was of course nothing new in either of the two positions. The circumstances, however, were significantly different by virtue of the new flexibility which potentially existed as a result of the Socialist reunification conversations. CISL's proposals, which had always been its basic position, now had to be focused to draw the Nenni Socialists, if they really did break away from the Communists in the trade union field, into a single unified democratic trade union confederation, however unhappy the CISL leadership might be at the prospect. Conversely, UIL more than ever opposed merging with CISL since it saw its chance for the first time to become a major or even predominant organization in the trade union constellation if the Nenni Socialists broke from CGIL and joined UIL.

The Nenni Socialists, meanwhile, and in the following years, simply

56. *Conquiste del Lavoro*, IX, 40, October 20, 1956, pp. 1–5.
57. *Il Lavoro Italiano*, VIII, 34, September 3, 1956, p. 1.

stayed put in the CGIL. Both CISL and UIL, however, in the aftermath of the unification polemics carried on vigorous campaigns, which were in fact organization drives on the basis of the positions they had assumed. The Hungarian affair and its aftermath on the Italian scene were merged into these campaigns as additional ammunition against CGIL.

The PSI trade unionists gave no encouragement to any speculation concerning their loyalties within the CGIL. In June 1957, several months after their Party congress at Venice, a conference of approximately 400 PSI trade union and party officials was held under the auspices of the party leadership.[58] Several themes dominated the general report made to the conference by the party official in charge of mass organizations, Vincenzo Gatto. The same themes characterized the conference discussion and the resolution later adopted by the party Directorate. The theme they most emphatically stressed was that the place of PSI trade unionists was in CGIL. Trade union unity came next, with emphasis on the fact that in achieving such unity "no one with common sense in Italy believes that in a climate of democracy, a democratic trade union . . . could develop within the organizational or ideological framework of any of the existing trade union centers." [59] Plant level trade union activity was described as basic to strengthening unity and promoting organization. Nevertheless, the Internal Commission was held to be the foundation of plant level worker protection and unity and therefore had to be defended at all costs. Significantly, the party was called on to help in strengthening the position of the PSI trade unionists as a faction within CGIL.

While critical of CISL, the conference as a whole was surprisingly balanced in its comments on the organization. On the other hand, UIL was attacked savagely by a number of the most prominent trade union representatives, taking their cue from the general report which had referred to UIL as "this organization without history, without ideals and without programs." [60] UIL appeared to be the more immediate threat as a pole of attraction — which UIL was actively attempting to exploit — to rank-and-file Socialists and militants dissatisfied with their CGIL affiliation. In fact, UIL was having considerable success during this period in Internal Commission elections, frequently running its lists under the banner of Socialist unity and including where possible PSI or ex-PSI workers among its candidates. In addition, UIL had been publicizing its claim that PSI trade unionists had little influence in CGIL and that they were complete prisoners

58. For proceedings of the conference and subsequent resolution adopted by party Directorate see I socialisti e il sindacato, Atti del convegno nazionale indetto dal Partito Socialista Italiano sui problemi e sulla vita del sindacato in Italia, Roma: 1, 2, 3 Giugno 1957 (Rome, 1957).

59. Ibid., p. 34.

60. Ibid., p. 17. For Viglianesi's answer to the attacks upon his organization see Il Lavoro Italiano, IX, 25, June 18, 1957, p. 1.

of the Communist apparatus. UIL circulated widely its analysis of the distribution of CGIL leadership positions showing the feeble representation allotted to PSI trade unionists in a number of the most important industrial regions. For example, according to UIL, in the province of Milan of the 15 leadership positions in the Chamber of Labor, 3 were held by PSI and 12 by Communist Party members; of the 34 secretaries of industry unions in the province, PSI had the least significant 7 industry secretaryships; and PSI had only 5 of the secretaries in the approximately 200 communes in the province.[61] Furthermore, Viglianesi and other Social Democratic UIL leaders, particularly Enzo Dalla Chiesa, were active within PSDI in promoting a favorable atmosphere toward Socialist reunification but were urging their trade union position as a cardinal precondition for PSDI-PSI agreement.[62] The official PSI attitude was therefore understandably sharpest in its antagonism against UIL.

CGIL Loses Support

During the course of 1958 a new period of stabilization among the trade unions was gradually achieved, as had occurred earlier in the year on the political scene. The repercussions of the political, economic, and international developments had spent themselves. A rough order of the magnitude of CGIL losses in support and gains made by the other trade unions during the previous years is given in the unreliable statistics of the organizations on their membership claims and the incomplete compilation of Internal Commission election results. CGIL by its own admission had lost one million members during the four years from 1954 to 1958, claiming a membership of 3,678,000 at the end of the latter year. CISL claimed a membership of 2,316,000 at the end of 1958, an increase of 13 percent over four years before. UIL claimed a doubling of membership during the same four-year period, with a claimed membership of approximately 1,150,000 at the end of 1958.[63] Both the CISL and CGIL compilation of Internal Commission election results showed the same tendencies.[64] According to the CGIL compilation, CGIL received 68.3 percent of the votes in 1954 and 53.6 percent in 1957, recovering slightly to 54.6 percent in 1958. The CISL compilation

61. *Il Lavoro Italiano,* IX, 29, July 16, 1957, p. 1. Data on other provinces were given as follows: Bologna, *ibid.,* IX, 25, June 18, 1957, p. 1; Turin, *ibid.,* IX, 26, June 25, 1957, p. 1; Genoa, *ibid.,* IX, 27, July 2, 1957, p. 1; Bari, *ibid.,* IX, 30, July 23, 1957; p. 1; Perugia, *ibid.,* IX, 31, July 30, 1957, p. 1.

62. See texts of Viglianesi and of Della Chiesa speeches at October 1957 Milan PSDI Congress in *Il Lavoro Italiano* IX, 43, October 29, 1957, pp. 3–4.

63. CGIL, *Discorsi e documenti del IV Congresso,* p. 114; *Lavoro,* XIII, 3, January 17, 1960, p. 5; CISL, *Il sindacato democratico per lo sviluppo,* p. 40; *Il Lavoro Italiano,* IX, 4, January 22, 1957, p. 1; *ibid.,* XII, 8, February 23, 1960, p. 6.

64. M. Neufeld, *Appunti sul funzionamento,* table 1, opposite p. 16; *Lavoro,* XI, 17–18, May 4, 1958, p. 5; *Ibid.,* XII, 4, January 25, 1959, p. 7; *Conquiste del Lavoro,* XI, 1–2, January 1, 1958, p. 4; *ibid.,* XIII, 2, January 15, 1959, p. 8.

showed CGIL falling from 64.7 percent of the votes in 1954 to 47.8 percent in 1957 and rising very slightly to 48.5 percent in 1958. During the same years CISL votes went from 23.9 percent to 33.8 percent and then fell to 29.9 percent according to the CGIL compilation, while it went from 27.1 percent to 38.8 percent and then fell to 35.9 percent according to its own compilation. About two-thirds of the CISL fall in votes between 1957 and 1958 is accounted for by votes lost at FIAT as a result of the expulsion of its affiliate at the FIAT plants immediately before the 1958 election. UIL went from 3.5 percent (1954) to 7.8 percent (1957) to 8.6 percent (1958) according to CGIL and from 3.8 percent (1954) to 8.1 percent (1957) to 8.1 percent (1958) according to CISL.

UIL, unlike the two other organizations, did not run slates in many plants. Its compilations, limited to those elections in which it participated, gave the following percentages of distribution of seats won on the Internal Commissions (it released no calculations based upon votes): CGIL had 50.3 percent of the seats in 1954, 38.1 percent in 1957 and 33.6 percent in 1958; CISL had 21.1 percent in 1954, 28.5 percent in 1957 and 26.8 percent in 1958; UIL had 25.0 percent in 1954, 29.1 percent in 1957 and 28.1 percent in 1958.[65]

As the national political election campaign got under way in 1958, the trade union organizations announced their general positions. While individual trade union leaders, particularly in CGIL and in CISL, actively campaigned for specific party support, the organizations as such continued their tradition of placing their emphasis upon programs. The type of program upon which the Communist and PSI trade union leaders were able to agree is interesting in reflecting how closely the PSI trade union leadership and presumably the Party itself stood to the Communists in their international policy position. To help the membership "select the party of their choice" a ten-point program was adopted, the first point of which called for "active defense of peace in the world; prohibition of installation of atomic bases or missile launching bases on national territory; initiative by Italy on behalf of easing of international tensions, peaceful coexistence, disarmament, the end of thermo-nuclear tests, prohibition of arms of extermination."[66]

Lest there be any mistaking the nature of the recommendations, Novella, who had taken over as secretary general of CGIL some months before, issued a press statement after the Executive Committee had approved the program in which he stated "The confidence of CGIL cannot go . . . to those parties and those groups which in the course of the last decade have supported the political monopoly of Christian Democracy and have not

65. UIL, *Relazione Organizzativa al 3° Congresso Nazionale dell' Unione Italiana del Lavoro, Roma, 9–10-11–12 Febbraio 1958* (Rome, n.d.), p. 9; *Il Lavoro Italiano*, XII, 8, February 23, 1960, p. 4.

66. Text of entire program in *Lavoro*, XI, 19, May 11, 1958, pp. 6–7.

succeeded in resolving or carrying to solution any of the fundamental economic and social problems of the country, nor to guarantee a solid basis for peaceful and democratic life."

While UIL's position reflected its Social Democratic-Republican leadership orientation, it played a passive role for the most part in the campaign and relatively few of its leaders did any campaigning on their own. CISL, on the other hand, took a much more active part, not directly through its organization, but through the extensive participation on an individual basis of a large number of its national and provincial leaders in electoral contests. Since they were almost all Christian Democrats, it was the campaign of this Party which was actively stamped in many areas by the CISL trade unionists. For some years CISL leaders had functioned as an organized faction within the Christian Democratic Party. They had been instrumental in helping to balance the Right elements within the Party and to push the Party apparatus into more liberal hands. Because of their work within the Party and the strength they added as trade union leaders to the Christian Democratic slates, a large number of CISL leaders were given prominent place on their party's tickets. As a result, 31 CISL trade unionists were elected to the Chamber of Deputies — fifteen for the first time — and three were elected to the Senate — two for the first time.[67]

Trade Union Leadership Changes

One result of the aftermath of the 1958 political election was a change in top leadership in CISL. In June, Giulio Pastore resigned as general secretary of the organization to accept a cabinet post in the Fanfani government, and was replaced by Bruno Storti. CISL thus followed CGIL by less than a year in replacing its top official.

Giuseppe Di Vittorio, who had led CGIL since it was set up during the war, died on November 3, 1957. He was replaced by Agostino Novella. Di Vittorio had been the popular leader who could move multitudes to deep emotion through his simple warm manner and his projected sincerity and humanity. He never seemed far from the destitute *braccianti* of Cerignola, from among whom he had started on his career as a worker leader. He had been a disciplined Communist for more than thirty years, yet such was the personality he had projected that speculation always continued that the Party found it necessary to assign "watch dogs" to CGIL to keep Di Vittorio from straying into straightforward consideration of worker interests. Novella was quite a different sort. He was reputed to be a principal party "watch dog" over Di Vittorio. Much more the "organization man" of the Communist apparatus than a natural leader of men, his choice to succeed Di Vittorio had clearly been planned in Communist Party headquarters as

67. *Conquiste del Lavoro*, XI, 13, June 1, 1958, p. 3 and *ibid.*, XI, 14, June 15, 1958, p. 3.

a guarantee that no question would arise concerning control and obedience to party interests. For CGIL as a trade union organization seeking to maintain its mass appeal among workers, Di Vittorio's death was an irreparable loss.

The succession problem is CISL when Pastore decided to leave the trade union movement for a full-time political career was of quite a different nature. Pastore had stamped the trade union movement with his own personality to an extent that Di Vittorio in the nature of things could not match in CGIL. A strong and stubborn man, Pastore had developed well beyond his own Catholic background in molding CISL gradually into an organization genuinely free of outside political or ideological controls. He kept decision-making in his organization narrowly based at the top, yet to an astonishing extent he devoted the relatively limited resources of CISL to training leadership on all levels of the organization.

Bruno Storti had come through the evolution of trade union events at Pastore's side from before the Christian faction's split away from CGIL in 1948. His development as a national trade union leader had been within the framework of the free organizational atmosphere of CISL. Coming from the same Catholic background as Pastore, he too had followed the same path as Pastore. He had the advantage, however, of not carrying the battle scars and personal antagonisms which Pastore had inevitably incurred as a result of the wars he had led, particularly with UIL and within the ranks of Christian Democratic leadership.

CISL and Political Action

A measure of the evolution of CISL over the years and the development within its ranks of a democratic spirit reflecting the progress toward the image CISL had from its inception attempted to convey, was demonstrated at its third congress held in March 1959. Storti could accurately write afterwards in an editorial in the CISL weekly *Conquiste del Lavoro,* that many observers had made a "discovery":

Accustomed to consider and define CISL to be at the service of this or that government, inclined toward the wishes of a particular party subjected to strong ideological bonds, they have been surprised to find themselves in the presence of an assembly of people who reason with their own heads, who do not have fur on their tongues, who say exactly what they think and who certainly do not commit the sin of excessive conformism. In short, they discovered that CISL is an authentically democratic, independent and autonomous organization where freedom of circulation of ideas has no other limits than those imposed by respect for the opinion of others.[68]

68. *Conquiste del Lavoro,* XII, 17, April 1, 1959, p. 1.

The aspect of the congress to which Storti was referring and upon which widespread comment was made in the press and elsewhere, was the wide and energetically articulate participation of the delegates, particularly on two matters about which considerable cyncism had always been expressed by critics of CISL. One was the question of support for all Christian Democratic governments, whatever their orientation, and the other was the question of relations of the trade union movement to political parties, that is, the Christian Democratic Party. The Segni government had replaced the Fanfani government shortly before the congress and represented a shift in the parliamentary base of the government to the Right. Donat-Cattin, head of the CISL trade union forces at Turin and a Christian Democratic deputy in Parliament, and a number of others at the congress were sharply critical of the government and insisted upon an attitude of separation by CISL. The attacks were only less striking than the wide and enthusiastic response they received from the delegates. Storti as a result found it appropriate to announce that "I have no difficulty in affirming that this government by virtue of its political formula is far, very very far, from the sympathy and expectations of the workers." [69]

Pastore, who had continued with his ministerial portfolio in the Segni government when assured that economic development programs for the south would not be cut back, had an honored place at the congress. He felt compelled, however, to intervene at one point in the discussion to underscore that his decision to accept a government post the year before and continue in it with the new government was a purely personal one. He had resigned from his trade union leadership position to accept the government office and in no way committed the organization by his action. [70]

The attitudes toward the Segni government expressed by Donat-Cattin and others who were active within the Christian Democratic Party were shared by another group of delegates who pressed hard their position that there should be a much greater separation between trade union and political activity. The latter were primarily young veterans of the CISL training school at Florence, and deeply imbued with the principles of militant trade unionism, accepting no political party commitments. In a sense, the CISL training center appeared to have performed its task too well, in that such principles as separation of trade union from political or ideological commitments for which CISL had stood throughout the years, were now being taken so seriously by some that they were insisting upon withdrawal of trade union leaders entirely from political activity, even as individuals. This was a position logically in opposition to that supported by those like Donat-

69. *Ibid.,* p. 20. The entire issue is devoted to a stenographic summary of the congress.
70. *Ibid.,* p. 10.

Cattin, who were opposed to the Segni government because their factional efforts within the Christian Democratic Party to prevent a move to the Right had failed, but who would no doubt have wanted support for the government had their position carried in the Party.

The congress never really got out of control, so far as Storti and the top leadership of CISL were concerned. It served the organization well both in its own ranks and for the public to have a spirited and controversial congress. The position being taken by the Donat-Cattin group was after all fundamentally shared by Storti, Dionigi Coppo, and the other national leaders of the Confederation. They were as much committed in the factional struggles within the Christian Democratic Party as Donat-Cattin and as much disappointed by the Segni government formula as he. It was a significant development, however, for CISL to present a posture so openly and thoroughly unfriendly toward a Christian Democratic government. In 1953 there had also been a question concerning the attitude of Pastore toward the Pella government, but by contrast with the 1959 position, Pastore had felt compelled at the time to deny any implications of antagonism toward the government in the activities of CISL.

The position of the Florence school veterans raised a problem of quite a different sort. None of the top leadership of CISL could seriously contemplate the complete reversal of increased political commitment on the part of trade union leaders, which during the previous four years had made them a power in the Christian Democratic Party. On the other hand, there was a distinction which they regarded as a real and desirable one: the distinction between political activity and parliamentary representation on the one hand and executive responsibility on political and governmental levels. How much further than this relatively clear separation to carry the issue, given the pressure at the congress, was the problem posed for the leadership. They did not, for example, regard it as realistic to think in terms of withdrawal of trade union officials from seeking election to Parliament, given the realities of Italian politics and the place of trade unionism in the political constellation. Yet they themselves ideally favored such a trend as a matter of theory. What the leadership proposed was a theoretical solution for the future, combining this in a special resolution with the immediate issue of attitude toward the government. While the Florence school veterans were an energetic vocal group, they had too little strength to challenge the approach taken by the leadership, and the congress disposed of the issue on a note of unanimity.

The special resolution set out guide lines of significant importance in defining CISL's political position. It provided:

> In confirming the political independence of the trade unions and their permanent duty to intervene in all domains in support of democratic freedom and the rights of the worker;

Expresses the grave concern of the labor world because of the danger of involution which characterizes the Italian political scene.

In the name of the essential contribution which workers have offered in constructing the democratic state, the Third Congress recalls to operative coherence the democratic parties which affirm in their programs the commitment to insert the workers within the state as the means and end of civil development,

And gives the new organs of the Confederation the mandate to define with opportune firmness positions and initiatives so that the trade union shall always be in the first line in the struggle in the defense of democracy.

For the purpose of rendering operative and clear in the eyes of the workers and the country the bases set out by CISL with most correct distinctions of functions in the unity of effort:

The Third Congress delegates to the General Council, on the basis of statutory principles and norms, the responsibility for establishing an objective regulation of the normal and gradual separation by trade union leaders from political responsibilities and from responsibilities on the legislative level.[71]

Employer Resistance and Unity of Action

The tone of militancy and the undertone of frustration which had characterized the general discussion, particularly by lower rank delegates at the CISL congress, reflected the change which had begun taking place in the general trade union area. The period from 1954 to 1958 had been very different from what appeared to be the position by 1959. In the earlier four-year period a great many things appeared to be stirring along lines favoring an improved position for the workers and the democratic trade unions. The Internal Commission election results, the plant level focus of CISL and its repercussions, the *conglobamento* agreement, the Nenni Socialist evolution toward autonomy, the repercussions of international Communist developments from the Twentieth Congress through the Hungarian intervention, all seemed to be weakening the CGIL and the Communist movement and redounding to the advantage of the free unions.

This was no longer the atmosphere by the time of the CISL congress. A new period of stability had set in during the previous year. The Communist Party and CGIL had succeeded in reorganizing, consolidating, and stabilizing their positions, as demonstrated by the national political election of 1958 and the Internal Commission elections in that year. The launching of the Sputnik into space had created a widespread psychological readjustment among the workers in viewing the Soviet Union as a backward country. The Moscow version of Madison Avenue salesmanship peddled by Khrushchev around the world, with its emphasis upon Soviet power and peace slogans made it easier for CGIL and the Communists to seek new ground for expansion of influence on the Italian scene. While Socialist re-

71. *Politica Sindacale,* II, 2 (April 1959), p. 201. Pages 196–201 of the same issue reproduce the texts of the general resolutions adopted by the congress.

unification and "opening to the Left" were still very much matters of interest and concern, there was no longer the expectant atmosphere of dramatic overnight developments.

On the industrial relations-collective bargaining front, too, matters seemed to have returned to an atmosphere of earlier periods. For management — *Confindustria* and the industrial employers — the recent period had been one in which concessions might occasionally be justified in the differentiated policy between CGIL and the other trade unions. *Conglobamento* and particularly the round of individual company agreements were the product of this policy. But by 1958 even such modest concessions to the principles of plant level collective bargaining were becoming fewer.[72] The predominant thinking appeared to be that the weakening of CGIL had been but a step in the process of the general weakening of the trade union movement, and that after the CGIL reversals during the earlier four years, the trade union movement could not successfully impose bilateral treatment of wage and other labor issues on the level of the plant. Since the trade unions were still in no position successfully to challenge management on the plant level, and were meeting with rigid positions on all levels, they found it necessary to concentrate their strength upon the regular traditional national industry negotiations, where their strength was traditionally greatest.

The earlier years had already reflected the weakening position of the trade unions in the few agreements negotiated by the Confederations with *Confindustria* on a national all-industry basis. There were only three agreements negotiated during the eight-year period following the *conglobamento* agreement. The first, in April 1956, was of minor importance, providing that the lunch allowance payment which was general in industry by that time, should be included in the calculation of the wage base for such purposes as discharge allowance, vacation and holiday pay and end-of-year bonus.[73]

The more important agreement replaced the agreement of March 21, 1951 on the subject of the sliding-scale cost-of-living allowance supplement to wages and was signed on January 15, 1957. *Confindustria* had taken the initiative in opening negotiations on modification of the old agreement, and the settlement represented significant concessions to management interests in addition to some concessions to wage earners. The cost-of-living adjustments were to be made every three months instead of every two months. Adjustments were to apply to decreases in cost-of-living as well as to increases, and in the same proportion. In return for these concessions, *Confindustria* agreed that the bonus adjustment would be made more realistically consonant with the change in general wage scales since the last agreement, by increasing the lire equivalent of each cost-of-living index point by 43 per-

---

72. *See, for example,* CISL letter to *Confindustria* of January 31, 1958, *Politica Sindacale,* I, 1 (June 1958), pp. 88–98.

73. CISL, *Il sindacato democratico per lo sviluppo,* 222–224.

cent or 53.75 percent, depending on the geographic zone. Finally, after a fixed number of point increases, the cost-of-living allowances would be absorbed into the regular wage rates (*conglobomento*).

Another agreement was reached on an all-industry basis after the January 1957 agreement. On July 16, 1960, an agreement was signed providing for equal pay for equal work for women.[74] The negotiations on the agreement had started more than three years before and had for a long time been bogged down in the claim of *Confindustria* that such parity between men and women was already provided for in agreements of 1945 and 1946.[75] The fact that the employers' association chose this ground and not opposition to the principle, made agreement eventually possible in the light of the differentials which obviously did exist in industry.

As already mentioned, at the opposite end of the scale, on the plant level, after several years during which significant progress had been made in a number of industries, the policy of management became more rigid. The fact that the Italian economy suffered from a mild recession in 1958 created stiffer opposition to such agreements in that year. *Confindustria* began to press harder among its affiliates against plant level negotiations and found a more receptive audience than during the previous years. CISL, which had remained the only Confederation actively pressing forward on this front, increasingly found itself too much involved in disputes over national industry agreements to concentrate on the issue. Management returned more uniformly to unilateral wage and compensation setting on the plant level within the framework of the national minima.

During 1959, when the Italian economy had resumed its rapid expansion, it was on the level of the traditional bargaining in setting national wage scales in individual industries that difficulties concentrated. During the previous several years such agreements had regularly been renegotiated on a basis which, while less than fully satisfactory to the trade unions, nevertheless provided for sufficiently large concessions on wages to avoid large-scale disputes. This was not the case during 1958–1959 and the result was a convergence of large-scale disputes in the spring and early summer of 1959. The installation of the Segni government early in 1959 with its parliamentary base to the Right had been taken by *Confindustria* as a sign that it could exercise a free hand on such matters as wage policy, and *Confindustria* did not hesitate under the circumstances to press its advantage.

The disputes were concentrated mainly in the maritime and metallurgical industries and the strikes during June were jointly supported by CGIL,

74. Text of agreement in *Notiziario della Confederazione Generale dell' Industria Italiana*, XVII, 16–17, August 20–September 5, 1960, pp. 1968–1974.

75. These agreements had provided that "whenever women are assigned to work which is traditionally performed by men with equal conditions of work and with equal qualitative and quantitative productivity, the contractual wage which is provided for the men shall be paid." CISL, *Il sindacato democratico per lo sviluppo*, p. 233.

CISL, and UIL. The innumerable declarations over the previous years against any unity of action with the Communist CGIL were swallowed reluctantly in the face of worker pressure. It had been possible to avoid unity of action when large-scale disputes were not taking place. But it was not judged possible in 1959 and the fact that Storti insisted that it was not "unity of action" but "unity for action" did not change the reality. CGIL, though much weakened, was still the predominant trade union force and circumstances forced the non-Communist trade unions to give it, however unwillingly, their blessing of respectability which had been unsuccessfully sought for several years.

As in 1953, CISL was accused of political motives in supporting the large-scale strikes of 1959. It was claimed that CISL's position reflected its dissatisfaction with the government more than with the collective bargaining situation. *Confindustria* was particularly vociferous on the subject and in a letter responding to *Confindustria*'s accusation, Storti on June 13 energetically rejected the accusations, pointing out in detail the specific circumstances in each of the disputes arising out of employer association intransigence which had resulted in the convergence of strike situations on a national scale.[76] Storti felt compelled early the next month to hold a press conference on the subject, again insisting that convergence of the expiration of a number of collective agreements and the rigid positions of employers were solely responsible for the situation.[77] The disputes were eventually terminated on the basis of compromise settlements. The accusations against CISL would appear to have been without foundation, except in the sense that the political support in the Segni government and the orientation of the government itself had reinforced *Confindustria*'s determination to remain rigid in its bargaining positions with the trade unions.

Labor Relations Legislation

The area of labor relations had been entirely free of specific legislative regulation or protection throughout the period since the war. Although numerous efforts had been made to establish a legal framework, sufficient consensus had never been obtained among the interested groups or among the political parties to press forward on labor relations legislation. For the first time, in July 1959, Parliament enacted legislation on a very limited aspect of the subject. The new law, referred to as the *Erga omnes* law, was similar in principle to French legislation for "extension" of collective agreements. The law made it possible for the government, at the request of one of the parties to a collective agreement, to extend the standards established in the agreement to cover all plants within the geographic and industry limits set in the agreement, thereby covering those employers — and their

76. *Bollettino d'Informazioni della CISL,* XII, 6 (June 1959), pp. 1–2.
77. *Conquiste del Lavoro,* XII, 14, July 15, 1959, p. 3.

workers — who were not members of the employer association signing the agreement.[78] Unlike the French legislation, the government was given the "extension" power for only a limited period. As a result, during the following year, in September 1960 the unions obtained parliamentary approval to extend the government's powers for an additional fifteen months.[79]

The enactment of the 1959 legislation was the result of several years of campaigning by the trade unions, particularly by CISL. On the other hand, while CGIL had for some years been pressing for general legislation to implement Article 39 of the Italian Constitution, CISL had opposed any legislation on the subject, preferring the flexibility of the existing situation.

The constitutional provision was not operative until implemented by legislation. It provided:

Article 39. Trade union organization is free. There cannot be imposed upon the trade unions any other obligation than their registration at a local or central government office in accordance with norms established by law.

It is a condition of registration that the statutes of the trade unions provide for an internal functioning on a democratic basis.

The registered trade unions have legal personality. They may, represented together in proportion to their membership, stipulate collective labor agreements having obligatory application for all those belonging to the category to which the agreement refers.

In the early 1950's a number of attempts by Ministers of Labor in several succeeding cabinets had been made to develop legislation implementing the constitutional provision, as well as the immediately following constitutional article which provided that "The right to strike shall be exercised within the limits of the laws which regulate it." In each case the proposals contained so many restrictive and regulatory provisions, that the political storms blown up around them buried them long before they found their way seriously into the legislative machinery. In those years, CGIL had been as energetically opposed as the other Confederations to such legislative proposals. As the CGIL lost relative strength and was faced increasingly with competition and sometimes with discrimination in collective agreements, it began to campaign energetically on behalf of legislation to implement Article 39. Implementation would have had the effect of guaranteeing its important position among the trade unions at the bargaining table, and undercutting any efforts to give the other organizations arbitrary advantages. It would well have served the CGIL tactical objective of

78. For text of legislation, law no. 741 of July 14, 1959, *see La Gazzetta Ufficiale,* no. 225, September 19, 1959. Also see reproduced in *Bollettino d'Informazioni della CISL,* XII, 8–9 (August–September 1959), pp. 22–23.

79. *Conquiste del Lavoro,* XIV, 40, October 2, 1960, p. 5; *Lavoro,* XIII, 41, October 9, 1960, p. 5.

imposing greater cooperation and even "unity of action" upon the trade unions.

CISL on the other hand argued against legislation. It preferred to avoid the rigidities of relationships which such legislation inevitably would impose and the advantage which it felt that this would necessarily give to CGIL. It argued that there would unavoidably result a certain amount of regulation of the trade unions and that its conception of trade unionism was one of complete freedom from government intervention in its internal affairs. Finally, it argued that implementation of Article 39 would automatically be accompanied by implementation of Article 40 and that in the political distribution of forces in Parliament this would mean severe limitations upon the right to strike.

UIL favored the CGIL position on the subject, although with increasing lack of enthusiasm, and eventually its position evolved to one of opposition in 1960. As the smallest of the three principal Confederations, it had felt that its position would be guaranteed against the discrimination always latent as a result of the antagonism of the other two organizations toward it. Its gradual gain in self-confidence and its concern over the implications of having the strike limitation provisions implemented, brought it around to a position which led its representatives to join CISL representatives in walking out on the government advisory commission which was considering the legislative proposal in June 1960.[80] The advisory body, the *Consiglio Nazionale dell'Economia e del Lavoro,* with representation from government, labor, management, and other economic groups proceeded slowly in its deliberations, despite the refusal of CISL and UIL to participate in its discussions of Articles 39 and 40, and despite CGIL opposition to consideration of Article 40. Nevertheless, as with so many earlier efforts in the 50's, it seemed doubtful that even with a *Consiglio* recommendation to the government, Parliament would act on the subject.

The growing differences of view within the trade union movement toward the Internal Commission as an institution also resulted in different positions on the question of legal recognition of the Commissions. Under the 1959 legislation the trade union organizations filed with the government the collective agreements for which they desired legal blessing for universal application within the areas defined by the agreements. CGIL and UIL included the March 1953 Internal Commission agreement among the agreements they filed, while CISL did not. In addition, during 1960 CGIL began

80. For the various positions taken by the trade union organizations and their criticism of each other, *see* CISL, *Il sindacato democratico per lo sviluppo,* pp. 5–8; *Politica Sindacale,* II, 4 (August 1959), pp. 349–353; *Conquiste del Lavoro,* XIV, 22, May 29, 1960, p. 3; *ibid.,* XIV, 27, July 3, 1960; *Rassegna Sindacale,* no. 30 (June 1960), pp. 1469–1471; *ibid.,* no. 31–32 (July–August 1960), pp. 1530–1531; *Lavoro,* XIII, 28, July 10, 1960, p. 4; *Il Lavoro Italiano,* XII, 5, February 2, 1960, p. 1–2; *ibid.,* XII, 27, July 5, 1960, p. 1.

a campaign supported by the Communist and Nenni Socialist deputies in Parliament to enact legislation making obligatory the establishment of Internal Commissions and giving them legal status. UIL also favored the measure, presumably since it might facilitate strengthening its relatively weak position on the plant level. CISL's opposition was a logical extension of the position it had evolved since 1953. It argued that its conception of the trade union as a voluntaristic association would be violated by such government intervention, that it inevitably would result in extension of the authority of the Commissions into business properly the affair of trade unions, and that it would weaken the trade unions.[81]

In its publications CISL went even further in reflecting its increasingly open criticism of the Internal Commission as an institution. In 1959, in its publication for its own activists, CISL had written, "The Internal Commission is the alibi of the non-unionized workers, who believe they are being shrewd and believe they have fulfilled a duty of conscience through the expression of an annual suffrage. How can one think of being able to create trade union strength with a renunciation of such a kind, which becomes a principal element for the de-unionization of the workers?"[82] CISL did not, however, officially attack the Internal Commission as such. It rather concentrated its fire on the extensive use made of the Commissions by the employers as an excuse for not dealing directly with the trade unions. It urged that the limited authority of the Internal Commissions be defined more precisely. In addition, it urged that the Commissions be renewed every two years instead of each year in order to permit a more stable situation among the workers in industry. In September 1960, in an effort to obtain implementation of its position, it wrote to *Confindustria* serving official notice of reopening the 1953 agreement in order to negotiate on these issues.[83]

CGIL criticized the move by CISL on the grounds that the door was being opened to the fundamental weakening of the Commissions, despite the fact that one of its own principal affiliates, the Federation of Metallurgical Workers, had officially taken a position late in August in favor of better defining the functions of the Commissions to prevent their intrusion into affairs properly belonging to the trade union.[84] It appeared likely in any event that the renegotiation of the 1953 agreement would involve almost insoluble differences with *Confindustria* and would not be settled for some time to come.

81. *See, for example,* Luigi Macario, "Potere sindacale e commissioni interne," *Conquiste del Lavoro,* XIV, 1, January 3, 1960, pp. 1–2; also *Conquiste del Lavoro,* XIV, 40, October 2, 1960, p. 3 and "Contro il riconoscimento giuridico dell'accordo sulle commissioni interne," *Politica Sindacale,* III, 4 (August 1960), pp. 301–304.

82. "Per creare il potere del sindacato nell'azienda," *Sindacato Nuovo* (CISL monthly for its activists) (July 1959), pp. 5–6. See also, *ibid.* (July 1960), pp. 10–14.

83. *Conquiste del Lavoro,* XIV, 38, September 18, 1960, p. 2.

84. *Lavoro,* XIII, 39, September 25, 1960, p. 12; *ibid.,* XIII, 40, October 2, 1960, p. 5.

Communist Respectability and Socialist Autonomy

The increased emphasis by the Soviet Union upon easing of tensions with the West, its drive toward a summit meeting and Khrushchev's visit to the United States in the fall of 1959 furthered the efforts of the Communists and the CGIL to win their way back to respectability in Italy. The unity of action with which the labor disputes had been fought in the middle of 1959 served further to lend emphasis to the trade union unity theme of CGIL. The trade union unity theme represented common ground for all the factions within the Nenni Socialist Party, from those favoring complete autonomy from the Communists across the spectrum of internal party divisions to those who represented the Frontist positions of the fellow travelers. At the PSI Congress in Naples in January 1959, while Nenni appeared to make progress with his political autonomy position, the commitment toward trade union unity was clamorously reaffirmed by all factions.[85]

When the Socialists held their second trade union conference in October 1959, the commitment to remain within CGIL was taken for granted and the principal emphasis was placed upon achievement of trade union unity. Nenni in opening the conference pointed to what he considered the three requirements for achievement of trade union unity: removal of party control (*departitizzazione*) from the trade union, democratization of the internal life of the trade union, and the participation of the masses in the fight for international easing of tensions.[86] The formula was a reflection of Nenni's dialectical reasoning and his preoccupation with the evolution of the international situation in the direction of coexistence which would make his own neutralist orientation more generally palatable in Italy.

The discussion at the Socialist conference placed great emphasis upon Nenni's first two points. Repeated reference was made to the necessity of continuing to press for less political control in CGIL. "The CGIL has achieved effective forward steps on the road toward autonomy from the parties . . . there still remain — it would be absurd to deny it — strong residues of *strumentalismo,* of subordination, particularly in the choice of trade union leaders." [87] In general the discussion was less sharply critical

85. The resolution on the subject affirmed "the principle of unity of all workers in their struggles over demands . . . has strengthened . . . the commitment of the Socialist trade union current in the CGIL to work for the creation of the necessary conditions for unity of action . . . and for re-launching the policy of trade union unity . . . refutation of any conception of a party controlled trade union." *Rassegna Sindacale,* no. 12 (January 1959), p. 466.

86. PSI, *I socialisti e l'unità sindacale, Atti del 2° convegno nazionale del PSI sui problemi del sindacato, Roma, 28–29–30 October 1959* (Rome, 1960), is an official stenographic summary record of the conference. See pp. 7–8.

87. From general report to conference by Giovanni Pieraccini, in charge of mass organization section of PSI, *ibid.,* p. 17.

of UIL than in the 1957 conference, and UIL and CISL were lumped together in a tone more of pain than of anger, as having been obliged to accept unity of action during the year, but not yet having seen the true light in their continued rejection of unity. With all the discussion of non-party unified trade unionism, the conference did not lose sight entirely of the Socialists' own relative position in CGIL, and urged the necessity of continued action to strengthen the Socialist faction *vis-à-vis* the Communists within the organization.[88]

It was part of the irony of the trade union positions during these years that the Nenni Socialist and particularly the Communists wrapped themselves up so articulately in the slogan of defense of trade unionism free of political party control as part of their attack against both CISL and UIL because of the opposition of these organizations to trade union unity. A typical example of the reasoning — unobjectionably logical in theory — pressed by CGIL was an editorial in one of the CGIL official periodicals in reaction to a press conference statement by Storti before the beginning of the January 1959 PSI congress in which he had expressed the hope that the congress would be the occasion for reconsideration by the Socialists of their trade union position:

> Whoever is interested in rendering permanent trade union pluralism is an enemy of the autonomy of the trade union . . . Pluralism pushes toward competition, exacerbates the patriotism of the organization, carries every trade union, even despite itself, to exalt the characteristics which differentiate it from the others, and therefore finally underlines its connections and its affinity with forces . . . to utilize them in competition with other trade unions. Pluralism . . . causes the trade union to accentuate its own subordination, ideal and practical, to certain reality external to itself . . . unity and autonomy are interdependent.[89]

Both the Communist Party congress and the CGIL congress in 1960 emphasized the same theme. At the January Communist Party congress Novella talked of leaving behind "those times which we have ourselves defined as those in which the transmission belt between trade union and party operated," and the congress theses expressed Communist hostility to "any tendency toward conceiving of the Confederation as an assembly of ideological and political currents and unity as the result of compromises among the exponents of various currents."[90] But even as the congress published its desire for an autonomous trade union organization, some discussion of reality could not be avoided. Lama, for example, who had succeeded Novella as head of CGIL Metallurgical Federation, said at the party congress

88. *Ibid.*, pp. 30–32.
89. *Rassegna Sindacale*, no. 12 (January 1959), pp. 465–466.
90. *Lavoro*, XIII, 7, February 14, 1960, p. 3 and *Sindacato Nuovo* (February 1960), pp. 2–4.

that it was necessary "that we insist upon a search for . . . those immediate demands which promote the development of an anti-capitalist conscience, in preparing the conditions for understanding the policy of PCI in its most general terms." [91]

The CGIL congress of April 2 to 7, 1960, made an all-out effort to present a new face to the public. It had sufficiently recovered its acceptability that for the first time since the trade union movement had split, the government sent an official representative, the Minister of Labor, to greet the congress. The government's motives in so doing were more specifically prompted by its attempt to overcome its increasing political difficulties (it fell later in the month) and to balance the fact that it had sent a representative to a congress of neo-Fascist trade unions some months before. Nonetheless, the fact that the Minister of Labor attended the congress added to the atmosphere CGIL was attempting to promote, that it had turned its back on the harsh period of extremist political unionism. The congress emphasized the importance of trade union unity in a context of moderation and reasonableness. It increased the Nenni Socialist representation on its executive bodies. In keeping with the emphasis given at the PSI trade union conference six months before, it emphasized collective bargaining within the framework of the existing economic system. It accepted the desirability of pressing for differentiated wage increases based upon the potentialities of specific situations. It dropped its opposition to increased productivity, accepting the desirability of obtaining the sharing of productivity gains by workers. Finally, it authorized the recasting of its statutes into terms more in keeping with the new lines it was adopting.[92]

To an extent which was surprising, CGIL succeeded in creating an impression that it was actually moving away from its previous orientation. Even CISL, in one of its official publications, after pointing to the limitations on the change in CGIL, wrote "Still, CGIL is today a new reality." [93] The "new reality" in its substance was an attempt by the CGIL more realistically to increase its popular appeal and make progress toward its tactical objectives and to build trade union strength on a pragmatic basis permitted by the general orientation and the flexibility of the Communist line of the moment. In terms of its general posture, however, the change from the Segni government to the Tambroni government and the atmosphere after the abortive Paris summit meeting, led to the exploitation of the expected

91. Quoted in *Sindacato Nuovo* (February 1960), pp. 2–4.

92. For general report to congress, *see Rassegna Sindacale*, no. 28 (April 1960), entire issue. For report on congress and resolutions adopted see *Lavoro*, XIII, 15, April 10, 1960; *ibid.*, XIII, 16, April 17, 1960; *L'Unità*, issues of April 1 through 9, 1960; and *Rassegna Sindacale*, no. 29 (May 1960), section "Vita e attivita della CGIL," no. 5. See *Lavoro*, XIII, June 24, 1960, pp. 11 and 14 for changes in statutes.

93. "Lezione della storia per la CGIL," *Sindacato Nuovo* (April 1960), pp. 5–8.

popular reactions against the MSI-scheduled congress in Genoa at the end of June and the turbulent riots in the following days. As has already been described, CGIL played a direct political role in the affair which contrasted sharply with the posture it had publicly assumed at its congress earlier in the year. Yet it had done so under circumstances which permitted it to march under the banner of defense of democracy and later to claim that it had sponsored the effective pressure which caused the fall of a government depending on Fascist votes.

The PSI trade unionists made common cause with their Communist colleagues in the 1960 general strike and riots, as did their Party. A large proportion of these trade unionists were less than enthusiastic about the Nenni position of autonomy precisely because they continued strongly to favor continuation of their own collaboration within CGIL and feared that the logic of a truly autonomous Socialist position would eventually involve ceasing to collaborate with the Communists in the labor area. Viglianesi struck up quite a storm in June 1960, when as part of his continuing campaign to press for Socialist exodus from CGIL, he obtained wide publicity for the results of a study UIL had made — similar to its study of three years before — of the relative distribution of leadership positions in CGIL. He claimed that the leadership positions were distributed between Socialists and Communists in the proportion of one to ten; that Socialist leadership was limited to areas and sectors of little importance; that even in these cases they were always flanked by a preponderance of Communist leaders; that the Socialist presence was never the result of organizational action but the consequence of "agreements." "In reality CGIL is a big Communist pot, in which — by Communist concession — some Socialist celery is accepted when and how and in the proportion decided by the Communist cook." [94]

The Viglianesi accusations were heatedly denied and strongly resented, particularly since they were directed principally at refuting the position which Nenni had argued on behalf of PSI at the Socialist International, where he had assiduously continued his efforts to obtain increased tolerance for eventual PSI admittance to the organization. It was argued in refutation of UIL that PSI had 31 percent representation in the Directive Committees of CGIL affiliates, that CGIL was "truly independent," that in any event issues were considered only on their merits within CGIL and that on most

94. *La Giustizia,* June 21, 1960, pp. 1–2. An English translation of the article, entitled "A Necessary Clarification" (mimeographed) and an accompanying "Survey of the Organizational Structure of the CGIL" (mimeographed and dated June 1960) which gives the details of the UIL survey, was widely circulated outside Italy under cover of a letter dated June 24, 1960, from Enzo Dalla Chiesa, international secretary of UIL. For an earlier full statement by Viglianesi on the Socialist question *see* pamphlet, *Rinnovamento Socialista, Discorso di Italo Viglianesi al XII Congresso Nazionale del PSDI, Roma, 26–29 Novembre 1958* (Rome, n.d.).

issues positions were not taken on the basis of factions.[95] Despite the self-justifications, however, the PSI trade unionists had increasingly found themselves on the defensive outside their organization. That the Communists were willing to pay a price for continued Socialist loyalty to CGIL had been demonstrated during the previous few years. The price, however, had not been a high one and CGIL as an instrument for Communist party advantage — blunted as it had become over the years — had proved its continued usefulness again in the turbulent days of June–July 1960.

CGIL had in fact made the adjustments it considered necessary to meet the new competitive situation on the trade union scene. Partly under pressure from the PSI trade union leaders within the organization, by 1960 CGIL was firmly focused toward a plant level bargaining policy parallel to that of CISL and UIL. During 1960 and 1961, after the national agreement renewals of the previous year, the emphasis of the trade unions was on company level negotiations. Despite *Confindustria* opposition, some progress was made during these years of enormous prosperity in industry. Most of the plant agreements were concerned with incentive payment systems and productivity bonuses. According to a CISL compilation there were 244 company agreements signed in the Lombardy region alone in 1960, covering almost 300,000 workers.[96] While CGIL was still excluded from many of the agreements, it could no longer be ignored on the basis of lack of interest. Indeed, Novella early in 1961 devoted the major portion of his annual press conference review of 1960 to the subject and underscored how thoroughly the CGIL had been converted to the tactical usefulness of the plant bargaining approach. What had a few years before been regarded as a CISL tactic betraying the interests of the working class, had by 1961 become in Novella's words "one of the fundamental aspects of the structural reform of contractual relations, an essential condition for improvement of wages and salaries, of reinforcing the contractual strength of the trade unions, of the development of the function and the democratic life of the trade union." [97]

The new emphasis given by CGIL to plant level problems and its efforts to promote concern with specific economic issues, within the setting of its much-publicized repudiation of "transmission belt" relationships with the Communist Party, lent strength to the CGIL campaign to regain some of the ground it had lost in the 1950's. During 1960 and 1961 it made modest gains in the Internal Commission plant elections. At FIAT, the bellwether of worker sentiment, CGIL received 24.3 percent of the votes in 1961 after having fallen as low as 21.1 percent in 1959. CISL lost slightly, receiving 15.6

95. Luigi Nicosia, "La dottrina Viglianesi, i socialisti, la CGIL," *Rassegna Sindacale,* no. 31–32 (July–August 1960), pp. 1541–1543.

96. *Notiziario Internazionale CISL News,* no. 3 (March 1961), pp. 6–7.

97. Text of press statement in *Rassegna Sindacale,* no. 37 (January 1961), pp. 1829–1839; quote at p. 1830.

percent. The FIAT independent union, which had been expelled from CISL several years before, and had received a plurality of 33.4 percent of the vote in 1959, fell to 28.5 per cent in 1961. UIL on the other hand, had steadily been increasing its strength at FIAT and in 1961 emerged as the strongest union with 29.7 percent of the vote.[98]

The enthusiasm with which local Communist CGIL leaders threw themselves into the specifically trade union and economic issues, popular as this was with their following, became a matter of concern to the Communist Party, however. In May 1961 the party held a national conference of Communist plant activists at Milan, which was attended by more than a thousand delegates. Giorgio Amendola, in charge of the mass organization office of the Party, stressed the dangers for the Party of abandonment by many of the plant activists of their "anti-capitalist political struggle" and their following the "reformist line" of concentrating on day-to-day trade union problems. Togliatti was even more explicit when he addressed the conference. "Trade unionism is not everything. Be active in trade union affairs but do not forget that beyond winning higher wages there are other objectives and that these objectives only the Party has responsibility to recall to you and it is to the Party that you must look in any activity and in any conquest in which you are committed." [99]

The PSI trade union leaders had played an important role in pressing for the new CGIL focus on specific plant problems. They had regarded with some satisfaction the earlier Communist pronouncements of separation between Party and trade union. Their position in favor of remaining in CGIL had been confirmed two months before the Communist plant activists' conference at the PSI Congress in March 1961.[100] The Togliatti and Amendola pronouncements, however, recalled sharply the realities of the limits set by the Communists upon "autonomous" trade union action. The CISL and UIL underscored the lesson to the Socialists in CGIL after the conference. The Socialists continued, however, to feel bound to CGIL and continued to urge reunification of all trade union forces.

Early in 1961, at their annual press conference reviews, both Storti and Viglianesi also dwelt upon the theme of unity, setting forth the respective positions of their organizations.[101] Storti urged the Socialists to

98. Computed from statistics given in *Rassegna Sindacale,* no. 40 (April 1961), p. 1966.

99. "I communisti nelle fabbriche," *Conquiste del Lavoro,* XIV, 20, May 14, 1961, p. 7. For CISL comment see "Gli innovatori socialisti," *ibid.,* XIV, 21, May 21, 1961, p. 7.

100. "Le mozioni del P.S.I. e il sindacato," *Sindacato Nuovo,* no. 3 (March 1961), pp. 11–12.

101. For text of Storti statement *see Politica Sindacale,* IV, 1 (February 1961), pp. 68–83, particularly pp. 74–75. For extracts from text of Viglianesi statement see *Rassegna Sindacale,* no. 39 (March 1961), pp. 1942–1943. For CGIL criticism of Viglianesi's comments on CGIL see *ibid.,* pp. 1941–1942.

leave CGIL and join in reunifying the democratic trade union forces. Viglianesi on the other hand, after rejecting any possibility of cooperating with CGIL because of the Communist domination of the organization, also criticized CISL because of its "pretensions to monopoly" and its invitation to the Socialists while ignoring the existence of UIL. The Viglianesi attack upon CISL was a public renewal of the resentment which had been increasing in each organization at the positions assumed by the other on the problem of trade union relations and the Socialists. UIL continued the efforts it had made over the years to channel into its organization those attracted by democratic Socialist traditions. CISL continued to regard its organization as the embodiment of non-Communist democratic trade unionism. With the Nenni Socialists as a potential important force determining the character of trade union reorganization, if they broke away from CGIL, the stakes were high enough to brush aside the relatively friendlier relationships which had haltingly developed between CISL and UIL in the previous few years.

In May 1961 one of the few important Social Democratic regional trade union leaders who had remained in CISL through the years, announced that he was shifting to UIL. Anselmo Martoni was the most influential Social Democratic trade unionist in the province of Bologna and the only Social Democratic CISL leader who was a member of Parliament. He carried with him into UIL the secretaries of the CISL Bologna provincial agricultural and metallurgical workers' unions as well as eight CISL commune union chambers and the autonomous unions of Molinella.[102] The Martoni shift and the sharp impact it had upon the relative positions of the two organizations in Bologna province led to further deterioration in the relations between CISL and UIL. The General Council of CISL, meeting several weeks after the Martoni affair, attacked UIL for placing ideological considerations in the way of any useful discussion between the two organizations. The atmosphere between the organizations had begun to return to that of almost ten years before.

Opening to Left in 1962

It was early in 1962 that a potentially historic shift in the relations of the political parties took place. The PSI Congress of March 1961, where 55 percent of the delegates had given their support to Nenni's autonomous position, had set the stage for renewed pressures during the rest of the year within the Social Democratic and Christian Democratic Parties for further exploration of the possibility of an "opening to the Left." The limitations upon adoption of any wide social reform measures imposed upon the Fan-

---

102. *Il Lavoro Italiano,* XIII, 18, May 6, 1961, p. 1. For text of Martoni's statement explaining his action *see ibid.,* XIII, 19, May 13, 1961, pp. 1 and 3. For Storti's rebuttal to Martoni's statement see *Conquiste del Lavoro,* XIV, 21, May 21, 1961, p. 7.

fani government by the nature of its parliamentary support had become increasingly frustrating to a wide spectrum within the Christian Democratic party going far beyond the Fanfani faction. There was also in the background the sobering experience of the 1960 disturbances fed by the precariously narrow base of Center government. As 1961 progressed, the atmosphere gradually became more favorable for a serious attempt to negotiate an arrangement with Nenni to permit organization of a government based upon support from his party.

The Christian Democratic Party Congress held at Naples at the end of January 1962 made the historic decision to turn to the Left for support. The powerful Center faction of Aldo Moro, secretary of the Party, joined forces with Fanfani supporters and other Left groups within the Party to obtain the decision. The Fanfani-Moro policy motion ruled out inclusion of Nenni PSI representatives in the government but pledged to seek PSI parliamentary support for a cabinet including Christian Democrats, Social Democrats and Republicans. The move was to be made without weakening Italy's commitments to the West and to NATO or to weaken domestic vigilance against communism. Domestic social reform measures were to be the sole basis of cooperation with PSI.[103]

The Fanfani government resigned immediately after the congress decision, and negotiations with Nenni went forward successfully during February. The Central Committee of PSI voted agreement with Nenni's decision to give support to a new government pledged to a series of social reform measures.[104] Fanfani thereupon proceeded to form a Cabinet on the basis of the formula which had been agreed to at the Christian Democratic Congress. The government received its vote of confidence in Parliament in March 1962, with the Nenni Socialists abstaining but pledged to support the social reform proposals of the government.[105]

The "opening to the Left" formula for the first time, after the many years of discussions, was put into practice. It was recognized as a dangerous experiment and yet was undertaken in the hope that the Nenni Socialists would break completely with the Communists and that the Communists would thereby be isolated. If this were eventually applied by the PSI in the trade union field, it would fundamentally affect the distribution of trade union forces. Meanwhile it was hoped that serious social reform programs, applied by a government freed of dependence on the Right, might help build a wider democratic consensus than had been achieved during the previous years.

103. New York *Times* (International Edition), January 27, 1962, p. 7; *ibid.,* February 2, 1962, p. 1.
104. *Ibid.,* February 3, 1962, p. 2; *ibid.,* February 20, 1962, p. 2.
105. *Ibid.,* February 22, 1962, p. 1; *ibid.* (New York edition), March 3, 1962, p. 1; *ibid.,* March 12, 1962, p. 7.

CHAPTER IX

The Pattern of Italian Trade Unionism

The most obvious characteristic of the trade union movement after the last war was the predominance of Communist control and the difficulties encountered in combatting this predominance. Significant progress was gradually made in this direction during the 1950's, yet the Communist-controlled CGIL, despite its losses, continued to be the most important single force in the labor field. Even more than the CGIL, the Communist Party succeeded in maintaining its popular electoral support despite the evident weakening of its apparatus and its gradual loss of membership. The specific circumstances of the postwar period and the illusions, shortcomings, and tactical positions of other trade union and political groups help explain the role the CGIL and the Communists continued to play. These factors have been discussed earlier and will be reviewed only briefly in the latter part of this chapter.

Underlying the diverse reactions of leadership and its following among the various factions were the traditions and characteristic reactions grounded partly in the distant past and partly in the history of the trade union and leftist political movements of modern Italy. The full sweep of the history, as developed in earlier chapters, has shed some light on its complexities. A review of the characteristics of the movement over time should help in shedding further light upon the general nature of Italian trade unions. As we have seen, the Italian trade union movement in its evolution has acquired certain characteristics even as it attempted to resist some of them.

Trade Union Evolution

The trade union movement can be divided into several distant periods. The first, which may be called the period of stage-setting, extended through Italy's unification period to the 1880's. It was characterized by the spread of the friendly societies, the impact of Mazzini's ideas, and particularly his encouragement of organization; the ascendency of Bakunin and the Internationalists in spreading a doctrine of social transformation which prepared the ground for the later diffusion of socialist ideas as they evolved both in their revolutionary form by successors to Bakunin among the Internationalists and in more moderate form in the regions of the industrializing north. The sharp antagonism of the Catholic church toward the national state in the immediate years after national unification led it to contribute toward an arousing of the lower classes, particularly in rural areas, against the "usurper" state, which facilitated the spread of socialist ideas and organization in succeeding years.

The next period, which covered the remaining years of the nineteenth century, may be described as the period of emergent trade union organization. Local trade unions began to emerge and spread in the industrial areas of the north and began to coordinate among themselves. Worker exclusivism developed in these areas, particularly its most industrialized area — Lombardy — and took political form as a supplement to trade union activity, but after a short time merged gradually into the Socialist movement. Under the impulse of evangelical fervor of its pioneers, the gospel of socialism spread rapidly in rural and urban areas. The period was one of widespread rural ferment and undifferentiated organization, frequently of an ephemeral sort. Finally, the government, after tolerating the emerging organizations with only occasional harassment, undertook a series of thoroughgoing repressive actions which left a lasting mark upon psychological attitudes toward the state.

A period of progress, "normalization" and "domestication" followed, lasting until shortly before the First World War. The economy progressed as Italy's "great push forward" toward industrialization proceeded. This was the period of Giolitti, who tolerated organization of labor and industrial strife as part of his expectation that the Socialists could be encouraged to evolve toward their incorporation into the normal democratic parliamentary process. For the trade unions it was a period of expansion, of development of normal coordinating machinery, the establishment of the *Confederazione Generale del Lavoro,* with the emerging National Unions competing against the Chambers of Labor for predominance in the structure of the movement. In the competition for control, the Reformist leadership which emerged oriented the movement strongly toward collective bargaining, building strong organization, responsibility in agreements, and achievement of moderate social reform. The Revolutionary Syndicalist minority, for whom these objectives were diversions from the principal focus of animating revolutionary ardor, continued to have strength outside the principal industrial centers, but represented no threat to the organizational predominance of the CGL. In the Socialist political movement, reform and moderation gradually took over, although a revolutionary minority wing continued to be active. A huge electoral machine was built, with municipal management and parliamentary representation a principal focus of the Party. The cooperative movement as it developed during the period also added to the Socialist stake in society, particularly through Giolitti's emphasis upon granting public works contracts to the producer cooperatives.

A period of revolutionary gymnastics and eventual disintegration followed during the first several years after the First World War. With the victory of the Revolutionaries in the Socialist Party shortly before the First World

War, the period of "domestication" was reversed. The trade union movement never escaped from the leadership of the moderate elements. On the other hand, these elements, particularly from 1919 onward, found themselves swept along or swept aside by a tide of activity arising out of the Socialist Party's propaganda and the social and psychological aftermath of the war. For a brief fleeting moment, enormous collective bargaining gains were made: the eight-hour day, significant wage increases, generalization of collective agreements, establishment of grievance machinery throughout industry. But they were achieved as part of the atmosphere of turmoil which appeared about to tear apart the old fabric of society. As the fury spent itself, reaction set in. Fascism did not save Italy from bolshevism, as was later claimed. The Socialists and their threatened revolution had been defeated long before fascism moved forward to grasp the reigns of power. Fascism simply exploited and dominated the tide of reaction.

The Fascist period from the early 1920's to the Second World War eliminated all autonomous trade union and political activity. The controlled Fascist syndicates functioned as part of the apparatus of government and party. In so doing, however, certain characteristics left their imprint upon the future: the membership-card psychology, the "desk" approach to worker organization, structure of national collective agreements, and neglect of local focus in organization.

What did these stages in the development of the trade union movement mean for the postwar post-Fascist atmosphere of organization? What were the traditions and heritages which left their mark? The discontinuity resulting from the twenty years of fascism did not, it appears, wipe out these traditions, but added another layer of additional characteristics to worker responses during the years that followed.

Fundamental to the molding of worker attitudes and worker organization was the economic and social conditions under which the people lived. The low level of economic opportunity, the residual heritage of a rigid social structure, the late and slow progress of Italian industrialization, the lack of fundamental transformation in much of agriculture, despite the intermittent periods of progress, combined to form a pattern of hostile environment made even less acceptable as workers and farm population were aroused by the efforts of political and trade union groups to channel discontent into specific organizational forms.

The Workers' Traditions

The revoltist traditions which characterize unorganized reaction against conditions in many rural pre-industrial societies remained firmly imbedded in modern Italy, encouraged and given ideological rationalization by Revolutionary Syndicalism and the activism of Revolutionary Socialism. The *piazza* demonstration, so characteristic of protest manifestations in both rural and industrial Italy, is in varying measure a continuation of the revoltist tradition. In the same way, the general strike, practiced so much more frequently in Italy than in other countries, is frequently less a disciplined effort to bring pressure calculated to obtain specific objectives than simply an organized manifestation of generic revolt attitudes. It is perhaps no accident that while Revolutionary Syndicalism had its home in France and only represented a minority movement among the trade unions of Italy before the First World War, the use of its principal tactical weapon, the general strike, was kept largely symbolic in France, but was a recurrent frequent practice in Italy.

The revoltist traditions were even more strongly entrenched in rural Italy than in the industrial cities where a more disciplined organizational pattern evolved in the new industrial atmosphere. Yet, they were not wholly absent in industry. They found expression, for example, after the Revolutionaries captured the Socialist Party before the First World War during the frequent difficulties which CGL encountered in preventing the activism of Mussolini's exhortations and that of the Revolutionary Syndicalists from dominating the actions of the trade unions in Milan. The most dramatic and tragic period in this regard was the post World War I years when the verbal barrage of the Socialist Party revolutionary propaganda resulted in futile exercises in unorganized and purposeless revoltism and found response among a population hopefully seeking answers to pressing problems through the miracle of activism which ultimately led them nowhere.

Vying with this tradition of revoltism were the organizationally disciplined pressure tactics of the CGL, the pattern of organization developed through cooperatives, and the electoral emphasis which the Socialist Party — sometimes despite itself — gave to its activities. Yet, it could not be said, even at the height of power of the Reformists in the Socialist Party and the Federalists in the CGL that they completely controlled the popular reaction along the disciplined channels which they favored. Despite themselves, and apparently as a price they felt they had to pay to maintain mass support for their positions, the Reformists never became quite as integrated into the institutional framework of society as similar Socialist leadership in other European countries did. The same was true on the trade union side, where the underlying social pressures and the competition with the Syndicalists prevented the trade union movement from developing firmly along gradualist lines, even at the time of greatest relative stability of CGL at the end of the first decade of this century.

The mistrust of government and its representatives is deeply rooted in the ancient traditions of the population. While the *Risorgimento* spirit aroused a sense of concern with public affairs in other groups of the general population, the popular masses in the towns and countryside were hardly touched by it. Furthermore, when political unification of Italy did come, it had none of the aspects of a revolutionary achievement which might have rallied these groups out of their apathy to give them a sense of participation or identity with the national institutions. Government remained a remote "they" which simply became another obstacle in the popular mind to their own advancement. During the last decades of the nineteenth century, the combination of successive appeals directed toward them helped to further these reactions. The clergy and their lay representatives hammered away at the theme of government usurpation of church authority and frequently oriented their appeal toward arousing the masses against government on the basis of alleged reactionary exploitation by those who controlled the government. The Bakunin propaganda attacking the very existence of state and government followed upon the heels of the Mazzini and Garibaldi repudiation of the nature of the state as it was established in unified Italy. Finally, the enormously widespread and effective proselytizing of the Socialists during the last decades of the last century built upon already fertile ground by crystallizing worker and rural sentiment around its own banners which identified government with forces opposing popular interests.

The widespread and repeated governmental repressions of all popular movements during the last years of the century — political, trade union, cooperative — confirmed and hardened attitudes already strongly felt. While the governmental atmosphere changed during the succeeding decade and the Socialists appeared to be evolving toward that "domestication" so assiduously encouraged by Giolitti, they never could bring themselves to compromise so far with the *"bourgeois"* state as to agree to participate in government. In the period immediately following the First World War, when participation might genuinely have permitted basic reforms of an economic and social character and later might at least have saved the country from fascism, the Socialists were so committed to their extremist doctrinaire ideological blinkers as to refuse in all circumstances to compromise their implacable opposition to the state — until it was far too late. If one excludes as myopic aberration the Socialist position of that period, one is still left with the continuous tradition of refusal to participate, although always, even in its most extremist period, playing the parliamentary game at least to the extent of building electoral machines, winning control of municipal governments, functioning on local levels as a municipal Socialism of a respectable character, and bidding for legislative concessions fairly successfully, especially under the Giolitti regime.

Fundamentally, through the combination of background circumstances and traditional cynical distrust, and heightened by the extremes to which Socialist Party attitudes carried, the government in the popular mind was something outside and frequently against its own identification of interests. It represented just another symbol of that combination of forces which in the worker's mind was the social system in whose unjust clutches he found himself.

By contrast with the Socialist tradition which had channeled the overwhelming proportion of articulate worker reaction to his total environment, there existed the Catholic social tradition. The Socialist tradition was represented by diverse and frequently inconsistent strands — revoltist, revolutionary and evolutionary — but aimed at radical transformation of the economic and social system. The Catholic traditions were also multiple and diverse. There were in the modern period the traditions developed and exploited by the *Popolari* and the CIL which genuinely sought reforms, particularly in agriculture. It is no accident that the CIL strength was heavily concentrated in rural areas among the sharecroppers and tenant farmers, who were the groups most actively interested in land reform but less given to the extremism which appealed more to the day laborers, the *braccianti*. The other areas of important strength were the industries employing a large proportion of women — the textile industry and the clothing industry. Geographically, the largest strength was in the traditionally strong Catholic areas, such as the Veneto. The strength of the CIL and *Popolari* was in their combining a Catholic appeal independent of church control with a social doctrine which sought greater justice without the revolutionary implications of traditional socialist doctrines. For large numbers of wage earners, however, such an appeal aroused little enthusiasm and frequently much antagonism. Socialism had preempted the field of representation of worker interests and in the process had built upon an anti-clericalism which existed both within and particularly without the Catholic movement, but which condemned any effort of the church to move beyond the spiritual realm. The extent to which this latter issue divides society and arouses deep-seated impassioned reaction is difficult to understand outside Italy. For many centuries the Catholic church had exercised temporal power in Italy, and had felt its interests so directly at stake that it had played a role in all secular matters, from government through economic and social affairs. It had been identified — and the decades of Socialist monopoly and near monopoly in the social field had driven the conclusion home — with the forces of reaction or at least of "order," of *status quo*. While the question of religion was not necessarily identified with anti-clericalism, the latter sentiment drew widespread support throughout Italian society as a direct consequence of the history of the manifold church activities in Italy. The problem represents, still, a basic cleavage in Italian society, adding to the unfortunate numerous centrifugal forces already at work.

Much has been made in the contemporary post-Fascist period of unity as a basic theme in the trade union and the working class arena generally. In retrospect, on the trade union side there had almost always been competition, even though CGL itself characteristically lightly papered over deep and fundamental differences of orientation among competitive groups within its own ranks. It is rather on the political side than in the trade unions that unity within the Socialist Party represented a long and remarkably strong force. It is true that the Revolutionary Syndicalists were ambivalent about their participation in the Socialist Party. They were, however, essentially anti-political party in ideology and yet even they were eventually expelled from the Party — they did not withdraw. The Communists split away from the Socialists in 1921, but they acted, as did Communists in other countries at the same time, according to the Communist International's tactics of the time by establishing a party unquestioningly accepting the Twenty-One Points of Communist loyalty.

Nevertheless, the remarkable characteristic of the Socialist Party was its ability to maintain unity, most particularly during the years following the First World War. The cleavage between the Reformists who had the bulk of Socialist parliamentary seats and the Maximalists who controlled the Party and its machinery during that period was so wide that it is difficult to understand the acceptance of continued unity and Party discipline on the part of the Reformists. Over and over again in those tragic years, the Socialist representatives in Parliament accepted the Party's veto of any position which involved compromise with all-out opposition to the government — any *bourgeois* government. Yet, the Reformists were aware that the position was leading to fascism. A split did eventually take place, but only after fascism had already been installed and it was far too late to reverse events.

In the contemporary period the myth that greater working class unity would have prevented fascism from taking power became an article of faith and for Nenni and the PSI became a powerful directional signal for what they regarded as the lesson of history. But the reverse of the myth is true. Unity with non-working class democratic elements would have prevented fascism, that is, if those who controlled the Socialist Party had accepted the thesis of the Reformists in the Party. In the absence of this possibility, why did the Reformists, convinced that the official Socialist position was leading to disaster, accept it nonetheless, rather than break with the Party? In part, no doubt, there was the conviction that in a break between themselves and the official Party, the Party would be supported by the mass of Socialists and the wage earners generally. However, this alone would not have been enough for some of those involved. The other element which probably played a role was the fact that they were obsessed by the inherent virtue of working-class unity and discipline to the point of accepting the Party's official position and marching in the ranks, however reluctantly, directly toward the disaster they themselves were predicting. Unity, then, has been a strong force in the political arena, but much less in the trade union arena, in the past. It has, however, been a slogan widely misused both in the past as well as in the present.

Trade Union Political Relations

Perhaps the most constant characteristic of the Italian trade union movement's evolution is the intimate relationship between the movement and political affairs. This is not to be taken to mean that the trade union movement has been controlled or dominated by a political party until the recent period of fascism. Certainly the effort to control or at least to promote common orientation is a constant throughout the history of the trade union movement. But the clear fact is that the political efforts at organizational domination had not been successful. It is not in these simple terms that the problem of relationship is best approached. The early period of development was characterized by a great deal of undifferentiated propagandizing and organizing on the part of Socialists, who frequently laid stress on whatever immediate problems came to hand, forming or promoting political groupings and trade union organizations wherever the opportunity presented itself. The differentiation, however, from an organizational point of view, was early insisted upon by the trade union leadership.

The Revolutionary Syndicalists represented a rather special case as their ideology dictated the principal emphasis upon trade unions as the instrument of transformation of society. The political party was theoretically superfluous in their framework, since only the direct action of workers through general strike was what counted. It is interesting that in this regard the Italian Revolutionary Syndicalists compromised sufficiently with their ideology to compete directly in the political field and even to run candidates in parliamentary elections at one time. Nonetheless, for them the trade unions were what counted, and in this sense the Revolutionary Syndicalists controlled a minority segment of the trade unions in pre-Fascist Italy.

Several aspects of the political relationship of trade unions in pre-Fascist Italy are significant for our understanding of this relationship. First, the trade unions were committed to a common ideological orientation as part of the Socialist movement. They accepted the desirability of general transformation of society, even as they insisted that their own role was to be concerned with immediate specific problems facing workers in their job relationships. In this regard, they were reacting and functioning as the Socialist-oriented trade union movements of other European countries were doing at the time.

Secondly, in the competition which the CGL faced from the Revolutionary Syndicalists, the CGL found that it could not always escape involvement in tactics dictated by its competitors. The leadership apparently felt that unless it bent in this regard it would lose in the competition. Yet, on the whole, despite these compromises, so long as the conditions of the Giolitti period of economic progress prevailed, the CGL leadership was able to establish its own imprint and bargaining trade union pattern as an acceptable alternative to "cyclone unionism."

It was the changed conditions of a Socialist Party in the hands of revolutionary elements which began the reversal of trends for the trade unions. In the period immediately before World War I, the combination of revolutionary-controlled Socialist Party efforts and those of the Revolutionary Syndicalists began to take control of the situation out of the hands of the CGL leadership. The leadership retained control of its organization in the sense that it continued to command majority support, but found that workers were responding more readily under some circumstances to the appeals of "outsiders" than to their own appeals. Fundamentally, they no longer could control the actual activity of their organizations. All this was only a prelude to the years of turmoil following the First World War, in which, as we have seen, the CGL found itself churning in a maelstrom which it neither chose nor could control but in which it played a role largely dictated to it by events and promoted by the propagandistic atmosphere created by the Socialist Party.

The fundamental question posed after the First World War was why the CGL had so little control and why the workers turned more willingly to the Socialist political leadership than to the trade union leadership. To some extent this was inherent in the situation at the time. The years after the First World War were turbulent ones in most countries. The sacrifices and disruptions caused by the war, the heightened expectation of radical social change and the dramatic example of the Russian revolution, combined to give a sharp degree of militancy and activism to the worker and other Left forces in most countries. In these terms, the situation was basically a political one and not primarily a trade union problem, except insofar as the trade unions could be drawn upon for support and implementation. One might maintain that the channelization of the expectations into purely trade union objectives might conceivably have been achieved were it not for the excess of futile revolutionary-appearing gestures promoted by the Socialist Party. The trade union achievements within eighteen months of the war's end were remarkable. Yet, it is far from certain that these very solid trade union successes met the expectations of the times sufficiently to have channeled the upsurge of active momentum. It might be argued that these would have been sufficient only if there had been a Socialist Party policy which accepted the role of political guarantor against reaction by accepting participation in government and proceeding to carry forward basic social reforms by parliamentary means. Since the Socialist Party made the trade union gains appear only minor incidents in an active class war leading immediately to revolution "as in Russia," the trade unions were in a hopeless situation so long as it was toward a political party that the mass of workers turned.

This then brings us back to what appears to be a characteristic of the entire pre-Fascist period, sharply highlighted after 1918: the workers' first allegiance to his party and only secondarily to his trade union. More accurately, since differentiation between trade union and political party was not a clear-cut one in his mind, and since transformation of society was a constant objective, it was first toward the party, especially in times of dramatic turmoil, that he would turn. In this sense the moderate trade union leadership itself contributed to some extent to the situation by teaching its lessons only too well — it had repeatedly held that it made common ideological cause with the Socialist Party on the desirability of social transformation, but that the function of the trade unions was limited to specific wage earner problems related to immediate terms and conditions of employment. The wider, more ambitious objective was that of the political party. The choice made by the workers in periods of stress would appear to support the view that they embraced the broader objective rather than that they were satisfied with the more limited one.

One of the continuing problems in the trade union movement, as we have seen, was the question of the relative supremacy of the National Unions (the Federations) and the Chambers of Labor. The ideological content of the struggle for supremacy between the Revolutionary Syndicalists and the Reformists, has already been described earlier in detail. Even where the competition had no ideological content, however, the problem was not solved as in other European countries. While the National Unions made progress in increasing their authority over the years, the Chambers of Labor continued for the most part to remain the repository of the confidence of the workers. They remained the organization to which the workers turned for help and with which they identified themselves much more than with the national unions. This was apparently not only a question of servicing on immediate worker problems. It was also a question of worker identification with the broader political (as well as trade union) concerns with which the Chambers of Labor were typically identified.

Whereas in other countries the geographic horizontal organizational equivalent of the Chambers had also played an important role in the early evolution of the trade union movement, they had, in varying degrees, gradually been submerged in the machinery which primarily was concerned with a specific trade or industry. While this tendency also developed in Italy and was a principal objective of the national trade union leadership — indeed, they were identified as Federalists, because of their firm position on this issue — it did not evolve as far as in other countries. Underlying the difference with other countries was the relative failure of a truly national economy to develop and the continued relative importance of the locality and region for economic problems with which the trade unions dealt. In its practical manifestation, the Italian industrial and rural workers continued to place their primary confidence in the Chambers of Labor for the very reasons which frequently earned the condemnation of the national trade union leadership: the Chambers' concern with broad political problems which went beyond specific trade union issues, although trade union tactics were frequently affected by these political concerns.

There still remains the question of the reason for the political commitment of the trade union movement itself. The orientation given by the national CGL leadership to day-to-day trade union affairs was a straightforward trade union one and they energetically pressed for the development of a type of trade unionism akin to that of other European countries: concern with immediate labor problems, collective agreements, strikes as a last resort only, loose relationship with political parties. Yet, they felt obliged to keep close ties with the Socialist Party both as individuals and as an organization. Actually, even in this regard they tried to avoid being rigidly bound and resisted giving the Socialist Party a monopolist position. The Republican and Radical parties were cultivated along with the Socialist Party, since these in combination represented the parties most sympathetic to the legislative and administrative assistance sought by the trade union movement. These objectives were normal trade union ones—protective labor legislation, social security and labor standards legislation, sympathetic government administration of such legislation and handling of labor disputes. In this regard, too, the CGL pressed for an orientation which was straightforwardly trade union. The fact that it refused a formal exclusive commitment to the Socialist Party for many years, however, was in part more form than substance in view of the actual relationships which existed, including an explicit agreement on division of responsibility with the Socialists.

Yet the CGL leadership was sincerely and energetically concerned with pressing forward the independence of the trade union movement. For some years, in fact, such rapid progress was made by them in this regard that they gave the impression of successfully leading the trade union movement, despite the harassment of the Revolutionary Syndicalists and the unwelcome intervention of Socialist politicians, toward an Italian style "bread and butter" unionism. Yet they never succeeded for long. Furthermore, while the principal architect of trade union independence, Rinaldo Rigola, fought the encroachments of the political party in the trade union area, he realized that he was losing the battle when he offered his resignation in 1913 and when he resigned in 1918. The issue over which he resigned in 1918 was the crucial question of whether there would be any collaboration with government in seeking economic and social reforms. The CGL leadership did not defy the orders of the Socialist Party to boycott all government-sponsored commissions concerned with economic and social reform, even though Rigola resigned from the trade union leadership over the issue. The leadership apparently did not feel it possible, on this crucial issue, to act independently of the Party and contrary to its directives. It apparently felt that while it disagreed with the Party's decision, the trade union-Party relationship was such that it could not risk personal expulsion from the Party and condemnation on an issue as politically important as the one posed. Whether this represented the conviction that it could not continue to control the trade union movement against a Party offensive if it defied the Party on this basic issue is not certain, but Rigola appeared to have held this view when he resigned rather than fight the issue as he had fought so many other issues of Party relationship in the past.

It can be seen that there existed a basic generic control by the political party which had nothing to do with controlling the trade union machinery or dominating its leadership. It was actually not a control, but a moral leadership and supremacy of the Party in the allegiances of the members of the trade union movement, and to a certain lesser degree of the trade union leadership itself. Even this may be reading too much into the situation after World War I, since the very exceptional psychological climate obtaining at the time played an important role in determining reactions which under other circumstances might have been different. Yet during the period after the Revolutionary wing gained control of the Socialist Party before the First World War, and Mussolini led the Socialist extremists in supporting the Revolutionary Syndicalist trade union approach, Rigola and his colleagues fought back and helped limit the repercussions of a situation which might otherwise have been completely lost to them.

The political trade union relationships in the pre-Fascist Catholic sphere were posed in a different fashion from those of the Socialists. Before the First World War, the Catholic trade unions were coordinated directly by the church-controlled Catholic Action section dealing with social matters. The *non expedit* order of the church had been modified by degrees to meet the evolving problem of opposing Socialist strength, but there was no specific Catholic contender in the national political arena. The situation changed after the First World War, when the Catholic trade unions cut loose entirely from other Catholic organizations and set up their own independent co-ordinating machinery, the CIL. At the same time a national Catholic political party, the *Partito Popolare,* was established. The experience of an independent Catholic political party alongside an independent Catholic trade union movement lasted but a few years before being submerged by the Fascist machine. During this short period the problems of relationships were not posed in as acute a form as for the Socialists. Both the trade union and the party shared a common view of Catholic social doctrine and an unquestioned loyalty to the church. On the other hand, while sharing common faith and ideology, they remained independent of each other while cooperating closely. Certainly they had joint identification in the attitudes of the adherents of the trade unions toward such matters as land reform and worker participation and collaboration in industry. It is, however, probably the case that the CIL unions, involved in such smaller degree in the dynamic and crucial segments of society and the economy than the CGL, were able to some extent to escape the great turmoil into which the latter organization was thrown by events after the First World War. Or more probably it was because the CIL was outside the traditions which the Socialists had monopolized and which had primary appeal to the workers that the CIL was outside the center of trade union affairs. But again, it was not on specifically trade union grounds that the issues of the time appear to have been posed.

In summary, while the trade unions valiantly sought independence from political domination and succeeded in general in maintaining their independent leadership and organizational apparatus, they failed to evolve a trade union movement oriented primarily toward industrial relations. The nature of political forces and political problems, the urge for — and resistance to — social transformation, the rigidity of the society's structure, the incomplete economic-industrial transformation, combined to determine the essential nature of the trade union movement. The trade union movement pressed hard to become a movement oriented toward industrial relations. It remained a movement in which, or over which, political forces influenced and at times held sway in determining the direction and nature of its activities. The heritage of bargaining practices and industrial relations remained, but it was overshadowed in a vital respect by the pressure of political and social events which unfolded in most dramatic fashion between the First World War and fascism.

To recapitulate, a number of characteristics, some conflicting in nature, evolved in the pre-Fascist trade union scene which continued to have an impact upon the contemporary movement. These included "revoltist" reactions, which competed at times successfully against the more organizationally disciplined activity promoted by CGL leadership. A deep-seated mistrust of government remained ingrained in the consciousness of wage earners. This did not eliminate the expectation of favorable action from government, although it was still regarded as fundamentally alien. The Catholic social reform traditions made some progress in light industry and in agriculture and competed against the longer traditions of apparent Catholic alignment with the "forces of order" and established social structure. Cutting across both these Catholic traditions were the more basic clerical and anti-clerical traditions which represented a fundamental cleavage in Italian society between those who rejected and those who urged a role for the church and those acting in its behalf in areas outside the spiritual realm. The clerical and anti-clerical traditions, centuries old, were carried forward into modern Italy both in the political and in the social arenas. The tradition of "unity of the working class" was strong in the political area, but much weaker in the trade union sphere. It was largely the victory of fascism and the search for explanations of that victory which later gave such potency to the myth of working class unity in Italy.

Finally, the traditions of trade union political relationships, which go to the heart of the nature of Italian trade unionism, are too complex to be accurately described as political unionism. The predominant trade union organization sought largely to establish an industrial relations trade unionism in the broad European — not American — tradition, that is, a trade union movement whose central interest was collective bargaining, but which maintained an interest in social reform and had mutually independent ties with a Socialist Party. It seemed to progress gradually toward this end, but only in a formal sense. The political events and the limited control by the trade union leadership of its own membership made it impossible to prevent the trade unions from becoming both a battleground and, more importantly, an instrument in political developments. Political developments, through a combination of background circumstances and specific events, and the nature of Socialist political leadership, overshadowed trade union developments to the point of engulfing the trade union movement and placing the trade union movement's central interest into the background despite its own leadership's orientation.

Influence of Fascism

Twenty years of fascism separated this history from the contemporary democratic period. To a surprising degree the gap of a generation had left still alive the imprint of the past. Added, however, was additional residue accumulated as a result of fascism. For some years, for example, the "membership card" psychology continued to prevail. The necessity under fascism to hold membership in the official syndicates or in the Fascist Party in order to remain within the good graces of the regime or even to obtain employment, had become sufficiently ingrained that in the new free atmosphere wage earners felt it safest to continue the "membership card" habit, this time in CGIL. While the longer tradition of reluctance to pay dues regularly, about which Rigola had complained for years, gradually whittled away the more recently acquired habit, membership still remained relatively high compared with previous periods both in the trade unions and the Left political parties. The trade unions took over from fascism the centralized collective agreement structure and continued a national focus in agreements which later created multiple problems for the trade unions and the wage earners. More important was a continuation of the Fascist practice of decision-making from the top and discouragement of assumption of responsibility or initiative at intermediate levels or among individuals. The Italian, who is the consummate individualist, never succumbed entirely, but was sufficiently affected by the prevalent atmosphere for a residue to be left in the post-Fascist period. Furthermore, the gap of a generation in training of democratic trade union leadership was sorely felt in the years after fascism and gave rise to many problems affecting the activities and relationships of the trade unions as well as the competition among the factions of the trade union movement.

The postwar contemporary years can be divided into three periods. The immediate years after the Second World War were characterized by economic reconstruction, rapid inflation, establishment of democratic governmental institutions, participation of Communists and Socialists in government with Christian Democrats. The trade union organizations were rapidly reconstructed from the top down and quickly fell to the dominance of the Communists. The next period was one of economic stabilization, victory of the Christian Democrats politically, Communist and Socialist opposition to government and the splitting up of CGIL as the Christian Democratic, Social Democratic, and Republican elements successively withdrew to set up organizations to compete against CGIL. The third period was characterized by rapid economic expansion, the beginnings of an ambitious land reform and the southern economic development program, gradual increased autonomy of the Socialists *vis-à-vis* the Communists and significant progress of the unions competing against CGIL.

Communists and Socialists

As we have seen in previous chapters in detail, the Communists emerged rapidly in the predominant position of control in the CGIL, which for the first time included all trade union elements within one organization. The confusion of the times, the single-mindedness of the Communists and their emphasis and ability to organize effectively for leadership made the Communist victory possible. The Socialists might have been expected to have offered keener competition and have had the prospect of predominance themselves. They were, however, for the most part so thoroughly imbued with an ideological mystification regarding "working class unity," common ultimate Socialist goals and the USSR as Socialist Fatherland that their subordination to their more able and determined partners inevitably developed during this period. This was the case particularly since deliberately competing against the Communists was regarded somehow as anti-Socialist, and while the Communists did everything they could to further this attitude, they themselves did not feel inhibited from simultaneously pressing rapidly forward to overcome the Socialists' natural advantages and organizing their own predominance. During this period the Socialists were thoroughly anaesthetized with ideological slogans, much of it self-administered, but with enthusiastic assistance from the Communists. Actually, within the trade unions, a large proportion of the Socialist leadership was more Reformist than Fusionist, but since Buozzi had been killed at the time of the German retreat from Rome, none of the Socialist trade union leadership had the stature or ability to challenge the Fusionist position of the party. Furthermore, the atmosphere of the times was such that just as in the post-World War I period, the political parties were what counted and the trade union machinery, built by party decision and subject to control, fell in with the political orientation followed by the Communists and Socialists.

On the political side, the Communists did equally well. Social Democratic beliefs were stigmatized as "vile reformism," and "reformism" became a word of opprobrium in official Socialist Party circles, equalled only by such terms as "class enemy" and "black clericalism." As in the period after the First World War, so in the years following the Second World War, the Socialists helped stage their own tragedy, with all the unfortunate consequences for the "working class" and for Italy as a whole. The promise of basic transformation of social structure in the later period, as in the earlier period, did not materialize. The Socialists must carry a heavy responsibility in this regard. As a result of the Fusionist policies during the early years after the fall of fascism, they were rapidly supplanted by the Communists as the predominant party of the working class and as the party effectively laying claims to the Left traditions of the workers. The irony of Nenni's position during those years is that he and his party made strategic blunders of the same nature as those for which he had so effectively criticized the Socialist Party of the post-World War I period in his published analysis of the earlier period, previously cited. By following a pro-Communist policy, the Socialists sacrificed their prestige symbols and their potential predominance to the Communists and at the same time made effective social reorganization and reform less possible by joining forces with the Communists in consistent opposition to Center-Left democratic policies. Furthermore, by their position, they furthered the plausibility of the "two alternatives" psychology — "black clericalism or Red communism" — which was so important in building Communist strength during those years.

It might be argued that the mood of the times was such that a Socialist Party policy genuinely committed to democratic reform and to democratic institutions might have offered no more effective competition to the Communists than did the Fusion policy. The failure of the Social Democratic break-away movements to develop more than a relatively small following does not present evidence either way, since these movements faced the overwhelming disadvantage of being break-away movements from official socialism. The policy followed by the Socialist Party, however, insured the failure to achieve social reform.

It was only in recent years that the Socialist Party, as we have seen, hesitatingly began moving to an autonomous position away from the Communists. In the process, it gained strength relative to the Communists, although it faced difficult problems internally as a result of factional differences over the Communist relationship issue. The considerable sentiment among democratic Center-Left Parties in favor of an "opening to the Left" government which would have the support of the PSI has been an understandable aspiration. Political arithmetic had made this an almost irresistible formula for insuring a solid political majority for basic social reforms and a government policy of democratic Left orientation. The mortgage of years of commitment to their Communist allies was a great and complex one for the Socialists, however, and the extent of their genuinely democratic orientation and commitment even in an eventual effective autonomy remained a troublesome question for the "opening to the Left" proponents.

Contemporary Trade Unions

For the trade unions, the recent years were ones of sharp competition within a general downward trend in over-all strength in contrast to the early postwar years. Within an atmosphere of improving economic conditions, of an economy in rapid expansion although achieving little basic social reform, the non-Communist trade unions made significant progress against CGIL. CGIL remained thoroughly and irreparably under Communist control, while the Socialists remained committed to the organization on grounds of "working class unity." Socialist autonomy could not be regarded as having been built on solid ground so long as this commitment continued.

The UIL offered itself as a natural ground for reunifying Socialist-oriented trade unionism, if PSI finally moved away from CGIL. This was a natural aspiration for those in UIL leadership who for years had struggled against great odds to maintain their organization and based their position on the need in Italy for democratic Socialist-oriented labor organization.

CISL, on the other hand, consistently urged the necessity of unity among all non-Communists for the building of a democratic trade union movement. It worked hard to develop a responsible independent trade union machinery which it insisted had to be non-political and oriented primarily toward industrial relations problems with economic reform as a secondary although important goal. It found itself, however, committed on the political scene in a multiplicity of ways which grew in significance as its own importance increased. As individuals, its leadership, as we have seen, played an increasingly influential role within the Christian Democratic Party as part of an organized faction pressing for reform in the economic and social spheres. Paradoxically, but with fundamental logic, as its influence within the Christian Democratic Party and in Parliament increased, so at the same time did the CISL leadership and the organization itself gain in its long hard battle to overcome the limitations of the label of "Catholic unionism" which had tended to restrict its appeal among wage earners. Its gradual demonstration of genuine commitment toward economic and social progress and its slow but effective building up of its organization reduced the potency of the labels attached to it by its critics.

As in the pre-Fascist period, fundamental forces of a political character sharply influenced the nature of the contemporary trade union organizations and the focus which they gave to their problems. But, unlike the previous period, there were new economic forces at work basically favorable toward development of stable viable trade union organization. Whether, despite the current Communist CGIL predominance, the democratic organizations could gradually exploit the situation in building strong organization, remained unsettled. In any event, the history of Italian trade unionism would appear to support the likelihood that regardless of verbal commitment, trade unions would combine in a measure larger than in other western European countries a political orientation with their purely economic concerns.

The pattern of Italian trade unionism has sharply demonstrated a fundamental instability in broad institutional relationships throughout the history of modern Italy. Such lack of stability — or "normalization" of relationships within an equilibrium of political, social, and trade union forces — has been a decisive factor in determining the character of the trade union movement. The changes which have occurred in the economic and social structure, in the character of political forces, and in the trade union movement itself, were, in their nature and degree, not sufficient to bring the three into enough congruence to achieve stability in Italian society. It is this lack of congruence which appears to be an outstanding characteristic of Italian trade unionism and of Italian society.

Congruence among a society's social and economic structure, its political forces and the trade union movement can be achieved in various ways in different societies. It has been achieved, in distinct fashion, in a number of Western democratic countries, including the United States, Great Britain, and the Scandinavian countries. It has not been achieved in Italy. Yet, slow as the process may be, economic progress in Italy may gradually have its impact upon the social structure of the country. Political and government policy may also play a crucial role in the years ahead. The democratic trade union forces have developed sufficient potential dynamism to offer the possibility that they, also, may contribute to a political, economic, and social congruence which would give Italy the democratic stability its people have so richly earned.

Selected Bibliography

The following list is a selected bibliography of more useful works on the Italian economic, political and trade union developments within the general scope of the text.

The trade union and political party official journals, periodicals and occasional publications as well as congress proceedings and reports are indispensible for research in view of the relatively little basic work which has been published on the Italian trade union movement.

Adams, John Clarke. "Italy," in Walter Galenson, ed., *Comparative Labor Movements*. (New York: Prentice-Hall, 1952)

Albrecht-Carrié, René. *Italy from Napoleon to Mussolini*. (New York: Columbia University Press, 1950)

Angiolini, Alfredo and Eugenio Ciacchi. *Socialismo e socialisti in Italia: Storia completa del movimento socialista italiano dal 1850 al 1919*. (Florence: Nerbini, 1919)

Angiolini, Eugenio. *Cinquant' anni di socialismo in Italia*. (Florence: Nerbini, 1900)

Anzi, F. *Il movimento operaio socialista italiano*. (Milan-Rome: Soc. ed. Avanti!, 1946)

Barbagallo, Corrado. *Le origini della grande industria contemporanea (1750-1850)*. 2 vols. (Perugia-Venice: "La nuova Italia" Editrice, 1930)

Bellini, Fulvio and Giorgio Galli. *Storia del partito comunista italiano*. (Milan: Schwarz, 1953)

Bonomi, Ivanoe, *Diario di un anno: 2 Giunio 1943-10 Giunio 1944*. (Milan: Garzanti, 1947)

————. *Leonida Bissolati e il movimento socialista in Italia*. (Milan: Martinelli, 1929)

Borgese, Giuseppe Antonio. *Goliath, The March of Fascism*. (New York: The Viking Press, 1937)

Borghi, Armando. *L'Italia tra due Crispi*. (Paris: Libreria Internationale, 1924)

Bruno, Tomaso. *La Federazione del Libro nei suoi primi cinquant' anni di vita*. (Bologna: Coop. Tipografia Mareggiani, 1925)

Bulferetti, Luigi. *Le ideologie socialistiche in Italia nell' età del positivismo evoluzionistico (1870-1892)*. (Florence: Felice Le Monnier, 1951)

Cabrini, Angiolo. *La legislazione sociale, 1859-1913*. (Rome: Bontempelli, 1913)

————. *La resistenza nell' Europa giovane (Viaggi e Congressi)*. (Imola: Coop. Tip. Editrice Pablo Galeati, 1905)

Candeloro, Giorgio. *Il movimento sindacale in Italia*. (Rome: Edizioni di Cultura Sociale, 1950)

Cannarsa, Spartico, *Il socialismo e i XXVIII congressi nazionali del Partito Socialista Italiano*. (Florence: Casa Editrice Avanti!, 1950)

Carbone, Salvatore. *Le origini del socialismo in Sicilia*. (Rome: Edizioni Italiane, 1947)

Colajanni, Napoleone. *L'Italia nel 1898: tumulti e reazione*. (Milan: Soc. Ed. Lombarda, 1899)

————. *Gli avvenimenti in Sicilia e le loro cause*. (Palermo: Sandron, 1895)

Colombi, Arturo. *Pagine di storia del movimento operaio*. (Rome: Edizioni Rinascita, 1950)

Confederazione Generale dell'Industria Italiana. *Labor Management Councils in Italy.* (Rome: Confindustria, 1951)

———. *I consigli di gestione: Experienze e documenti sulla participazione dei lavoratori alla vita delle aziende nell' ultimo trentennio.* 2 vol. (Rome: Confindustria, 1947)

Confederazione Generale Italiana del Lavoro. *La C.G.I.L. dal patto di Roma al Congresso di Genova.* 3 vols. (Rome: CGIL, 1949, 1952)

Conti, Elio. *Le origini del socialismo a Firenze (1860–1880).* (Rome: Edizioni Rinascita, 1950)

Corbino, Epicarmo. *Annuali dell' economia italiana 1861–1914.* 5 vols. (Città di Castello: Tipografia "Leonardo da Vinci," 1931–38)

Croce, Benedetto. *A History of Italy, 1871–1915.* (Oxford: Clarendon Press, 1929)

Dal Pane, Luigi. *Storia del lavoro in Italia dagli inizi del secolo XVIII al 1815.* 2nd ed. (Milan: A Giuffre, 1958)

DeRossi, D. Giulio. *Il Partito Popolare Italiano.* (Rome: Editore Francesco Ferrari, 1919)

Di Vittorio, Giuseppe. *L'unità dei lavoratori.* (Rome: Editori Riuniti, 1957)

Einaudi, Luigi. *Le lotte del lavoro.* (Turin: Piero Gobetti, 1924)

Einaudi, Mario and Francois Goguel. *Christian Democracy in Italy and France.* (Notre Dame: University of Notre Dame Press, 1952)

Einaudi, Mario, Jean-Marie Domenach and Aldo Garosci. *Communism in Western Europe.* (Ithaca, New York: Cornell University Press, 1951)

Einzig, Paul. *The Economic Foundations of Fascism.* (London: Macmillan and Co., Ltd., 1933)

Fanfani, Amintore. *Catholicism, Protestantism and Capitalism.* (New York: Shield and Ward, Inc., 1935)

———. *I problemi del lavoro in Italia prima del 1900.* (Florence: Casa Editrice Poligrafica Universitaria, 1936)

———. *Storia dell' lavoro in Italia dalla fine del secolo XV agli inizi del XVIII,* 2nd ed. (Milan: A. Giuffre, 1959)

Fenica, Salvatore. *La cooperazione in Piemonte.* (Turin: Fratelli Bocca, 1901)

Field, George L. *The Syndical and Corporative Institutions of Italian Fascism.* (New York: Columbia University Press, 1938)

Finer, Herman. *Mussolini's Italy.* (New York: Henry Holt and Co., 1935)

Foa, Bruno. *Monetary Reconstruction in Italy.* Published for the Carnegie Endowment for International Peace. (New York: King's Crown Press, 1949)

Foerster, Robert F. *The Italian Emigration of Our Times.* (Cambridge: Harvard University Press, 1919)

Forlani, Arnaldo. *Il PSI di fronte al comunismo dal 1945 al 1956.* (Rome: Edizioni 5 Lune, 1956)

Fossati, Antonio. *Lavoro e produzione in Italia dalla metà del secolo XVIII alla seconda guerra mondiale.* (Turin: G. Giappichelli, 1951)

Galli, Giorgio. *La sinistra italiana nel dopoguerra.* (Bologna: Il Mulino, 1958)

Gentile, Panfilo. *Cinquanta anni di socialismo in Italia.* (Milan: Longanesi, 1948)

Gerschenkron, Alexander. "Notes on the Rate of Industrial Growth in Italy, 1881–1913," *The Journal of Economic History,* XV, 4 (December 1955), pp. 360–375.

Giolitti, Giovanni. *Memoirs of My Life.* Translated from the Italian by Edward Storer. (London: Chapman and Dodd, Ltd., 1923)

Gnocchi-Vianni, Osvaldo. *Le borse del lavoro.* (Alessandria: Partito Operaio Italiano, 1889)

———. *Dieci anni di camere del lavoro.* (Bologna: Camera del lavoro della città e provincia di Bologna, 1899)

Gorresio, Vittorio. *I carrissimi nemici.* (Milan: Longanesi, 1949)
——. *I moribondi di Montecitorio.* (Milan: Longanesi, 1947)
——. *Un anno di libertà.* (Rome: Edizioni Polilibraria, 1945)
Greenfield, Kent Roberts. *Economics and Liberalism in the Risorgimento (A Study of Nationalism in Lombardy, 1814-1848).* (Baltimore: Johns Hopkins University Press, 1934)
Griffith, Gwileym O. *Mazzini: Prophet of Modern Europe.* (London: Hodder and Stoughton, 1932)
Grindrod, Muriel. *The New Italy: Transition from War to Peace.* (London: Royal Institute of International Affairs, 1947)
Gualtieri, Humbert L. *The Labor Movement in Italy.* (New York: S. F. Vanni, 1946)
Guarnieri, Mario. *I consigli di fabbrica.* (Città di Castello: Il Solco, 1921)
Haider, Carmen. *Capital and Labor Under Fascism.* (New York: Columbia University Press, 1930)
Halperin, Samuel William. *Italy and the Vatican at War.* (Chicago: University of Chicago Press, 1939)
Hilton-Young, W. *The Italian Left: A Short History of Political Socialism in Italy.* (London: Longmans, Green and Co., 1949)
Hostetter, Richard. *The Italian Socialist Movement.* vol. I *Origins (1860-1882).* (Princeton: Van Nostrand, 1958)
Hughes, H. Stuart. *The United States and Italy.* (Cambridge: Harvard University Press, 1953)
I Sindacati in Italia: Saggi di G. DiVittorio, G. Pastore, I. Viglianesi, G. Rapelli, F. Santi, E. Parri, G. Canini. (Bari: Laterza, 1955)
Jacini, Stefano. *Storia del Partito Popolare Italiano.* (Milan: Garzanti, 1951)
Jemolo, Arturo Carlo. *Chiesa e stato in Italia negli ultimi cento anni.* (Turin: Giulio Einaudi, 1949)
Joll, James. *The Second International, 1889-1914.* (New York: Praeger, 1956)
Kaplan, Jacob J. *Economic Stagnation in Italy* (New Haven: Yale Institute of International Studies, 1949)
King, Bolton. *Mazzini.* (London: J. M. Dent and Co., 1902)
Labriola, Arturo. *Riforma e rivoluzione sociale.* (Lugano: Soc. Ed. "Avanguardia," 1906)
La Palombara, Joseph. *The Italian Labor Movement: Problems and Prospects.* (Ithaca, New York: Cornell University Press, 1957)
Leonetti, Alfonso. *Mouvements ouvriers et socialistes (chronologie et bibliographie): l'Italie (des origines à 1922).* Collection dirigée par E. Dolleans et M. Crozier. (Paris: Les Editions Ouvrières, 1952)
Lorwin, Louis L. *The International Labor Movement.* (New York: Harpers, 1953)
——. *Labor and Internationalism.* (New York: Brookings, 1929) (An earlier edition of Lorwin's *The International Labor Movement,* containing considerably more detail on earlier periods.)
Luzzatto, Gino. *Storia economica dell' età moderna e contemporanea.* 2 vols. (Padua: Casa Editrice Dott. A. Milani, 1948)
Mack Smith, Denis. *Italy: A Modern History.* (Ann Arbor: University of Michigan Press, 1959)
Magri, Francesco. *Controllo operaio e consigli d'azienda in Italia e all' estero (1916-1947).* 2nd ed. (Milan: Editrice Academia, 1947)
——. *Dal movimento cristiano al sindacalismo democratico.* (Milan: La Fiaccola, 1957)
Manacorda, Gastone. *Il movimento operaio italiano attraverso i suoi congressi dalla origini alla formazione del partito socialista (1853-1892).* (Rome: Edizioni Rinascita, 1953)

Meda, Filipo, *Il socialismo politico in Italia.* (Milan: Societa Editrice "Unitas," 1924)

Michels, Roberto. *Il proletariato e la borghesia nel movimento socialista italiano.* (Turin: Fratelli Bocca, 1908)

———. *Storia critica del movimento socialista italiana dagli inizi fin al 1911.* (Florence: Editrice "La Voce," 1926)

Ministero di Agricoltura, Industria e Commercio, Ufficio del Lavoro. *Le organizzazioni di lavoratori in Italia, Federazioni di mestiere. I: La Federazione dei Cappellai.* (Series B, No. 10.) (Rome: Officina Poligrafica Italiana, 1906)

———. *Le organizzazioni di lavoratori in Italia, Federazioni di mestiere. II: La Federazione Edilizia.* (Series B. No. 11.) (Rome: Officina Poligrafica Italiana, 1906)

———. *Le organizzazioni d'Impiegi* (Series B, No. 27.) (Rome: Officina Poligrafica Italiana, 1910)

———. *Le organizzazioni operaie cattoliche in Italia.* (Series B. No. 35.) (Rome: Officina Poligrafica Italiana, 1911)

———. *Le Organizzazioni padronali — I. Le Agrarie.* (Series B, No. 40.) (Rome: Officina Poligrafica Italiana, 1912)

Ministero per la Costituente, Commissione per lo Studio dei Problemi del Lavoro. vol. I: *Relazioni-Questionari-Interrogatori-Inchieste.* vol. II: *L'Ordinamento del lavoro nella legislazione comparata.* vol. III: *Memorie sui argomenti.* (Roma, Economici stabilimento tipogra. U.E.S.I.S.A., 1946)

Montagnana, Mario. *Ricordi di un operaio torinese.* 2 vols. (Rome: Edizioni Rinascita, 1952)

Morandi, Carlo, *I partiti politici nella storia d'Italia.* (Florence: F. Le Monnier, 1945)

Morandi, Rodolfo. *Storia della grande industria in Italia.* (Bari: Laterza, 1931)

Murri, Romolo. *La politica clericale e la democrazia.* (Rome: Ascoli Pisceno, G. Cesari, etc., 1908)

National Industrial Conference Board: European Commission. *Problems of Labor and Industry in Great Britain, France and Italy* (Spec. Report No. 6) (Washington: U.S. Government Printing Office, 1919)

Nettlau, Max. *Bakounin e l'internazionale in Italia dal 1864 al 1872.* (Geneva: Il Risveglio, 1928)

Neufeld, Maurice F. *Italy: School for Awakening Countries.* (Ithaca, New York: New York State School of Industrial and Labor Relations, Cornell University, 1961)

———. *Labor Unions and National Politics in Italian Industrial Plants.* (Ithaca, New York: Institute of International Industrial and Labor Relations, Cornell University, 1954)

Nenni, Pietro. *Storia di quattro anni.* (Rome: Guilio Einaudi, 1946)

Olgiati, Francesco. *La storia dell' azione cattolica in Italia (1865–1904).* 2nd ed. (Milan: Societa Editrice "Vita e Pensiero," 1922)

Olschki, Leonardo. *The Genius of Italy.* (New York: Oxford University Press, 1949)

Palumbo, Beniamino. *Il movimento democratico-cristiano in Italia.* (Rome: Tipo. "Cidi M," 1950)

Perticone, Giocomo. *La repubblica di Salò.* (Rome: Edizioni Leonardo 1947)

———. *Storia del socialismo.* (Rome: Edizione Leonardo, 1945)

Por, Odon. *Guilds and Cooperatives in Italy.* (London: The Labour Publishing Co., Ltd., 1923)

Rigola, Rinaldo. *Cent' anni di movimento operaio.* (Milan: Edizioni dell' A.N.S. Problemi del Lavoro, 1935)

———. *L'evoluzione della Confederazione Generale del Lavoro* (Florence: Edizioni della Critica Sociale, 1921)

———. *Manualetto di tecnica sindacale.* (Florence: Edizioni U — Biblioteca di Critica Sociale, 1947)

————. *Storia del movimento operaio italiano.* (Milan: Editorial Domus S.A., 1946)

————. *Rinaldo Rigola e il movimento operaio nel Biellese.* (Bari: Laterza, 1930)

Riguzzi, Biagio. *Sindacalismo e riformismo nel Parmese: L. Musini-A.Berenini.* (Bari: Laterza, 1931)

Romani, Egisto. *L'organizzazione del ceto operaio nelle società di mutuo soccorso.* (San Benedeto: Tipografia Rozzi Carlo, 1895)

Romano, Salvatore Francesco. *Storia della questione meridionale.* (Palermo: Pontea, 1945)

————. *Storia dei fasci siciliani.* (Bari: Laterza, 1959)

Rosenstock-Franck, L. *L'économie corporative fasciste en doctrine et en fait: ses origines historiques et son évolution.* (Paris: Librairie Universitaire J. Gamber, 1934)

Rosselli, Nello. *Mazzini e Bakounin: 12 anni di movimento operaio in Italia (1860-1872).* (Turin: Fratelli Bocca, 1927)

Rossi, A. *The Rise of Italian Fascism, 1918-1922.* (London: Methuen and Company, Ltd., 1938.) The Italian edition, which has considerably more documentation in footnotes, was published under Rossi's real name, Angelo Tasca, as *Nascita e Avvento del Fascismo.* (Florence: La Nuova Italia, 1950)

Rossi-Doria, Malio. *Dieci anni di politica agraria nel Mezzogiorno.* (Bari: Laterza, 1958)

Sacco, Italo Mario. *Storia del sindacalismo.* 2nd ed. (Turin: Societa Editrice Internazionale, 1947)

Salomone, A. William. *Italian Democracy in the Making: The Political Scene in the Giolittian Era (1900-1914).* (Philadelphia: University of Pennsylvania Press, 1945)

Salvatorelli, Luigi, ed. *Giolitti.* (Milan: Casa Editrice R. Caddea e Cia., 1920)

Salvatorelli, Luigi. *A Concise History of Italy.* Translated by Bernard Miall. (New York: Oxford University Press, 1940)

Salvemini, Gaetano. *Under the Axe of Fascism.* (New York: Viking Press, 1936)

Sanseverino, Luisa Riva. "Collective Bargaining in Italy," in Adolf Sturmthal, ed. *Contemporary Collective Bargaining in Seven Countries.* (Ithaca, New York: Institute of International Industrial and Labor Relations, Cornell University, 1957)

Sanseverino, Luisa Riva. *Il movimento sindacale cristiano.* (Rome: Zuffi, 1950)

Schmidt, Carl T. *The Plough and the Sword.* (New York: Columbia University Press, 1938)

Sforza, Carlo. *Contemporary Italy.* (London: Frederick Muller, Ltd., 1946)

Società Umanitaria, Ufficio del Lavoro. Publication No. 18: *Origini, vicende e conquiste delle organizzazioni operaie aderenti alla Camera del Lavoro in Milano.* (Milan: Ufficio del Lavoro della Società Umanitaria, 1909)

Spriano, Paolo. *Socialismo e classe operaia a Torino dal 1892 al 1913.* (Turin: Einaudi, 1957)

Sprigge, Cecil, J. S. *The Development of Modern Italy.* (London: Duckworth, 1943)

Sturzo, Luigi. *Italy and the Coming World.* (New York: Roy Publishers, 1945)

————. *Italy and Fascism.* (London: Faber and Gwyer, 1926)

Thomas, Ivor. *The Problem of Italy: an Economic Survey.* (London: George Routledge and Sons, Ltd., 1946)

Toldo, Antonio. *Il sindacalismo in Italia.* 2nd ed. (Milan: Centro Studi Sociali, 1953)

Tremelloni, Roberto. *Storia dell' industria italiana contemporanea.* Vol. I: *Dalla fine del settocento all' unita italiana.* (Turin: Giulio Einaudi, 1947)

————. *Storia recente dell' industria italiana.* (Milan: Garzanti, 1956)

Turati, Filippo. *Trent' anni di "Critica Sociale."* (Bologna: Nicola Zanichelli, 1921)

Trevisani, Giulio. *Lineamenti di una storia del movimento operaio italiano.* (Milan: Ed. Avanti!, 1958)

————. *Piccola enciclopedia del socialismo e del comunismo*. (Milan: Il Calendrio del Popolo, 1958)

Ubertazzi, G. *Il Partito d'Azione*. (Genoa: Ceva, 1945)

Valente, Giovanni Battista. *Il programma sindacale cristiano*. 3rd ed. (Rome: Luigi Buffetti, 1921)

Valiano, Leo. *L'Avvento di DiGasperi: Tre anni di politica italiana*. (Turin: Francesco de Silva, 1949)

————. *Tutti le strade conducono a Roma*. (Florence: La Nuova Italia, 1947)

Vallardi, Antonio, ed. *Mezzo secolo di vita italiana: 1861–1911*. (Mlian: Vallardi, 1911)

Vercesi, Ernesto. *La democrazia cristiana in Italia*. (Milan: Tip. e libr. dell' Unione, 1910)

————. *Il movimento cattolico in Italia (1870–1922)*. (Florence: Editrice "La Voce," 1923)

Volpe, Gioarchino. *L'Italia in cammino: L'ultimo cinquantennio*. 3rd ed. (Milan: Trivea, 1931)

Wiskeman, Elizabeth. *Italy*. (London: Oxford University Press, 1947)

Zanella, Emilio. *Dalle "Barbarie" alla Civiltà nel Polesine: L'Opera di Nicolo Badaloni*. (Milan: Edizioni dell' A.N.S. Problemi del Lavoro, 1931)

Zibordi, Giovanni. *Saggio sulla storia del movimento operaio in Italia: Camillo Prampolini e i lavoratori reggiani*. 2nd ed. (Bari: Laterza, 1930)

Index

ACLI, *see* Christian Associations of Italian Workers

Action Party, 189–191, 193; elections, *1946,* 203. *See also* Committees of National Liberation

Agriculture, 4, 9, 58, 85, 326, 329; protected by tariff, 7; hostility toward unification of Italy, 11–12; economic transformation in, 40–41; strikes in, 54–55, 58–59, 78, 140–141; acceptance of Syndicalist doctrine, 79; Catholic mutual-aid societies concentrated in, 100; CIL success in, 123, 125; armed bands, 155. *See also* Land reform

Albertario, Don Davide, 98

Altabello, Argentina, 92

Anarchist movement, 20–23, 30, 71, 92–93, 176–177

Anardelli, Giuseppe, 36

Anti-clericalism, 13, 329, 336–337, 339

Associazioni Cristiane dei Lavoratori Italiani (ACLI), *see* Christian Associations of Italian Workers

Avanti, 46, 57, 88, 89, 90, 93, 147, 158

Aventine Parliament, 119, 172–173

Badoglio government, 193–194

Badoglio, Marshall Pietro, 183, 185, 189

Bakunin, Michael, 18–22, 324, 328

Bari trade union conference, 189–190

Benedict XV, 115–116, 129

Benefits, workers'; in friendly societies, 12, 14, 17; in Workers' Party program, 25–26; in early trade unions, 37–38; in Socialist Party program, 55, 85; in CIL program, 121; in CGIL program, 197–198, 200. *See also Conglobamento* agreement; Education; Eight-hour day; Insurance, social; Legislation; Vacations with pay; Wages

Benevento episode, 22

Bianchi, Professor Antonio, 123–124, 162

Bignami, Erico, 24, 27

Bissolati, Leonida, 56, 57, 58

Bittosi, Renato, 212

Black Years, 35, 44

Blacklisting, 61, 149

Bombacci, Nicola, 92, 130

Bonomi, Ivanoe, 57, 167, 183

Bonomi government, 168, 170, 194

Bordiga, Amadeo, 158

Borghi, Armando, 177

Buozzi, Bruno: FIOM general secretary, 92, 143, 148, 151, 159, 161–162; CGL general secretary, 175, 180, 189, 251; commissioner of Fascist Confederation of Industrial Workers, 185, 186; assassination, 186, 339

Buozzi-Mazzini agreement, 186, 197

Cabrini, Angiolo, 57, 62, 64, 65, 66

Cafiero, Carlo, 20

Canini, Giovanni, 217, 220, 224, 258

Carbonari, 11

Catholic Action, 116–117, 120, 261–263, 266, 335

Catholic church in Italy: relations with state, 2, 17–18, 95, 109–110, 261, 324–325, 328, 329; state repression of organizations, 35–36, 111; *non expedit* policy, 95, 104, 105, 106–109, 116, 325; encyclicals, 96, 98, 99, 100, 103–104, 106; Pius X, 105, 106, 108; Benedict XV, 115–116, 129; Pius XI, 119; Pius XII, 263–264, 265–266. *See also* Anti-clericalism; Catholic Action; Christian Associations of Italian Workers; Christian Democratic movement, Party, Democrats; Free Italian General Confederation of Labor; Italian Confederation of Labor; Italian Confederation of Trade Unions; Murri, Father Romolo; Mutual-aid societies; National unions, Catholic; *Opera dei Congressi;* Popular Party; Trade union movement, Catholic

Catholic Congresses: *1891,* 99; *1892,* 99–100, *1894,* 100, 101–102; *1900,* 104; *1901,* 105; *1903,* 105, 106, 110–111, 114

Catholic Popular Party, *see* Popular Party

Catholic trade union movement, *see* Trade union movement, Catholic

Cavour, Count Camillo Benso di, 7, 10

CGIL, *see* Italian General Confederation of Labor

CGL, *see* General Confederation of Labor

Chambers of Labor, 41–45; source of authority, 61–63; relations with Socialists, 64;

and National Unions, 67, 69, 77, 325, 333–334; relations with CGL, 71–72, 76–78, 176; taken over by Revolutionaries, 67, 87, 89, 176; not supported by Catholic leadership, 99–100; role during *1919* riots, 138–139; after liberation of Italy, 199; affiliation with CGIL, 200; political concerns, 333–334. *See also* Italian Federation of Chambers of Labor

Chiesa, Pietro, 62, 64

Christian Associations of Italian Workers (ACLI), 217, 218, 263–266

Christian Democratic movement, 102–107, 110–111. *See also* Christian Democratic Party

Christian Democratic Party, 3, 193–194, 262; criticism of communism, 204; and Catholic trade unions, 266–267; attitude toward "opening to the Left," 278;
    congresses, national, *1962,* 323;
    elections: union, *1945,* 204; national, *1946,* 202; *1948,* 213, 228; *1953,* 229–230; *1958,* 284
See also Christian Democratic movement; Christian Democrats, Committee of National Liberation

Christian Democrats, 202, 278, 286, 338; participation in trade union unity, 185, 189, 195; relations with CGIL, 204, 208–210, 212–218. *See also* Christian Democratic Party

CIL, *see* Italian Confederation of Labor

Circolo Operaio, 24–25

CISL, *see* Italian Confederation of Trade Unions

Class struggle, 1, 18, 96, 99, 160, 161, 162, 332–333

CLN, *see* Committees of National Liberation

CLNAI, *see* Committee of National Liberation for Northern Italy

Colajanni, Napoleone, 34

Collective bargaining, 39, 61, 84, 206–208, 325, 326, 337. *See also* National agreements; Plant level policies

Colombino, Emilio, 162

Cominform, 210, 213

Comitato d'Azione Diretta, 89, 176

Committees of National Liberation (CLN), 183–184, 187, 189, 199

Committee of National Liberation for Northern Italy (CLNAI), 184, 199, 252

Commune, Paris, 21, 22, 24

Communist Party (Italian), 3, 158, 182, 309–310, 316; "Transmission Belt," 1, 296–298; membership, 181, 244, 284; participation in government, 193–194, 230–231, 285–286; policy and tactics, 194–195, 196, 200, 209,

276, 287–288; basis of strength, 244-250; and Hungarian revolt, 280, 298; controversy with PSI, 283–284; internal crisis, 284; relations with CGIL, 296–297, 320, 321, 324;
    congresses: *1955,* 291–292; *1956,* 297–298; *1960,* 317–318;
    elections: communal, *1951* and *1952,* 229; national, *1921,* 165; *1924,* 172; *1946,* 202–203; *1948,* 181, 213, 266; *1953,* 181, 229–230; *1958,* 181, 284; union, *1945,* 204
See also Communists; International, Communist (Third)

Communist Party (Soviet Union), 278–279, 283, 297

Communists, 202, 210, 338; in CGL, 159–160, 178–180; and Socialists, 184–187, 188, 189, 330; domination of CGIL, 203–204, 208–209, 250–253, 324, 338–339. *See also* Communist Party

Confederation of Fascist Corporations, 175

Confederation of Lombardy Workers, 24

Confederazione Generale dell' Industria Italiana, see Confindustria

Confederazione Generale Italiana del Lavoro (CGIL), *see* Italian General Confederation of Labor

Confederazione Generale del Lavoro (CGL), *see* General Confederation of Labor

Confederazione Italiana dei Lavoratori (CIL), *see* Italian Confederation of Labor

Confederazione Italiana Sindacati Lavoratori (CISL), *see* Italian Confederation of Trade Unions

Confindustria, 234, 239, 310–312; pact of Palazzo Vidoni, 126; eight-hour day negotiations, 137; Buozzi-Mazzini agreement, 186; wage policy, 237-238; and national agreements, 207–208; agreements on Internal Commissions, 290–291; plant level policies, 293, 295. *See also Conglobamento* agreement

Conglobamento agreements, 236, 240, 242–243, 309, 310–311

Congresses, Catholic, *see* Catholic Congresses

Congresses, political, *see* names of political parties

Congresses, trade union, *see* Trade union congresses

Congresses of Worker Societies, *see* Worker Societies Congresses

Consigli di Gestione, 252–253

Consiglio d'azienda, 144–147

Consiglio Nazionale dell' Economia e del Lavoro, 314

Consolato Operaio, 24, 26, 41

Cooperatives, 13, 24, 50, 155, 156, 325, **327**

Costa, Andrea, 23, 26, **73**

Councils of Administration, 252–253
Crispi, Francesco, 34
Croce, Giuseppe, 24–25, 30
"Cyclone unionists (unionism)," 1, 78, 332

D'Aragona, Ludovico, 135–136, 147, 151, 159, 162, 166
De Gasperi, Alcide, 202, 210, 214, 230, 262
Democratic Labor Party, 183, 193
Demonstrations: of *1869*, 20; of *1873*, 22; of Black Years, 35; of *1919*, 138–140; Communist-inspired, 286–287; *piazza*, 326–327. *See also* Strikes
Depretis, Agostino, 3
Direct Action Committee (*Comitato d' Azione Diretta*), 89, 176
Di Vittoro, Giuseppe, 186, 305–306; head of CGIL, 190, 192, 196–197, 206, 209, 212, 298, 300; quoted, 208, 221, 289–290, 297
"Domestication," 50, 56, 58, 149, 325, 326
Donat-Cattin, 307, 308
Dossettiani, 269

Economic crisis, 22, 166, 168, 192, 201-202, 210-211. *See also* Black Years; Food riots
Economic expansion: favorable to socialism, 23; during Giolitti period, 48, 50; effect on trade unions, 58, 60–61; since *1950*, 8–9, 228, 274, 338
Education, promotion of: by friendly societies, 14–15, 16, 18, 24; in political parties' programs, 25, 51, 55, 117; by Chambers of Labor, 43
Eight-hour day, 137–138, 142, 326
Einaudi, Professor Luigi, 46, 210
Elections, communal: *1920*, 118, 153, 166; *1951* and *1952*, 229;
 national: *1895* and *1897*, 35; *1900*, 36, 51; *1904*, 106, 109; *1905*, 110; *1909*, 55, 85, 108, 109, 110; *1913*, 55, 90–91, 109, 110; *1919*, 117, 132, 154–155, 165–166; *1921*, 165–166, 167; *1924*, 119, 172, 174–175; *1946*, 202–203; *1948*, 181, 213–214, 226, 228, 229–230, 244; *1953*, 181, 229–230, 231, 239, 240, 241, 244, 277; *1958*, 181, 244, 283–285, 304–305, 309;
 union: *1945*, 204; *1953*, 289; *1954*, 243, 289–290, 303–304; *1955*, 243, 289, 296; *1957*, 303–304; *1958*, 304, 309; *1959* and *1960*, 320; *1961*, 320–321
 See also Suffrage
Encyclicals, 96, 98, 99, 100, 103–104, 106
Exclusivism, *see* Worker exclusivism

Facta, Luigi, 170
Factory councils, 144–147
Fanfani, Amintore, 95, 230, 262, 288

Fanfani governments, 285–286, 287–288, 322–323
Fanfani-Moro policy, 323
Fasci dei Lavoratori (the *Fasci*), 31–34
Fascism: rise to power, 118–119, 125–126, 153–156, 170–180, 330; end of regime, 181–183, 186; imprint left on trade unions, 326, 337. *See also* Fascist Party; Mussolini
Fascist Confederation of Industrial Workers, 185
Fascist Party, 157, 165–166;
 elections: *1919*, 165–166; *1920*, 166; *1921*, 165–166; *1924*, 119, 172
 See also Fascism
Fascist Social Republic, 181
Federation of Chambers of Labor, *see* Italian Federation of Chambers of Labor
Federation of Italian Workers (FIL), 220–221, 222–224, 268–269; congress, *1950*, 223, 270
Federations, the, *see* National Unions
Federazione Italiana del Lavoro (FIL), *see* Federation of Italian Workers
Ferri, Enrico, 53
FIAT, 144, 166, 289–292, 304, 320–321
FIL, *see* Federation of Italian Workers
FIOM, *see* Metallurgical Workers Federation
First International, 13, 19, 20, 21, 324
Food riots of *1919*, 138–140
Four Days of Milan, 35
Free Italian General Confederation of Labor (LCGIL), 218–219, 222–224, 264–265, 267–269
Freemasonry, *see* Masons
Friendly societies, 12–17, 18, 24, 29, 324

Garibaldi, Giuseppe, 2, 10–11, 21, 328
General Association of Workers' Mutual Aid of Milan, 24
General Confederation of Labor (CGL), 70–94, 135–142, 325; membership, 75, 125, 141, 173–174; and CIL, 126; antiwar activities, 128–129; and Socialist Party, 133, 334–335; orientation, 136, 160, 334–335; and occupation strikes, 146, 149–153; and Communists, 159–160, 178–180; destroyed by fascism, 166, 168–170, 173–175; and minority trade union groups, 175–178; and Revolutionary Syndicalists, 327, 331–332, 334; after World War I, 332–333; and revoltism, 327; relations with Republican and Radical Parties, 334;
 congresses: *1908*, 72, 76, 79, 82, 83–84, 85; *1911*, 76–77, 85–86, 87, 114; *1914*, 77, 83, 86–87, 91–92; *1921*, 77, 157, 159–160, 164–165, 178; *1924*, 175, 179
Gennari, Egidio, 151–152

Gentili, Dino, 189, 190, 191, 192
Gentiloni Pact, 109
Giolitti, Giovanni, 48–50, 52; and the *Fasci,*
    33; Minister of Interior, *1901,* 36; prime
    ministership after World War I, 142; en-
    couragement of "domestication," 149, 328;
    and occupation strikes, 149, 152–153; during
    rise of fascism, 156; resignation, 165, 167
Giolitti period in Italian history, 3, 48–94,
    325, 328, 332
Giovani (Youth), 98, 102
Gnocchi-Viani, Osvaldo, 24, 42, 101
Gramsci, Antonio, 144
Gramsci Communists, 145, 158
Grandi, Achille, 125, 185, 186, 189, 191, 208,
    251
Graves de Communi re encyclical, 103–104
Grieco, Ruggero, 247
Grievance machinery, 142–143, 326
Guilds, 12, 96, 97

Hatters, 38, 41, 62, 67, 72
Hungarian revolt, 279–280, 297, 298–299, 302

IFTU, *see* International Federation of Trade
    Unions
Il Fermo Proposito encyclical, 106
Il Lavoro, 214, 246
Il Popolo d'Italia, 154
Industrialization of Italy, 5–9, 86, 274, 275,
    325, 326.
    See also Strikes, Textile industry, Trade
    unions
Istituto per la Recostruzione Industriale (IRI),
    198
Insurance, social, 55, 85
Integralist bloc, 53–54, 55
Internal Commissions, 143–144, 186, 315. *See
    also* Factory councils
International Association of Workmen, *see*
    First International
International Confederation of Free Trade
    Unions (ICFTU), 236
International Federation of Trade Unions
    (IFTU), 160, 162, 164–165, 192
International, the First, 13, 19, 20, 21, 324
International Labor Organization, 162
International, Third (Communist), 158, 162–
    163, 178, 180
Internationalist (First), Italian, 19, 21, 22–23
Italian Communist Party, *see* Communist Party
    (Italian)
Italian Confederation of Labor (*Confederazione
    Italiana dei Lavoratori;* CIL), 116, 120–126,
    148, 175, 329, 335–336
Italian Confederation of Trade Unions (CISL),
    224, 231–234, 241–243, 303–309; relations

with UIL, 225–226, 235–237, 322; member-
    ship, 228, 303; policy, 268–269; and PSLI
    trade union leadership, 270–271; orientation,
    340–341;
    congresses: *1951,* 228; *1959,* 306-309;
    elections: *1954,* 290, 304; *1957* and *1958,*
    304; *1961,* 320–321
    See also Conglobamento agreement; Legisla-
    tion, labor relations; Plant level policies
Italian Federation of Chambers of Labor, 45,
    62–66, 68.
    See also Chambers of Labor
Italian Federation of the International Work-
    ing Men's Association, *see* Italian Interna-
    tionalists
Italian General Confederation of Labor
    (CGIL), 187, 190–192, 197–198, 200, 226–
    227, 239–244; orientation, 195, 201-202,
    209–210; dominated by Communists, 203–
    204, 208, 250–253, 338–339, 340; and na-
    tional bargaining, 207; membership, 208,
    228, 299, 303; unity destroyed, 210–212,
    269–271, 338; and competitor organizations,
    218–219, 233, 237–238, 267–269, 274; *piano
    del lavoro* (national economic plan), 226,
    238, 253; policies, 238–239; Socialists in,
    257–261; reversals, 289–292, 303–304; rela-
    tions with Communist Party, 296–297, 320,
    321, 324; internal crisis, 298–299; reunifica-
    tion proposals, 299–303; *1958* national elec-
    tions, 304–305; expansion of influence after
    1958, 309–310, 316;
    conferences: Rome, *1944,* 191–192; Rome,
    1950, 226–227;
    congresses: Naples, *1945,* 192, 196–198;
    258; Florence, *1947,* 208, 209–210, 223,
    258, 269, 271; *1949,* 226, 294; *1952,* 228;
    1956, 294; *1960,* 317, 318;
    elections: *1953,* 289; *1954,* 289, 303–304;
    1955, 289; *1957,* 303–304; *1958,* 304; *1959,*
    320; *1961,* 320–321
    See also Conglobamento agreement; *Il La-
    voro;* Legislation, labor relations; Plant level
    policies
Italian Internationalists (First), 19, 21, 22–23
Italian Social Movement (neo-Fascist MSI),
    286–287;
    elections: *1948,* 213; *1953,* 229; *1958,* 284
Italian Social Republic (Republic of Salò), 183,
    252
Italian Union of Labor (UIL), 148, 177–178,
    224–225, 234–237; membership, 228, 303;
    and CGIL, 176, 231; gain of PSLI members,
    269; plant level policies, 295; reunification
    proposals, 301–303, 340; *1958* national elec-
    tions, 305; relations with CISL, 322;
    congress: *1953,* 223, 235;

elections: *1954, 1957* and *1958,* 304; *1961,* 321
See also Conglobamento agreement; Legislation, labor relations

King of Italy, 171, 182–183, 189, 193

La Plebe, 24
Labor Democrats, 183, 193
Labor force, 4, 8, 9, 58
Labriola, Arturo, 53
Land reform, 247, 329, 336, 338
Lavoro, see *Il Lavoro*
Lazzari, Constantino, 55, 128, 130, 158
LCGIL, *see* Free Italian General Confederation of Labor
League of the Sons of Labor of Milan, 26
Lega Democratica Nazionale, 107, 112
Legislation: protective labor, 48, 85, 117, 334; labor relations, 312–315
Leo XIII, 99, 103, 104, 105
Libera Confederazione Generale Italiana del Lavoro (LCGIL), *see* Free Italian General Confederation of Labor
Liberal Party, 183–184, 189, 199; elections: *1948,* 213; *1953,* 229; *1958,* 284
See also Liberals
Liberals, 34–35, 193–194, 230, 278, 286
Libyan war, 3, 56, 86–87
Lizzadri, Oreste, 206, 257–258
Lockouts, 149

Maglione, Battista, 175
Malon, Benoît, 24, 27
"March on Rome," 171
Marchetti, 89, 92
Margotti, Don Giacomo, 95
Martoni, Anselmo, 322
Marx, Karl, 13, 19, 20, 22
Marxist ideology, 21, 27
Masons, 57–58, 92
Matteotti, Giacomo, **172–173**
"Maximalist" Socialists (Maximalists), 134, 158, 160, 330
Mazzini, Giuseppe, 10–11, 13; and unification of Italy, 2, 328; views on Worker Societies Congresses, 15; and Bakunin, 19–20; attack on Paris Commune, 21; impact on trade union movement, 324
Mazziniani, 15, 16–18
Meda, Filippo, 103
Metallurgical Workers Federation (FIOM), 137, 143–145, 148–149, 152, 161, 296
Miglioli, Guido, 123
Milan, 87–88, 89, 103, 149, 155
Moderates, 15, 16, 17, 24

Modigliani, Giuseppe, 57
Monarchists, 213, 229, 284
Morelli, Luigi, 224
Moro, Aldo, 323
MSI, *see* Italian Social Movement
Murri, Father Romolo, 102–103, 105, 107–108
Mussolini, Benito, 153–155, 165–166, 167–174; Revolutionary Socialist, 56, 88–90; editor of *Avanti,* 57, 88; followed by some UIL leadership, 178; deposed, 182–183; head of Republic of Salò, 183, 252; and revoltism, 327; fought by Rigola, 335. *See also* Fascism
Mutual aid organizations, *see* Friendly societies
Mutual-aid societies (Catholic), 100

National agreements, 142, 206–208, 294
National Democratic League (*Lega Democratica Nazionale*), 107, 112
National Federations, *see* National Unions
National Unions, 61–72, 76–78, 325, 333–334. *See also* Chambers of Labor
National unions, Catholic, 114–115
Nenni, Pietro, 277–282; head of Nenni Socialists, 206, 230, 254, 283, 285, 289; commitment of PSI to CGIL, 299–300, 316; and working class unity, 330, 339. *See also* Nenni Socialist Party
Nenni Socialist Party (PSI), 3, 202, 210, 283–286, 323; and CGIL, 208, 209, 259, 269, 270, 289, 301–302, 316–317; autonomy movement, 221–225, 258, 271, 276–282, 287, 289, 319–323, 338–340; and Hungarian revolt, 279–280; pact with Communist Party, 281; participation in Communist-sponsored demonstrations, 289; congresses: *1949,* 221; *1957,* 280, 282, 283, 302; *1959,* 316, 317; *1961,* 321, 322; elections: *1924,* 172; *1953,* 229–230, 277; *1958,* 284
Non expedit policy of Vatican, 95, 104, 105, 106–109, 116, 325
Northern Italy, 3–5, 10, 155–156, 198–201
Novella, Agostino, 296, 300, 304–306, 317–318, 320

Obstructionism, 148–149
Occupation strikes, 147, 149–153, 178
"Opening to the Left" formula, 277, 278, 280, 285, 310, 322, 323, 340
Opera dei Congressi, 97–98, 101–102, 103, 105, 106, 110. *See also* Catholic Congresses
Ordine Nuovo, 144

Pact of Palazzo Vidoni, 126, 175
Pact of Rome, 186–187, 190–191, 208, 212, 217, 219, 250–251
Paris Commune, 21, 22, 24

Parri, Enrico, 216, 220, 223, 224, 272
Parri, Ferruccio, 202
Partito Popolare Italiano, see Popular Party
Partito Social-Democratico Italiano (PSDI), *see* Social Democratic Party
Partito Socialista dei Lavoratori Italiani (PSLI), 206, 256, 270
Partito Socialista Unitario, 172
Pastore, Giulio, 1, 306–307; leader in CGIL, 214, 216; secretary general of LCGIL, 218, 222, 237–238; secretary general of CISL, 224, 232, 241, 269; Minister in Fanfani's cabinet, 285; resignation from CISL, 305
Pelloux, Luigi, 36
Pius X, 105, 106, 108
Pius XI, 119
Pius XII, 263–264, 265–266
Plant level policies, 292–296, 320
Po Valley, 4, 40, 59, 169, 177
Popolari, see Popular Party
Popular Party (*Partito Popolare; Popolari*), 115–120, 170, 172, 335; and Socialists, 133; reform goals, 329;
    elections: *1919,* 117, 132; *1920,* 118; *1921,* 165; *1924,* 119, 172
Population, 4, 5
Prampolini, Camillo, 132
Price lists (wages), 37, 38
Protectionism, 7
PSDI, *see* Social Democratic Party
PSI, *see* Nenni Socialists
PSLI, *see* Saragat Socialist Party

Quaglino, Felice, 62
Quarello, Gioacchino, 185

Radical Party, 24, 26–27, 83, 85;
    elections: *1900,* 36; *1958,* 284
    See also Radicals
Radicals, 29, 34–36
Railroad workers, 61, 67–69, 72
Rapelli, Giovanni, 208, 214
Red Trade Union International, 162, 164–165, 180
"Red" unions, 188
Red Week, 57, 92–94
Reformists: in Socialist Party, 51, 53–56, 58, 71, 85, 86; in trade union movement, 57, 65, 67–70, 72, 78, 88, 91, 325; tradition of unity, 330
Reformists (Turati's Concentrationists), 158
Reina, Ettore, 62, 92
Republic of Salò, 183, 252
Republican Party, 223, 271–272;
    congresses: *1906,* 83; *1948* and *1949,* 272;
    elections: *1900,* 36; *1946,* 203; *1948,* 213;

1953, 229–230; *1958,* 284
    See also Republicans
Republicans, 34–36, 71, 278; in trade unions, 83, 85, 214–215, 219–221; participation in Red Week demonstrations, 92–93. *See also Mazziniani;* Republican Party
Rerum Novarum encyclical, 96, 98, 99, 100, 103
Revoltism, 326–328, 336
Revolutionaries: in Socialist Party, 21, 51, 53–54, 56–58, 325–326, 327; in trade union movement, 65–69, 72, 85–88, 90–91
Revolutionary Syndicalism, 326–327. *See also* Revolutionary Syndicalism
Revolutionary Syndicalists: in trade union movement, 1, 65, 69–71, 74, 75, 78–94, 176–178, 325, 327, 331; in Socialist Party, 52–57, 330; support of Mussolini, 154. *See also* Revolutionary Syndicalism
Rigola, Rinaldo, 40, 62, 64, 72–74; CGL leader, 1, 82–83, 84, 86, 88–94, 337; resignation from CGL, 72, 135–136, 334–335
Risorgimento, 10, 13, 253, 327–329, 336
Rocchi, A. Claudio, 223, 272
Rome, Pact of, *see* Pact of Rome
Rosselli, Nello, 184
Roveda, Giovanni, 185, 189, 208
Rudinì, Antonio di, 34, 36

Salandra, Antonio, 127, 128
Salerno trade union conferences, 189–190
Santi, Fernando, 206, 221, 258, 300
Saragat, Giuseppe, 206, 230, 256, 277, 278, 281
Saragat Socialist Party (PSLI), 208–209, 214–215, 219–221, 269–271
Scelba, Mario, 216, 230–231
Scelba government, 241, 242–243, 278
Segni government, 278, 286, 307, 308, 311
Serrati, Giancinto Menotti, 157–158
Sicily, 3, 20, 31–34, 117–118, 123
Social insurance, 55, 85
Social Democratic Party (PSDI), 230, 269–271, 278, 280–283, 288; *1957* congress, 283; elections: *1953,* 229, 277; *1958,* 284
Socialist International Stuttgart Congress, *1907,* 80
Socialist movement, 45–47, 95–96, 325–326, 328–330. *See also* Socialist Party
Socialist Party, 29–32, 44, 130, 146, 327, 332, 339; and Chambers of Labor, 43; program, 51, 55; and Masons, 57-58; and CGL, 80–81, 83–85, 87, 90–94, 135–137; represented by Mussolini, 88–90; antiwar activities, 128–129; following World War I, 131–135; failure to assert leadership after World War I, 132–134, 139–140, 141, 167, 170, 245, 253,

338–339; left-wing faction, 144–145; and revolution issue, 149–153; in post-Fascist period, 193–194; torn by factions, 195–196, 206; orientation, 253–257, 325;

congresses: *1892*, 30; *1893*, 30; *1900*, 51; *1904*, 53; *1908*, 54, 81; *1910*, 55; *1911*, 56; *1912*, 57; *1914*, 57–58, 91; *1919*, 134; *1921*, 157–159; *1946*, 255–256; *1948, 1949, 1951*, 257;

elections: communal, *1920*, 118, 153; national, *1895* and *1897*, 35; *1900*, 36, 51; *1909*, 55, 85; *1919*, 117, 132; 154–155; *1921*, 165, 167; *1924*, 172; *1946*, 202–203; *1948*, 213; *1953*, 229–230; *1958*, 284; union, *1945*, 204

See also Committee of National Liberation; Socialist movement; Socialist trade union conferences; Socialists; Stuttgart resolution

Socialist trade union conferences: *1957*, 317; *1959*, 316–317

Socialists: repression of, 34–36; promotion of agricultural trade unions, 40; promotion of trade union unity, 184–187, 188, 189; in CGIL, 204, 257–261; relations with government, 328, 338. *See also* Socialist Party

Sonnino, Sidney, 127, 128

Sorel, Georges, 53

Southern Italy, 3–4, 5, 9, 275, 338

Storti, Bruno, 1, 305, 306–308, 312, 321–322

Strike funds, 21–22n, 81–83

Strike, right to, 25, 175

Strikebreaking, 114, 169

Strikes: Worker Societies Congresses against, 15, 16–17; Anarchists' approach to, 21–22n; in industry, 38–40, 58, 60, 78, 182; increase in, 41, 44, 45, 58–60; in agriculture, 54–55, 58–59, 78, 140–141; employer resistance to, 60–61, 140, 147–148; in *1901–1914*, 78–79; CGL approach to, 82, 88–89, 136; Catholic approach to, 101–102, 114; violence in, 133–134, 138–139, 142n; during depression of *1921*, 166–167; Communist-sponsored demonstrations of *1960*, 286–287; in *1959*, 311–312;

factors in: education for socialism, 53; political purposes, 57, 88, 122, 139–140, 203; wage increase principal issue, 59, 60, 140; trade union recognition principal issue, 59–61; revolutionary approach to industrial relations, 66–67; education for revolution, 78–79; sympathy strikes, 79, 141; manifestation of revoltism, 327;

printers', 37, 41, 61, 67, 72; in textile industry, 38–40, 41; in Genoa, *1900*, 45; general, of *1904*, 54, 68, 106; during Red Week, 92–94; occupation, 117, 122, 147, 149–153; general, of July *20–21, 1919*, 139–

140; in Turin, April, *1920*, 146–147; general, of August *1, 1922*, 169; in Rome, Dec. *1947*, 211–212; railroad, of *1953*, 233

See also Demonstrations; Strike, right to

Sturzo, Father Luigi (Don Sturzo), 116, 118–119

Stuttgart Congress, Socialist International, *1907*, 80

Stuttgart resolution, 80–81

Suffrage: at time of unification of Italy, 2–3; advocated by Worker Societies Congresses, 15, 16, 24; extended to workers, 24; in Workers' Party program, 25; in *1890*'s, 35; in Socialist Party program, 51, 85; in Giolitti's program, 55; elimination of literacy requirements, 109. *See also* Elections

Syndicalists, *see* Revolutionary Syndicalists

Tambroni government, 286

Tasca, Angelo, 159

Tax reform, 25, 51, 117

Textile industry, 7, 38–40, 41, 122, 137–138, 329

Third International, 158, 162, 178, 180

Togliatti, Palmiro, 150n, 276, 292; Moscow-endorsed leader of Italian Communists, 193–194, 247, 288, 292, 321; attempted assassination of, 215; negotiation of pact with PSI, 282; concern with Socialist unity, 285

Tomasini, Dario, 62

Toniolo, Giuseppe, 98, 102

Trade union conferences: Bari and Salerno, 189–190; Socialist, 316–317;

congresses: *1905*, 68; *1906*, 70–72

See also names of trade unions; Workers Societies Congresses

Trade union movement, Catholic, 95–126, 156, 261–268, 335–336

Trade unions: evolution of, 10, 58, 59–64, 324–327; repression of, 35–36, 44–45; promoted by Workers' Party and Socialists, 40; early leadership, 41; attacked by fascism, 156; in post-Fascist period, 184–192, 196–201, 203, 337–338; membership drop, 226; competition among, 227–228; unification proposals, 299–303, 316–318, 321–322; employer resistance to, 309–312; *vs.* Internal Commissions, 315; political domination of, 324–341. *See also* names of trade unions; Chambers of Labor; Elections, union; National Unions; Strikes; Trade union conferences, congresses; Trade union movement, Catholic Traditions, workers', 1–2, 326–331

Trasformismo, 3, 27, 49

Turati, Filippo, 30, 94; leader of Reformist forces in Socialist Party, 51, 54, 57, 130, 132, 134, 158

Turati's Concentrationists, 158
Turin, 143–147, 149–151
Twentieth Congress of Soviet Union's Communist Party, 283, 297

UIL, *see* Italian Union of Labor
Unemployment, 4, 86, 166, 203, 211, 275
Unification of Italy, 2, 3, 5–6, 10–11, 17, 327–328
Union shop, 38
Unione Economico-Sociale, 108, 111–112
Unione Elettorale Cattolica Italiana, 108–109, 110
Unione Italiana del Lavoro (UIL), *see* Italian Union of Labor
Unione Sindacale Italiana (USI), 87–88, 148, 175–178
Unioni del Lavoro, 125
Unions, trade, *see* Trade unions
Unitary Communists, 158
Unitary Socialist Party (PSU), 269
United Nations Relief and Rehabilitation Administration (UNRRA), 201–202
United States European Recovery Program Administration, 8
USI, *see* Unione Sindacale Italiana

Vacations with pay, 142
Valente, Giovanni Battista, 120
Vanoni plan, 9
Vercesi, Ernesto, 107
Viglianesi, Italo, 1, 235, 236, 301, 319, 321–322
Vita Operaia, 73

Wages: increases in, 8, 86, 275–276, 326; Worker Societies Congresses attitude toward, 15, 16; increased by Chambers of Labor, 48; issue in strikes, 59, 60, 140, 311–312; cost-of-living adjustments, 197, 204, 207; women's, 311. *See also Conglobamento* agreement; Strikes
"White unions," 121, 122, 188, 189
Wollemborg, Leone, 101
Worker exclusivism, 23, 24, 26, 28–29, 325
Worker Societies Congresses, 14–17, 29–30. *See also* Friendly societies
Workers' benefits, *see* Benefits, workers'
Workers' Party, 25, 26–29, 30, 40
Working class unity, 10, 80, 330, 337, 338, 340

Young Italy movement, 11, 13

Zoli government, 278, 283

WERTHEIM PUBLICATIONS IN INDUSTRIAL RELATIONS

Published by Harvard University Press

J. D. Houser, *What the Employer Thinks*, 1927
Wertheim Lectures on Industrial Relations, 1929
William Haber, *Industrial Relations in the Building Industry*, 1930
Johnson O'Connor, *Psychometrics*, 1934
Paul H. Norgren, *The Swedish Collective Bargaining System*, 1941
Leo C. Brown, S.J., *Union Policies in the Leather Industry*, 1947
Walter Galenson, *Labor in Norway*, 1949
Dorothea de Schweinitz, *Labor and Management in a Common Enterprise*, 1949
Ralph Altman, *Availability for Work: A Study in Unemployment Compensation*, 1950
John T. Dunlop and Arthur D. Hill, *The Wage Adjustment Board: Wartime Stabilization in the Building and Construction Industry*, 1950
Walter Galenson, *The Danish System of Labor Relations: A Study in Industrial Peace*, 1952
Lloyd H. Fisher, *The Harvest Labor Market in California*, 1953
Theodore V. Purcell, S.J., *The Worker Speaks His Mind on Company and Union*, 1953
Donald J. White, *The New England Fishing Industry*, 1954
Val R. Lorwin, *The French Labor Movement*, 1954
Philip Taft, *The Structure and Government of Labor Unions*, 1954
George B. Baldwin, *Beyond Nationalization: The Labor Problems of British Coal*, 1955
Kenneth F. Walker, *Industrial Relations in Australia*, 1956
Charles A. Myers, *Labor Problems in the Industrialization of India*, 1958
Herbert J. Spiro, *The Politics of German Codetermination*, 1958
Mark W. Leiserson, *Wages and Economic Control in Norway, 1945–1947*, 1959
J. Pen, *The Wage Rate under Collective Bargaining*, 1959
Jack Stieber, *The Steel Industry Wage Structure*, 1959
Theodore V. Purcell, S.J., *Blue Collar Man: Patterns of Dual Allegiance in Industry*
Carl Erik Knoellinger, *Labor in Finland*, 1960
Sumner H. Slichter, *Potentials of the American Economy: Selected Essays* edited by John T. Dunlop, 1961
C. L. Christenson, *Economic Redevelopment in Bituminous Coal: The Special Case of Technological Advance in United States Coal Mines, 1930–1960*, 1962
Daniel L. Horowitz, *The Italian Labor Movement*, 1963

STUDIES IN LABOR-MANAGEMENT HISTORY

Lloyd Ulman, *The Rise of the National Trade Union: The Development and Significance of Its Structure, Governing Institutions, and Economic Policies*, 1955
Joseph P. Goldberg, *The Maritime Story: A Study in Labor–Management Relations*, 1957, 1958
Walter Galenson, *The CIO Challenge to the AFL: A History of the American Labor Movement, 1935–1941*, 1960
Morris A. Horowitz, *The New York Hotel Industry: A Labor Relations Study*, 1960
Mark Perlman, *The Machinists: A New Study in Trade Unionism*, 1961
Fred C. Munson, *Labor Relations in the Lithographic Industry*, 1963

Published by McGraw-Hill Book Co., Inc.

Robert L. Alexander, *Labor Relations in Argentina, Brazil, and Chile*, 1961
Carl M. Stevens, *Strategy and Collective Bargaining Negotiations*, 1963